Tents and Tent Stability

A month-long camping adventure in the national parks and nature reserves of Germany - in a rather dodgy tent!

Chris Lown

My sincere thanks to Paolo Barone for his efforts and expertise editing the original manuscript.

This book is dedicated to the memory of Barbara, John, Denis and Ben

Tents and Tent Stability:

A month-long camping adventure in the national parks and nature reserves of Germany – in a rather dodgy tent!

Chapter One – My Next-Door Neighbour's Cat

"A journey of a thousand miles begins with a single step."
Unknown author – Chinese proverb

My next-door neighbour has a cat called Fifi. She's a sweet little thing – full of mischief and joie de vivre. She spends much of her time scurrying playfully about the house, and in the summer can often be found snoozing in her favourite spot in the garden, basking in the warmth of the sunshine.

But enough about my next-door neighbour – it's her cat that I wish to focus your attention on. Like all cats, Fifi will make you work hard for her affection. She'll sleep for unfeasibly long periods of time, waking only occasionally to eat, drink or answer the call of nature. Every so often she'll poke her head through the cat-flap to conduct a rather brief and desultory visual surveillance of her territory – but it's always something of a half-hearted effort. She is, without a shadow of doubt, the laziest, most indolent animal on the planet. My wife always refers to her affectionately as *'Little'* Fifi – but given that Fifi is a cat and therefore no more than thirty centimetres tall the epithet seems rather superfluous. I prefer the more pejorative *'Bloody'* Fifi.

Every so often, my next-door neighbour finds herself having to travel abroad. And on those occasions when her work commitments drag her away to exotic tropical paradises around the world, my wife and I will take the cat in as our temporary house guest, and we'll devote a week or so of our lives tending to the insatiable needs of the world's most demanding and ungrateful creature.

Actually, suggesting that my wife and I share the burden of this responsibility is a little erroneous. It's my wife who tends to the demands of the cat – providing the food, topping up the water bowl, cleaning out the litter tray. My role tends to be that of a casual observer. Sometimes several days will go by before I'm even vaguely aware of any feline presence in the house. I'll be mystified as to why my eyes are itching; puzzled by the peculiar scratches that have suddenly appeared on my nose during the night; confused by the strange smell of '*Jonny-Cat Clumping Litter*' that assaults my senses whenever I open the kitchen door – only to be enlightened when my wife eventually informs me that for the past week or so we've been looking after our next-door neighbour's cat. But please don't misunderstand me – I don't find the task of cat-sitting objectionable as such. It's just I'm not much of a 'cat' kind of person – and whenever we have Fifi as a house guest, I look forward to my neighbour's homecoming every bit as much as Fifi does.

Although I may be loath to admit it, I suspect there may be a perfectly plausible explanation as to why I find Fifi's presence in my home so incredibly irritating. The inconvenient truth of the matter is that, as I head towards my fifties, I am slowly but surely turning into a miserable and cantankerous old git. My wife of course would argue that 'miserable' and 'cantankerous' are two traits that have always featured predominantly in my personality profile – my age having nothing to do with it. And I suppose she must be right. But the thing is, I've noticed it more of late. I've reached that milestone of middle age, when your broad mind and narrow waistline begin to trade places; that time of life when you become irritable over the most inconsequential of issues – like the languid behaviour of the council refuse collectors or the atrocious parking skills of the man who lives across the road. My grouchy behaviour is, I suspect, a natural consequence of midlife boredom. I've reached that time of life where the kind of event that I get excited about is the imminent arrival of a new range of men's winter pullovers at *Marks and Spencer*. It's not that I don't *do* anything any more – I do paint the town red occasionally. But I find myself having to take a long rest before I can muster enough enthusiasm to apply a second coat.

"You're having a midlife crisis," my wife tells me – but she's wrong. If I were having a midlife crisis I'd be spending my money on a shiny new six-cylinder sports convertible. I'd be cruising the streets with the top down; a stunning nubile blonde by my side; the sun reflecting off my bifocals and the wind rushing through my receding hair with its ever expanding bald patch. No, it's probably not a sports car that's lacking in my life. But there is definitely *something* that's missing – an indescribable or indefinable *something* – a certain 'je ne sais quoi'.

However, I digress. Let us return to the subject of Fifi – my next-door neighbour's cat. As I've said already, it's not that I harbour any personal antipathy towards cats per se – I suspect that, in the immortal words of 10cc's *Stewart* and *Gouldman*: 'it's just a silly phase I'm going through.' Nor for that matter, over the years that my wife and I have been volunteering our services as cat-sitters, have I harboured any feelings of animosity towards my neighbour for asking us to help out. But if there's one emotion I *do* have regarding the woman who lives next door, it's an overwhelming feeling of envy.

Now, *envy* I know is a very dangerous trait – one of seven deadly sins if I'm not mistaken. It's right up there with wrath, greed, sloth, pride, lust and gluttony in its propensity to condemn one to eternal damnation. But the truth is, the woman next door has a most enviable occupation – one that enables her to travel to every corner of the globe, drawing a substantial salary for the privilege of doing so, whilst her cat skulks around our house pining for her to return. Yes, my neighbour has more stamps in her passport than James Bond, and although I'm fully aware of the possible

7

consequences of this envy I have for her globe-trotting lifestyle, I just can't seem to shake it off.

My neighbour, you see, works in the travel industry. Her job, as far as I can ascertain, is to travel to exotic locations in far-flung corners of the globe and return a week or so later to file a report on the sort of things that discerning holidaymakers might wish to know about. Does the resort have its own private beach? Does the hotel provide guests with spa treatments and their own private masseuse? Will a tall, handsome waiter in a cream-coloured jacket and a black bow tie bring me a tray of lobsters and champagne while I top up my suntan on the golden sands of some remote sub-tropical archipelago? It's the sort of job that most people would be perfectly willing to do for no remuneration whatsoever, yet my neighbour wanders around the globe with the advantage of a most munificent expenses budget.

But in recent months my dear neighbour has done nothing but complain. She'll return from a trip abroad and spend an hour in conversation on our doorstep, grumbling about the shabbiness of the holiday destination from which she has recently returned and criticising her employer for having the impudence to send her there. You see, a year or so ago, my next-door neighbour's employer introduced some changes to the company's internal structure, and as a result, several members of staff (my neighbour included) were given changes of responsibility. My next-door neighbour was beside herself with fury. Whereas previously she would have been sent to relax beneath swaying palms on the smooth white sands of Mexico's Caribbean beaches, or dive among the corals in the crystal-clear turquoise waters off the coast of Mauritius, she was now responsible for reporting on the number of deckchairs available on the beaches of Torremolinos, and checking out the times of 'happy hour' in the bars in Benidorm. But as my wife and I stood at the front door listening to my neighbour chunter about the misery and

8

the indignity of having to spend a week on the Costa del Sol, it suddenly occurred to me that despite the caustic nature of her comments and the venom with which they were delivered, most of my neighbour's opinions on the subject of package holidays seemed to be entirely justified. And that was when it hit me – I suddenly found myself becoming overwhelmed by a feeling of middle-age restiveness – if such a condition exists.

Now, you may be wondering what any of this has to do with my next-door neighbour's cat, or why the very mention of the name 'Fifi' somehow manages to whip me into a frenzy of prickly petulance. Well, as strange and inexplicable as this may seem, it was my next-door neighbour's cat – this fluffy little bundle of irksome feline nonsense – that was indirectly responsible for helping me realise what was lacking in my life. It was during a doorstep conversation with my neighbour (that marked the end of another stretch of cat-sitting duties and the official handover of *bloody* Fifi to her rightful guardian), that I began to realise that on every occasion I'd travelled abroad I had seen nothing of the country I'd visited. I had spent my time there cocooned inside a hotel complex – inveigled into a state of general lethargy by the presence of the pool and the sunloungers.

Wouldn't it be wonderful, I thought, if my wife and I could ditch plans for our next insipid annual package holiday and do something exciting in its stead – something adventurous – something brave and intrepid. Of course! *That* was the ingredient that had been missing from my life – it was so obvious I couldn't believe it hadn't occurred to me sooner. My wife and I could travel across Europe, carrying the accoutrements of a pair of intrepid wayfarers in our backpacks – blithely roaming from one town to the next. We could immerse ourselves in a marinade of European culture and sleep under canvas beneath the stars. Yes, that truly would be an adventure. There was no need for meticulous planning either – we could leave tomorrow – go wherever the fancy took us – destination irrelevant. After all, there was nothing preventing us, was there?

Rucksacks: – check.

Passports: – check.

Sleeping bags: – check.

My wife's consent to accompany me on this whimsical fantasy of mine: – ah, now there's something I perhaps should have given a little more consideration to. You see, deep down I was fully aware this notion was just wishful thinking on my part. I knew my wife would never agree to it. Travelling hundreds of miles across Europe with a backpack would be her idea of holiday hell. And I couldn't go it alone. Travelling by myself would undoubtedly be the perfect solution, but it simply wouldn't be fair. The fact is, my wife and I go on holiday *together*. That's how it is and that's how it's always been.

So in light of the fact that this dream of traipsing across the continent was one I would be unlikely ever to fulfil, I tried to put those restive feelings behind me and focus instead on whether I could afford the monthly payments on a shiny new six-cylinder sports convertible.

Now, they say that miracles never happen – and I must confess that until recently, I was one of those sceptics who would have readily agreed with such a sentiment. But a few months ago a most extraordinary thing occurred. One of my wife's closest friends won first prize in a competition – two tickets for an 'all expenses paid' cruise around the Caribbean. It was the trip of a lifetime – a twenty-one-day tour setting off from Bridgetown, then sailing to ports of call in Grenada, St. Vincent, St. Lucia, St. Kitts, St. Maarten and Tortola. She had won this spectacular prize by entering a competition she had spotted in a women's magazine – sandwiched between a riveting article on Kerry Katona's prodigious collection of handbags and a compelling story

10

entitled 'Help, I'm Addicted to Cheesecake!" It was one of those rather absurd competitions which seem to be popular these days, where contestants simply have to choose the correct answer to a question from a choice of three possibilities. You know the sort I mean – ludicrously simple questions like 'What is the capital of France?' Followed by the three possible answers:

A) Paris, B) Stoke on Trent or C) Lady Gaga.

There's no skill involved – which is just as well, as I'm pretty sure that some of the many thousands of subscribers to this tawdry brand of publication would have deliberated for some considerable time over which of the three answers might be correct. But despite the huge number of competition entries, my wife's friend (who I'm going to call *Joanna* for the sake of a more apposite pseudonym) had been miraculously chosen at random from the list of thousands who had submitted the correct answer (and yes, apparently there *are* people out there who managed to get it wrong).

So, just a few weeks later, two tickets for a luxury Caribbean cruise came winging their way by courier – an event celebrated with the opening of several bottles of champagne during one rather bibulous evening last summer at Joanna's compact little studio apartment in Putney. But here's the thing: Joanna is neither married nor in a steady relationship – and as far as I know isn't on speaking terms with any of her relatives. So it was almost a foregone conclusion in my mind that my wife would be offered the spare ticket. And deep down, my wife felt sure that this would be the case too. I must admit that because of this, I felt a little sorry for my poor wife. I knew this would put her in a very awkward position. As I've already mentioned, it's an axiom of our annual summer holiday arrangements that we always travel *together* – I had never been anywhere without her or vice versa. The prospect of her cruising around the Caribbean without me was something I felt sure my wife

11

would consider unthinkable. So when that awkward moment came for Joanna to offer my wife the spare ticket, I was certain that my beloved spouse would be searching for a tactful way of letting her dearest friend down as gently as possible. And as I sat there supping on a glass of champagne in Joanna's rather cramped little apartment, wondering what words of skilful diplomacy my wife would employ to convey the bad news, I noticed Joanna heading towards my wife with two tickets in hand and a beaming smile on her face.

"You *will* come with me on this Caribbean cruise, won't you?" Joanna asked.

"Of course I will," my wife replied without any hesitation whatsoever, "Wild horses wouldn't stop me!"

For a moment I was speechless – astounded that my wife had so readily agreed to bugger off to the Caribbean with her best friend, without any hint of consultation with her husband!

My dear wife, it has to be said, is not a great maritime traveller. The last time the two of us ventured on a seafaring expedition she was violently sick and spent most of the journey with her head over the side of the boat. [1] But as time passed I started to come round to the idea of my wife and her friend going off on a cruise together. It would be good for them both to spend a bit of 'quality' time in each other's company, assuming of course that it didn't coincide with my next-door neighbour being summoned to an emergency karaoke competition in Alicante – and me being left to look after *bloody* Fifi on my own. And of course, there was another rather expedient advantage – it would enable me to fulfil my own travel aspirations. Yes, if my wife was swanning off to the Caribbean with her best friend, then I

---

[1] *We were foot passengers on the Woolwich Ferry.*

was pretty sure she'd have no objection to my heading off on a backpacking journey across Europe. And I was right.

But with my wife's consent in the bag came the troublesome question of where my adventure should take me. I didn't want to travel anywhere too remote – one of the countries in mainland Europe was far enough, I decided. I only wanted to dip my toes into the water rather than immerse myself in an ocean of unfamiliarity – lest there be sea monsters. And so, after much deliberation, I eventually decided I would backpack my way around Germany – for three main reasons:

Firstly, I can't help feeling a teeny bit sorry for the Germans. The fact is that very few people in the UK choose to visit Germany compared to other European countries – and I think that's a great shame. Germany and its people tend to get something of a bad press. Much of it, of course, can be attributed to the country's rather turbulent political history – that, and the fact that many of us Brits cling on to the same prejudices that we held in the 1940s.

In a poll of one hundred people conducted for the television quiz show 'Family Fortunes', contestants were asked to name something associated with Germany. The top answer was 'Hitler', with both 'World War II' and 'using towels to reserve sunloungers' also submitted as popular answers. I suppose that just about sums up the shallow opinion we have of our European neighbours. But we shouldn't take this too seriously of course – this is 'Family Fortunes' we're talking about here – the same show on which hapless contestants suggested 'The Yellow Brick Road' as something associated with Liverpool and 'the lamps' as something one might take from a hotel as a souvenir.

But it's the country's geography, I think, that explains the real reason why we Brits have a tendency to give Germany a wide berth. When we're choosing a European summer holiday destination we're inclined to opt for countries like Spain, Portugal, France or Italy. Germany doesn't usually get a look in. But that's because most of us will be searching for sun, sea, sand and speedboats that tow huge inflatable bananas. Germany has hardly anything to offer in this regard. [2] It shares 3,734 kilometres of border with nine other countries, and has just two comparatively short lengths of coastline on the North Sea and the Baltic. But it's the capricious nature of the weather in northern Europe that makes Germany's beaches far less appealing to sun worshippers than those on the Mediterranean – so tourists have a tendency to stay away. And even as a winter holiday destination, intrepid souls who venture out on the piste are inclined to plump for Austria or Switzerland as their destinations of choice. Germany, which in point of fact has a number of first-rate ski resorts, is regarded as the poorer brother.

In 2010, we Brits made just over two million visits to Germany. Now that may sound like an awful lot of visits, but when you consider just how big the country is, together with the size of her population, you begin to realise that two million visits is an astonishingly small number. Germany is a vast country covering an area of around 357,000 square kilometres. You could stick the whole of the United Kingdom into a space that big and still have enough room to squeeze in Switzerland, Belgium, Luxembourg and the Netherlands. The country has a huge population too. It may surprise you to learn that there are more Germans than any other nationality in Europe – more than 82 million of them. Compare that with the 68 million people living in France and the 47 million in Spain. And yet we Brits make only two

[2] *Actually, I'm sure there are plenty of speedboats in Germany – the country has a thriving speedboat manufacturing industry and exports them all over the world – it's the inflatable bananas that are in scant supply.*

million visits to Germany each year, compared with the nine million we make to France and the eleven million to Spain. There are far more trips made by UK citizens to Ireland, Portugal, the USA and even the Benelux countries than are made to poor old Germany.

Secondly, Germany is renowned as being a major producer of two of the greatest wonders of the modern world – beer and cheese. And this fact alone is another good reason for choosing Germany as my camping holiday destination. I'll start with cheese if I may – which I accept is a little unconventional, given that the cheese usually arrives as an alternative to dessert at around the same time as the coffee and the wafer-thin chocolate mints. Cheese is, without a shadow of a doubt, the most wonderful food on the planet – period. There's nothing out there that can possibly beat it (although I am prepared to acknowledge that bacon sandwiches and lemon meringue pie are both very strong contenders). Cheese is quite simply *ambrosial* – and I'm sure there will be thousands of turophiles out there who will willingly concur. [3] And the fact is that, when it comes to making cheese, the Germans are far better at it than anybody else. My wife didn't believe me when I told her that. She thought it would be the French who would be the proud holders of such an acclaim. But the reality is this: it's the Germans who hold all the major cheese accolades, and not the French. Germany, for example, produces more cheese than any other European country and is second only to the United States as the largest cheese producer in the world. Germany is also the world's largest exporter of cheese as well as the world's biggest consumer. [4] But the most

[3] *I'm a bit worried about my use of the word 'turophile'. My spellchecker insists on underlining it in red, suggesting that no such word exists. I couldn't find it in my dictionary either. However, I am of the opinion that it is a genuine word meaning 'lover of cheese' although not used in common parlance I admit.*

wonderful thing of all is that German cheeses (there are around 150 different varieties I could potentially gorge myself on during my visit) have such splendid-sounding names – all completely unpronounceable even if you're stone-cold sober. They have names like *Tilsiter, Wilstermarschkäse* and *Edelpilzkäse* – the sort of names that could potentially tie your tongue into knots whilst you're attempting to pronounce them. And then there are those 'even-tougher-to-pronounce' varieties, such as *'Odenwälderfrühstückskäse'* and *'Altenburgerziegenkäse'* which I suspect even the Germans have difficulty enunciating.

They may be world-class cheese producers, but when it comes to brewing beer, the Germans are, quite simply, in a league of their own. There are around 1,300 breweries in Germany, which between them churn out more than 5,000 different brews. I don't know whether any previous attempt has been made to sample all 5,000 varieties over a thirty-two day period (there was no mention of it in this year's *Guinness Book of Records*) but as part of my camping trip itinerary I decided it would be churlish of me not to give it a damn good go.

Thirdly, and I suppose this was my primary motivation – Germany is a country I have visited on numerous occasions in the past. Now, I suppose one could plausibly argue that this fact alone could be regarded as a very good reason *not* to visit Germany. After all, why go again if I've already been?

[4] *Germany produces marginally less than two million metric tons of cheese annually against 4.2 million produced by the US. France ranks as the third biggest cheese manufacturer, producing around 1.8 million metric tons per annum – but produces more varieties of cheese than Germany. Regarding consumption, the average German eats around 31 kilograms of cheese every year (the greedy bastard). This compares with around 22 kilos consumed by the average Frenchman (presumably accompanied by a glass or two of fine wine), and around 11 kilos scoffed by the average Brit.*

Why not visit uncharted territory instead? Well, yes maybe you're right. But the thing is this: I like Germany. It's a country crammed with beautiful historical towns and cities and quaint medieval villages. It has a wealth of unspoilt natural landscapes in the form of nature reserves, biosphere reserves and national parks. Its flora and fauna are wonderfully diverse and often unique. And then of course, there are the German people – so often stereotyped as being officious and dour; efficient, but lacking humour. Well, I can assure you the reality is very different. In my experience the German people are generally rather warm, friendly and welcoming, well behaved and punctiliously polite. And to top it all – I can speak a bit of the lingo. Not fluently by any stretch of the imagination, but enough to get me through any impromptu exchanges with the indigenous population and hopefully enough to enable me to convince the Polizei that the whole sordid incident was indeed regrettable but was, in fact, all just a terrible misunderstanding.

So my mind was made up – I would embark on a camping tour of Germany. From Schleswig-Holstein in the north to the foothills of the Bavarian Alps, I would make my way through each of Germany's sixteen states (staying at least one night in each of them) and visit as many of her twenty-three officially-designated national parks and nature reserves as I possibly could in the time allowed. I would explore the country's historical towns and cities; meet the local people; immerse myself in their culture; eat their cheese; drink their beer and familiarise myself with their quirky little ways. And I'd spend the best part of five weeks doing it.

I began my preparation for this trip by compiling a detailed list of all those items I would need to take with me – a task which I set about with gusto – and was delighted to discover that the vast majority of camping accoutrements listed on my inventory were things I already owned. This was indeed an auspicious start, although there were one or two minor exceptions and one rather major one – which I'll return to presently. I was, for example, already in possession of a rucksack – proven to be suitable for pan-European travel and a most congenial travelling companion, it having accompanied me on a previous trip from Hammerfest to Syracuse. However, the one major item that I didn't already possess was a tent.

Now, it's been a while since I last purchased such a thing, and I'm pretty sure that over the years, styles and fashions in the tent world would undoubtedly have changed – such is the way of most things – it's an inexorable fact of life. The last time I purchased a tent was about twenty years ago – it was a large family frame tent aptly named the '*Paradox 1900*'. It was a complex and cumbersome affair that took an eternity to assemble. But with the help of dogged determination, a small measure of good fortune and a set of positively Byzantine assembly instructions, the *Paradox 1900* transformed into a rather splendid temporary dwelling for a family of four – windproof, waterproof, and complete with kitchen area and three separate bedrooms. Of course, for this latest adventure of mine the *Paradox 1900* would have been entirely unsuitable – too large, too unwieldy and impossible to transport without a motor vehicle with capacious boot space. Not only that, I had no idea where I might find it. It was probably rotting away in the cellar having been unceremoniously dumped there after our last family camping holiday – the frame slowly rusting, the groundsheet moulding and the canvas gradually being devoured by moth.

And so, on one warm and sunny Tuesday morning (with me feeling rather smug and sanguine), I repaired to my local 'outdoor' shop – which I was delighted to discover was a retail outlet specialising in tents, camping equipment and outdoor clothing, rather than a shop with its roof missing, as I had momentarily envisaged. I was greeted almost immediately by one of the shop assistants who ran the entire length of the store to welcome me the moment he saw me walking in. Gary was a scrawny-looking young man, about seventeen years old with a ruddy complexion and blighted with more than his fair share of acne. He had an assortment of piercings in his ears and eyebrows, wispy stubble on his chin and his hair was tied at the back with a ponytail. I knew his name was Gary because it was emblazoned across his chest on a large name badge that was pinned onto his tangerine-coloured overalls – the corporate colours of this particular 'outdoor' shop. So, unless he had swapped his name badge with another of the store's employees in a puerile effort to add a little mirth to his otherwise wearisome day, I assumed that Gary was his name.

"I'm looking for a tent," I said, having decided it would be preferable to come straight to the point rather than go off on a tangent by indulging in irrelevant idle banter. There was a portentous pause while Gary perfected his look of total exasperation.

"Yeah, well there's a lot of different sorts, innit," he said rather boorishly. He was right of course, although his discourtesy and impertinence were unnecessary in my opinion. I suppose I should have turned around at that point and left the shop, with a view to taking my business elsewhere. But there weren't that many camping and leisure shops in my neighbourhood – a conclusion I had reached earlier in the day following a meticulous and exhaustive examination of my local Yellow Pages. Not only that, I wanted to get the task of 'tent purchasing' over and done with as quickly as possible, and taking my business elsewhere would only have delayed the process unnecessarily. So I decided to persevere with young Gary – give him the opportunity to redeem himself and turn his rather unpromising start into one of his more triumphant sales successes.

"Are there?" I replied, with just a small hint of sarcasm. Gary took a deep breath and launched into the following outburst of verbal diarrhoea:

"Yeah, well you've got yer Khyam tents, yer tunnel tents, yer pod tents, yer geodesic and yer semi-geodesic tents." He paused momentarily for breath, leading me into a false sense of optimism that he may have exhausted his catalogue of tent types. But before giving me the chance to interrupt, he continued where he'd left off, as if someone had lifted their finger off the 'pause' button.

"Then there's yer basic ridge tents, yer dome tents, yer frame tents, yer vis-à-vis tents, yer family tents, tepees, trailer tents, not to mention a whole range of inflatable and quick-pitch tents."

"Well, I'll tell you what, Gary," I said, "why don't you give me the benefit of your superior knowledge on the subject, and advise me what type of tent I should purchase?"

Realising at last that his encounter with me might actually result in his first commission-yielding sale of the morning, Gary dropped his acerbic and churlish stance and decided instead to adopt a degree of civility – a trait in his personality that clearly wasn't allowed out very often. Having realised that he was standing face to face with someone who was genuinely interested in his advice, Gary smiled the sort of smile that suggested he had been waiting his entire life for this moment to arrive. It was Gary's chance to shine – and it wasn't an opportunity Gary was going to waste.

"What are you planning to use it for?" he began, which sounded to me like a very sensible place to start.

"I'm planning a trip around Germany," I said. "It's just me on my own so I'll only need something small and preferably easy to assemble. I'll also be carrying it around with me in a rucksack so it'll need to be lightweight and portable."

Gary sucked air in through his teeth and shook his head disapprovingly.

"Be very wary of 'lightweight and portable,'" he said, eventually.

"You see, the trouble with 'lightweight and portable' is that the two things that really matter get compromised."

"Really? And what are the two things that really matter?" I ventured rather audaciously.

"Strength and stability," declared Gary emphatically. "Never underestimate the importance of tent stability. You see, the thing is," he continued, "lightweight and portable is all very well – but all it takes is one strong gust of wind and your tent will be lifted off the ground and blown around like the wicked witch's bicycle in the Wizard of Oz." I tried to visualise Gary's analogy but struggled to picture it. I felt certain that the Wicked Witch of the West never owned a bicycle; a broomstick, maybe – but not a bicycle.

"So what would you suggest?" I asked. Gary frogmarched me through the store to a small section at the rear housing a number of pre-assembled display tents.

"This one," said Gary, pointing at one of them. "This little beauty is the *Vaude Power Tokee UL,*" he said proudly. "It's the smaller single-person version of the successful two-person *Power Lizard* ultra-light tent. The *Power Tokee* has the same double wall, single arch construction as the *Power Lizard* but in a smaller version. It's got a single entrance, a single vestibule and a laminated formic acid-resistant floor. The *Power Tokee* offers maximum stability and yet weighs only 800 grams."

I must admit, this '*Power Tokee*' did look rather splendid.

"How much is it?" I asked.

"Two hundred and ninety-nine pounds," he replied.

Later that day, I bought a fine-looking tent from a well-known retail chain store specialising in catalogue shopping, for the princely sum of twenty-nine quid – with a sleeping mat thrown in for free as part of a special promotional offer. My tent of choice was called the *Wind-Breaker DeLuxe* which, despite sounding like a medicinal treatment for chronic flatulence was, in fact, a one-man tent that combined strength and stability (the two things that apparently really matter), together with being lightweight and portable (two qualities which I would personally have considered crucial but, it turns out, are things I should be very wary of). 'Guaranteed waterproof' and weighing around 1.5 kilograms, I will admit that my *Wind-Breaker DeLuxe* was a little heavier than the *Power Tokee* lightweight tent that Gary had recommended, but to the naked eye it appeared every bit as sturdy. I was also intrigued to discover that it came with what the shop described as a *'limited lifetime guarantee'* – which sounded to me like an oxymoron if ever I heard one. But its greatest advantage over the *Tokee* was simply this: if my tent were to blow away in a tornado of the sort of Kansas-style ferocity that Gary was expecting, then for less than thirty quid, I could dump into a skip those pieces that weren't sucked up into the vortex and simply buy myself a new tent.

After a great deal of debate, dithering and vacillation, I decided that my trip through Germany should run concurrently with my wife's cruise in the Caribbean. The dates of her cruise weren't flexible like mine were of course – the *'Oasis of the Seas'* would be setting sail from Bridgetown on its preset date of June 8th whether my wife was onboard or otherwise. *My* trip however, could happen pretty much anytime I wanted it to. But the month of June seemed like a propitious time of year to trek across the German countryside – the weather should be reasonably reliable and each day would bring a profusion of daylight hours. Our detached holiday arrangements wouldn't coincide precisely of course – my wife would return home after three weeks, whereas I would be away for thirty-two days. But since our next-door neighbour would be predominantly office-based throughout June and much of July, our services as cat-sitters would not be necessary, and my neighbour could keep an eye on our house as a safeguard against it being destroyed by fire, flood or gas explosion. Not that our absence would contribute to the possibility of such a catastrophe I hasten to add – but our languorous twenty-year-old son would be home alone whilst my wife and I were away, and so the propensity for an incident resulting in severe structural damage to our property would be significantly enhanced during this period.

And so, on the evening prior to our departure, my wife and I packed our bags in readiness for our respective journeys to foreign climes – I with my rucksack and she with her three (yes three!) huge 90-litre trolley-suitcases in a hideous matching pink peony floral fabric. Heaven knows why my dear wife believed she needed half the things she was planning to take with her. Had there been room in one of her cases, I'm quite certain she would have taken the fridge.

But since I would be carrying all my worldly possessions in a single rucksack, I needed to be far more disciplined – my spine and my shoulder blades were quite resolute about that. So with a miscellany of appurtenances spread out over the bed, I set about the task of dividing everything I had into three separate categories which I labelled 'essential', 'functional' and 'extravagant'. With so many items vying for the limited space in my rucksack, this system enabled me to create a 'pecking order' – with 'essential' items taking priority as you'd expect. Among my list of travelling 'essentials' were my *Wind-Breaker DeLuxe* tent, my sleeping bag and mat, my passport, ferry ticket, wallet, and my thirty-day *Deutsche Bahn* rail pass. Of course

I threw a few clothes in too, but I decided only to take the bare essentials as I figured that most of the campsites I'd be staying at would boast a laundry room among their amenities.

After the '*essentials*' had been crammed into my bag, I endeavoured to find room for the items on my '*functionals*' list. These included my 'Hand-Forged Feasting Utensils' – purchased from the same catalogue shop that supplied me the tent – an LED torch, my camera and several books comprising a number of illustrated guidebooks and a couple of fictional paperbacks, which I had been intending to read for some time but hadn't quite got round to. I shan't bother to reel off any of the items on my '*extravagant*' list as doing so would be largely academic. None would fit into my rucksack, and so were put back onto the shelves or into the drawers and cupboards whence they came and were ruthlessly disqualified from accompanying me on my trip.

And that was that. After precisely sixteen minutes and twenty-five seconds my rucksack was packed and I was ready to roll – so I cracked open a bottle of *Peroni* to celebrate. My wife's packing of her own suitcases was an event that continued long into the night.

A taxi turned up outside our house the following morning. I gave my wife a big hug and a kiss goodbye and watched her climb inside, leaving the harried taxi driver to struggle on his own as he lifted her suitcases into the boot. My wife had a rendezvous with her friend Joanna at Heathrow Airport – a detail which they had worked into their itinerary many weeks earlier. The two of them had allowed 'plenty of time' for some duty-free shopping before their departure gate opened for boarding. What is it with women and shopping? Their flight wasn't scheduled for another nine hours! Go figure.

I too had a few hours to kill before it was time to leave (I wouldn't be heading off on my own adventure until around nine o'clock that evening), but unlike my darling wife and her comrade in retail therapy (for whom spending money frivolously was almost an obsessive compulsive disorder), I had no intention of killing it by wandering around a bustling airport terminal, browsing the shelves of tax-free shops in search of discounted perfumes, shoes and handbags. Instead, I took a leisurely stroll along the towpath at Richmond upon Thames and stopped for lunch at a riverside bar – a chance to enjoy the sunshine, a glass of cold beer and make some last minute checks to my travel itinerary.

oOo

Chapter Two – On a Bike on Borkum

"I've got a bike, you can ride it if you like, it's got a basket, a bell that rings, and things to make it look good; I'd give it to you if I could – but I borrowed it."
From 'Bike' by Pink Floyd. Lyrics by Syd Barrett (1946 – 2006) singer, songwriter, guitarist, painter, genius

If ever you're considering a journey from the UK to Germany, then you'll find your route options are both varied and numerous. But only, that is, if you're planning to fly. If, like me, you prefer to travel at the more leisurely and hypnotic pace that only a ferry crossing can achieve, then you'll find your options somewhat limited. Actually, if you're looking for a *direct* ferry crossing to Germany from anywhere in the UK, then you'll find your options are non-existent.

There used to be direct ferry services from the port of Harwich to the German cities of Bremerhaven, Cuxhaven and Hamburg, but sadly all three have now disappeared. It was the Bremerhaven route, operated by sister ships *'Prins Oberon'* and *'Prinz Hamlet',* that was the first to go back in 1984. DFDS, who operated all three services, later closed the Harwich to Hamburg route in 1999, leaving Cuxhaven as the only port in Germany with a direct ferry link to the UK. But low demand raised questions over the long-term commercial viability of the service – and in 2005 (sadly, yet inevitably), this route was also discontinued. The demise of the Harwich-Hamburg route was particularly disappointing, since the journey across the North Sea culminated in a 130-kilometre cruise along the River Elbe into the heart of Hamburg's bustling port. I used this service on a couple of occasions in the early 1980s – the trip along the Elbe was indeed the main highlight. There may no longer be any direct passenger ferry services to Germany but there are a multitude of alternative ferry routes available via Denmark, France, Belgium and the Netherlands. Which of these I would plump for would depend, of course, on where my camping tour of Germany was to begin.

After a great deal of deliberation, I chose a route that would take me from my home in West London to the Island of Borkum in Lower Saxony – a journey which, by my reckoning, would take around twenty hours to complete. Now, if you've never heard of the island of Borkum, then you're not alone. I hadn't heard of it until I began planning this trip, and I have it on good authority that there aren't many Germans who are familiar with it either.

Borkum is one of the East Frisian Islands (*Ostfriesische Inseln*) – a chain of small islands strung out like pearls just a few kilometres off the North Sea coast. The islands extend for some 90 kilometres from west to east between the mouths of the Ems and Weser rivers. There are seven East Frisian Islands in total – the largest and most westerly of which is the island of Borkum – which is not exactly what you might call gargantuan – it covers an area of a little less than 36 square kilometres. This may seem like an anomalous place to begin my tour of Germany – but I chose it for two very good reasons.

Firstly, the island of Borkum lies in the far north-western tip of the country – so much so that both the Dutch and the German coastlines are visible from its shores. Actually, it's geographically closer to the Netherlands than it is to Germany, but only just. And if, like me, you're planning to zigzag your way through all sixteen German states, then Germany's top-left hand corner seemed to be a jolly sensible place to begin.

Secondly (and I think this swung the decision for me), the East Frisian Islands are located in an area of outstanding natural beauty. You see, the North Sea on the Lower Saxony coast is really quite extraordinary. At times it isn't there at all – it comes and goes with the rhythm of the tides. At low tide the sea bed is exposed to reveal slimy mudflats with occasional water channels running here and there – some of which are deep enough for ships to navigate their way through. This North Sea coastal area is known as the *Niedersachsen Wattenmeer* (the Lower Saxony Mudflats). It's a protected nature reserve, one of Germany's official national parks and a UNESCO World Heritage site. The East Frisian Islands form part of the *Wattenmeer National Park*, and since the Borkum Tourist Authority seemed so eager for me to visit '*the North Sea's most glittering jewel*', I chose the island of Borkum as the starting point for my camping trip across Germany.

My twenty-hour journey would begin with a ride on a tube train to London's Liverpool Street station, followed by a train to Harwich International, and an eight-and-a-half-hour ferry crossing to the Hook of Holland (*Hoek van Holland*). Once I had crossed the North Sea and was back on terra firma, my journey would continue by train across the Dutch-German border, arriving on Borkum Island almost eight hours after leaving the ferry port at Hoek. All in all, a bit of a palaver I admit, particularly since the rail journey from the Hook of Holland would necessitate four separate changes of train at Rotterdam, Gouda, Groningen and Leer – and I'd still have a ferry to catch to get me to Borkum. This may not be the fastest route to the East Frisian Islands, but it's certainly the least circuitous – and it had another significant advantage over the other routes I'd considered.

The ferry service between Harwich and the Hook of Holland operates twice daily – a daytime and a night-time sailing. By choosing the night service, I could sleep through the entire sea crossing in a comfortable bed in my own private cabin and wake the following morning feeling refreshed, rejuvenated and ready for the train journey ahead. That was my theory, anyway. It would also mean arriving on Borkum in the early afternoon, giving me enough time to find the campsite, set up my *Wind-Breaker DeLuxe*, and still have most of the afternoon and evening to explore the island.

And so my journey began.

After seventy-five minutes on a train from Liverpool Street I arrived at *Harwich International* – a pretentious name for a railway station serving a drab and rather unattractive ferry port. The railway first arrived in Harwich in 1854 on the line from Colchester and was known as the *Mayflower Line* – named of course after the ship that carried the English pilgrims to Plymouth, Massachusetts in 1620. [5] The station was originally called *Parkeston Quay* until 1995 when it suddenly underwent a bizarre and inexplicable metamorphosis – re-emerging as '*Harwich International*' without any visible change to its function or its physical appearance.

With daylight rapidly fading and ominous grey clouds scudding across the skies over the Stour Estuary, I boarded the *Stena Hollandica* – one of two ships operated by Stena Lines on the Harwich-Hook of Holland service. Acclaimed as the 'largest combined freight and passenger ferry in the world', the *Stena Hollandica* truly is a monster. Weighing 62,000 tons and costing over £200m, this extraordinary 240-metre-long vessel was built in Wismar in 2007 and delivered to Stena Lines in 2010 along with her sister ship the *Stena Britannica*. As I stepped aboard, I grabbed a handful of Stena Line's publicity brochures from a dispenser mounted on a wall beside the bureau de change, before making my way to the *Riva Bar*, where I parked my backside on a bar

[5] *The Mayflower was based in Harwich at one stage during its lifetime, and Christopher Jones, the master and quarter-owner of the Mayflower was a resident of the town.*

stool for over an hour while I studied the brochures and polished off a pint of lager.

"Our onboard facilities..." the brochure proudly explained, *"...include buffet and à la carte restaurants, two bars, children's playroom, teenager area, cinema and the Stena Plus Lounge – a media room filled with magazines and newspapers where you can keep up with the latest local and world news".*

I was fascinated by some of the on-board facilities described in the brochure. I was particularly intrigued by the existence of a *teenager area*. In my mind's eye I had conjured an image of a messy enclosure hidden deep in the bowels of the engine room – where spotty teenagers were kept under secure conditions in the interests of the health and safety of other passengers. With large piles of dirty laundry on the floor jostling for space among the discarded sweet wrappers and empty beer cans, hundreds of languid teenagers were held in storage, where they could wear their trousers halfway down their backsides, shuffle around making absurd grunting noises and practise on each other the art of stringing comprehensible sentences together. I could almost hear the voice of the ship's captain as he welcomed his passengers on board:

"I see you have teenage children, madam. Don't worry – we have a special teenager area you can put them in."

I was also somewhat intrigued by the media room – *filled with magazines and newspapers*. I knew an elderly lady once who filled every one of her rooms with magazines and newspapers – so much so that the doors wouldn't open. In her case however, it was attributed to a mental illness.

With an eight-and-a-half-hour sea crossing ahead of me, I decided there was time enough for me to explore the on-board facilities, so I decided instead to seek the whereabouts of my overnight accommodation. The booking confirmation that Stena Lines had e-mailed me several weeks earlier confirmed my reservation of an 'outside' cabin – another of those ambiguous adianoetas that add to the splendour of the English language. But I was soon to discover that an 'outside' cabin was one with a window overlooking the sea, rather than one fully exposed to the elements. The cabin was compact, I admit, but it was clean and tidy and the bed was comfortable enough, so I lay there for a while reading more of Stena Line's advertising brochures and wondering whether the on-board cinema would be screening *The Poseidon Adventure* as a cruel stunt devised by the ship's embittered Entertainments Officer on his final shift prior to his retirement.

I don't know if it was the gentle swaying motion of the ferry as it sliced its way majestically through the choppy waters of the Stour Estuary and out into the North Sea; or the fresh salty air; or whether I was mesmerised by the mellow hum of the ship's engines – but whatever the contributing factors, I began to feel my eyelids getting heavier as I studied the brochure, so I abandoned my plans to investigate the true nature of the *teenager area*, and fell asleep instead.

I woke the following morning far later than I had originally intended. Sunlight was streaming through the window of my cabin as I lay there still half asleep; my sub-conscience stuck in the weirdest of dreams. I was vaguely aware of a change in the noise of the ship's engines – the gentle, soporific hum had suddenly become a sonorous drone as the captain negotiated the delicate task of docking 62,000 tons of steel onto its berth at the Hook of Holland. But while all this activity was going on outside, I was stuck in a broken elevator with Ronnie Corbett, and the sound of the ship's engines was the noise made by the lift as it suddenly sprung back into life again, thanks to the elevator repair skills of Ant and Dec and a polar bear wearing orange overalls and a fez. But I woke from my dream rather suddenly as an announcement was made over the ship's public-address system, advising passengers that we had reached our destination and that we should make our way *immediately* to the car deck to be reunited with our vehicles. Not all of us had a vehicle of course, so I was delighted when a further announcement was made advising foot passengers to await further instructions before disembarking. It gave me a vital extra few minutes to change into a fresh pair of undercrackers; put my trousers on; find a clean T-shirt in the murky depths of my rucksack and splash my face with a drop of lukewarm water.

It was 8.00am and I had arrived in the Netherlands – a veritable integrated transport Utopia, where transport connections are designed to make the lives of travellers as simple and as painless as possible. So it was no great surprise to discover that the railway station at the Hook of Holland was more or less adjacent to the point of disembarkation from the *Stena Hollandica,* where a train was scheduled to depart on the first leg of my onward journey. As I've mentioned already, my route from here to Borkum Island comprised five separate train journeys. So rather than suffocate you with laborious detail which I know can be terribly enervating, I'll try to summarise the highlights for you as briefly and succinctly as I can.

Train number one: would only take me as far as Rotterdam – a short sprint of around thirty minutes from the ferry port. I had never been to Rotterdam before and I can't pretend to know very much about the city or its people. I do, however, have it on good authority from a very reliable source that 'the whole place is pickled, and the women tug their hair like they're trying to prove it won't fall out'. [6] But whether this is true or not would have to remain

[6] *From the lyrics of the song 'Rotterdam', written by Paul Heaton and David Rotheray and performed by The Beautiful South.*

unconfirmed, as I had just twelve minutes at Rotterdam station to change platforms and connect with the train operating the second leg of this five-stage railway escapade.

Train number two: a remarkably short hop of less than twenty minutes to the town of Gouda. Now, even if you're not a big fan of cheese as I am, you will surely be aware that the town of Gouda in the Netherlands is famous for its creamy, semi-soft cheese – smooth and rounded, with a pale yellow interior dotted with a few tiny holes. Despite having a texture analogous to something a builder might use for filling cracks in walls, Gouda cheese accounts for more than 60% of Holland's total cheese production and the stuff is exported in huge quantities to countries across the globe. The thing is, Gouda cheese is not made in the city of Gouda as you might have assumed – it's produced in the surrounding region. But its name is derived from the fact that the cheese is traded in the city as a commodity and Gouda city council imposes stringent quality controls. I was hoping that the station at Gouda would house a small cheese shop, where I could spend the twenty-minute waiting time for my onward connection to Groningen, simply browsing its shelves, taste-testing the various Gouda variations and purchasing a small amount to keep me going during the next stage of this seemingly interminable journey. But there was no cheese shop at Gouda station, which was a pity because I didn't have time to stroll into the city centre to buy some authentic Gouda at one of the numerous cheese stalls in the market square. In fact, there wasn't anything of any interest at Gouda station, save for a small kiosk selling snacks and refreshments. I purchased a coffee served in a rather flimsy take-away polystyrene cup, together with a chocolate bar with the comical brand name *'Big Nuts'* – manufactured by the Belgian confectionery giant *Meurisse*.

Train number three: very different from the previous two. This was a swanky, modern, high-speed Inter-city affair

33

– although the driver managed to restrain his machine from breaking any land speed records. The journey from Gouda to Groningen took a little over two hours, but it was smooth and comfortable and I managed to fill the time supping my coffee and munching away on my Big Nuts. [7] It was a pity I didn't have any cheese as a savoury accompaniment.

Train number four: a time for celebration. The train crossed a bridge over the River Ems at Weener – out of one country and into another. It had now been a little over seventeen hours since I'd left my home in west London and I had finally made it into the Federal Republic of Germany – a milestone which I celebrated by smiling inanely at the young lady sitting opposite me, much to her obvious disapproval. Just a minute or two later, our train wheezed into the station at the somnolent little town of Leer – so bereft of life that the sight of tumbleweeds blowing across the station concourse wouldn't have surprised me in the slightest. It was here at Leer that I waited for a mind-numbing forty-five minutes for my fifth and final rail connection.

Train number five: one of the those little sprinter trains with only two carriages and plastic seating designed to cause maximum irritation for those who suffer haemorrhoid problems, and create haemorrhoid problems for those who don't. This was the train that would take me the final twenty

---

[7] *That was both vulgar and puerile I admit, but I simply couldn't resist it. The 'Big Nuts' chocolate bar is listed on the official top 10 products with comical brand names, so I was delighted to have found it on sale in the platform kiosk at Gouda station. Others on the list include Jussi-Pussi dinner rolls (Finland), Fart (Polish fruit juice drink), Dickmilch (German milk drink), Prick (Brazilian potato chips), Bum-Bum (German ice cream), Creamy Balls (Japanese confectionery product), Plopp (Czech candy bar), and Finger Marie (Swedish biscuit brand – manufactured by McVities of all people – whose marketing bods really should have known better). The final product listed in the top ten is Horlicks – a brand name which we in the UK have become so accustomed to over the years, its name is no longer funny.*

kilometres of my railway journey to the small seaport of Emden.

The AG Ems car ferry '*Münsterland*' was waiting at her berth at the Emden dockside – this was the aging and decrepit-looking vessel that would take me on the ninety-minute crossing to the island of Borkum. There was nothing luxurious about the *Münsterland*. She was slow, noisy, she reeked of engine oil, and listed wildly from side to side – qualities identical to those of a girl I once knew from my college days. After her valiant battle against every ripple in the choppy waters of the North Sea, the *Münsterland* arrived in Borkum's little dockyard, and was secured to a dockside cleat by a pair of burly, bearded stevedores.

Along with my dozen or so fellow passengers, I clambered cautiously down the gangway and onto the quayside, holding tightly to the handrail as I made the descent. Immediately, I headed for a small dockside coffee shop for an urgent caffeine injection. This was top of my list of priorities, I decided, given the wan, dishwater-style nature of the coffee that had been on sale aboard the *Münsterland*.

The geographical shape of Borkum Island is not easy to describe without drawing you a map – but I'll try to give it my best shot, even at the risk of both over-simplification and wild inaccuracy. So, imagine if you can, an upside down equilateral triangle – with one of its three sides lying horizontally across the top. In the bottom corner of the triangle is the dockyard, where the *Münsterland* has recently docked and where I am currently enjoying a rather splendid cappuccino accompanied by an obscenely calorific blueberry muffin. In the top left-hand corner is the only town on the island, which for the purposes of saving both of us from having to remember too many complex and unpronounceable German place names, is also called Borkum.

Connecting the dockyard with the main town is a seven-kilometre stretch of road – the only significant road on the whole of the island and something of a rarity in these parts, as the majority of the East Frisian Islands have been designated 'car-free zones'. And running parallel with the road along the entire seven-kilometre stretch is a railway line – which I shall return to in just a moment. Other than that there's not much else on Borkum. The rest of the island is largely bereft of anything man-made – save for the occasional lighthouse, coffee shop or isolated farm building – oh, and a camping site of course. Fortunately though, Mother Nature manages to fill the vacuum rather well.

The area of the Lower Saxony Mudflats is believed to be the second most productive ecosystem after the tropical rainforests of South America – with only the latter surpassing it in terms of its living biomass. There are up to 4,000 animal and plant species to be found here – including diatoms, snails, mussels and lugworms. It's a natural breeding ground for thousands of gulls, ducks, geese and waders; and the sandbanks off the island's coast attract many hundreds of seals. The vegetation typically found in the island's sand dunes comprises beach grass, wild roses and sea buckthorn – all of which makes the island of Borkum a rather attractive place to visit. It became a popular and somewhat well-to-do holiday resort in the late 19th century when visitors began to realise the medicinal value of the bracing North Sea air, and the restorative qualities of the high levels of iodine in the water. But the weather here can be a challenge for holidaymakers. The East Frisian Islands are flat – pancake flat. Just a few metres above sea level, their geographic position in the North Sea means that the weather is often inclement, to put it mildly. Even now, in early June, as I sat there in the dockside café supping on my coffee and wolfing down my blueberry muffin, a strong northerly wind was doing its best to liberate a pair of elderly ladies from their rather

36

elegant cloche hats – one of the disadvantages of opting to take afternoon coffee al fresco at one of the café's outdoor tables.

I reduced my muffin to a small pile of crumbs and decided to head towards the main town – a seven-kilometre journey either by bus or train. I had no difficulty deciding which of these two options I would go with – and here's why. During the planning of my camping trip around Germany, I discovered that the island of Borkum boasted a miniature railway among its many tourist attractions – the *Borkumer Kleinbahn* to give it its proper title.

At the mention of a miniature railway, there are some who might instantly conjure up an image of a giant train set. They'll envisage children sitting on top of the carriages – their legs splayed over the sides, holding on for dear life with one hand whilst waving nervously to mum and dad with the other. Pulling the carriages is a replica steam train in miniature, driven by an elderly railway enthusiast who always wanted to be a proper train driver, but sadly missed his vocation in life. This ebullient septuagenarian will be enjoying himself far more than any of his passengers. He'll have huge sideburns and a portly physique, and will be wearing the obligatory train driver's cap.

Well, the *Borkumer Kleinbahn* is nothing like that at all. Built originally in 1879, the trains run on a 900mm-gauge track – only marginally narrower than a standard-gauge railway line.[8] This almost life-sized railway operates a combination of both steam and diesel locomotives, many of which date back to the 1940s or even earlier. But along with the rolling stock, these charming locomotives are lovingly maintained and cared for by an army of volunteers and

[8] *The 'gauge' of a railway track is the distance between the inside edges of the rails, the standard for which is 1,435mm. This 'standard gauge' or 'Stephenson gauge' is used on approximately 60% of the world's railway lines. 900mm, however, is something of a rarity.*

37

railway enthusiasts who keep them looking immaculate and in pristine condition. The train I was about to board was probably the weirdest looking contraption I have ever seen operating on a railway. Known as the 'Wismar Railcar', this extraordinary single-carriage train was built in 1936, but after twenty years in storage was restored, refurbished and returned to the *Borkumer Kleinbahn* in 1997. The engines on both the front and rear of the car are housed in a long, elongated casing which protrudes from the body of the carriage. Little wonder that these trains are known affectionately as *Schweineschnäuzchen* or 'pig snouts'.

By the time I arrived at Borkum's town centre the weather had begun to deteriorate. The wind had strengthened; the skies (which had been grey for much of the afternoon) were looking even darker and more foreboding; and I could feel a few spots of rain in the air. At first glance, the town appeared to have a great deal worthy of further exploration – there were two fine-looking beaches, an aquarium and a small shopping precinct. But having spent the best part of twenty hours travelling, I was eager to find the campsite and assemble my tent before the rain started in earnest. And so I set off on a four-kilometre trek away from the town centre, across the island's flat, wind-swept landscape and along a seemingly endless network of pathways lined on either side by spur dykes. The wind blew relentlessly, throwing fine particles of sand into my face, and by the time I reached the campsite *'Insel-Camping'* I was cold, tired and not in the cheeriest of spirits.

Insel-Camping is the only official campsite on Borkum. It's a well-maintained site boasting a great many amenities and is managed with emblematic German efficiency. As I wandered around the grounds in search of a suitable pitch, I stumbled upon the toilet block, which included a smartly furnished washroom and shower facility, the campsite shop and the children's play area. By now though, the rain was beginning to fall rather more persistently, the raindrops tapping out perfect paradiddles on the tin roofs of the surrounding caravans. So I took temporary refuge beneath the boughs of an oak tree in a more secluded area within the campsite compound. When the rain eased, I decided to take full advantage of the temporary ceasefire and ventured out from my shelter in search of a suitable spot to pitch my *Wind-Breaker DeLuxe.* Most of the primary pitches at *Insel-Camping* were reserved for caravans and motorhomes – of which there was a multitude, with stand-alone tents confined to a small corner of the site. It wasn't a great spot, to be honest. To begin with, the area designated for tents wasn't terribly well sheltered. There were a few trees offering *some* protection from the wind, but all the best spots had already been taken. Moreover, the tent area was at the rear of the grounds – a long way from the site's main amenities and some considerable walking distance from the nearest toilet block. Still, I suppose I could always nip behind a tree should I get caught short in the middle of the night.

During a break between rain showers, I chose what looked to me like a decent enough patch of ground and made a start on setting up my tent as quickly as I could – conscious that the rain might start again at any moment. My pitch was very close to where a large green family-sized frame tent had already been erected. It reminded me of the *Paradox 1900* that had accompanied me on my family camping holidays when my children were small. This tent belonged to one of my fellow countrymen – a short but sinewy-looking Englishman with a tidy grey beard, wild wispy hair and a pair of thick-lens spectacles. He stood beside his tent in his khaki three-quarter-length trousers, brown sandals and white socks, smoking a pipe and staring at me continuously as I assembled my tent. Since not a word was spoken between us during the construction of my *Wind-Breaker DeLuxe*, you may be wondering how I knew that he

39

and his family were English. Well, parked adjacent to his tent was a car – a vomit-yellow Ford Mondeo with a roof rack, bicycle carrier and British registration plates. Now, whilst I accept that registration plates alone do not necessarily constitute irrefutable evidence of a person's nationality, you must admit it's a pretty good clue.

With my tent now fully assembled, I took a few steps backwards to inspect my workmanship. It was a proud moment as I'm sure you will understand. As I stood there admiring the fruit of my labours, the man removed the pipe from his mouth and struck up a conversation with me in his broad Mancunian accent – which instantly eliminated any doubt regarding his nationality.

"Is that your tent?" he asked.

Now, what sort of a damned silly question was that? He had been standing there for the last twenty minutes watching in silence as I battled with the assembly instructions, trying to erect the bloody thing. Whose tent did he think it was, for pity's sake? And who, exactly, did he think *I* was – some sort of benevolent guardian angel who went about charitably erecting other people's tents out of kindness of heart?

"Yes," I said, holding back on something more sarcastic. "Why do you ask?"

"Well, it just don't look all that stable to me," he replied, "I've been listening to the forecast, you see, and the weather over the next twelve hours ain't looking all that clever. It's gonna be wet and windy, and that tent don't look like it's man enough to cope."

Well, that was *all* I needed – an interfering, self-righteous busybody harping on about that now familiar old chestnut – *tent stability.*

"I think my tent will be fine," I replied confidently, hoping *that* would terminate this rather depressing conversation that I appeared to have unwittingly stumbled into. But I was wrong.

40

"It just seems a bit flimsy," he continued, "If a tent like that manages to survive the sort of winds that we're in for tonight, then my name's not Joseph!"

This, I thought, was an extraordinary thing to say. Who the heck did he think he was? What made him such an expert on tent stability? And what gave him the right to cast aspersions on the quality of my *Wind-Breaker DeLuxe* or question its manliness? I decided there and then that I didn't like this strange little man whose name may or may not have been Joseph. Not only had he offended me with his derogatory comments about my tent, his pipe smoke had now wafted into my personal space and was wreaking havoc with my nasal chemoreceptors. But as luck would have it, at that very moment the man's wife poked her head out from behind one of the tent flaps, and she summoned him inside for whatever culinary masterpiece she had conjured up on the camp stove. A courteous nod was about all I could muster as our meeting came to an end.

At around three o'clock in the morning my tent collapsed. Not completely, thank goodness – I was still able to clamber inside it, but a couple of the supporting poles buckled causing the entire structure to tilt sideways and sag a bit in the middle. I suppose the circumstances in which my tent managed to depart from its original upright position deserve explanation – otherwise I suspect that you too will draw all sorts of hasty conclusions regarding the resilience of my *Wind-Breaker DeLuxe* – or the lack of it. Well, the truth is that my tent coped admirably with the weather that night – she survived everything that Mother Nature threw at her. Sure, it *was* a squally night – the wind was gusty at times and the rain unrelenting – but not on the biblical scale that the bearded doomsayer in the neighbouring tent had so gloomily predicted. But shortly before 3.00am I woke up in desperate need to use the toilet. I didn't relish the prospect of walking as far as the nearest toilet block – it was dark

41

after all, and the weather was particularly poor, so I opted to take a leak behind a tree. As I fumbled my way in the darkness on my way back to the tent, I somehow managed to trip over one of the guide ropes, dropping my torch and falling rather clumsily on top of my tent. It was difficult to tell the extent of the damage. It was the middle of the night, I was cold and wet, and all I really wanted to do was get back into my sleeping bag and go back to sleep. So the official damage evaluation, I decided, would have to wait until daylight.

When I woke the following morning the wind had mercifully relented, the rain had stopped and the campsite at *Insel-Camping* was bathed in glorious sunshine. Unfortunately, the sun reflecting on the canvas had raised the temperature inside my tent to that of a pottery kiln and I could feel myself being slowly roasted at gas mark six. Still half asleep, my hair unkempt and with a whole heap of clutter behind my eyes, I stepped outside to inspect the damage I had inadvertently inflicted on my tent during the night. But I wasn't the only one scrutinising the extent of the destruction – the man whose name may or may not have been Joseph was there too, grinning at me inanely and wallowing in his own self-righteousness.

"Looks like it didn't fare too well," he announced smugly. "That's the difference between you and me," he continued, "*I* bought a tent that survived the storm unscathed."

---

[9] *The term 'Morton's fork' originates from the late 15th century, although nowadays has perhaps been superseded by the expression 'damned if you do, damned if you don't.' The term refers to the philosophy of John Morton, Lord Chancellor of England in 1487, who believed that if a man showed signs of wealth, then he could clearly afford to pay taxes to the King. If however, a man lived frugally and showed no sign of wealth, then the man must clearly have substantial savings hidden away somewhere and must therefore be able to afford to pay his taxes.*

"Yes," I replied, "And another difference between you and me is that I don't have shit for brains and a wife who is hideously ugly." Actually, I didn't say that at all, but only because it was way too early in the day for cleverly thought-through witticisms of that calibre. But I felt his conceited comments surely warranted a response of some sort. I was now faced with what I believe is commonly known as Morton's Fork [9] – a choice between two equally unpleasant alternatives. I could, of course, go for the truthful option – confess to having tripped over a guide rope during the night and fallen on top of my *Wind-Breaker DeLuxe*. But that would serve only to highlight my own stupidity and ineptitude, and would leave me with a cavernous dent in my dignity. But if I were to lie to him, and agree that it was *indeed* the wind that had caused the damage – well, that would simply have given him the smug satisfaction of believing he was right. So I decided instead to say nothing and chose simply to ignore him.

By far the best way to explore Borkum is to hire a bike – and a small '*Fahradverlieh*' or bicycle rental shop was one of the many surprises on offer at *Insel-Camping*. The shop was located just outside the main entrance to the campsite, adjacent to a small wooden construction with a sign reading 'Borkum Weather Centre' emblazoned across its facia. This easy-to-understand weather forecasting system simply comprised of a stone suspended from a supporting wooden frame by a short length of chain. There was a notice board alongside it offering the following explanations:

Stone cold - cold weather, winter.
Stone warm - fine weather, sunny.
Stone dry - no rain.
Stone white - snow.
Stone under water - flood.
Stone topped with seagull poo - shit weather.

Stone wiggling about - changing winds.
Stone bouncing – wind.
Stone bouncing a lot - storm.
Stone bouncing wildly - gale.
Stone invisible - fog.
Stone missing - no weather.
Stone dancing up and down - earthquake.

There, who says the Germans don't have a sense of humour?

After yesterday's wind and rain, the weather this morning was beautiful. I knew this, not simply because the stone in the weather centre was both warm and dry, but because the sky was a turquoise blue and deficient of cloud, and the sun was so strong I was forced to don my prescription shades. As I entered the bicycle rental shop I was greeted by a teenage girl with blond hair tied in pigtails. She was wearing shorts and a T-shirt with the slogan *'cyclists do it on a saddle'* printed on it. The girl welcomed me as I entered the shop with the curious greeting "*moin moin*" – not a phrase I had been familiar with prior to my arrival, and certainly not the customary *guten Morgen* or *guten Tag* that are the more orthodox salutations. But the language spoken in northern Germany is *low-German* – almost Dutch in fact, and virtually incomprehensible compared to the *high-German* or *Hochdeutsch* that Mr. Stevenson taught me in German lessons all those years ago. The word *moin*, I discovered, meant 'nice' and was an abbreviation for *'moin Dach'* or 'nice day'. So, in acknowledgment of the young girl's politeness I reciprocated with a *'moin moin'* of my own and we immediately got down to the business of renting a bicycle, she, very thoughtfully adapting her accent to accommodate my audibly limited German-speaking skills.

Choosing a suitable bike wasn't difficult – the number of bicycle varieties on offer in this little shop totalled – one. No choice between town bikes, trekking bikes, mountain bikes or hybrids. No selection of colours or styles. Not even the option of a men's or a women's model. Just like Henry Ford's original Model-T motorcar in matt black, it was one style fits all – Hobson's choice, I do believe. [10] The height of the saddle and the handlebars was adjustable of course, and the young girl with the pigtails went to scrupulous lengths to ensure that both were tweaked to meet my fastidious demands. And so, with saddle and handlebar heights both attuned to accommodate my short legs and my portly frame, I thanked the girl for her outstanding customer service skills, and wheeled my bicycle out of the shop. If the 'outdoor' store that I had visited a few days earlier had employed this assiduous young woman rather than Gary (that uncouth adolescent with the ponytail) – then I may well have been persuaded to fork out almost three hundred quid for a tent after all.

My bike was a magnificent contraption. It looked resplendent with its wicker-style basket at the front, aluminium rack at the rear, and one of those old-fashioned 'ting-a-ling'-style bells which I couldn't resist ringing pointlessly, just for the sake of listening to its enchanting sound. It answers that age-old question, *'is a bell necessary on a bicycle*?' Well, yes it is – it gives the rider something wonderful to play with. Conscious of annoying the throng of people gathered outside the campsite, I stopped ringing the bell and set off on the bike.

[10] *Well, we've done Morton's fork, so we might as well do Hobson's choice. In the early seventeenth century, Thomas Hobson ran a thriving horse rental business in Cambridge – renting out horses primarily to university students. To ensure the rotation gave his horses adequate resting time, he would only hire them out in the order of his choosing. Hobson gave his customers the option of taking the horse they were given or none at all.*

I've said this once, but I'll say it again – there really is no better way to explore Borkum than on a bike. The island has an impressive network of *Radwege* (cycle paths), and much of Borkum is off limits to motor vehicles. In fact, the eastern half of the island is totally car-free. But above all, Borkum Island is completely flat – no mountains, hills or knolls. Not even a gentle undulation here and there. And that of course, makes it something of a cyclist's paradise. In fact, the only disadvantage to cycling around Borkum is the wind. It's always blustery here – even on a bright day like today, the northerly wind just doesn't yield. So I cycled for twenty minutes or so to Borkum town where I stopped beside the grand promenade and chained my bicycle to one of the railings.

There are three main beaches on the island – two of which (the *Südbad* or *southern beach* and the *Hauptstrand* or *main beach*) are located near Borkum town centre. The third, known as *Nordstrand* (north beach), is located on the other side of the island and faces the open sea. The *Hauptstrand* was busy that morning. Not overcrowded as it apparently tends to be in the height of the summer season, but busy nonetheless. I considered renting a *Strandkorb* for a couple of hours from one of the little huts along the edge of the promenade – but changed my mind when I realised there was a minimum hire period. A *Strandkorb*, in case you've never experienced the joy, is literally a beach basket – a large enclosed wicker chair with a cover that provides its occupant with protection from the sun or from sea breezes (or in the case of the beaches on Borkum Island – protection from squally gales). Each *Strandkorb* is capable of seating two people, so they're popular with courting couples. The back can be reclined and footrests can be pulled out from underneath the chair. All in all, *Strandkörbe* are really rather comfortable to sit in, terribly romantic if you happen to be one of those courting couples, and above all, they're

46

quintessentially German. The problem for me was that the *Strandkörbe* on the *Hauptstrand* were not available for rental by the hour – only by the day or by the week (in which case you'll get a key for the cover so you can lock up your towels and other beach-related equipment to save you the hassle of carrying it home).

I took a stroll along the *Hauptstrand* until I reached a barrier that prevented me from strolling any further. This was the line that separated the tourists' half of the beach from the protected nature reserve. Beyond the barrier I could see a large number of seals resting on the sandbanks. I tried counting them, but it's not easy counting objects of identical size, shape and colour. I reached thirty-five before I lost count, but there were at least twice that number. It was fascinating just standing there watching them. There was a sign on display cautioning people not to cross the barrier, and warning too of heavy fines for those who failed to comply. The barrier is monitored by the coast guards and anyone ignoring the regulations can expect severe admonition from the authorities. Not that I had any intention of crossing the barrier. Apart from respecting wildlife in its natural environment, it occurred to me that seals also have a rather vicious bite – a fully grown bull can inflict a very serious wound.

The exertion of cycling and the invigorating sea air had given me something of an appetite – which, I decided, would have to be satiated before my cycle tour around Borkum could continue. I wasn't exactly spoiled for choice – Borkum isn't renowned for its culinary excellence. But the options, although limited, seemed reasonable enough. The *Il Faro* was a family-run Italian restaurant specialising in pizzas, but chose to promote its 'excellent views of the lighthouse' rather than the quality of its food, so I was understandably nervous. Alternatively, there was a restaurant called the *Nordsee-Grill* – offering Bratwurst, Pommes-frites, Schnitzel and Sauerkraut – typical fast food – German style. But ultimately, I settled on the *Kartoffelkäfer* – a small establishment specialising in dishes made from the humble potato. I chose this particular restaurant for three very good reasons. Firstly, it had a rather quirky name. Unless Mr. Stevenson wasn't as competent a teacher as I thought he was, I was of the opinion that the word *Kartoffelkäfer* translated as 'Potato Beetle' which seemed to be a rather bizarre name for a restaurant. (*Kartoffel* being the German for potato and *Käfer* the German for beetle - as any enthusiast of Volkswagen motor cars will concur.) [11] I was hoping the name wasn't derived from the restaurant being blighted by an insect infestation. Secondly, the restaurant was located on the beachfront promenade and the panorama overlooking the sea was simply wonderful. And finally (and I suppose, in fairness, this ought to have been the primary consideration for choosing where to eat), the food was great. I opted for the jacket potato with chilli con carne followed by a cup of East Frisian tea – a strong blend of black teas served in the traditional East Frisian style, with cream and rock sugar.

I spent the remainder of the day cycling around Borkum – exploring the island, and stopping every now and again to visit any landmarks I happened to stumble upon or that I found to be of particular interest. I wasn't expecting to find the Monastery of Petra or the Taj Mahal here on Borkum Island (I may not have a masters degree in the subject, but my geography isn't *that* bad) – or anything of such majesty or architectural significance. But I did find one or two little gems worthy of investigation. The island, for example, has two lighthouses – an old one and a new one, aptly named '*the old lighthouse*' and '*the new lighthouse*'. The small

[11] *Everybody in the 1960s wanted to be seen cruising the streets in a Volkswagen Potato.*

spectator gallery on top of the old lighthouse cost me the princely sum of €1,50 to climb up to, and offered spectacular views of the entire island as well as the German and Dutch coastlines. I took a rain check on climbing to the top of the new lighthouse – I'm not even sure whether it was possible to do so. I also visited the North Sea Aquarium. Visitors expecting something comparable to the Sea Life Centre should brace themselves for a bit of a disappointment. It was a modest affair to say the least and one which I managed to have pretty much covered in less than twenty minutes.

By the time I arrived back at *Insel-Camping* and had returned the rental bike to the delightful young woman with the pigtails, dusk had already fallen. The campsite was now a hive of activity – the restaurant full to bursting point with hungry campers, the sound of raucous laughter emanating from the barbecue area and the tumult of the games room as boisterous teenagers competed for highest score on the pinball machines. Despite the allure of a karaoke competition that was underway in the campsite bar, I decided not to allow myself to be led into temptation, but to take a couple of bottles of *Jever Pils* back to my tent instead. It was a wise move, I thought. I had promised myself one or two riotous nights during this trip, but tonight, I decided, would be a night of sobriety. I intended to leave Borkum the following morning and I was hoping to be awake in time to catch the early ferry.

So my plans for the remainder of the evening were relatively uncomplicated. I would begin by dismantling my tent, bending the buckled support poles back into shape again (following the previous night's unfortunate toilet-run incident), and then reconstruct it again – all of which would need to be completed before nightfall. After that, it was just a simple matter of settling myself snugly inside my sleeping bag and drinking my beer whilst reading one of my paperbacks under torchlight. It would be the perfect end to a perfect day. But the best laid plans do not always come to fruition.

When I arrived back at my tent, the man from the neighbouring one – yes, *him* – the bearded Mancunian, was standing beside his tent, smoking his pipe, and staring at me as I made my approach. I couldn't possibly repair my tent poles with him standing there watching. I simply wasn't in the mood for his derisory commentary, which I knew would be inevitable. So I nodded at him in acknowledgement of his presence, and clambered inside my misshapen tent which, thanks to a couple of awry tent poles, had a tilt more prominent than the Leaning Tower of Pisa.

At three o'clock in the morning my mobile telephone rang. I'm always a little apprehensive when this happens. After all, phone calls at that time in the morning are usually bad news aren't they? So, still half asleep, I fumbled around in the darkness until I found my phone, and I answered the call with a fair degree of trepidation. It was my wife calling. Immediately, I feared the worst – something dreadful had clearly happened. *The Oasis of the Seas* had been hijacked; the passengers and the crew taken hostage – and now the blighters were demanding our entire life savings to secure her release. That, I concluded, would be the only plausible explanation as to why she was calling me at such an unearthly hour.

"Hi," she said rather serenely. "How's the camping trip going?"

This certainly didn't sound like the anxious ramblings of a terrified woman with a gun held to her head. I could hear her friend Joanna giggling in the background, so I figured that the pair of them had been enjoying a rather boozy night together.

"Guess what!" she said, giggling mischievously. "We've been invited to join the captain at his table for dinner this evening! How cool is that?"

"Well, that sounds great," I said, still half asleep and not entirely sure whether any of this was really happening. "But it's three o'clock in the morning!"

This revelation was greeted by an awkward pause.

"Don't be ridiculous," she said eventually. "It's only nine o'clock in the evening. Why would Joanna and I be going down for dinner at three o'clock in the morning?"

I tried to explain the concept of international time zones and how the world was divided by meridian lines of longitude, but it all seemed to go in one ear and out the other. My fault entirely – perhaps I should have explained it with a little less ambiguity than I did. But please spare at least a modicum of pity for me – it was 3.00am – way too early for conversations about matters as complex as this. And besides, I desperately needed the toilet.

oOo

Dear Diary,

__The Beer, Cheese and Tent Report for the State of Lower Saxony:__

__Beer: Jever Pilsner:__

The brewers claim that it's the Frisian water that distinguishes Jever Pilsner from any other beer. I must admit it was rather good – a sort of malty taste with a kick of lemon and herbs.

__Cheese: Sauermilchkäse (Quark Cheese):__

Quark cheese is produced all over northern Germany, mainly on small farms in Lower Saxony. It's a soft, creamy cheese and I found some on sale in the campsite shop. It's a wee bit bland in my opinion, and has a powdery aftertaste.

__Tent Stability:__

Structural support pole buckled and slight distortion also to some of the other poles. One tent peg is completely bent. However, I think the damage looks worse than it is – relatively superficial and easily repairable – although I was denied the chance to attempt any unhindered repairs by the wanker in the tent next door.

oOo

Chapter Three – A Stranger on a Train

*"Never like seein' strangers. Guess it's 'cause no
stranger ever good newsed me."*
*Frank Borden (1900 – 1971) US Screenwriter. From the
film 'Red River' as two men on horseback approach
Tom Dunston's (John Wayne) land - 1948*

As I've mentioned already and probably more than
once, the Federal Republic of Germany is formed of sixteen
states or *Länder* – each state having its own partial
sovereignty. Thirteen of them are known as *Flächenländer*
or *area states,* which between them cover 99.4% of
Germany's total land area. The remaining three are the
Stadtstaaten or *city states,* which, in terms of their
geographical size, are diminutive compared with the area
states. The cities of Hamburg and Berlin are two of the
Stadtstaaten and the third is Bremen – which was the next
port of call on this decadent jolly of mine around Germany.

The state of Bremen is a little different from the others –
the odd one out, so to speak – and for a number of reasons.
To start with, it's the smallest of Germany's states, covering
an area of just 419 km² – that's about 0.12% of Germany's
total land area, so we're talking almost infinitesimal. It's also
the least populated – the state of Bremen is home to just
over 660,000 people – much less than 1% of Germany's
overall population. That said though, it is Germany's third
most densely populated state. Finally – and this perhaps
highlights the main disparity between Bremen and the other
states – it comprises two separate geographic enclaves. The
City of Bremen is the state capital. It is located on the river
Weser, and, along with its sprawling suburbs, forms one of
the two enclaves. The other is the town of Bremerhaven
(literally '*Bremen's Harbour*') – also on the river Weser, but
approximately   fifty   kilometres   further   downstream.

Bremerhaven, you'll remember, is one of the North Sea ports I mentioned earlier – as I recall, I was lamenting over the fact that the city once boasted a direct ferry service to Harwich. Both Bremen and Bremerhaven are completely surrounded by the neighbouring state of Lower Saxony, which at nearly 48,000 km² is the second largest of Germany's *Länder* and completely dwarfs the state of Bremen.

Having ticked off Lower Saxony already (represented on this trip by the East Frisian island of Borkum), Bremen was my next stop, and a state which I had been particularly looking forward to visiting. I wasn't planning to visit very many cities during this trip – the journey was supposed to be about camping in the great outdoors – enjoying the natural beauty of Germany's lush countryside and her national parks and nature reserves. But I had planned to stop over in all sixteen of Germany's states – *that* being the whole point of the trip – and to achieve that goal I would *have* to visit the cities of Hamburg, Berlin and Bremen – simply because they are states in their own right.

Yes, I suppose I could have chosen Bremerhaven rather than the city of Bremen to represent the next state on my tour – but here's the thing: Bremen is a 1,200-year-old Hanseatic City filled with architectural treasures of breathtaking beauty. It is home to the world-famous Town Musicians (which we'll return to later), promotes itself as 'the pulsating, multifaceted heart of North West Germany', and, according to the Bremen Tourist Authority, is 'a metropolitan city experience like no other'. I'm not sure whether a city experience can be anything other than 'metropolitan', but these are the words of the Bremen Tourist Authority and not mine. Bremerhaven, by stark contrast, offers a North Sea ferry terminal; a container port; a number of multi-storey car parks and an industrial estate of titanic dimension. Not only that, I have it on very good authority from somebody I know who has recently visited Bremerhaven (and is therefore the definitive expert, in my opinion), that the whole place smells of fish. So I chose Bremen over Bremerhaven, which was why I found myself in a platform waiting room at Emden railway station at just after eleven o'clock on this fine, sunny morning.

I hadn't slept too well the previous night – what with my tent sagging in the middle and my wife phoning me with her frivolous tales of pointless gibberish at three o'clock in the morning. So I had woken early, dismantled my tent, and left the campsite while most of the other campers were still sound asleep. Having caught the early ferry from Borkum back to the mainland, I now found myself here, at Emden station, eating a couple of warm 'breakfast panini', made with tomato, ham and processed cheese. A balding man with nicotine-stained teeth (who worked in the '*Schnell Imbiss*' snack kiosk on the station platform), had employed the full extent of his culinary skills by heating them up for me in his microwave oven.

The train crept sluggishly into Emden station, and along with everybody else in the waiting room, I climbed aboard. I found a vacant seat next to a window and promptly struggled with the weight of my rucksack as I lifted it onto the overhead luggage rack. It had been my intention to while away the journey by reading a few pages of my paperback – Jeffery Deaver's '*The Empty Chair*' which my wife had recommended several months earlier but I'd never managed to get around to reading. So I placed the book on the table in front of me with the intention of making a start on it just as soon as we were on the move. But as I sat there waiting patiently for that moment to arrive I was joined by an elderly man who, having evidently noticed the book on the table, chose to address me in English in preference to his native German.

"Is this seat free?" he asked, pointing at the seat opposite.

"Yes, I believe so," I replied.

The man sat down, removed his hat and placed it carefully on top of the table. He adjusted his posture by fidgeting repeatedly, until he finally settled into a position in which he felt comfortable.

"Hello. My name is Heinrich. I am seventy-eight years old and I am a retired accountant," said Heinrich, who was a seventy-eight-year-old retired accountant.

"I'm Chris," I replied, shaking Heinrich's hand in a spirit of camaraderie. Heinrich had a rather flaccid handshake – which I suppose was pardonable for a man of his age. He was immaculately dressed in a grey suit with a faint pinstripe, a smart cream-coloured Winchester shirt and a black necktie – tied with a perfect half-Windsor knot. Pinned to the lapel of his jacket was a gold Saint Christopher brooch which he wore, presumably, as an amulet.

Now then, here's a question for you: how long does it take to make friends with a complete stranger? More specifically, how long does it take to make friends with a stranger who is thirty years your senior and with whom you have nothing palpably in common? Answer: one hour and forty-seven minutes – the precise amount of time that Heinrich and I sat chatting to each other on the train that took us from the somnolent little station at Emden to the bustling rail terminus at Bremen city centre. After our initial introductions were over and the ice had been broken, Heinrich just wouldn't stop talking. Now, you may think that the incessant ramblings of a seventy-eight-year-old man throughout the entire train journey from Emden to Bremen would have been a source of irritation to a cantankerous old git like me. And under normal circumstances you'd be right. After all, it *had* been my intention to make a start on my Jeffery Deaver that morning. But Heinrich turned out to be a most affable, charming and personable individual – one of a rare breed of truly old-fashioned 'gentlemen'. Making conversation with Heinrich seemed effortless. His repartee was interesting and lively – his stories really rather beguiling. So Jeffery Deaver was abandoned in favour of Heinrich – at least for the time being.

Heinrich's command of the English language was unimpeachable – his use of grammar and his extensive range of vocabulary were a standing reproach to my German-speaking skills which appeared decidedly amateur by comparison. But his voice had a somewhat monotonous intonation and his accent was rather clichéd – almost slightly comical, I thought, a bit like the accent adopted by *'Herr Flick of the Gestapo'* in the TV comedy series *'Allo 'Allo*. Heinrich would say things like *'vun'* instead of 'one'; *'zee'* instead of 'the' and *'sank you'* instead of 'thank you'.

I always thought that people who had devoted their lives to a career in accountancy also harboured secret aspirations to become lion tamers. Then again, maybe I misspent my youth watching too many episodes of Monty Python. But unlike Mr. Anchovy, Heinrich had been leading something of a double life for the past fifty years – a chartered accountant by day, and a percussionist in a jazz quartet by night. It is extraordinary how quickly the time passes when you're engaged in captivating conversation – especially with somebody as sweet and as unassuming as Heinrich. It transpired during our conversation that in his home town of Bremen he was regarded as something of a local celebrity – although this little snippet of information was something I gleaned after a great deal of badgering – Heinrich was far too modest; too diffident to simply blurt out such a revelation.

Heinrich's band, *'Jazz zum Frühstück'* (which translates as 'Jazz for Breakfast') was, in its heyday, a jazz quartet of international renown – regarded as one of the leading semiprofessional jazz bands of its day. Heinrich mused over many of the band's achievements and their tours of the bars and clubs of Europe – where they spent night after night churning out a repertoire of classical jazz numbers in poky, smoke-filled venues until the early hours of the morning.

"Of course, in those days I was a young man and I had an eye for the ladies," he said, with a mischievous grin. I bet he did – the randy old bugger.

Heinrich, it turned out, regarded himself as something of an anglophile. His band had toured the jazz bars of London, Manchester and Liverpool back in the heady days of the 'swinging' 1960s, and he had visited London on many occasions subsequently. But nothing could have surprised me more than Heinrich's next revelation – I would have been less surprised had I woken up that morning to find my ears stapled to my groundsheet. Although he had retired from his career in accountancy almost twenty years ago, Heinrich's interest and participation in jazz drumming was still very much alive. Yes, after fifty years of touring the smoky jazz music venues of Europe, *Jazz zum Frühstück* was still going strong. The line-up had changed a bit over the years, which I suppose is not surprising. A new guitarist had to be recruited following the death of the original back in the late 1990s, and a whole string of saxophonists had made guest appearances since the original ran off to the Caribbean with a Jamaican girl he'd met at a gig in 1977. Nobody had seen or heard from him since. But Heinrich and his colleague Klaus or *'Klavier-Klaus'* as he was affectionately nicknamed ('Klavier' being the German for 'piano'), both remained active members of the quartet and had been so since the genesis of time. And through a combination of both coincidence and good fortune, it just so happened that *Jazz zum Frühstück* were performing that very evening at a venue in Bremen.

"You must come to see us," Heinrich insisted, offering me a complimentary ticket which he produced from an inside pocket of his jacket. "We can have a beer together during the interval, and I can introduce you to the other members of my band."

Now, I'm not fanatical about jazz, I admit. But all music, regardless of the genre, is always superb when it's performed live. There's something quite inspiring and really rather magical about watching gifted musicians perform. And that, I think, is especially true of jazz – simply because of its complexity. The guitarist will be lost in a world of his own, manoeuvring his fingers frantically up and down the fret board, whilst the saxophonist and the keyboard player will be wandering off on a tangent of their own. It's as if they are all playing their own separate, individual tunes – and yet, somewhat enigmatically, it all combines into something that sounds really rather exquisite.

But percussionists I particularly admire. They always seem to get something of a bad press, and yet it's the drummer who is there holding the whole thing together. There is a standing joke that does the rounds in the music world from time to time: what do you call somebody who hangs around with talented musicians? Answer: the drummer. But despite the jokes, I hold all drummers – and jazz drummers especially, in very high esteem. Those complicated rhythms for which jazz music is notorious, call for a considerable degree of deftness and dexterity. So I was delighted to receive Heinrich's invitation to *Jazz zum Frühstück's* performance that evening. I accepted the ticket with gratitude – but I began to have second thoughts almost immediately afterwards.

The venue for tonight's show was in the heart of the city, and was called '*Jazz Club Bremen*' – which I suppose as venue names go, tells you all you need to know about where it is and what you can expect when you get there. But the campsite I had chosen to stay at wasn't in Bremen as such – it was further *out* in the city's sprawling suburbs. And although I rather fancied a night of listening to jazz in the company of a bunch of septuagenarian musicians, I wasn't sure how practical it would be to accept Heinrich's kind invitation.

"I'm staying at the lakeside campsite at *'Campingplatz Stadtwaldsee,'*" I said, "How easy will it be to get back there from the city centre late at night?"

"It will be an absolute breeze," Heinrich replied, demonstrating how his command of the English language extended beyond what might be considered rudimentary, since it included figurative phrases too.

"There's a tram that will take you from the main station to the university campus just outside the city. You can catch a number 28 bus from there that will take you directly to the camping site."

When our train eventually arrived at Bremen's *Hauptbahnhof*, Heinrich and I shook hands once again and we headed off in our separate directions – he to his luxury riverside apartment with its veranda overlooking the river Weser, and me to the tram stop in the street outside the main railway station.

Getting to the Stadtwaldsee campsite was indeed a breeze, as Heinrich had rightfully predicted – a fifteen-minute tram ride to the University of Bremen, followed by a five-minute ride on a single-decker bus. But I had been lucky to make it here as quickly as I did. Although the tram service runs every few minutes, the number 28 bus operates considerably less frequently, and it was purely by luck rather than judgement that I made the connection just as the next bus was due. So before entering the camp, I studied the timetable posted at the bus stop by the side of the road to acquaint myself with the times of the late night buses. It wasn't great news. Although the trams ran until late into the night, the last bus from the university to the campsite was at 10.30. This would mean having to leave the *Jazz Club*

Bremen by 10.00pm at the latest to be sure of making the connection.

Now, I know what you're thinking. If the bus journey from the university to the campsite takes just five minutes, then surely it wouldn't take all that long to get up off my lardy arse and walk. Well, yes that would indeed be a very valid point – except for one thing. The journey from the university may only have taken five minutes, but the route was less than straightforward. The bus wound its way along narrow country lanes which snaked their way through the countryside. There were no pavements to walk on or street lamps to light the way – just acres of woodland on either side of the road. I'm afraid to say that on reflection, any attempt to walk from the university after dark would be the act of a deranged individual – if I was going to see my newly-found friend performing at the jazz club this evening, then I would simply have to make my apologies before the performance ended, and slope off at ten o'clock. The last thing I wanted was to have my clothes reverting to rags and my carriage turning back into a pumpkin. Wait a minute! My clothes were already rags! Whatever I was planning to wear this evening would be scrunched up in the bottom of my rucksack – and probably in urgent need of a wash. I would have to make a trip to the laundry room top of my 'to do' list.

The camping site at Stadtwaldsee was a pleasant affair – typical of most campsites in Germany. It had all the usual amenities that modern campsites offer including the obligatory laundry room, which was equipped with at least a dozen washing machines – all of which were in use when I first poked my head around the door. It also had the advantage of a lakeside location – the *Stadtwaldsee*, where one can swim, or for a small fee, even scuba-dive.

I found a suitable spot on the area of grassland set aside for small tent pitches, and assembled my *Wind-Breaker DeLuxe,* before returning to the laundry room a short while later. I was delighted to discover that one of the machines was available for use. Armed with my fairly modest load of dirty laundry: three pairs of socks; two T-shirts; a pair of jeans that had been soaked through during the rain showers in Borkum two days earlier (which I had shoved into my rucksack rolled up and still damp), two towels and three pairs of undercrackers, I read the instructions (in German) that were displayed on the panels of one of these mysterious coin-operated mechanical contrivances.

Now, I'm sure my dear wife will be raising her eyebrows and tutting derisively at what I'm about to tell you, but it was only at the point of my reading the instructions for use, that it occurred to me that some sort of detergent might be necessary – a requisite in which I was unequivocally lacking. And that wasn't the only thing I didn't have with me. The machine accepted €1 and €2 coins only – neither of which I could find in the mound of loose change that I'd been carrying around with me for much of the day. It was the bald man with the nicotine-stained teeth who sold me the two breakfast panini earlier in the day who had given me change for my ten-euro note in a miscellaneous bundle of assorted shrapnel. Now, I know that what I am about to confess to may seem like an act of terrible selfishness, but it seemed to me that demand for washing machines at this time of day was at its peak – and one doesn't make any friends during washing machine rush hour. I was lucky to have found a machine that wasn't in use – in fact my surprise on discovering such a rarity would probably have surpassed that of Howard Carter when he inadvertently stumbled upon the tomb of Tutankhamen. So rather than risk losing the only vacant machine in the laundry room, I stuffed my dirty clothes into the drum, closed the door and headed off to the campsite shop in search of washing powder and the correct denomination of coins needed to operate these confounded contraptions. I was only gone for five minutes at most. But when I returned to the laundry room, the machine I had reserved was in the early stages of a wash cycle – and in the process of washing somebody else's clothes. *My* clothes had been discarded in a corner of the room – in a pile – on the floor. Whoever had callously dumped my clothes onto the floor had also taken the time and trouble to scribble a little note for me – which had been placed on top of the pile, wedged inside one of my dirty socks. It read:

'Liebe Arschloch' (dear arsehole)

'Die Bereithaltung einer Waschmaschine ist verboten!!!!' – I shan't bother with the translation for that last bit – I'm sure you get the general gist. So I abandoned my plans to wash my laundry, and I waited for the bus to take me back into Bremen.

I spent the remainder of the afternoon wandering around the quaint little streets of Bremen's *Altstadt* – or old town. It would be another four hours before the jazz club opened its doors, so I had time aplenty to explore the city and find somewhere to eat.

The Bremen Tourist Authority describes Bremen as 'multifaceted' – and indeed it is. It's a contrasting blend of old and new; of elegant and shabby; of nice and nasty. Bremen's main attractions are concentrated almost exclusively in the Altstadt – a tiny, oval-shaped section of the city on the banks of the River Weser. I wandered into *Marktplatz* (the market square) where the guidebooks tend to steer most of the two million tourists who visit Bremen every year. It's a pretty spot I admit – dominated by Bremen's medieval town hall. This beautiful edifice was built between 1405 and 1410 in the gothic style, but the building's rather opulent façade was built two centuries later in the style of the Renaissance. The town hall is a UNESCO World Heritage site, but it's not the only architectural gem in Bremen's old town. To the east of the square I found the magnificently impressive 13th century Cathedral of St. Petri, together with the *Schütting* – the Flemish-style guildhall dating from the 16th century. Two statues stand at the west side of the town hall. The first is the statue of *Bremen Roland*. Roland was the city's protector, and he stands facing the centre of the square with his 'sword of justice' in one hand and his shield, decorated with an imperial eagle, in the other. The other statue is more contemporary. It was created in bronze in 1953 by the artist Gerhard Marcks. The statue is of a donkey, a dog, a cat and a rooster – all standing one on top of the other. (The rooster is at the top and the donkey at the base – just in case you had visions of a rooster with a pained facial expression.) These four creatures are the *Stadtmusikanten* or the '*Town Musicians of Bremen*' made famous by the Brothers Grimm in their fairy tale of the same name.

There are lots of towns all over Germany that celebrate their association with fairy tales. Jacob and Wilhelm Grimm grew up in the town of Steinau, in the Main-Kinzig region in the state of Hesse, and used real locations as their settings for many of their stories. And there were plenty of them – the Grimm Brothers wrote around 240 children's stories in all. Little Red Riding Hood, for example, was set in the region along the Schwalm River near where the brothers spent much of their childhood. Trendelburg Castle, also in the state of Hesse, was the setting for the story of Rapunzel – where the handsome prince climbed to the top of the castle to rescue the fair maiden, by clinging tightly to her long, flaxen tresses as he made his ascent. And perhaps the most famous of them all is the little town of Hamelin – best known as the location for that most macabre of fairy tales – the Pied Piper. And then there's Bremen – the setting for the story of *The Town Musicians* – except it wasn't.

In the story, the four animals set off on a journey to Bremen to become musicians, following a lifetime of mistreatment by their owners. But on the way, they discover a cottage occupied by four robbers enjoying their ill-gotten gains – and in the hope of being rewarded with food and water the four creatures climb on each other's backs to perform for them. But the sound of the animals' 'music' is enough to frighten the felons half to death, so they flee the cottage, leaving the 'musicians' to take up residence there and live happily for the rest of their days. There is a bit more to it than that of course, but that's the potted version. It seemed a little odd to me that Bremen should celebrate so proudly its association with four fictitious creatures who only ever *intended* to visit the city, but never actually made it.

As dusk began to fall, I repaired to the *Schnoor* district of the city – a small but extraordinarily well preserved area of crooked and narrow cobbled streets, 17th century fishermen's cottages, and a miscellany of artisan shops, antique dealers, art galleries and quaint little restaurants and cafés. The Schnoor district is hidden away very neatly between the cathedral and the River Weser and it was here that I took refuge in a riverside restaurant for a what was described on the menu as a 'traditional German' *Wienerschnitzel* (an escalope of veal coated in breadcrumbs in the 'Viennese' style – which by my reckoning makes it traditionally Austrian, surely?), followed by a colossal portion of '*Streuselkuchen*' (which, unless my eyes and taste buds had joined forces in a conspiracy to deceive me, was essentially a generous helping of apple crumble).

When I arrived at the club, *Jazz zum Frühstück* were already on stage – performing to the small but nonetheless appreciative crowd of jazz aficionados who were there to pay homage to four of the oldest swingers in town. The two original band members, Heinrich and '*Klavier-Klaus*' were 78 and 76 years old respectively. The other two – Joseph the saxophone player, (aka '*Saxophon Sepp*'), and Volkard the guitarist, (aka '*Gittarre Volk*' – which is where the alliteration theme completely falls apart) were both in their mid sixties and were therefore relatively youthful by comparison. As I sat down at a table beside the stage, the quartet began to play a piece that I didn't recognise. That said, I wasn't familiar with *any* of the tunes that *Jazz zum Frühstück* performed throughout the entire evening. But I suppose that, not being au fait with the modern jazz scene, my ignorance was hardly surprising – but they were playing a euphonious and lively tune with an upbeat tempo, and I couldn't fight the urge to tap my foot along to the rhythm.

I ordered a glass of Beck's beer – one of the many German beers with which we Brits are already familiar as the UK is one of almost a hundred countries the stuff is exported to. Beck's is brewed here in Bremen and the huge brewery building on the west bank of the River Weser dominates the skyline. The Beck's brand name is ubiquitous throughout the city – on poster boards and on signs above the doorways of shops and cafés. I'm not sure whether the *Jazz Club Bremen* sold anything else actually – the waiter who took my order seemed to imply that 'Beck's' was the only option available.

Waiter: (notebook and pencil poised at the ready) "Bitte?"

Me: "Ein Bier, bitte."

Waiter: "Ein *grosses* Bier oder ein *kleines* Bier?"

Me: "Ein *grosses* Bier bitte."

Waiter: Ein grosses Beck's Bier – danke."

Perhaps he was on some sort of commission arrangement.

The Jazz Club Bremen was a charming venue – cosy and congenial, with tasteful, elegant decor and mood lighting – a far cry from some of the more tawdry music venues that I've been to. The chairs were preposterously comfortable – so much so that it was a pity to have to leave my seat to go to the toilet – something which I did with aberrant regularity as the evening rolled on and my beer consumption increased. After a while my interactions with the waiter seemed to become increasingly brief.

Waiter: "grosses Beck's?"

Me: "Ja, bitte".

The brevity of my exchanges with the waiter was a worrying development, I thought. It would only be a matter of time before any verbal communication between us ceased altogether and successive glasses of beer would magically appear on the table in front of me, simply because we happened to have made eye contact. But the beer was sliding down like nectar, and so the waiter's assumption that I would inevitably want another just as soon as my glass was empty, was something I felt disinclined to contest.

At around 9.00pm, the music stopped and '*Saxophon Sepp*' stepped up to the microphone to announce a thirty-minute interlude – "a chance for you to order another ice-cold glass of deliciously-smooth Beck's," he said, in the sort of deep, gravelly voice that only a lifetime on sixty cigarettes a day could have fashioned. Yep, there *definitely* was some sort of commission thing going on here.

Heinrich seemed delighted that I had made the effort to show up that evening, and he joined me at my table along with Klaus and Volkard, while Sepp stepped out into the street for a smoke.

"That was fantastic," I said, once the introductions were out of the way. "I've never been a huge fan of jazz music but that was truly awesome. You'll forgive me for not recognising any of the tunes though – I haven't heard any of them before."

"Neither have we," said Heinrich. "We make the whole thing up as we go along."

For a moment I was nonplussed – not able to tell whether Heinrich was pulling my leg or not.

"What? You're joking! Are you telling me that your whole repertoire is improvised?"

"Of course," he replied very matter-of-factly. "All our music is improvised. Klaus usually decides which key we'll play it in; I will set the tempo, and we'll take it from there. When one of us decides to change key then we communicate with each other using our own special code that we have developed over the years – a nod or a wink, or some other head movement will indicate our intentions to make changes. Maybe go up or down an octave, or change the tempo completely."

"But isn't that risky?" I asked rather naively, and immediately wished I hadn't.

"But jazz *is* risky," Volkard interrupted. "That's the whole point of it. It's the unpredictability of the music that makes jazz such a wonderful genre."

"You've heard of Leon Beiderbecke, I assume?" said Heinrich as he held his empty glass aloft in an attempt to attract the waiter's attention. I had to confess that I hadn't.

"Well, 'Bix' Beiderbecke was an American jazz pianist and cornet player – one of the greatest of his era. The poor man died in 1931 – just 28 years old. But he once said, 'the one thing I like about jazz is that I don't know what's going to happen next.' And he was absolutely right. That's what all jazz lovers like about it. It's the unpredictability of it. And yes, we do cock up from time to time. We made a thousand mistakes during that last set. But I bet you didn't notice a single one of them, did you?"

Saxophon Sepp joined us a few moments later. At just 64, he was the youngest member of the quartet and seemed far less convivial than the other three. His hair was matted and greasy, his fingers stained by nicotine, and his breath smelled of cigarette smoke. When Sepp discovered I was from west London the conversation changed direction. Heinrich and Klaus began to reminisce about their jazz tours in London in the 1960s, and all four of them began rattling off the names of pubs, clubs and other assorted venues that the original *Jazz zum Frühstück* had performed at.

"Is the London Jazz Club still there?" Klaus asked.

"What about the Bull's Head in Barnes?" Heinrich interjected.

"And the Jazz Café in Camden?"

There was little point in them firing a list of names of London jazz venues at me. Most of them I hadn't heard of, and with around 7,000 pubs in London I was hardly in a position to know all of them. I asked Heinrich and Klaus what their impressions were of London in the 1960s.

"They were difficult times for us," Heinrich admitted. "The war had ended less than twenty years earlier and the horrors of those terrible days were still fresh in the memories of both the Germans and the British. It was difficult to be German in London in the 1960s. We were treated with suspicion and hostility – many Londoners still held feelings of enmity towards us. But the music seemed to solve all of that. At night when we played in the clubs and the bars, our efforts were rewarded with rapturous applause. Suddenly everybody wanted to embrace us and the rancour was temporarily forgotten. When we played our music the people didn't see 'Germans' any more – they saw jazz musicians – at least until the show ended. Music is a very powerful thing, you know. It can unite people in times of crisis. It can bring old enemies together – reconcile their differences."

It was a very poignant and eloquent soliloquy – but one which Sepp was about to contaminate with an observation of his own.

"Yeah, and the English money was just a fucking nightmare," he said. "What was it now? Shillings? Halfpennies? What the fuck was that all about?"

Despite his earthy and colourful use of our language, I understood immediately what Sepp was talking about. I really can't imagine how anybody who visited our country prior to the decimalisation of our currency managed to grasp what on earth was going on. But throughout history the British have maintained an extraordinary ability to make life as complicated for themselves as possible – by sticking rigidly to elaborate and convoluted systems.

In February 1971, the United Kingdom (and Ireland) had the good sense to introduce a decimalised currency – finally replacing one of the most baffling currency systems in the world – such a Byzantine system in fact, that it was a small wonder that any of us understood how it worked. Whilst virtually every other nation in the world operated a simple decimalised currency, the UK operated a system where the *pound* (symbolised as £ or L), was subdivided into 20 *shillings*, or 240 *pennies* or *pence*. A shilling was subdivided into 12 *pennies*, or 24 *halfpennies*, or 48 *farthings*. To add further complication, a number of coins of quite random value were in general circulation, much to the bemusement of Klaus and other tourists visiting this strange country of ours. These included the *threepence*; the *florin* (two shillings); the *crown* (five shillings); the *half-crown* (two shillings and sixpence); and the *guinea* (the most extraordinary multiple of them all, representing one pound and one shilling, or twenty-one shillings, or 252 pence). And as if that wasn't confusing enough, shillings were represented by the symbol '*s*' (not 's' for 'shilling' as one might expect, but from the Latin *solidus* – although I'll concede that since the word 'shilling' also begins with an 's', this is indeed a lucky coincidence); and pennies were represented by the symbol 'd' (from the Latin *denarius* – a Roman monetary unit whose origins can be traced back to 211BC). And the most extraordinary thing of all was that despite its bizarre complexity, everyone seemed to be able to grasp it. This was particularly true of the elderly. My grandmother for example – a woman hardly blessed with a sizable degree of intelligence (or common sense for that matter) – would not have flinched at all had her milkman presented her with a bill for *one pound, fourteen shillings and threepence-ha'penny.* But her head would have exploded with befuddlement had he asked her for £1.73.

Anyway, I digress. It was now 9.30 and the thirty-minute intermission had come to an end. Heinrich, Klaus, Sepp and Volkard made their way back to the stage for their next one-hour session (they still had three more sessions to get through before bedtime), and I sat back to enjoy another selection of swinging melodies that neither I nor the band members, nor anybody in the audience had heard before, or would ever hear again. I couldn't stay long though. It was imperative that I caught the tram in time to make the last bus connection to the camping site. I could hang around for another half an hour perhaps, but certainly no longer than that – I would have to slope away at ten o'clock and leave the oldest jazz swingers in town to carry on improvising into the early hours.[12] There was still time for one more beer though. I made eye contact with the waiter across the crowded bar. Two minutes later a large glass of Beck's appeared on the table in front of me. It was gone ten o'clock by the time I left the jazz club. I waved goodbye to Heinrich as I made my escape, which he acknowledged with a courteous nod – probably all he could realistically manage with a drumstick in each hand. The tram rattled and clattered its way through the shadowy streets of the city centre and out along the dark avenues of the city's suburbs. By the time the tram arrived at the university campus, I was in desperate need to use the toilet. In fact, nature wasn't just calling, she

[12] *Renowned for their mix of parody, slapstick and double entendres, Gerald Thomas and Peter Rogers directed and produced twenty-nine 'Carry On' films between 1958 and 1978. An additional (30th) film was made in 1992 but with hardly any of the original cast. Sadly, 'Carry On Improvising' wasn't one of them but certainly it should have been, in my opinion.*

was yelling in my ear through a megaphone. You see, I have this infernal bladder problem. After five glasses of beer (I think I had five...or was it six maybe?) I find myself having to visit the gents with alarming regularly. I suppose, on hindsight, I should have spent a penny before I left the jazz club (or whatever the equivalent may be in euros). But the thing is, I didn't need to go at the time – I thought I'd be able to hold out. I was wrong.

As soon as we'd reached the university campus and the pneumatic doors had swung open, I leaped out of the tram with the alacrity and determination of a man whose pants were ablaze – and immediately made a beeline for the public toilet which, on the two occasions I had been to the university campus earlier in the day, I hadn't noticed was there. [13] It was afterwards that I realised the reason why I hadn't spotted the toilet block before. I hadn't been here before. In my desperation to answer nature's call, I somehow managed to alight the tram at the wrong stop. To say I was cross with myself would be understating it – I was beside myself with rage. How could I have made such a stupid mistake? I think part of the problem was that there is more than one tram-stop serving the university campus. It was dark too, which didn't help – neither did the fact that I had managed to sink copious volumes of beer and was, perhaps, just a teensy-weensy bit inebriated. Nevertheless, it was a disastrous error. The last bus of the day which could have taken me back to the campsite was due to depart in just two minutes' time – from a bus stop at least half a mile

[13] *The term 'beeline' derives from the extraordinary behaviour of bees. When a forager bee finds a source of nectar it returns to the hive and communicates its location using a surprisingly sophisticated 'dance' routine, with the angle of the body indicating the direction of the nectar and the duration of the dance denoting the distance from the hive. This enables the other bees to fly directly to the source.*

further down the road. The chances of me making the connection now were zero.

I sat down for a while on a bench in the manner of Forrest Gump to contemplate my options – of which, I concluded, there were three. The first was to walk – along those dark country lanes back to the campsite. The second was to telephone for a cab and the third was to take a tram to the next stop and wait there for the next scheduled number 28 bus to take me to the camp – which, according to the timetable, was due just after 06.00 the following morning – in a little under eight hours. Having dismissed options one and three as being equally as absurd as each other, I dialled the number of a taxi firm which was displayed on a poster-board.

"The taxi will be with you in fifteen minutes," said the officious-sounding man on the other end of a very crackly telephone line. And it was – almost to the second.

I woke the following morning feeling a little jaded. My mouth felt like I had gargled with a dead possum and any head movements had to be negotiated delicately. But as I climbed out of my tent and stepped into the great outdoors, I was thumped in the face by a fresh, crisp summer's morning. The sky was overcast admittedly, but the grass was wet with the early morning dew, and the air smelled as fresh as a spring daisy blowing in the mountain breezes.

There are only two known cures for a hangover. The first is to bury yourself up to the neck in moist river sand. The second is a bacon sandwich. I chose the latter, simply because the campsite restaurant had been open since 7.00am and was serving cooked breakfast and strong coffee.

Aside from a German family with a geeky-looking teenage daughter who looked bored out of her mind, and a ratty-faced ten-year-old son with wayward hair – I was the only person in the restaurant. I ordered my sandwich and coffee, chose a seat strategically positioned to provide me with a perfect view of the television (which was mounted on the wall and had its sound muted) and I contemplated the day's agenda. It was a toss-up between two possibilities – one of which was to spend another day in Bremen. There were many attractions in the city that I hadn't yet visited. The Modern Science Museum of Space Technology sounded both interesting and educational. Or I could join one of the Beck's Brewery tours – one of which is conducted in English. Apparently the tour culminates with a 'tasting' event, which I suppose is something to look forward to – but before reaching this much anticipated grand finale one has to sit through the 'technical bit', delivered by a didactic science geek with a white coat and a clipboard, who'll drone on and on about hops, fermentation techniques and *'saccharomyces cerevisiae',* before allowing you the chance to guzzle down your complimentary glass of beer. The alternative option was to leave Bremen this morning and head for Hamburg – another of the *Stadtstaaten* of course, being both a major city and a state in its own right.

According to the forecast, the weather today was destined to be a little bit shit. That wasn't the actual meteorological terminology used by Joerg Kachelmann – Germany's leading meteorologist and presenter of *'Das Wette'* on the RTL Channel (at least I assumed not – the sound on the television had been muted after all, so I suppose it couldn't be completely ruled out) – but his weather map of northern Germany was wholly obscured by a plethora of gloomy-looking cloud and rain symbols, so *shit weather*, I think, was the gist of it. And so, after much indecision I finally reached the conclusion that if the heavens were going to open and deliver a deluge of rain, then I'd be better off sitting on a train than wandering the streets of Bremen. But before I could go anywhere there was something I urgently needed to do – and with all twelve of the campsite's washing machines currently available for use, right *now* was the best time to do it.

oOo

Dear Diary,

The Beer, Cheese and Tent Report for the State of Bremen:

Beer: Beck's:

A strong, steady beer that packs a bit of punch and slips down rather well especially if accompanied by jazz music. Beck's has a metallic, almost industrial flavour – you can almost taste the factory that produces it.

Cheese: Tilsiter:

Produced mainly in northern Germany, Tilsiter has a creamy texture and a mild flavour. I purchased some from a cheese shop in Bremen and the variety I sampled had added herbs, pepper and caraway seeds. Verdict: sublime.

Tent Stability:

I have straightened the main structural support pole and it appears to be holding out well. The bent tent peg was damaged beyond repair but has been replaced by another I found lying on the grass.

oOo

Chapter Four – Things to do in Hamburg When It's Raining

"It always rains on tents. Rainstorms will travel thousands of miles, against prevailing winds for the opportunity to rain on a tent."
Dave Barry – American journalist

Hamburg – a member of the medieval Hanseatic League; a free imperial city of the Holy Roman Empire; the second largest city in the Federal Republic of Germany and the bustling conurbation where I lost my umbrella during a visit back in 1982. Hamburg is less than an hour's train journey from Bremen – and since it had been more than twenty-eight years since I last stepped foot in the city's lively streets, I was delighted to be back here again today. Hamburg is a city boasting sixty museums, forty theatres and more than a hundred clubs and music venues. There are enough shops, in terms of both volume and diversity, to satiate the demands of just about everybody – and sufficient bars and restaurants to gratify even the most discerning of palates. Yes, there was plenty for me to explore in Hamburg, and if I also happened to stumble upon my missing umbrella during my visit – that would indeed be a bonus, if not a tiny bit miraculous.

Joerg Kachelmann's gloomy prediction that inclement weather would dominate much of northern Germany seemed to be accurate enough – I felt the first spits of rain as I dismantled my tent at the campsite in Bremen, and it was raining in torrents as I reconstructed the damned thing at the *Campingplatz Blauholz* a few hours later.

Now, in the interests of imparting a 'balanced' review, I find myself having to dig deep into the inner sanctum of my soul to come up with something positive to say about the *Campingplatz Blauholz*. But in the words of the late Johnny

Mercer, it is important, I think, to 'accentuate the positive' whenever possible – even if everything around you is looking worryingly grim. So here goes: The highlight of the *Campingplatz Blauholz* is its proximity to Hamburg city centre. There, I knew that if I tried hard enough I would find something nice to say. With the campsite located just a little over four kilometres from the heart of town, I was only a short bus ride away from Hamburg's main tourist attractions. And as if that wasn't good news enough, the bus in question stopped right outside the camp's main entrance. But other than its propinquity to the city, I'm afraid there was nothing about the *Campingplatz Blauholz* that made me smile – it had nothing going for it that filled me with a burning desire to hug the person standing next to me, or plant them with a slobbery wet kiss as an expression of my unrestrained joy. It was expensive, for a start. Now, I may by my own admission be a miserable and cantankerous old git, but nobody can accuse me of being parsimonious. I don't mind paying a little extra for something when it represents good value for money or where the additional cost is patently justified. I fully expected to have to pay a little extra for a city centre location, but the cost of pitching my tiny little tent at Blauholz was, in my opinion at least, preposterously excessive. The ground was hard and gravelly – more suitable for use as a car park than a campsite. Trying to drive a tent peg into ground that solid was like hammering a matchstick into concrete – I managed to destroy several of my pegs in the process. The site offered no facilities, save for a rather poorly maintained toilet and shower block and a small café/bar which was open for breakfast for a couple of hours in the early morning but closed for the rest of the day. No laundrette, no games room and no campsite shop – which surprised me somewhat, given that a shop here would have made a small fortune from the sale of replacement tent pegs alone. It was a noisy site too, with only a feeble wire fence separating the campsite from one of Hamburg's busiest arterial thoroughfares.

I suppose my spirits might have been lifted had the weather been better – after all, even the drabbest of places seem so much nicer in the sunshine. But the rain was unremitting and continued incessantly throughout the afternoon. So, it was a case of either taking the defeatist option – sitting here moping inside my tent, quietly wallowing away in my own self pity – or heading into town to explore what Hamburg had to offer – and cocking a snook at the appalling weather. I chose the latter.

My bus arrived at Hamburg's main railway station where it pulled into its allocated bay and wheezed to a pneumatic halt. As I stepped off the bus and onto the rain-drenched pavement, I felt for the first time on my trip so far, just a tiny bit despondent. The weather was to blame of course – I had allowed the rain to dampen my spirits in much the same way as it had dampened Hamburg's streets and sidewalks. The weather was doing its level best to ruin everything. The parks should have been brimming with people out strolling, walking their dogs, or otherwise enjoying the freedom of the open spaces in the warmth of the early summer sunshine. The upper decks of the city tour buses should have been overflowing with tourists – their cameras at the ready – snapping away feverishly at every opportunity as the buses ambled their way along Hamburg's lively streets. But the rain had put a stop to all these things. Hamburg's red open-top tour buses looked decidedly sorry for themselves as they cruised the streets with nobody on them. I usually enjoy an open-top bus tour. It is, in my opinion at least, one of the best ways to explore a city's historical and architectural highlights without having to deviate from the sitting position. But I didn't fancy the idea at all – not today. There were one or two intrepid souls wrapped from head to toe in plastic mackintoshes, who seemed determined to complete at least one circuit of the tour – but they didn't appear to be enjoying the experience. They sat on the upper deck of the tour bus looking glum and wretched – the rain falling on them from above and water seeping in through the seats of their trousers from the wet plastic bench seats they were sitting on.

The parks and the tour buses weren't the only attractions that were suffering as a result of the miserable weather. Hamburg has much to offer the seven million tourists who visit each year, but much of it is best explored in drier conditions. The bustling 300-year-old fish market for example, with its fresh seafood, exotic fruits and nuts, and teas from all over the world, is decidedly less bustling when the weather's grim. The historic port – the third largest in the world and over 800 years old – would be the perfect place for a boat tour or just a casual stroll along the waterfront – unless of course it happens to be raining. And adjacent to the harbour – the historic warehouse district – where narrow cobblestone streets and a network of historic canals are lined with 100-year-old warehouses, originally built for storing luxury imports from every corner of the globe – cocoa, silks and oriental carpets. The perfect place to stroll, assuming of course that it isn't bucketing down with rain.

As I stepped into the main square where the bus had dropped me, I was greeted by a parade of fibreglass statues – all depicting the same character, but each of them painted differently with bold, colourful designs. The character portrayed in the statues was that of *Hans Hummel* – a man with whom I share something of an affinity, and there are hundreds of fibreglass statues of him all over Hamburg. It's an idea that seems to be popular in many cities nowadays – Berlin has its bears, Zurich its cows and London its elephants. Well, Hamburg has its *Hans Hummels* – and since this character is based on a real person who lived here over two hundred years ago, I shall offer you this little snippet of insight as to who Hans Hummel was and why his image appears in statues all over the city.

A man by the name of *Johann Wilhelm Bentz* lived in Hamburg from 1787 until 1854 and was employed as a water carrier. In the days before Hamburg's intricate network of canals had been constructed, the water carrier was an omnipresent sight in Hamburg's narrow thoroughfares. They could be found walking along the streets carrying up to thirty litres of water in two large pails supported by a wooden frame mounted across their shoulders. The water carriers supplied the residents of 18th century Hamburg with fresh water, and it was arduous work as I'm sure you can imagine. Bentz lived in a small flat which had once belonged to a soldier named Christian Hummel. Hummel had been a popular character – well liked by the general citizenry and a favourite of the children who lived and played in the streets nearby. But when Hummel moved out and Bentz moved in – well, the poor man struggled to live up to the reputation of the previous occupant. Bentz, it seemed, was a man after my own heart – a miserable and cantankerous old git – and a little peevish too by all accounts. The local children would hurl abuse at him as he struggled through the streets carrying his load. They would regularly traduce his character with a stream of invective and hurl taunts of *'Hummel Hummel'* at him as he passed – something they knew to be a sure-fire way of rubbing the poor man up the wrong way. And Bentz would always reply in exactly the same way – by muttering *'Mors Mors'* in response to the children's taunts. I've hunted high and low to find you a suitable translation for *'Mors Mors'* that isn't too vulgar or offensive – so I'm going to settle for *'sod you, sod you'*, which I suppose will just have to do. Actually, *'Mors Mors'* is a shortened form of an old saying in the Hamburg regional dialect *'Klei mi an Mors'* – which translates more literally as *'go lick my arse'*. Over the past two hundred years the phrase *'Hummel Hummel, Mors*

Mors' has developed into a traditional Hanseatic greeting, more commonly referred to as the 'Hamburg salute.' [14] So, Johann Wilhelm Bentz became known as Hans Hummel, and more than 150 years after his death, the good people of Hamburg are still hurling abuse at the poor man every time they greet one another – metaphorically speaking of course.

I took temporary sanctuary at a small but nonetheless elegant coffee shop just across the square. The café had a number of tables and chairs spilling out into the street from its shadowy interior, but despite the presence of huge umbrellas covering every one of them – none was occupied. The rain had driven the café's clientele inside, so it was rather busy as you might imagine – and it was only through fortuity that I managed to find a vacant table. As I sat there supping on my cappuccino, staring despondently through the rain-soaked windows and watching the water droplets trickling slowly down the panes, my attention was suddenly drawn to an advertising poster which was displayed on one of the walls. *"Was ist los in Hamburg?"* the poster asked (what's on in Hamburg?). 'Good question,' I thought.

As I waded through the plethora of advertisements for antique dealers, wine merchants and hairdressing salons, I stumbled upon one that immediately caught my eye – an advertisement for the Borgweg Pool Halls. Now it's been a little while since I last played a game of pool. In my younger days I played a lot, although I'd rate my talent for the game as 'decidedly average' at best. But it seemed to me that a game of pool would be the ideal indoor pursuit on a rainy day like today, and the perfect vehicle for me to meet a few native Hamburgers and share an evening of merriment with

---

[14] *Hummel', coincidentally, is also the German word for 'bumblebee' – so I suppose the greeting 'Hummel Hummel, Mors Mors' would translate literally as 'bumblebee bumblebee, sod you sod you'. It may have been abusive in its origins, but it's intended nowadays as a friendly and welcoming salutation.*

them. The pool halls didn't open until later that evening, so I scribbled down the address on a paper napkin and stuffed it into the pocket of my cagoule. With plans for the evening settled, it was time to decide how best to occupy myself for the remainder of the afternoon. I couldn't sit in the café all day – although I will admit that its charming ambience, together with the wonderful aroma of coffee beans, made the prospect of doing so decidedly appealing. But with cappuccino costing seven euros a piece, it would have been an expensive way to kill a wet and windy afternoon.

My Hamburg guidebook offered a number of suggestions in its *'wet weather'* section – the *Hamburger Kunsthalle (Hamburg Halls of Art)*, for example – home to a diverse collection of both modern and classical paintings including masterpieces by Rembrandt, Caspar David Friedrich and Edvard Munch; or the Church of St. Michaelis – Hamburg's signature landmark and perhaps the most famous church in northern Germany. I decided I would visit neither. Not because of any lack of interest on my part – I just wasn't in the mood. Traipsing around art galleries or exploring ecclesiastical architecture demands a significant attention span. It's an educational experience and one has to be prepared to absorb copious amounts of information in order to fully appreciate the true wonder of what's on offer. And to be brutally honest, I didn't really want to work that hard. Not today anyway. I wanted something entertaining rather than educational – a place where I could leave my brain at the door, and collect it again on my way out. And on page 27, my guidebook suggested what appeared to be the perfect solution – The *'Hamburg Miniatur-Wunderland'*. I shan't insult your intelligence by offering a translation.

The guidebook described the experience as *'not just for model railway geeks – normal folk will love it too!'* – which I suppose was reassuring in its own strange little way – even if there was a hint of suggestion that model railway enthusiasts weren't normal. But the best thing of all was that, although my guidebook included the full postal address of this most intriguing of tourist attractions along with a brief explanation of how to get there, none of this information was either useful or necessary – for the simple reason that Hamburg's 'world-famous' *Miniatur-Wunderland* was just across the square – I could see it through the window of the café.

I joined a long queue of people waiting outside before eventually paying my twelve-euro entrance fee to a morose-looking woman who was sitting behind a glass kiosk. After some confusion over the number of tickets I needed (for some reason she seemed to be under the impression that I was in charge of a group of Japanese schoolgirls who were lined up behind me, each wearing school uniform, carrying identical satchels over their shoulders and waiting patiently and obediently for instructions from their group leader who was outside in the rain rounding up the stragglers), the barrier was lifted and I was allowed to step inside what I can only describe as the most enchanting tourist attraction I have ever experienced – a veritable Aladdin's Cave of joy and wonder.

The *Miniatur-Wunderland* is an indoor model village exhibition – or rather several model villages – but on a most impressive scale. The exhibition covers 6,400m² of floor space – although there are plans in place for future expansion. *Miniatur-Wunderland* is divided into eight separate exhibits including recreations in miniature of Harz, Hamburg and the North Sea coast, Austria, the fictitious village of Knuffingen, the United States of America, Switzerland and Scandinavia. Plans to add models of France and Italy are in progress too, and the construction of the attraction's latest exhibit – the Alpine airport, was already 'work in progress' during my visit here. Everything on display at the exhibition is created in miniature in painstaking detail and with meticulous precision. There are life-like models of well-known landmarks; reconstructions of the Grand Canyon, Las Vegas, Area 51, the Everglades and Cape Canaveral, as well as stunning miniature Alpine scenery. In all, the *Miniatur-Wunderland* boasts 900 model trains; 300,000 lights; 5,500 cars; 3,500 buildings and bridges; 200,000 figurines and 12,000 metres of railway track (making this the largest model railway exhibition in the world). Unfortunately though, the exhibition hall is able to accommodate only a limited number of visitors in any one session, so my time here was restricted to around an hour or so before an officious-looking woman with a severe facial expression and a clipboard ushered me towards the nearest exit. But I had no cause for complaint. The one hour time restriction was understandable, I suppose, given the number of visitors the exhibition attracts. But as far as I was concerned, even if I had been allowed to stay here for the rest of the day, it still wouldn't have been anywhere near long enough. You can browse the exhibits over and over again and notice something new and exciting every time. As soon as the sullen attendant had kicked me out into the street (figuratively speaking of course), I rummaged through my wallet in search of another twelve euros, and once again joined the queue to get in.

Since there was no chance whatsoever of being reunited with the umbrella I lost here in 1982, I began my afternoon tour of the city by stopping at a shop near to the main station to purchase a new one – a gentleman's classic style umbrella in black, that was sturdy enough to protect me from the elements and had a retractable telescopic handle making it easy for me to carry – a snip at just ten euros. There are, in point of fact, a large number of shops in Hamburg selling umbrellas. Northern Germany is prone to the occasional deluge of torrential rain – and Hamburgers (for that genuinely is what the natives are called) don't like to be caught in a downpour any more than the rest of us.

Feeling delighted with my new purchase (which was both functional as well as decidedly 'au courant'), I headed towards the *Reeperbahn* – arguably Hamburg's best known thoroughfare, and the street where some guidebooks urge tourists to head towards, and others advise visitors to steer clear of. If there is anybody out there who hasn't heard of Hamburg's *Reeperbahn* (and I can't imagine there will be many), then it's similar to *La Pigalle* in Paris, the *Halmtorvet* in Copenhagen or just about any of the streets in Amsterdam's notorious red-light district. The word 'Reeper' means 'roper' in German, and the *Reeperbahn* takes its name from the rope makers who supplied the ships docking at Hamburg's bustling port. But over time it became a popular spot for sailors who, after many months at sea, came here in search of a bellyful of alcohol and a couple of hours in the company of an obliging young lady. And nothing much appears to have changed since then. Nowadays the *Reeperbahn* is a veritable den of iniquity – a street alive with pubs, strip joints, lap dancing clubs, casinos, sex shops and the like. You'll find licentious ladies plying their trade and drugs being bought and sold in the squalid little lanes and alleyways that branch off of the main thoroughfare. And somewhat paradoxically, right in the middle of all this sleaziness and sandwiched between a cinema showing adult movies and a sex shop having a sale on dildos and vibrators, is a branch of the discount supermarket chain *Lidl* – having a sale of their own on tins of tuna and family packs of toilet roll.

So, you may well be wondering what innocent explanation there could possibly be for a forty-nine-year-old happily married man to be wandering the length of the *Reeperbahn* in the pissing rain. Well, in my defence, Your Honour, I was walking along here in broad daylight, and I am

86

given to believe that the ladies of the night as well as many other elements of Hamburg's sleazy underworld prefer to wait until after dark before coming out to play. Secondly, my guidebook suggested that the *Reeperbahn* had done much in recent years to clean up its act, by introducing a number of elegant new haunts including chic nightclubs and trendy new bars and restaurants. And this, I decided, required my personal verification.

I stumbled upon a splendid looking establishment called *Teatro*, where I took refuge from the rain – a chance to dry out a bit and fill a hunger gap. The menu was in German, and from what I could ascertain from a cursory glance through its listings, seemed to offer a wide choice of culinary options. Among the offerings was a dish known as *Finkwarder Scholl*, which I thought might be a seafood dish of some kind, although without my German-English pocket dictionary to hand I couldn't be sure. So I decided to ask the man behind the bar – a tall, lean, giant of a man with a chiselled jaw line and cheek bones sharp enough to carve the Sunday joint with.

"Entschuldigung," I said rather humbly, "der *Finkwarder Scholl* – ist das ein Fisch?"

The barman looked at me as if I was a complete idiot.

"Ja, natürlich," he replied.

At this point I decided it might be necessary to justify to the barman why I had asked the question – after all, judging from his answer, he had clearly thought my question was a particularly stupid one. So I decided to go with the explanation of *"ich bin English"* as if it were my 'get out of jail free' card. The barman shrugged his shoulders.

"Your nationality is not relevant," he said, "it's still a fish."

As it turned out, the *Finkwarder Scholl* was a piece of pan-fried plaice, served with *Bratkartoffeln* (pan-fried potatoes) and a curious north German delicacy known as

'*Birnen, Bohnen und Speck*' (green beans cooked with pears and bacon). It was, quite simply, sublime.

I managed to find the Borgweg Pool Halls later that day. They were exactly where the poster suggested they would be – on the junction of *Barmbekerstraße* and *Wiesendam* and within a short walking distance of the U-Bahn (underground railway) station at Borgweg. It was a large building, spotlessly clean, stylishly decorated and adorned with glittering ceiling chandeliers. As I stepped into this vast explosion of space I was greeted by the soothing clatter of colliding cue balls and the welcoming aroma of freshly-brewed coffee. It was a busy night at the pool halls too – the numbers swollen, I suspect, as a result of the squally weather outside. All of the pool tables were in use and there were a large number of people waiting patiently at the sidelines for their chance to play.

Now, in my experience, the established method of registering one's intention to enter a pool tournament with a group of total strangers is to place your money on the side of the pool table – in this case the princely sum of two euros. There is a flaw in this methodology of course – a rather major one actually, in that my €2 looks strikingly similar to everybody else's €2, so unless you're keeping a very close eye on proceedings, this system offers no guarantee that games will be played in the correct sequential order. Add to the mix the influence of alcohol and teenage high spirits and you have a recipe for a good old-fashioned bar brawl. But the convention at the Borgweg Pool Halls seemed much simpler, far more equitable and considerably less likely to result in a punch-up. Players wishing to throw their hat into the ring, so to speak, would simply add their name to the list of those already waiting by scribbling it onto a chalk board mounted on the wall beside each of the pool tables. As each game was played, so the player's name would have a line scratched through it. I dutifully added my name to the list and sat down at one of the tables. There were three other people ahead of me on the list, so I had time to kill before my turn would come – my chance to unleash my pool prowess on this unsuspecting crowd. So time enough, I thought, to make myself comfortable, order a glass of ice-cold beer and check out the skill of the competition while I waited.

The preponderant pool player in the Borgweg Pool Halls was a man named Lars. I knew he was so called as *'Lars'* was one of the many names that appeared on the chalkboard. It was a long way up the list as it happened, having been scribbled up there much earlier in the evening – but his skills as a pool hustler were such that he had won the last six games in succession – and some of them pretty convincingly. Not only that, a number of people in the club had addressed him as 'Lars' during general conversation, including a few of the bar staff – so I figured that Lars was one of the regulars here, and clearly proficient at his game. Lars was what I can only describe as a leviathan – a tall, brawny lad with biceps as thick as tree trunks and pectorals like Arnold Schwarzenegger's. With every shot he took, he leaned awkwardly over the pool table – his posture lacking in grace on account of his muscular physique. Clumsy as his technique may have seemed, Lars managed every shot with razor-sharp precision. He stood out from the rest of the crowd in the pool halls that evening – not only because of his burly stature, but also because he was the only person I saw using his own personalised pool cue. Everybody else seemed content to use the house cues. But not Lars – he carried his own cue with his name engraved on the side of what I'm going to describe as 'the thick end' – on account of my being wholly ignorant of pool-related terminology. There was a hideously ostentatious cue case made from walnut, which leaned precariously against a wall throughout the entire evening. It too had Lars' name engraved on its side.

I had calculated, perhaps rather naively, that I would probably have to wait around 45 minutes before my turn would come. I based this on a supposition that the average game of pool lasts approximately fifteen minutes and there were three games to be played before it would be my turn to step into the limelight. It was a logical enough hypothesis, but was alas flawed – a theory with more holes in it than a Swiss cheese. Lars made proverbial mincemeat out of his next three opponents. One by one, each of them valiantly stepped into the frame exuding an initial air of buoyant self-confidence, only to have their self-esteem crushed into a fine powder at the mercy of Lars and his unassailable skills in the art of pool. In less than twenty minutes flat, Lars had wiped the floor with all three of them – leaving them to recoil into a corner of the room to consider whether they would prefer to suffer their humiliation in silence or to whimper like puppies licking their wounds.

Before my glass of beer was even half empty my name was called out, and I was summoned to the pool table to face the wrath of Neanderthal Man. I stepped gingerly towards the cue rack, picked up a couple of cues in each hand and began shaking them a few times – as if I were testing them for weight and balance. It was something I'd seen professional pool players doing on the television. It was a rather pointless gesture obviously, but it was all part of my wily plan to persuade Lars that, for the first time that evening, he was up against some formidable opposition. It's called psychological warfare I think – I'm sure I've watched something on the telly about that too. Of course it was all a charade – deep down I knew that I probably wouldn't be able to beat him, but I was determined to give it my best shot (if you'll pardon the pun), and hope that my imminent defeat wouldn't be too humiliating. I selected a cue which I thought might be suitable (any one of them would have done), and I set about arranging the balls into the triangle while Lars

90

paced menacingly up and down beside me. He had a serious, rather austere look about him and he breathed deeply as if he were psyching himself up into a heightened state of mental preparedness. Lars was a man of few words – he acknowledged my presence with just a menacing nod. My only hope was that along with his brawny physique, Lars also had a calm and placid temperament.

"Shall I break the balls?" he asked, which didn't help to set my mind at rest. I hoped that Lars was referring to the task of dispersing the balls on the pool table rather than threatening to inflict injury to a certain rather sensitive part of my anatomy.

"Yes, you can if you want to," I obligingly replied.

And so he did. Lars kept the tip of his cue low on the cue ball and hit it with the force of a charging bull. There was an almighty crack as the cue ball collided with the others, destroying their perfect triangular formation and scattering them in every direction around the table. As one yellow ball dropped into one of the corner pockets and another yellow ball disappeared into a second – I could feel my heart sinking into a third.

"Looks like I'm playing yellow and you're playing red," said Lars – as if I needed to have the rules explained to me. Having potted the first two yellow balls, Lars set about systematically potting the remaining five, calmly and nonchalantly, one after the other, until only the black ball and all seven of my red balls remained in play.

"I'll nominate this pocket here," said Lars, pointing to one of the corner pockets with the tip of his '*Nimbus 2000*' or whatever pretentious sobriquet he had given his personalised pool cue. Lars effortlessly smashed the black ball into his nominated pocket as I fully expected he would, and that, as they say, was that. The game was over with me not having played a single shot.

With my tail between my legs, I placed the cue back into the rack and returned to my table, where my half-filled beer glass was waiting patiently for me to return like a loyal Labrador puppy. Without even as much as a 'danke schön' from Lars, he glanced at the chalkboard and read aloud the name of the next victim on his hit list.

"Günther!" he shouted, as a short and scrawny-looking man with short hair and geeky spectacles made his way meekly towards the pool table.

Mine had been a humiliating defeat I admit, but I have never regarded myself as being *easily* defeated. I came out this evening with the intention of playing a game of pool, and having lost the only game of the evening without playing a single shot, I felt I had been a little short-changed. The convention at the Borgweg Pool Halls was a system of 'winner stays on' – where the winner of a game continues to take on fresh opponents one after the other until he or she (the incumbent champion) is eventually defeated. But to me, such a system didn't seem fair. It simply meant that somebody like Lars, who was clearly a gifted pool player, would pay two euros for his first game of the evening and spend the rest of the night hogging the table without having to pay a penny more. And that, I decided, seemed like a travesty of justice and was not how I'd intended my evening to pan out. Pool was supposed to be a pleasurable experience – a fun game where two people of a similar skill level can knock a few balls around a table whilst having a bit of laugh in the process. It wasn't meant to be a serious pursuit. This 'winner stays on' malarkey only encouraged people like Lars to make the whole thing way too competitive – stifle any hint of merriment and turn a fun night out into a tedious ordeal.

Now, I suppose that with the benefit of hindsight I should have taken a stroll around the room in search of another pool table where the competition was perhaps a little less fierce, or the opposition not quite so intimidating. But in my opinion, this 'Lars' character needed bringing down a peg or two – he was far too big for his boots in my view and for that reason alone, I decided to order another beer and scribble my name onto the chalkboard once again. My decision to do so raised a few eyebrows among some of the Borgweg Pool Halls' clientele, including the barman, whose eyebrow movements were accompanied by a look of utter disdain. If it were possible to capture the phrase *'what the fuck are you thinking?'* in a facial expression, the barman had managed to pull it off perfectly.

Günther's efforts to defeat Goliath were short-lived, although admittedly not quite as short-lived as mine had been. Theo – a middle-aged man wearing a pair of hideous turquoise trousers and a garish Hawaiian shirt managed to sink a couple of balls before Lars finally lost patience and made short work of him; and Greta – a plucky little girl in her mid to late twenties, managed to give Lars a bit of a run for his money until she too became another victim of his merciless game strategy and his infinitely superior pool skills.

And then it was my turn again. Lars gave me a wry smile when he saw me approach the table. There was nothing menacing about it – in fact it felt almost complimentary, as if he was trying to tell me how much he admired my spirit. I smiled back and set about the task of arranging the balls into the triangle.

"Shall I break the balls?" Lars asked for the second time that evening. Well, it was the second time he'd asked *me* anyway.

"No," I replied. "I think I'll break this time, if you've no objection."

"OK - go ahead."

I decided I would take a leaf out of Lars' book – give the man a taste of his own medicine. I kept the tip of my cue low on the cue ball and hit it with the same vigour as Lars had done in the opening break of our previous game. There was a deafening crack as the cue ball smashed into the mass of yellow and red balls, once again destroying their perfect triangular formation and scattering them around the table in every conceivable direction. I desperately hoped that one of the balls would find its way into a pocket. Either of the colours would have done – red yellow – I really didn't care – just so long as I could pot enough balls to beat the standard set in my previous game – a standard which I'd set at such a low level that potting just one ball now would have been enough. And then one of the balls *did* find a pocket to fall into. Was it red, maybe? Yellow, perhaps? No – the bastard ball that dropped into one of the pockets was black. Black! It was one of those Victor Meldrew '*I don't believe it*' moments. On my second game of the evening I had managed to pot the black ball on my opening break. It was game over. Lars was once again the victor – not this time as a result of his skills, but as a result of my ineptitude. My humiliation was complete.

As I placed my cue into the rack I could hear the sound of sniggering emanating from certain quarters of the room, and was incensed to discover that Theo – the middle-aged arsehole with the turquoise trousers and the Hawaiian shirt – was among the perpetrators. Nobody lacking in fashion sense to such an unpardonable degree, I decided, had the right to deride anybody. I guzzled the last drop of beer from my glass and made a hasty retreat from the Borgweg Pool Halls.

The first thing I noticed when I stepped into the street was that the rain had stopped. I was delighted at the time of course, but bizarre as this may sound, I rather wish the rain had still been bucketing down. You see, had it still been raining, I would have realised in an instant that I'd left my umbrella on the table in the pool hall. But since the rain had stopped, it simply didn't occur to me. The strange thing was that I knew there was *something* missing. You know how it is sometimes – you get that bizarre feeling where you know instinctively that something is wrong, yet you're unable to fathom what it is. I checked my pockets a couple of times, but on discovering that both my wallet and my rail pass were exactly where they should have been, I hastily concluded that all was 'present and correct' and didn't realise that it was my brand new umbrella that was missing until I was back at the campsite.

That wasn't the only piece of bad news that greeted me on my arrival at Blauholz. The campsite's ground with its almost impenetrable stony surface had absorbed so much rain that day that its saturation point had been reached and surpassed many hours earlier. The campsite was awash with thousands of puddles, some of which were large enough to sustain multifarious marine species. And what was probably the largest puddle of them all was located just outside the entrance to my tent. For those of you who have never experienced the pleasure of camping, getting in and out of a one-man tent isn't terribly easy – one has to adopt something of an undignified corporal posture, by getting down on all fours and crawling in backwards. [15] And by adopting such a position I managed to immerse my hands and knees into a puddle of water six inches deep. There was water inside my tent too – another puddle (albeit smaller than the one outside, thank goodness) had appeared at one end of the groundsheet. The water covered a small area of

[15] *You can, if you prefer, crawl in head first, but there isn't enough room in a Wind-Breaker DeLuxe for a 180-degree turn, so doing so would necessitate crawling out again backwards. It's just a matter of personal preference I suppose – one either crawls in frontwards and out again backwards or vice versa. I prefer the latter as you never know what might be lurking outside your tent in the middle of the night, and I'd rather be able to see it than shove my arse into its face inadvertently without knowing it's there.*

the tarp and had soaked the corner of my pillow. My 'guaranteed waterproof' *Wind-Breaker DeLuxe,* it seemed, had sprung a leak. On closer inspection under torchlight, I discovered a small hole in the roof – a tiny rip in the canvas where the water was seeping through. I could only assume that this tiny tear was supplementary damage sustained during the incident on Borkum Island, where I tripped over a guide rope and fell on top of my tent in the middle of the night. There hadn't been very much rain since then – the odd shower here and there, but nothing heavy or persistent – until today of course. So only now was the true extent of the damage caused by my clumsiness that night becoming clear.

As I lay there in my sleeping bag, my head positioned awkwardly to avoid the soggy bits of my pillow and with tissue paper strewn around the floor soaking up the small puddles of water, I felt crestfallen and dispirited. What the heck was I doing here? I *could* be sitting on the veranda in a five-star luxury hotel, looking out across the crystal-clear waters of the Mediterranean, soaking up the rays wearing only my shorts and sunshades, and supping champagne from a crystal flute. But I was here instead – cramped inside a tiny canvas capsule, my body wrapped in a damp sleeping bag and my head resting on a soaking wet pillow. And although the rain, which had been falling more or less persistently throughout the day, had at last mercifully relented, I could still hear droplets of water dripping rhythmically onto my groundsheet from the tiny hole in the roof. All I wanted to do at that point was cut my losses and simply go home – back to the comfort and warmth of my own house in west London, assuming of course that my son hadn't burnt it down or opened its doors as a refuge for vagrants and wayward strays. There was no point staying here for the sake of it. The wet weather was ruining everything, and right now I would rather have been home and dry.

This, I decided, would be my last night under canvas in Germany. I would terminate my trip across the country the following morning. Yes, after all that planning and preparation I was ready to throw in the towel, having visited just three of the sixteen states. I was absolutely determined that first thing the following morning I'd be gathering my belongings together and heading back to dear old Blighty.

oOo

Dear Diary,

The Beer, Cheese and Tent Report for the State of Hamburg:

Beer: St. Pauli Astra:

Not too bad a flavour – it slides down a treat and is not too gassy. I didn't have a headache in the morning, thank goodness, but I only managed to drink a couple in the pool hall before having to leave for the sake of my humility.

Cheese: Gouda:

And there was I thinking that Gouda was an exclusively Dutch product. Wrong! Germany has been making Gouda for almost 200 years and it remains one of the country's most popular cheeses. They make it from full cream milk which gives it a mild and buttery taste when it's young. If the cheese is allowed to age, it becomes more piquant. I bought a small piece from a shop in Hamburg which specialised in local regional cheeses.

Tent Stability:

Don't ask! Today has been a disaster. Six tent pegs are now buckled due to the hard ground at Blauholz – two of which may be salvageable but the others are damaged beyond repair. A small hole in the canvas is leaking water and is in urgent need of taping up. Maybe I should have spent £300 on a 'Power Tokee Ultra-Light' after all.

oOo

Chapter Five – From Hamburg to Saint Tropez – Well, Almost

*"I love blackjack but I'm not addicted to gambling,
I'm addicted to sitting in a semi-circle."*
*Mitch Hedberg – American Comedian - February 1968 to
March 2005*

We all have our good days and bad days. Yesterday had been one of those truly awful ones where everything that could possibly have gone pear-shaped went pear-shaped. The deleterious effects of the weather had left me feeling disconsolate and ready to throw in the towel. But life has an adept way of suddenly lifting your spirits doesn't it? Yes, in the immortal words of Joan Armatrading, 'some days the bear will eat you; some days you'll eat the bear' – and this morning I was having a whole roasted grizzly for breakfast. (Not literally of course, I'm still running with the Joan Armatrading song lyrics theme, so stick with me for a while longer if you will.) It was one of those mornings where everything seemed right with the world – and being woken by the ethereal song of a skylark nesting in a nearby tree was certainly a good way to start the day.

In stark contrast to yesterday's gloom, the weather this morning was beautiful – the sun was bursting through a cloudless turquoise sky. There was a soft, gentle breeze too – just enough to take the edge off the searing morning temperatures. And to top it all, the campsite's so-called 'restaurant' was not only open for business (which was a rarity in itself), but was serving coffee together with a selection of Danish pastries, warm croissants and pains au chocolat – perhaps not as rich in protein as a grizzly bear, but certainly as high in cholesterol and equally as likely to cause a chronic dose of heartburn. But what did it matter?

Pains au chocolat are always utterly irresistible – so I gorged myself anyway regardless of the inevitable consequences.

My threats to cut my losses and head back to the UK this morning had been idle – spoken in the heat of the moment, I suppose. I decided instead, to persevere with this decadent jolly of mine through Germany's sixteen states. And today I intended to conquer state number four on my list – Schleswig-Holstein – famous for its unspoiled dunes and sandy beaches, its North Sea shrimps, its medieval cities and its internationally renowned music and film festivals. The state of Schleswig-Holstein is also one of the few German states to have its own 'national' anthem – a melancholy ditty composed in 1844 entitled *'Wanke nicht, mein Vaterland'*, which translates as *'Don't falter, my fatherland'* and has nothing to do with what you were thinking. Schleswig-Holstein is Germany's northernmost province, bordered by Denmark in the far north and set between the harsh, unpredictable North Sea and the calmer, gentler Baltic.

My plan for today was to head for the affluent and rather salubrious little town of *Travemünde* on the outskirts of Lübeck – which manages to combine the role of a delightful Baltic seaside resort with that of a major ferry terminal. (Ferries trundle in and out of Travemünde from Malmo, Gothenburg and Helsinki.) Travemünde is located on the estuary of the *River Trave ('Mund'* being the German for *'mouth'*, so it's clear to see how the name was derived). The town became popular in the early 1800s when sea bathing was in vogue among the gentry, and has been known ever since as the 'German Saint Tropez'. Quite why the town is referred to as such does seem to me to be something of a mystery though. Germany's Baltic coast is hardly the French Riviera, and whereas Saint Tropez is renowned as a playground for the well heeled – a rendezvous for jetsetters, fashion models, millionaires and general bons vivants – Travemünde is a place where wealthier Germans move to following their retirement – where there is space aplenty for the elderly to stroll the tree-lined avenues with the support of their Zimmer frames and admire the town's impeccably manicured lawns and flourishing flowerbeds. The fact that Travemünde has the highest number of funeral parlours per capita than any other town in Germany gives you some idea of the average age of the folk who live here. But in times gone by, Travemünde *did* attract the rich and famous. The town was favoured by a young Thomas Mann for example, and Dostoevsky came here for the curative and restorative qualities of the iodine-waters and for the town's famous casino – a subject which we shall return to later.

The train journey from Hamburg to Travemünde is relatively short – less than ninety minutes even allowing for the connection at Lübeck, so I was in no great hurry to get going. In fact, since there had been such a dramatic and unexpected improvement in the weather, I decided to delay my departure from Hamburg until later that morning, concentrating my efforts instead on dismantling my tent and heading back into Hamburg's city centre, where I resolved to do something I would have done the previous day had the weather not been prohibitive. I spent the morning riding atop one of Hamburg's city tour buses. I managed to capture the majesty of most of the city's architecture in my camera – but it wasn't easy. Every time I had my camera poised at the ready and a major landmark in the frame, the bus would hit another pothole and I'd be catapulted from my seat. Four of the photos I took whilst our driver negotiated Hamburg's potholes had to be deleted from my camera. There were two interesting shots of my lap, one of my feet, and a photograph of the back of a Japanese woman's head.

My base for the next two nights would be *Campingplatz Windmühle* – Travemünde's premier campsite with a host of amenities and the additional benefit of one of the most stunningly attractive women I have ever seen sitting behind a reception desk. The moment I saw Loreley I was instantly smitten. I'm guessing she must have been in her late teens or early twenties – blond-haired, blue-eyed, with a smooth unblemished complexion and a smile that could illuminate a football stadium. Loreley wasn't her real name of course – I just made that up. [16] I had no intention of asking what it was in case she thought there was something creepy or sinister about me and arranged for her boyfriend to set fire to my tent in the middle of the night. A girl as stunning as Loreley was bound to have a boyfriend, I decided – a tanned hunk called Sherman or Panzer or something similar – mean, moody and built like a tank. Having liberated me of the €10 pitching fee, Loreley dutifully handed me a leaflet (in English) and a map of the site before undergoing a most extraordinary metamorphosis. Suddenly and without warning, Loreley dropped the bashful and adorable sweetheart façade, and launched into the following outburst of bumptious, overbearing and bureaucratic verbal diarrhoea:

"Please note the following rules," she said, in perfect English, albeit with a distinct American brogue. "Make sure you only use the designated pathways to minimise damage to the environment. Make sure your pets are kept under control and always clean up after them. All rubbish must be placed in the litter bins as you may be fined for dropping litter on the ground. No loud music is allowed at any time of

[16] *German folklore tells of a maiden who lived on a rock in the River Rhine, who would lure fishermen to their death with her song. The maiden's name was Loreley – from the German verb 'lureln' (to murmur) and the noun 'Ley' (a small rock). The name Loreley therefore means 'murmuring rock'. For some reason I always imagined that this maiden from German mythology would look something like the gorgeous young woman sitting at the reception desk at Campingplatz Windmühle – which is why I chose to name her Loreley.*

the day or night. Please make sure you stick to the speed limit in the park and remember that campfires are strictly prohibited. Don't drop cigarette butts on the grass – these should be properly extinguished and disposed of carefully. If you use the campsite facilities, please be thoughtful to other users – leave the bathrooms clean and don't take longer than necessary in the showers. And finally, please respect the local wildlife – it is their home after all and not yours."

As Loreley so condescendingly rattled off her list of campsite dos and don'ts, I stood there both nonplussed and utterly bemused. Just who the heck did she think she was? She had simply taken the list of campsite regulations as they were printed on the leaflet and quoted them at me verbatim. Did she think I couldn't read? Did she think I looked like the type of person who needed to have the rules explained to me in such a pompous and patronising manner? I think what irritated me more than anything was the fact that she found it necessary to quote *all* the rules – even those that clearly didn't apply to me. I didn't have any pets to clean up after – nor would I be likely to break any speed limits with the weight of my rucksack pressing down on my shoulders – and as for cigarette butts – I gave up smoking months ago! Her lecture was both inappropriate and unnecessary in my humble opinion – and despite that beautiful blond hair and those blue eyes of hers, my first impressions of her suddenly fell by the wayside – I decided I didn't like Loreley all that much after all. Still, there was one good thing to emerge from my encounter with this girl – I needn't have worried about her boyfriend setting fire to my tent, seeing as how keen she was to see the ban on campfires being observed.

As I assembled my *Wind-Breaker DeLuxe* yet again, I had the good fortune of making the acquaintance of James and Andrew – two gentlemen from south-west London in their mid to late forties – who, it transpired, were brothers. Quite coincidently, I had pitched my tent alongside theirs not realising they were English until I heard them chatting together – a lively and occasionally sardonic discussion about which of their favoured premiership football teams would be the likely winners of a match scheduled that coming weekend. I waited for a suitable lull in their conversation before brashly introducing myself. In my experience it's always a bit of gamble trying to make new acquaintances when you're travelling. Some people will be pleased to meet you and you'll gel with them almost from the outset. Others can be more aloof. But James and Andrew were warm and sociable and welcomed me into their world as if they had known me since their childhood. The three of us had much in common as it happened. Other than being approximately coeval and all hailing from roughly the same part of London, all three of us had travelled here by train from Hamburg earlier in the day – the two brothers just a couple of hours before me with their bicycles conveyed in the baggage car. After the hearty round of handshakes that followed our introductions, Andrew took a packet of cigarettes from the pocket of his jeans and placed one in his mouth.

"Be very careful how you dispose of the butt," I said sarcastically, "you don't want to suffer the wrath of the girl on the reception desk."

They both laughed.

"Adolf Hitler wasn't a particularly handsome bloke was he?" Andrew asked.

"No," I replied, failing to understand the relevance of his question. "Why do you ask?"

"Well, I was just wondering how his great-granddaughter turned out to be such a great-looking woman."

"I couldn't believe what I was hearing," James interjected, "when I first clapped eyes on the lass, I was smitten. I wanted to marry the girl and father her babies. And then, out of the blue, she starts rattling off a whole list of rules like the bloody Gestapo – do this, don't do that! I'm glad she gave you the same lecture. I thought it was just me and Andrew she had taken a dislike to."

Andrew was in the process of boiling a kettle of water on a small Calor-Gas burner and set about making tea.

"Fancy a brew?" he asked – an offer I readily accepted having not had a decent cup of tea since the day I left home.

As we sat and waited while the kettle boiled (I'll save the rest of the *Waltzing Matilda* lyrics until later in the story), James gazed inquisitively at my *Wind-Breaker DeLuxe*.

"Is that a small hole in your tent?" he asked – pointing at what was quite obviously a small hole in my tent. I nodded.

"I have just the thing to fix that," he said, much to my delight.

"I have some waterproof tape in my bag," he continued. "It's not a permanent solution though. Ideally you should sew another piece of canvas over the top of the tear and seal the seams with a waterproof spray. But in the absence of a needle and thread you can stick a few bits of tape over the tear, and with a bit of luck it'll hold for a few days."

I liked James and Andrew – affable characters who seemed willing to go that extra mile to help a fellow camper in need. I had met them only ten minutes earlier and already they were making me tea and helping me fix the hole in my tent. Add a beautiful sunny day into the mix and you have a recipe for perfection. No wonder I was feeling so sanguine. With tea consumed and tent temporarily repaired, I left the two brothers to enjoy their afternoon and I headed into the centre of town.

Now, I mentioned earlier that the novelists Thomas Mann and Fyodor Dostoevsky both had associations with Travemünde – and indeed they did. Thomas Mann's first novel, *Buddenbrooks,* was published in 1901 and won him the Nobel Prize for Literature, albeit twenty-eight years after its original publication. The book portrays the downfall of the Buddenbrooks – a wealthy mercantile family who, over a period of four generations, lived in the city of Lübeck. In the novel, the town of Travemünde is depicted by Mann as a place of freedom and happiness – a favoured retreat for several members of the Buddenbrook family as an escape from the problems and traumas of business life.

As for Dostoevsky – well, he too was a frequent visitor to the town – lured here it would seem by Travemünde's famous casino. Dostoevsky had something of an addiction to roulette, which in many ways was his inspiration for writing *The Gambler* – a short novel about a young tutor in the employ of a formerly wealthy Russian general who develops a gambling addiction of his own. The novella was first published in 1867.

But in the decades since the likes of Dostoevsky and Thomas Mann visited Travemünde, the town has lost a little of its cachet, and the comparison with Saint Tropez, in my view at least, is stretching things a little too far. But the town does have its attractions, not least of which is the seafront, where the crowds appeared to be heading.

It was a beautiful sunny afternoon and the beach was packed – every square centimetre of sand claimed by somebody in a swimsuit making the most of this rare glimpse of the early summer sunshine. Not wishing to miss out on the fun, I changed into my yellow floral swimming trunks – an item of my garb that rarely sees the light of day under normal circumstances, but one which I'd brought to Germany with me in the hope that there would be at least one day of blazing hot sunshine coupled with an opportunity to don them. And today, it seemed, was just such a day. Had I been on holiday on the Mediterranean I probably wouldn't have bothered to put them on. It would have been too embarrassing to place my pallid and portly body on public display among the perfectly toned and nutmeg-tanned torsos you always find on Mediterranean beaches. But my hideous, pale, hairy, beer-bellied frame was not particularly conspicuous among the other hideous, pale, hairy, beer-bellied frames on display on the beaches of Germany's Baltic coast (and that was just the women! – the local pharmacy must have sold out of depilatory cream). So I didn't feel too self-conscious in my yellow floral bathing trunks.

I tiptoed rather gingerly into the Baltic Sea – one step at a time until the water was just above my knees, and then promptly turned around and headed back to the beach. It was a cowardly, almost pusillanimous thing to do, I agree, but not only was the Baltic Sea bloody freezing (that alluring image from the shore of a warm, aqua-marine ocean with the sun glistening on its surface was cruelly deceptive), but it was also teaming with jellyfish – thousands of the bastards, which every so often would rub against my legs and make me wince and yelp like a silly schoolgirl. The Moon Jellyfish of the Baltic Sea aren't the venomous variety, mercifully, nor are they particularly large specimens, so there was really no excuse for my asinine behaviour, particularly as there were hundreds of people, adults and children alike, who were splashing around in the water, evidently unfazed by their presence. But I wasn't prepared to share my bathing experience with a multitude of ugly, pulsing, bell-shaped, translucent blobs – and that was the end of the matter. I wasn't terribly happy about sharing my bathing experience with the jellyfish either. I spent half an hour or so simply lying recumbent on the sand, soaking up the remains of the afternoon sunshine, until a coach-load of sun-worshipping geriatrics (I suspect on a day out from the nursing home) arrived on the beach and pitched beside me – invading my personal space and making the whole sunbathing experience less of a pleasure than it had been before their arrival.

In a bid to escape the melee, I headed towards Travemünde's attractive riverfront and sauntered firstly around the beautiful 16th-century *St. Lorenz-Kirche*, and then along the riverside. Visitors to Travemünde could very easily be seduced by the extravagant cake shops with their mouth-watering displays of gateaux and pastries – and there is nobody more easily tempted by such things than I. So I sat for a while watching the world passing by at a pleasant little pavement café where I ordered a cappuccino and an obscenely calorific slice of *Erdbeerkuchen*.

Anchored beside a jetty in the mouth of the River Trave, and visible from the street café where I was sitting, is the four-masted barque *'Passat'* – once the pride of the *'Flying P-Liner'* shipping fleet and now a youth hostel cum floating museum. I was going to describe the *'Passat'* as being either a schooner or a clipper – but to do so would simply have revealed my unmitigated ignorance of all matters nautical. Part of the Travemünde skyline since she was moored here in 1960, the *Passat* is actually a *windjammer* – the grandest of the merchant sailing ships designed to carry bulk cargo on ultra-long voyages. Windjammers were built with steel hulls and equipped with between three and five perfectly square sails, which give them their characteristic profile. Passat, which means 'trade wind' in German (once again I call upon Volkswagen motor car enthusiasts to verify this for me), was launched in 1911 at the famous Blohm & Voss shipyard in Hamburg, and prior to her final retirement in 1960 she had circumnavigated the globe twice and sailed around Cape Horn on at least thirty occasions. She now sits proudly and serenely at her permanent berth on the Trave quayside looking resplendent in a fresh coat of paint.

It was early evening by the time I arrived back at the campsite. The sun was still shining, and I found James and

Andrew sitting on the grass drinking bottled beer and smoking cigarettes – both looking decidedly relaxed.

"We're going to have dinner in the campsite restaurant," Andrew shouted as I made my approach. "Then maybe a few beers in the campsite bar. You're very welcome to join us if you've nothing else planned."

I didn't have anything else planned as it happened, and Andrew's invitation was very much appreciated.

"Love to," I said.

The campsite restaurant served typical north-German fayre – not exactly haute cuisine by any stretch of the imagination – the food in this part of the world has a tendency to be a little bland in my view. Some of the dishes on offer reminded me of Scandinavian cuisine. Although by no means identical, the food of Schleswig-Holstein, Norway and Denmark seem to have a great deal in common. All three, for example, have a predilection for toasted sandwiches of various sorts, especially topped with smoked or pickled fish. After a great deal of vacillation on my part (which James clearly found a little irritating), I eventually settled for a dish known as *Labskaus* – a mixture of corned beef, mashed potatoes and beetroot. *Labskaus* is a local variation of the Norwegian dish *lapskaus* and the Liverpudlian *lobscouse* – all of which are derivatives of a traditional stew-type meal that was once served on board ships – the main component of a sailor's often humdrum diet. For dessert, I opted for a *Rote Grütze* (spelled and pronounced *'Rode Grütt' in low German)* – a summer pudding made mostly from berries and drowned in cream. Again there's a Scandinavian connection – the Danes have a similar dessert known as *rødgrød.* After dinner the three of us retired to the campsite bar where we set about the task of destroying several bottles of *Flensburger Pilsener* – a local Schleswig-Holstein brew.

Now, I should probably point out at this juncture that I have never been very good at this drinking malarkey. So long as I pace myself and take little sips every now and then, I can comfortably accommodate three, maybe four pints of beer in any single sitting. Any more than that and I start to feel bloated and a little nauseous. Not only that, my brain has a tendency to switch to 'bullshit mode' after a few beers, and I start talking garbage – usually rather loudly and very enthusiastically. It occurred to me fairly early in the proceedings that an evening in the company of James and his brother, Andrew, was likely to turn into a bit of a 'session', and *that* being the case, I would have to pace myself accordingly. Fortunately for me, it turned out that both Andrew and James spoke fluent garbage themselves, which helped the flow of conversation enormously.

"What are your plans for tomorrow?" James asked. I shrugged my shoulders before replying.

"Nothing in particular," I said. "Another stroll around Travemünde maybe, or perhaps I'll venture a little farther afield – to Timmendorfer Strand or one of the other seaside towns along the Scharbeutz coast. None of my plans are ever set in concrete."

"James and I are planning to check out the Casino. You're welcome to tag along if you're interested."

"Is there a dress code?" I asked.

As soon as I had asked this question I immediately wished I hadn't – for the simple reason that it may possibly have been an incredibly stupid thing to ask. The thing is you see, I have never visited a casino before – at least not a proper one. My knowledge and experience of casinos comprise solely of what I've seen in the movies – I've been taught everything I know by Sam 'Ace' Rothstein – the consummate high roller who was always immaculately turned out, and James Bond of course, who could often be found at a casino with an attractive young lady in tow, looking dapper in his freshly laundered tuxedo and his sharply creased trousers. It was Bond's image that I had in mind when I asked Andrew about the dress code. I had this mental picture of Bond looking completely unruffled in his ceremonial finery as the dastardly Kamal Khan leans over his shoulder and says, "*Spend the money quickly, Mr. Bond.*" If Andrew had answered my question with 'don't be ridiculous – you've clearly watched too many Bond films', then it would have been nothing less than I deserved. But as it just so happened, my question wasn't stupid at all, for it transpired that Travemünde's casino did indeed impose a dress code. Andrew went on to explain that whereas trainers, jeans and T-shirts would certainly be '*strengstens verboten*' under the casino's house rules, patrons were required to wear shoes, full-length trousers and a collared shirt and tie. In a bid not to overload my rucksack, I had been economical with the amount of clothing I'd brought with me on this trip – but as luck would have it, I did bring sufficient apparel to meet three of the four criteria. Shoes and full-length trousers wouldn't be a problem (although my 'shoes' were actually 'walking boots' rather than shoes), and I did bring a suitable shirt too – well, almost. It was a white linen short-sleeved shirt – probably more suitable for a casual stroll on the promenade than for a formal occasion, but it did have buttons up the front and a collar – so I figured it complied with the casino's stringent requirements. I didn't have a tie though – and since neither James nor Andrew had a spare one they could lend me, I reasoned it would be necessary to purchase one. It would have to be a cheap one, of course. I had a drawer at home that was full of ties of every conceivable design and colour, many of them having cost me a small fortune and most of them hardly ever worn. The last thing I needed was another to add to my collection. As the conversation flowed and the pace of our beer consumption accelerated, my plans to 'drink responsibly' (as the advertisers constantly and so patronizingly advise us) fell completely by the wayside. It wasn't my fault, obviously – it was Andrew and James who were to blame. If the two of them hadn't been such agreeable company and such droll raconteurs, I wouldn't have felt compelled to sit in the bar with them for as long as I did.

I woke the following morning with a pounding headache, coupled with a feeling of nausea and a vampire-like aversion to natural daylight. I felt comfortable enough, I discovered, as long as I lay perfectly still. Even the slightest of head movements sent a sharp shooting pain across my forehead, causing a dull throbbing in my temples. Now, whilst I accept that I have previously expressed a devout belief in bacon sandwiches as the ultimate hangover cure, I'm afraid that on this occasion my advocacy for such things was not as strong as it might have been. Apart from the campsite restaurant's failure to include such a delicacy on their breakfast menu, this feeling of nausea would have prevented me from eating one even if it had. And I'm afraid the thought of pickled eel sandwiches (a delicacy of Schleswig-Holstein that *was* on the restaurant's breakfast menu) did nothing to help rid me of this feeling of queasiness. I crawled out of my tent as delicately as I could and made my way to the shower block to perform my morning ablutions – a task made all the more difficult by my inability to move my head. The brothers stirred a short while later, and by the time I'd finished showering and had returned to my tent, the two of them were brewing tea – both of them full of energy and irritatingly chirpy. It was as if they'd been early to bed following an evening of sobriety and had woken up with their batteries fully recharged. No headaches, no nausea, no clutter behind the retinas – they simply went about their business with sparkle and verve. I found it painful to watch.

"Fancy a brew?" Andrew asked.

I didn't. I really didn't. Luckily for me both Andrew and James instantly recognised my symptoms – both being experts in the field of hangover diagnosis and well versed in the subject of potential treatments. James began to offer me a variety of remedies from his medical bag – including Alka-Seltzer antacid tablets, paracetamol, and two unidentified and dubious-looking orange-coloured pills that had been lying loose in the bottom of his bag for heaven knows how long. James believed they were anti-veisalgia tablets of some kind although he couldn't be sure – veisalga being the correct medical term for a hangover. The Germans have their own word for it – '*Katzenjammer*' – literally 'a wailing cat'. And this morning I was nursing the worst Katzenjammer I'd had in a very long time. I decided against any of James' medicinal remedies. It was kind of him to offer but I didn't want to take any headache pills just in case I was unable to keep them down – and to bring them back up again would seem terribly ungrateful. So I declined the offer and hoped that 'fresh air' and 'the fullness of time' would combine forces to deliver a more natural remedy for my ills.

The three of us hadn't planned to hit the casino until the evening, and it had originally been my intention to spend the time between now and then exploring the town of *Timmendorfer Strand* – one of several quaint little seaside resorts further along the coast. But I really wasn't feeling all that great. All I craved was the opportunity to sit quietly in some secluded little spot and make a start on Deaver's '*The Empty Chair*' which I still hadn't started despite my good intentions. So that was exactly what I did. While James and Andrew headed off on their bicycles, I found a tranquil spot in a small wooded area that was isolated from the rest of the campsite by a natural partition of trees and hedgerow, where Jeffrey Deaver and I sat down on a little wooden bench beneath the shade of an elm tree. And there we sat enjoying the morning sunshine – in my own little haven of peace and serenity. And as a natural cure for a Katzenjammer, I'm pleased to report that it was remarkably effective. By the time I had reached chapter eight my headache had all but disappeared and I found myself able to eat a small piece of crispbread without feeling an uncontrollable urge to throw up. By chapter fifteen I felt confident enough to progress to a hotdog – purchased from the campsite restaurant and made with *Katenrauchwurst* (literally a 'smoked cottage sausage' – 100% pork meat that had been prepared through a long and complex smoking process), which I washed down with a can of Coca-Cola. By chapter eighteen I had managed to digest my lunch and my general state of health had improved from critical to stable. I was feeling considerably better. Well enough, I decided, to explore what the *Campingplatz Windmühle* had to offer its guests, other than a gorgeous receptionist with ambitions to become a despotic tyrannical political dictator just as soon as she'd completed her studies and graduated from university.

I was soon to discover that among the facilities on offer at the campsite was a children's play area, which according to the sign above the entrance was 'for children and grown-ups of all ages'. It was a remarkably well-equipped play area I thought. Along with the conventional equipment – the swings, the slide, and the children's roundabout, there were a ball pit, a bouncy castle, a go-cart track, a small boating lake with motorised boats operated by remote control, a giant chess board, skittles and a miniature golf course. Although I harboured a strange and secret desire to immerse myself into a pit full of plastic balls just to experience the sensation of doing so, I decided it would be a completely inappropriate thing to do. So instead, I found myself strangely drawn to the giant chess board, the sight of which brought back a few very happy memories.

You see, the last time I played a game of chess was on a particularly wet and windy weekend in Copenhagen a couple of years earlier. For my two-day stay in the Danish capital I had booked a room at the Marriott – a large hotel, spa and conference centre near the *Kalvebod Brygge* in Copenhagen's city centre. At the time of my visit, the hotel was hosting the annual 'Copenhagen Board Games Convention' organised by children from primary schools throughout the city – an event designed to reintroduce younger children to 'shared' entertainment, and to encourage families to play together. I must admit, it all sounded perfectly laudable to me. I'm afraid it's a sign of the times that in many households today you're very unlikely to find any trace of the traditional board game. Children prefer to sit alone in their bedrooms, frantically pressing buttons on their handheld portable games consoles and manoeuvring various game characters into carrying out brutal and bloody assassinations on the orders of the kingpins of the city underworld. During my visit to the board games convention I was challenged to a game of chess by Kristian – a sweet-looking blue-eyed, blond-haired seven-year-old Danish boy who I assumed would be no match for my polished chess skills. As it happened, he turned out to be formidable opposition – wrapping the game up in less than twenty minutes. It wasn't so much the humiliation of being beaten at chess by a seven-year-old that bothered me per se – it was the fact that Kristian (a boy whose native tongue was Danish of course) had the audacity to explain the meaning of 'checkmate' to me in perfect English. That syrupy 'butter-wouldn't-melt-in-his-mouth' persona that he managed to portray so well turned out to be merely a charade. Kristian, it transpired, was nothing other than a precocious little shit. The only thing I liked about Kristian was his mum – she also had blond hair and blue eyes and was drop-dead gorgeous.

The chessboard at the *Campingplatz Windmühle* was approximately sixteen metres square – the sixty-four chequered squares made from polished stone tiles. Each of

115

the chess pieces was made from toughened Bakelite plastic – the larger pieces standing almost a metre high, with the army of black and white plastic pawns only marginally smaller. As I paced up and down beside this Goliath-sized chessboard, I had the curious feeling that I was being watched. Standing on the opposite side of the board with his hand resting on top of one of the chess pieces was a middle-aged man of medium build wearing a gabardine shirt, a pair of khaki-coloured three-quarter-length trousers and an elegant black and white Panama hat. He smiled at me as we made eye contact and pointed to the chessboard.

"Wollen Sie spielen?" he asked (do you want a game?).

I nodded. The man in the Panama hat invited me to choose between playing 'black' or 'white'. He had a passive, soothing tone to his voice – the sort of voice that a sweet-tempered nurse might adopt when humouring a spoilt and irascible infant. Our skill levels were pretty evenly matched it seemed, and we managed to make the game last for over an hour. I was the victor in the end – my worthy opponent finally conceding defeat after losing every one of his pieces – with the exception of the king of course. When the game was over I shook hands with the man in the Panama hat, and I headed back to my tent.

As I strolled casually along the roadway (walking as slowly as I could so as not to fall foul of the campsite's draconian speed limit regulations), I heard the ringing of bicycle bells as James and Andrew approached me from behind and eventually pulled up alongside me on their bikes.

"We've been cycling around Travemünde" said James excitedly.

"And we bought you a little present!" Andrew added.

James handed me a small paper bag which I opened with gusto – like a child opening a gift on Christmas morning. Inside the bag was a polyester bow tie in a gaudy shade of yellow with a tacky floral pattern. It was cheap, utterly hideous, probably fashionable once upon a time but now completely passé and certainly not the sort of fashion accessory I would usually want to be seen wearing. But for the purpose of enabling me access to Travemünde's famous casino, it was absolutely perfect.

"Thanks guys!" I said – none of us quite sure whether I'd said it with any degree of sincerity. "How can I repay such a kind gesture?"

"It cost us one euro!" said James with a mischievous grin. "We found it on a market stall and thought of you!"

"I'll tell you what," Andrew interjected. "If you win a million euros in the casino tonight you can buy us both a beer. How does that sound?"

"It sounds like a deal to me," I replied, as I placed the bow tie back into its paper bag and tucked it into my pocket.

That evening, James, Andrew and I arrived outside the main entrance to the Travemünde casino looking resplendent in our evening attire – James and Andrew looking particularly spruce and debonair in their sharply creased trousers, shiny black leather shoes, freshly laundered shirts, ties and matching cream-coloured jackets. Yes, the two brothers had managed to capture that 'James Bond' image spectacularly well. I, by stark contrast, looked like Coco the Clown. My brown corduroy trousers which had been rolled up in the bottom of my rucksack for the past few days looked decidedly shabby, as I had no means of being able to iron out the creases. But I wore them anyway, along with my walking boots, my white short-sleeved linen shirt and an outrageous yellow floral bow tie. As we marched single file into the main entrance lobby, the doorman, dressed in all his finery, looked me up and down and said "*Oh my God – what the fuck are you wearing*?" Actually, he didn't say that at all. He didn't have to – the expression on his face said it for him. I smiled politely as we filed past him.

"Guten Abend," I said. The doorman simply nodded in response – either in awe of, or simply dumbstruck by, my unconventional yet considerably courageous fashion sense.

As I have already said, until that moment I had never stepped foot inside a casino – but thanks to the magic of Hollywood (and quite possibly Pinewood Studios) I had a clear mental image of what the inside of such an establishment looked like. And as it just so happened, my mental image turned out to be surprisingly accurate. The first thing that hit me as I stepped into what the casino described as 'the gaming lounge' was the tumult of the hundreds of slot machines that lined the perimeter of the hall – an endless vista of flashing lights and a perpetual din of whining and clattering in *Surround Sound*. Stepping into a casino for the first time made me feel a little disorientated and slightly overwhelmed. I found it rather sobering to study the faces of some of the punters who were feeding their money into the slot machines. Their arms moved in a robotic, almost animatronic manner – their expressions conveying glassy-eyed blankness in some, and in others a hollow-faced disappointment. The casino was already well attended when the three of us arrived, despite the fact that its doors had only been open for around thirty minutes. But it wasn't crowded by any means. The tables that seemed to be attracting the most attention were those proffering roulette or blackjack. Now, being a novice at both these games and therefore wholly ignorant of their respective rules, I had no option other than to seek advice from James and Andrew, and follow their lead. The two of them, it emerged, had played roulette twice in their lives and blackjack only once – which as far as I was concerned made them experts in both disciplines. I soon discovered that the rules for blackjack weren't all that taxing after all, and I soon got to grips with it. After a couple of games I felt confident enough to remain at the blackjack table while Andrew went off to play roulette and James headed towards a bank of slot machines at the far end of the lounge. I played five games of blackjack in total, and managed to lose every one of them.

"How's it going?" James asked me when I eventually joined him at the slot machines, having managed to prise myself away from the blackjack table.

"Not great," I replied. "I've played five games of blackjack and I placed a bet of five euros on each game."

"Did you win any of them?"

"No. I'm twenty-five euros down."

"Don't worry about it," said James rather unconvincingly. "There are never any winners at casinos – the odds are always stacked against you – but you have to admit it's a lot of fun."

And James was right – it *was* a lot of fun. I sat down at one of the slot machines near to where James was sitting which had the incongruous name '*The Palace of Riches*'. I dropped a one-euro coin into the slot and pressed the 'play' button before sitting back in my chair as the machine launched into a chorus of electronic whirring noises. The three reels spun furiously around, then one by one, came to a sudden and dramatic halt. And as the third and final reel stopped spinning, the machine suddenly lit up like a Christmas tree and an electronic voice began singing '*Let the Good Times Roll*' to a dramatic musical accompaniment.

"You lucky bastard!" James said, as an avalanche of one-euro coins tumbled down the coin chute like a waterfall – and clattered into the hopper below. With a stroke of astonishing good fortune I had managed to win fifty euros with a one-euro stake. Despite James imploring me to shovel my winnings back into the coin slot, I decided to do the sensible thing and quit while I was ahead. It was a wise move, I thought, although James clearly didn't think so – I had to endure taunts of 'coward!" and "chicken shit!" as I scooped up my winnings from the machine's coin hopper. It was meant in jest of course, although I suspect with just a small hint of the 'green-eyed monster of envy' lurking in its undertones. [17]

I now found myself in the enviable position of being twenty-five euros better off than I had been two hours earlier – when I first stepped foot into Travemünde's famous casino. Impelled by the philosophy of 'easy come, easy go', I decided to spend my twenty-five euros on something more worthwhile than simply shovelling it back into a slot machine. I purchased a round of drinks for James and Andrew – my newly-found friends who had been my mentors in the art of roulette and blackjack and of whom I had become really rather fond. The two brothers were back on the beer of course, whereas I opted for soft drinks, having committed to an alcohol-free evening following the excesses of the previous night. I used the remainder of the cash as stake money for the few games of roulette that followed – which, under Andrew's expert guidance, I managed to get the hang of relatively quickly. Along with my initial stake money I also reinvested my roulette winnings. Yes, I did manage to *win* some money during one of the games – the princely sum of thirty euros to be precise, when that little silver ball finished buzzing around the wheel of fortune and finally came to rest, much to my delight, on 32-red.

It was late by the time we left the casino. What had been a beautifully warm day with unbroken sunshine had now evolved into a clement and balmy night, with a full moon shining through a cloudless sky to reveal a constellation of a billion stars. The three of us chose to walk back to the

---

[17] *It was William Shakespeare who first coined the phrase 'the green-eyed monster' to denote jealousy – firstly in the Merchant of Venice and later in Othello. The number of words and phrases used in common parlance that can be attributed to Shakespeare is extraordinary. They include phrases such as 'lie low'; 'fair play'; 'salad days' and 'woe is me' – but there are hundreds of other examples.*

campsite rather than call for a taxi to take us there – a chance for us to breathe some fresh air into our lungs. This would be the last time I would see James and Andrew. We exchanged contact details of course – telephone numbers, e-mail addresses and the like, and we agreed we would stay in touch. I realise of course that many people make such pledges, and yet despite the good intentions, they rarely manage to fulfil them. But I hoped this wouldn't be the case with Andrew, James and me. The two brothers were a warm and generous couple who, despite the brevity of our acquaintance, made my visit to Travemünde a particularly enjoyable experience.

I would be leaving the campsite early the following morning – probably long before either of them would be up and about – so we said our goodbyes before turning in.

oOo

Dear Diary,

The Beer, Cheese and Tent Report for the State of Schleswig-Holstein:

Beer: Flensburger Pilsener:

Flensburger is light and refreshing. It slides down like nectar – but brace yourself for a blinding Katzenjammer in the morning.

Cheese: Wilstermarschkäse:

Like the Tilsiter I sampled in Bremen, Wilstermarschkäse is believed to have been created by Dutch immigrants. It is made uniquely in a dairy in Itzehoe, using partially skimmed milk from the region, and, I'm told, is not generally very easy to find. But as luck would have it, I managed to find some – in a small shop on Travemünde's waterfront. Wilstermarschkäse has a tangy, slightly sour flavour but tastes simply wonderful.

Tent Stability:

The small leakage in the canvas has now been repaired, thanks to the ingenuity and resourcefulness of my new friends, Andrew and James. There's no telling whether the repairs will hold out though – I'll just have to keep my fingers crossed.

oOo

Chapter Six – Rocket Science

"At the rate science proceeds, rockets and missiles will one day seem like buffalo – slow, endangered grazers in the black pasture of outer space."
Bernard Cooper (born 1936) – U.S. physicist reporting in Harper's (New York January 1990)

If you travel just a few kilometres east from Travemünde, you'll reach the provincial boundary that separates Schleswig-Holstein from the state of Mecklenburg-Vorpommern. There is nothing dramatic about the boundaries that separate the German states – I had already crossed between Lower Saxony, Bremen, Hamburg and Schleswig-Holstein without really noticing, and this one would be no exception. Other than a large signpost at the side of the road bearing the Mecklenburg coat of arms and the words '*Wilkommen in Mecklenburg-Vorpommern*', there was nothing else to indicate that I was crossing from one state to another. But that hasn't always been the case.

After 1945 and prior to the reunification of Germany in 1990, the line I was about to cross wasn't simply a state boundary as it is today – it was an international frontier marking the border between two independent sovereign nations – the Federal Republic of Germany (West Germany) and the German Democratic Republic (East Germany). Now, if you've conjured up in your mind an image of a jovial little man sitting at a sleepy security post, checking passports and raising the barrier every now and then to allow people to cross the border, then I would ask you to think again. This boundary wasn't merely an international border between two countries – it was a demarcation line separating two opposing political ideologies – the (supposedly) egalitarian, communist regime of the east, and the capitalist system in the west – and it was vital for the preservation of both that

123

these two disparate political systems were kept apart. So the borderline between the two wasn't a particularly pleasant affair. Known as the 'inner German border' (*innerdeutsche Grenze)* it was defined by a continuous line of barbed wire, high metal fences and walls, foreboding watchtowers, anti-vehicle ditches, alarms, booby traps and minefields – and, just for good measure, it was heavily guarded. (Around 50,000 GDR troops were employed to guard the entire length of the border.)

Mecklenburg-Vorpommern is one of six German states that were once part of the communist east, and for the next eleven days I intended to pass through all six before heading west once again to revisit territory with which I was more familiar. To help explain the geography, Mecklenburg-Vorpommern lies in the far north-eastern corner of Germany (in the top right-hand corner if you will). Like Schleswig-Holstein, the state has a long stretch of Baltic Sea coastline (almost 2,000 kilometres of it if you count the shores around the dozens of Baltic islands), and in its far eastern extremity Mecklenburg-Vorpommern shares an international border with Poland.

This was one of the German states that I had been particularly looking forward to visiting, having read many positive reviews from a number of eminent travel writers – and I was eager to discover for myself whether the profusion of superlatives used in many of their reports was justified. According to the state tourist authority, 'Mecklenburg-Vorpommern invites you to slow down, breathe deeply, relax, and prepare to live the experience' – a slogan designed to give you an enticing foretaste of what's to come. Mecklenburg-Vorpommern is Germany's self-proclaimed 'nature state', boasting more than two thousand lakes, three hundred nature reserves, seven nature parks, one hundred and forty landscape conservation areas, three biosphere reserves and three of Germany's twelve official national parks. It's a land of steep coastal cliffs, lush green hills, sandy dunes and unspoiled woodlands, interspersed with lively towns and tiny, dreamy little villages. And for those of you with an interest in local fauna, the denizens of Mecklenburg-Vorpommern include beavers, cranes, storks, European Bison and the white-tailed eagle. There are more nature trails, footpaths and cycle routes in this state than you can shake a proverbial stick at, and the sheer volume and variety of campsites available for me to choose from was enough to make my head spin.

Needless to say that with all this rural tranquillity, the state of Mecklenburg-Vorpommern is rather sparsely populated. There are around 1.7 million people living in an area of a little over 23,000 km² - making it the most sparsely populated province in Germany. To save us both from long and complex mathematical calculations, that works out at around 74 people per square kilometre – compare *that* to the city state of Berlin, where there are 3,800 people vying for every square kilometre of space. And I was particularly keen to meet some of the local people too, who I'm told, generally speaking, are happily ensconced in Mecklenburg-Vorpommern. They would have seen some changes too, I suspect – especially the older generation. Over a period of less than seventy years, they'd have lived under the politics of National Socialism, communism and capitalism. From the extreme right to the extreme left, and then finally settling for a political ideology somewhere in the middle – and I was hoping that during my stay here, or in any of the other former East German states, I'd be able to strike up a conversation with somebody in their dotage who might elucidate what life was like under each of these profoundly contrasting regimes.

For my two-day Mecklenburg-Vorpommern experience, I had elected to stay at a campsite on *Usedom Island* – the entire island being one of Germany's official national parks and an area of outstanding natural beauty. It would take me a long time to get there though – Usedom Island lies near the easternmost boundary of the state – about as far to the east as one can travel before tripping over into Poland. In fact, the German-Polish border runs through Usedom, splitting the island into two separate sections. Usedom National Park is approximately 280 kilometres from Travemünde, and in view of the complexity of the rail journey, I decided to make an early start.

The vast majority of Germany's railways are operated by *Deutsche Bahn* – the world's second largest transport company. Deutsche Bahn (more commonly referred to by its initials 'DB'), was created in 1994 following the reunification of Germany, as a result of an amalgamation between West Germany's '*Deutsche Bundesbahn*' ('German Federal Railway' – which, coincidently, was also known universally as 'DB') and the East German '*Deutsche Reichsbahn*' ('German Imperial Railway'). [18] Despite the fact that it's been almost seventeen years since the new network was created, many of the old regional services of the former East Germany remain in use, with scarcely any money being invested to improve the tracks, the signalling or even the trains themselves. So the journey from Travemünde to Usedom Island was scheduled to take around six-and-a-half hours, and would involve three changes of trains at Lübeck, Pasewalk and Züssow, with the final leg of the journey from Züssow to Zinnowitz (an elegant and rather regal seaside town on Usedom) operated by Usedom Island's own private railway network – the *Usedomer Bäderbahn*. Assuming

---

[18] *It is extraordinary that the former East Germany chose to retain 'Deutsche Reichsbahn' as the name of its national railway network. The name was originally created from the railways of the individual states of the German Empire following the end of the First World War. But the name is, of course, more synonymous with Adolf Hitler's Third Reich in the 1930s and 1940s – when the name 'Deutsche Reichsbahn' was created to reflect Germany's imperialistic political leaning.*

everything was to go according to plan and I managed to make all my connections on time (some of the connection times were pretty tight – just three minutes at Züssow!) – I would reach my destination at around 4.00pm.

And so I set off from the railway station at Travemünde on a journey that would involve changing trains more times than I'd changed my undercrackers since leaving my home in London. [19] The route was long and circuitous and the trains trundled along at what seemed at times like a snail's pace. But the journey took me through the heart of the Mecklenburg Lake District and through two of Mecklenburg-Vorpommern's National Parks, and the view from the window was, for the most part at least, stunningly beautiful.

Unlike the island of Borkum (which as you may recall is located some distance from the mainland and accessible only via a vehicle ferry), Usedom Island is separated from the rest of Germany by a narrow causeway which can be crossed via a road bridge. Actually, there are two road bridges – there's one accessing the *town* of Usedom on the south of the island, and another approximately 25 kilometres further north which carries both road and railway traffic. It was this one, at the town of Wolgast, that I crossed from the German mainland onto Usedom Island – across a bridge that linked the causeway at Wolgast. This bridge, incidentally, happens to be Germany's largest single-leaf bascule bridge. [20] The moment you arrive on the other side

[19] *Actually that isn't true at all – I had been changing my undercrackers on a daily basis – I only put that bit in for comic effect. I may have been economical with my clothing allowance when I set out on this trip, but I'd like to assure readers that I brought plenty of smalls.*

[20] *A bascule bridge, in case you were wondering, is a drawbridge or swing bridge that can be raised to allow ships to pass underneath – 'bascule' being the French for 'seesaw'. London's Tower Bridge, of course, is probably the best-known example of a double-leaf bascule bridge.*

of the causeway, the contrast in the landscape is immediately apparent. The colours change – asphalt-black and concrete-grey are both replaced by the colours of nature. The air smelled fresher too – or perhaps that was just my imagination. It was another blisteringly warm afternoon – uncharacteristic of the Baltic climate even at this time of year, and I had just landed in nature's very own Utopia.

Unquestionably the most impressive I had stayed at during my trip so far, the campsite *'Natur-Camping Usedom'* had everything the discerning camper could possibly wish for: a shop, bar, restaurant, games room, laundry room, communal kitchens – it even had an indoor heated swimming pool (which, I decided, I would have to utilise at some point during my stay here). There was also a spa and wellness centre. But as if that wasn't enough, the campsite had an idyllic lakeside location – occupying a small peninsular of coniferous woodland on the shores of the *Achterwasser* – the saltwater lagoon that separates Usedom island from mainland Germany. The Achterwasser is a popular spot for sailing, surfing and waterskiing and when I arrived at what I decided was the perfect spot to pitch my tent (a small, enclosed wooded area with a fabulous lakeside view), the surface of the water was carpeted with a multiplicity of sailboats – their tranquillity and apparent motionlessness disturbed only occasionally by one of the plethora of speedboats slicing their way through the serene water with their intrepid water skiers in tow, and creating a disruptive swell in their wake.

With my *Wind-Breaker DeLuxe* only half assembled, I made my way to the campsite's surprisingly well-stocked shop. It had been my intention to purchase a few tent pegs to replace those that had suffered collateral damage during their recent and valiant battle against stony terrain. But as I said, the shop was surprisingly well-stocked – a veritable Aladdin's Cave of camping paraphernalia. As I stepped inside I was greeted by a diverse selection of everything a camper might need, together with a vast array of stuff that I neither needed nor recognised. One of the treasures I found hidden among the extendable shnoglers and the adjustable nib-ribblets was a compact, lightweight, portable gas stove called the 'Pocket Rocket', which came complete with a small disposable butane gas cartridge. Now, I had deliberately avoided bringing such extravagancies with me on my camping trip around Germany – they were lavish and profligate in my opinion – they'd simply take up valuable space in my rucksack and add unnecessary weight. But my recent encounter with James and Andrew had softened my hard line attitude. With their stove and their kettle and their little tin mugs, they had all the equipment necessary for making tea and coffee. Until a couple of days ago I'd had to quell any urges I had for hot beverages. I'd have to wait until I found a café or a coffee shop in order to satiate such cravings – not always convenient or opportune. But Andrew and James' enviable ability to rustle up tea on demand had been a revelation – a small insight into a happier world – a taste of how much better my life could be, if only I had the apparatus necessary for making my own tea. I knew that buying a stove would be a risky venture. It wouldn't just be the stove and the gas canister – they would be merely the tip of the iceberg. I'd have to buy a kettle too, and a mug, and a box of teabags. And of course, when the time came for me to pack up my belongings and leave 'Natur-Camping Usedom' – I would have to find space in my rucksack for all this additional baggage.

What I did next may shock you. It shocked me. I have always considered myself to be a law-abiding citizen – a man of reasonably strong ethical and moral conduct. But I'm afraid that what I did next was nothing short of reprehensible. At least I think it was. You may not consider it so – in fact, you may consider that what I'm about to confess to is nothing other than petty and trivial – and barely worth mentioning in this chapter, especially in the unnecessary and nauseous detail in which it's written. But, like a penitent catholic seeking absolution from his sins through the sacrament of confession, I feel compelled to share with you the sordid details of this iniquitous, criminal indiscretion of mine – and hope that you'll find it in your heart not to judge me too harshly.

I stole some milk and a spoon from the campsite cafeteria. There, I said it. The thing is, I knew that if I was going to purchase all the necessary equipment for making my own tea, then *milk* would be a vital ingredient. I've experimented with black tea once or twice, but despite the dogged determination of certain members of my family to persuade me to relinquish milk from my morning cuppa, I'm afraid I have no taste for it – a mug of tea needs a little drop milk in it to make it drinkable – and that's the end of the matter. The campsite shop sold milk of course – as I fully expected it would. But it was sold only in two-litre cartons, which seemed a little excessive for my requirements. By my calculations (actually this is probably more of a wild estimate than a 'calculation'), two litres of milk would be enough to make approximately forty mugs of tea – and since I was planning to stay at *Natur-Camping Usedom* for just a couple of days I'd struggle to find the time to brew tea in such plenteous volume. (I don't think that *drinking* forty cups of tea over a period of two days is necessarily a good idea either.) Unlike my box of teabags, I wouldn't be able to take a two-litre carton of milk with me on the next stage of my travels. Aside from milk being a rapidly perishable commodity when left unrefrigerated, those cardboard Tetra cartons are impossible to reseal once you've torn them open

– and if it were shoved precariously into my rucksack for onward transportation then it would inevitably spill, leaving my books, shirts, socks and my freshly-laundered undercrackers soaked in a pool of milk. So I didn't bother to buy any – I just headed for the checkout and paid for my *Pocket Rocket*, my kettle, my teabags and my little tin mug. But on my way back to my tent, I called into the campsite cafeteria – one of those 'self-service' affairs where corpulent Germans with their impatient and unruly children in tow can be found pushing plastic trays along the tubular chrome counter, piling on sausages, fries, sauerkraut, pretzels, strawberry gateaux and fizzy drinks in cardboard buckets – before eventually reaching the point where the apathetic gum-chewing cashier sits, impatiently waiting to liberate them of their euros. Once inside, I headed straight for the condiments counter, which was conveniently located behind the tills and out of the cashier's line of vision. For it was here, among the freshly rinsed stainless steel cutlery, the tiny sachets of pepper and salt and the individual portions of tomato ketchup and mayonnaise in their small, hermetically-sealed, plastic packages, that I found the perfect solution to my lactose-related dilemma. Fresh milk – sealed in tiny plastic pots of twelve-millilitre portions. They were available free of charge to anyone purchasing hot beverages from the cafeteria (a trifling detail that I momentarily chose to ignore). But they were there for the taking – so I grabbed a couple of handfuls and filled my pockets. But what made this heinous crime of mine so odious and utterly deplorable was the fact that I felt no remorse whatsoever – quite the opposite in fact. I had committed an act of larceny without compunction – just an element of smug appreciation of my own devious ingenuity.

As soon as I arrived back at the thicket of woodland where my partially-assembled tent had been patiently awaiting my return, I realised at once that I'd forgotten to buy any tent pegs – the very reason for my visit to the camp shop in the first place. I had been so caught up in the excitement of acquiring my very own *Pocket Rocket*, that the need to purchase tent pegs to enable me to finish assembling my *Wind-Breaker DeLuxe*, had completely slipped my mind. I went back to the shop.

I returned to my tent with six new pegs; finished assembling the tent; and then set about making some tea – realising at once that I didn't have any matches to light the burner. I went back to the shop.

Matches purchased; burner lit; tea made. I burned my fingers trying to remove the teabag from a cup of boiling water and realised at this point that I needed a teaspoon. I went back to the shop.

The shop didn't sell teaspoons – at least not individually. I could have bought one as part of a 'camper's cutlery pack' which included knife, fork, teaspoon and dessertspoon, but I already had a knife and fork in my set of 'Hand-Forged Feasting Utensils'. Purchasing an entire cutlery pack for the sake of acquiring a single spoon would have been a frivolous waste of money. So I stole a teaspoon from the cafeteria.

I chose to stay at the campsite that evening rather than venture out into the world beyond its perimeters. I'd spent the entire day travelling after all, so a night in seemed like a sagacious plan. There was live music on offer at the '*Pott & Pann*' – the campsite's bar and clubhouse. A hastily-scribbled notice on a chalkboard outside the main entrance proudly proclaimed that '*Onkel Tom & Huckleberry*' would be performing live 'by popular demand' and 'for one night only'– and tonight just so happened to be the night in question. Onkel Tom and Huckleberry, it transpired, were two lads from Dresden – both in their early thirties, and both blessed with long, flaxen tresses, decent singing voices and a talent for playing guitars. The pair of them wore jade-coloured T-shirts with their names emblazoned across their chests – so their audience had no difficulty identifying which of them was Huckleberry and which was Onkel Tom. Olive-coloured three-quarter-length trousers and emerald-green bandanas completed the duo's stage costume. The two songsters played a diverse range of popular hits – an eclectic mix of musical genres, ranging from Country & Western to traditional folk and heavy metal. One minute they'd be skilfully harmonising a mellow version of John Denver's *'Country Roads, Take Me Home'* (or is it *'Take Me Home, Country Roads'?)* before suddenly launching into 'Lemmy' impersonations with their own unique adaptation of Motörhead's *'The Ace of Spades.'* Their performance was bizarre as well as rather unique – but above all, it was utterly compelling. So much so, that I felt dutifully obliged to remain in the *Pott & Pann* for the rest of the evening and witness Onkel Tom and Huckleberry perform their repertoire in its entirety. Naturally, I felt equally compelled to purchase a few beers while I was there – it would have been churlish not to.

My plan had been to spend the following day exploring as much of Usedom Island as possible, by travelling from the historic coastal town of *Peenemünde* (located at the island's westernmost point), to the elegant resort of *Ahlbeck* – a town with the acclaim of being the easternmost seaside resort in Germany. The towns of Peenemünde and Ahlbeck are thirty-five kilometres apart and are connected by the island's own railway system, the *Usedomer Bäderbahn* or 'UBB' – which conveniently serves a number of the island's resorts and tourist attractions. For a mere €11 a 'UBB Day Pass' would enable me to hop on and hop off whenever I wanted.

But the day didn't start well for me.

After a night of disturbed sleep, I woke in the early hours of the morning in desperate need of an emergency visit to the campsite toilet block. I'm not sure whether it was something I'd eaten that had contributed to my condition, or whether something in the water had provoked this sudden eruption within the inner depths of my anatomy, but at 6.00am, whilst my fellow campers were sleeping soundly in their tents, I was sitting on the throne suffering from what I believe is colloquially known as an arseplosion. I've heard a number of terms to describe this particular malady: a dose of the trots; the green apple splatters; the Hershey squirts – call it what you will, a name cannot alter the nastiness of such an ailment. I was suffering from a particularly pernicious case of acute diarrhoea – one of an intensely explosive nature. I sat on that damned toilet for almost an hour while my bowels evacuated in a violent and awesome deluge, grateful only for the fact that I had made it to the toilet block just in the nick of time. Luckily though, I still had the lyrics of *'Country Roads, Take Me Home'* buzzing around my brain, which helped take my mind off my predicament and saw me through the ordeal. Although the worst of it was over, I still felt a little delicate when I eventually left the campsite and boarded the train to Peenemünde a couple of hours later. I gave breakfast a miss, which was a wise decision, I thought, given the circumstances.

There is a fiery disagreement raging between me and my Usedom Island guidebook. The guidebook claims that the town of Peenemünde is home to four museums – but following my visit I would argue that there are, in fact, five. Most dictionaries, you see, will describe a *'museum'* as a building where old, interesting or valuable artefacts are kept on public display. If you were to accept *that* as the authoritative definition of the word, then yes, Peenemünde does indeed have four – the *Historisch-Technisches Museum*; the *Phänomenta* (a museum of physical experiments); a nautical museum (part of which is outdoors and features a Russian submarine docked in the harbour);

and a toy museum. But I would argue that a museum does not necessarily have to be a *building* as such – it could simply be a site – a patch of land perhaps, or even an entire town. And that's where my idea for a fifth museum comes from. The town of Peenemünde is a museum in its own right. Just like the ruined city of Pompeii (although perhaps with a little less grandeur or historical significance), Peenemünde is a town frozen in time – virtually abandoned since its heyday in the 1940s. Actually, the town had a ghostly feel about it and walking through its deserted streets felt just a little unnerving. Despite the fact that approximately three hundred people still choose to live here, the town has been more or less forsaken – and what remains is in a parlous state. The buildings, many of which were built in the 1950s and 1960s, are sad and grey-looking – having all the charm of archetypal communist architecture from the immediate post-war period. Through decades of abandonment they now stand decrepit and decaying – their windows broken, their façades crumbling. Graffiti was everywhere – daubed over walls and signposts, covering every square inch of Peenemünde's ramshackle concrete structures as if to efface the memory of the old communist order. Walking through Peenemünde was like taking a day-trip to Chernobyl – there was something rather eerie about the whole experience.

You may recall that I earlier described Peenemünde as an 'historic' town – and indeed it is – because despite its current dilapidated condition, the port of Peenemünde serves up a fascinating dose of history. Until 1936, Peenemünde had been a somnolent fishing village, before the Nazis came along and destroyed its serenity with the construction of an enormous research and testing facility for the development of rockets. But the rockets that were developed here were not designed for interplanetary research or for studying the composition and physics of those heavenly bodies which make up our solar system – their development was for more sinister reasons altogether. For it was here at the Peenemünde rocket research centre that the infamous V-1 and V-2 flying missiles were developed.

The V-1, better known as the *'Doodlebug'* or the *'Buzz-Bomb'*, was an early pulse-jet-powered predecessor of the cruise missile and was used by the Nazis in World War II to destroy the city of London and claim the lives of over six thousand Londoners. The sonorous drone of a doodlebug's engines in the skies above the city was enough to strike fear into the hearts of Londoners in the early 1940s. Well, actually that's not strictly true – it wasn't so much the *sound* of the engines that Londoners needed to worry about – it was the sudden outbreak of silence that occurred after the engines cut out. The V-1 was powered with enough fuel to reach its intended destination – and once depleted, its engines would cease and the eighty-ton flying bomb armed with ten tons of explosives would fall from the sky resulting in the complete obliteration of whatever happened to lie directly beneath it. Despite its formidable power as a weapon of war, the V-1 had all sorts of technical flaws that inhibited its operational effectiveness and kept the Nazis awake at night trying to resolve. The doodlebugs were complex machines – technologically years ahead of their time and very expensive to manufacture. And much to the Nazis' frustration, those pesky British defence battalions with their anti-aircraft guns that lined the coast along the south of England had this irritating habit of blasting their precious doodlebugs out of the sky long before they had reached their intended target.

And so it was that, here at Peenemünde, the Luftwaffe began the development of the V-2 – a rocket capable of flying so high that it almost touched the borders of space. Since British anti-aircraft guns were completely ineffective against a weapon capable of flying at such altitude, allied forces decided on an alternative strategy which they hoped would resolve the problem of German rocket technology once and for all – they embarked on a series of air raids on the research and testing facility at Peenemünde, and blew it to smithereens. Since then, the town of Peenemünde has never quite recovered. After the war, the communist regime cleared away the rubble and constructed unsightly, unprepossessing high-rise apartment blocks in its place – and here the citizenry resided until the shackles of communism had been released and they were at last free to choose somewhere more salubrious to live.

I visited the *Historisch-Technisches Museum.* Among its threadbare collection of exhibits I found a V-1 and a V-2 rocket – both on display outdoors in the museum grounds and standing perpendicular, as if ready for launch – their tail fins cemented firmly into the ground and their nose cones pointing skywards. And as I stood there gazing with incredulity at these extraordinary-looking contraptions, something about them made me smile. I shouldn't have smiled of course. When I reminded myself of just how many thousands of innocent people had lost their lives to these evil machines, I immediately felt remorseful. But it was the simplicity of them that amused me. They looked like children's toys – albeit on a somewhat grander scale, obviously. They were the shape of...well, rockets, I suppose – but the basic, simplified version. Give a bunch of five-year-olds pieces of paper and crayons and ask them to draw you a rocket – I'm sure you can imagine what the resulting images would look like. Well, that's exactly what the V-1 and the V-2 bore an uncanny resemblance to. The design was amateurish by modern standards – almost laughably so. I could have been looking at a crudely-built papier mâché prop from a 1950's science fiction movie, or maybe two early prototype versions of Thunderbird 3.

In the outskirts of Peenemünde I stumbled upon the Café am Deich – an elegant coffee house boasting 106 different varieties of coffee, 26 brands of tea and the best hot chocolate on Usedom Island. This immodest claim, I decided, needed substantiation – so I stopped for a while and indulged shamelessly in a mug of hot chocolate, before heading back to the railway station to continue my tour of Usedom.

I travelled as far as *Heringsdorf* – by far the most stylish of all the island's seaside towns – officially declared a health resort in 1825 and quickly becoming fashionable with the rich and famous of that time. The main street from Heringsdorf station is lined with a row of grandiose villas – originating from the early 1800s, and now restored and converted into hotels and holiday apartments. It all looked rather affluent and well-heeled. Almost every one of the streetlamps supported a hanging basket of Lobelia, Pelargoniums, Petunias and Clematis – which looked gorgeous of course and filled the air with their sweet perfumes. When I reached the seafront I discovered a stone-free beach of fine, white sand, understandably popular with holidaymakers and day trippers – and as you may well imagine, it was packed when I arrived. Heringsdorf marks the midpoint of a five-kilometre promenade which follows the Baltic coastline to the towns of Bansin in the west and Ahlbeck in the east. Of course, I could have continued my journey to Ahlbeck by train – the carriages of the *Usedomer Bäderbahn* were comfortable enough and fully air-conditioned. But by alighting at Heringsdorf, I could walk into Ahlbeck along the promenade and gawp inanely at Usedom's spectacular coastal scenery whilst simultaneously filling my lungs with the fresh sea air.

Founded in about 1700, Ahlbeck is one of the oldest of the Baltic Sea resorts, and like Heringsdorf is a stunningly beautiful town. Many of the hotels and guesthouses here were built in the early 1900s in the art nouveau style, and are tastefully decorated – with ornate façades, oriels, pilasters, balustrades – and even small towers with coned turrets. All of which add to Ahlbeck's unparalleled charm. From Ahlbeck it's possible to cross the border into Poland, although not by car – the checkpoint here is open only to pedestrians and cyclists. So I decided I would do exactly that.

I had two reasons for wanting to visit Poland – even if it was for just a couple of hours. Firstly, Poland is a country I have never previously visited, but I had been urged to do so by a Polish gentleman (a plumber by trade, and a particularly competent and reliable one I might add) by the name of *Lechoslaw*, who came to my house to replace the washers on my leaky bath taps just a few weeks earlier. Secondly, things tend to be a lot cheaper in Poland than they are in Germany. So as I crossed the border at Ahlbeck, it was no surprise to discover that the main road from the border to the town centre at Swinoujscie was lined on either side by a plethora of market stalls along its entire two-kilometre length. And trade was brisk. It is possible to buy almost anything here, from groceries to souvenirs and clothing. Of course, cigarettes and alcohol are especially popular among the German day trippers. But I didn't linger too long on the Polish side of the border – I was getting hungry and eager to return to the campsite before the cafeteria closed.

By the time I arrived back at camp my energy level had almost reached zero. It had been a long and exhausting day and I'd not slept all that well the night before, what with my infernal bowel trouble and all. To be honest, all I really wanted to do was snuggle up in my sleeping bag with Jeffery Deaver (metaphorically speaking of course), read a couple of chapters of my book and settle down for an early night. So given my general state of lassitude you won't be surprised to learn that after emptying the cafeteria of the scraps that remained from its evening menu, I settled into my tent and began to doze off from the moment my head hit the pillow.

Now, if there's one thing (other than diarrhoea, of course) that can ruin a good night's sleep – it's an arsehole with a guitar. As I lay there blissfully drifting in and out of consciousness (as one does in the early stages of a normal sleep pattern), I was rudely interrupted by a discordant wailing (which I think was supposed to be a rendition of Simon and Garfunkel's *'Bridge Over Troubled Water'*) emanating from a tone-deaf Finnish student strumming a badly-tuned acoustic guitar whilst sitting cross-legged on the grass outside my tent. A group of his friends, also sitting cross-legged, were gathered around him in a semi-circle – and as he screeched his way through the lyrics, they stared at him in wonder and admiration as if he were some sort of latter-day Messiah. I'm not sure how it's possible to confuse a drunken teenage idiot with a deity, but after a skinful of booze and a few puffs of the old wacky weed, then I suppose anything's possible. The thing is, it wasn't so much his singing that I found so incredibly irritating – it was more his choice of song. In my opinion, there are certain songs that *nobody*, be they professional or otherwise, should ever attempt to reproduce regardless of the circumstances. Who, for example, could ever forgive *The Corrs* for their disgraceful cover version of Fleetwood Mac's classic song *'Dreams'*? And what on earth were the *Scissor Sisters*

[21] *I am prepared to forgive the following artists for either recording or performing cover versions of the song 'Bridge over Troubled Water' – simply because of who they are: Aretha Franklin, Elvis Presley, Dionne Warwick, Gladys Knight, Whitney Houston, Roberta Flack, Neil Sedaka, Eva Cassidy and Perry Como. I am not, however, prepared to be so readily forgiving of the following – whose cover versions of the same song were, quite frankly, bordering on offensive: Elton John, Nana Mouskouri, Anita Baker, Amber Riley and Charlotte Church. I'm willing to forgive Stevie Wonder and Roy Orbison only out of sympathy for their visual impairments.*

thinking when they completely mutilated Pink Floyd's *'Comfortably Numb'?* Well, *'Bridge Over Troubled Water'* is just such a song. It's a classic; a song that belongs exclusively to the original artists and will only ever sound good so long as it's Messrs. Garfunkel and Simon (not necessarily in that order) who are singing it. Any attempt to create one's own unique version of this song is, quite frankly, tantamount to heresy – sacrilegious even. [21] Intoxicated Finnish students with silly curly hair and girly voices simply don't have the right. Secondly, it's a song that calls for a singer capable of hitting some pretty high notes – way beyond the vocal range of most people. Even Art Garfunkel, a man with the vocal range of a tooth-billed hummingbird, had to have electrodes clamped to his testicles before he was able to hit that highest of F-sharps in the final chorus. Needless to say, our Finnish friend had no such vocal skill (or *any* vocal skill, for that matter). For all of these reasons, I decided enough was enough – the singing and the guitar strumming had to stop. Something had to be done – the question was – *what?*

The late John Belushi faced a similar dilemma as I recall – back in 1978 in the film *National Lampoon's Animal House*. Belushi, dressed in a toga (he was at the fraternity house toga party after all), was incensed by a student with a guitar who was sitting on the stairs singing an appalling variation of the song *'The Twelfth of Never'* (memorable if only for the lyric *'I gave my love a chicken without a bone'*). Belushi's classic response was to take his guitar from him and smash it against the wall – only to hand the remaining pieces back a few moments later whilst muttering a half-hearted apology. I, of course, would have to settle for a slightly less violent or destructive solution – even though my heart longed to smash his guitar to pieces.

Much to my delight, *Bridge over Troubled Water* suddenly reached a welcome conclusion, and was followed by a brief ripple of applause from the small posse of students sitting cross-legged on the grass. But my joy was short-lived. As soon as the applause had ended, the Finnish student launched into an acoustic version of Katrina and the Waves' *'Walking on Sunshine'* – which, I decided, was the last straw. I crawled out of my tent in the usual undignified manner, unzipped the entrance flap and poked my head out.

"Please be quiet!" I exclaimed, my voice raised, but in my best German. The singing and the strumming stopped immediately, and the eyes of several drug-fuelled students stared in my general direction in a fusion of astonishment, confusion and utter derision.

"I am trying to sleep!" I continued, and with that, I crawled backwards into my tent and zipped it up again. It seemed to do the trick. I didn't hear any more from the Finnish student or his guitar, so I assumed that he and his friends had wandered off to set up another pow-wow elsewhere on the campsite.

But the following morning, as I crawled out of my tent to fill my lungs with fresh, crisp morning air, I observed to my horror that some bastard little oik had daubed the word *'Schwanz'* in large, bold letters across the side of my tent – using a black marker pen with indelible ink. Now, in case you're not familiar with this word, *'Schwanz'* in German has two possible meanings – one literal, the other more colloquial – although it doesn't take a genius to work out which of the two was intended in this particular context. 'Schwanz', literally, is the German word for 'tail' – as in that of an animal. But it's more commonly used to describe a certain part of the male anatomy. Perhaps I'll spell it out for you – it's used as a colloquial word for 'penis' – and, just as it is in English, can be adapted as a term of abuse. In a nutshell, I had the German equivalent of the word 'PRICK' emblazoned across the side of my tent in ineffaceable ink.

Riled by this show of gratuitous vandalism, I made my way to the campsite's swimming pool, which you may recall had the dual advantage of being both 'heated' as well as 'indoor'. There's nothing quite like an early morning swim to turn anger into placidness and to dust away those *ante meridiem* cobwebs. So armed with my yellow floral bathing trunks I set off down the road like a man on a mission – like Dorothy from the Wizard of Oz, without the accompanying Toto of course. (Or the lion, the scarecrow or the tin man – so all in all, a pretty lousy analogy.) I reasoned too that at this time in the morning there was a strong probability that the pool would be virtually empty. And I was right – the pool *was* empty – empty in every conceivable sense of the word. Bereft of people and bereft of water. It seemed I had chosen to stay at *Natur-Camping Usedom* on the only two days of the year that the heated indoor swimming pool was closed for cleaning.

So I decided it was time to leave Usedom Island. I headed back to the little enclave of woodland where my graffiti-covered tent stood, and I once again began the process of dismantling it.

oOo

Dear Diary,

The Beer, Cheese and Tent Report for the State of Mecklenburg-Vorpommern:

Beer: Zwickelfritz Dunkel Naturtrüb:

I particularly enjoyed this one. Zwickelfritz Dunkel Naturtrüb is a dark beer with a hazy amber colour, crowned by a substantial head that remains frothy until the bottom of the glass. It tasted of caramel and roasted malt and had the aroma of cereal.

Cheese: Steinbuscherkäse:

First produced in the mid nineteenth century in the town of Steinbusch, (now Choszczno in Poland), this is one of Mecklenburg's oldest cheeses and was on sale at a market stall during my trip to Świnoujście. A nice rich flavour, I thought – it complimented the Zwickelfritz Dunkel Naturtrüb perfectly.

Tent Stability:

My Wind-Breaker DeLuxe remains stable, although she now has the German equivalent of the word 'PENIS' painted in large letters across the side of her flysheet. The temporary repairs made to the holes in the canvas seem to be holding though.

oOo

Chapter Seven – Trabant

To enable you to fully understand the extraordinary series of events which, over the next couple of days, would ultimately lead to my spending a night sleeping in a car belonging to a perfect stranger, it is necessary for me to furnish you with a little background information. So I'll start, if I may, by introducing you to a friend of mine.

Back in the mid 1990s I worked in the financial services industry with a smart and irritatingly intellectual German chap by the name of Jan Henke. Jan was a corporate analyst and a particularly good one if the truth be told. He had qualities about him that were quintessentially German. He had an extraordinary ability to remain calm under intense pressure; he took enormous risks which always seemed to pay off; and somehow he managed to maintain his sense of humour even when the world appeared to be crashing down around him. But Jan had another characteristic not normally associated with a corporate analyst – he was a thoroughly nice bloke. The two of us gelled almost from the day we met and, I'm pleased to say, we've remained friends ever since. Jan now lives with his lovely wife Stella and their two adorable children in the small town of Wittlich in Rhineland-Palatinate, about as far to the west of Germany as one can get before tripping over the border into Luxembourg. Jan is the same age as I am, a slip of a lad at just forty-nine, yet he managed to retire from the insanity of the corporate world a few years ago. He is now the proud owner of a twelve-acre tract of farmland where he breeds pigs and chickens and grows an assortment of vegetables. The farm is more of a labour of love for Jan and his family than a money-making venture – something to keep them occupied whilst Jan's investment portfolio is busy accumulating hundreds of euros in dividends on pretty much a daily basis. I'm not envious you understand. Well, just a bit maybe.

The last time I saw Jan was a couple of years ago, when the two of us spent a disastrous weekend in Rome – a trip that was cut short rather suddenly when Jan managed to fall down a flight of stone steps and break his left ulna. It was his own fault entirely. At the time, the two of us were on a wine tasting excursion to Rome's Frascati region, and the stone steps which Jan managed to fall down were the steps leading to the wine cellar at the Pallavicini Wine Estate – a restored 15th century farmhouse where the event was being held. Just prior to the accident, Jan had been engaged in two of his favourite pastimes – drinking wine and chatting up women – two things that he managed to achieve simultaneously and really rather admirably. Who says men can't multitask? Needless to say he'd downed several glasses of wine before attempting to negotiate the steps, so his general level of inebriation was undoubtedly a contributing factor.

So, why am I telling you all this? Well, for two reasons really. Firstly, you'll be meeting Jan later in the story anyway, as I had planned to stay with him and his family when I eventually reach Rhineland-Palatinate in about eleven or twelve days' time. So although there are still a few chapters of this book to wade through before you meet Jan properly, it's always nice to know a little about somebody before you make their acquaintance. Secondly, it was during a chance conversation with Jan just a few weeks earlier that I discovered he knew somebody who could let me borrow a Trabant.

A *Trabant,* for those of you to whom the name is unfamiliar, is a car. Well, in a manner of speaking. There are some Trabant owners who would argue that the word 'car' is a misnomer, in that it only ever aspired to be such a thing. Most Trabants spent long periods of time in garages, whilst their owners rued the day they ever bought one, or dreamt of the day when they could afford to trade their Trabant in for something infinitely superior – like a *Lada* or a *Yugo* for example. Powered (originally) by a two-stroke pollution generator that maxed out at an eardrum-piercing 18 brake horse-power, the Trabant was the car that gave communism a bad name. Constructed from *Duroplast* (a type of crude, recycled fibreglass), it was a virtual antique from the day it first rolled off of the production line at the *Sachsenring* factory in the late 1950s. It was East Germany's answer to the VW Beetle – a "people's car", as if the people of the German Democratic Republic didn't have enough to worry about. The Trabant remained in production until the fall of communism in the early 1990s – by which time just over three million of them had been produced. Trabants generated more smoke than a fire in an oil refinery, assuming they ran at all, and often lacked even the most basic of amenities, such as brake lights or indicators. At a time when people in the UK regarded the 'Mini' as the car to be seen driving, the East Germans had the Trabant to pose around in, although most of them were only too eager to trade their Trabants for a Mercedes just as soon as the shackles of communism had been released. Their eagerness to be rid of their vehicles is all the more surprising since the average East German would have waited somewhere between nine and fifteen years for delivery of a new Trabant – such was the length of the waiting list for these vehicles at the peak of their popularity. In fact, those who were 'lucky' enough to be able to afford it chose to pay that little bit extra for a second-hand one – which seems a little anomalous I admit – but second-hand Trabants were more readily available than brand new ones, and so commanded a higher price. But surprisingly, history has been kind to the dear old 'Trabbi'. Thousands of East Germans drove their Trabants over the border when the Wall fell, which made it a kind of icon of its era – an automotive liberator, if you will. And for reasons that I'm afraid I can't really explain, I have always harboured a secret desire to drive one. Not for any prolonged period of time you understand – I'm not that much of a masochist – but I've always wanted to borrow one, just for a couple of days. And it was during my chat with Jan a few weeks ago that I happened to mention this – it simply cropped up in conversation.

Now, as it just so happens, Jan is one of those people with a flair for networking – a man with more contacts than you can shake a proverbial stick at. Some people would call it a gift; a skill perhaps. Call it what you will, Jan seems to have the enviable knack of making friends with everyone he meets, and has this galling habit of calling on people for favours whenever a favour is needed. So when I mentioned that I'd always wanted to drive a Trabant, I wasn't in the least bit surprised when Jan (or 'Mister Fix-It' as he's occasionally nicknamed) declared that he knew somebody who would lend me one. Actually, Jan wasn't being wholly truthful when he said this. The reality was that he *didn't* know somebody who *would* lend me a Trabant. He knew somebody who knew somebody who knew somebody who *might* lend me a Trabant – although I didn't know that at the time of course. But in the weeks that followed, Jan went all out to deliver on his promise. He contacted his friend, who contacted their friend, who, in turn, contacted the man who owned the Trabant, and by a stroke of good fortune, the person in question just happened to agree to the deal. (I suspect that Jan handed over a considerable amount of money to make this happen, although he vehemently refutes this allegation.)

The man who would (allegedly) be lending me his car for the next couple of days was called Günter Schneider. That, I'm afraid, was pretty much all I knew about him, other than the fact that he lived in an apartment block in *Friedrichshain* – one of East Berlin's less privileged suburbs. All I had to do, according to Jan, was pick the car up from Schneider's home and drop it back again once I'd finished with it. It sounded simple enough. But I must admit that, whilst I trusted my friend Jan implicitly, I felt a little uncomfortable about this rather bizarre arrangement. I was borrowing a car from a man I had never met – indeed, a man Jan had never met. I had no idea who he was; what he did for a living; or why he had so readily agreed to lend his car to a total stranger. He could have been a gangster for all I knew. The Trabant could have been used as the getaway car on a major heist – its boot still laden with bars of gold bullion – its registration number top of the 'alert list' on every police computer in Europe. Not only that: borrowing Schneider's Trabant would necessitate making something of a detour on my part, which was a tad inconvenient.

Now, you may think I'm being a little ungrateful, and yes, perhaps you're right. After all, both Jan and this man Günter Schneider, along with all the middlemen who negotiated the deal between them (whoever they may be), had gone to an awful lot of trouble on my behalf. I was, after all, going to have the use of a Trabant for a couple of days which, as I've already rather shamefully admitted, was something I had always wanted to experience. But here's the thing: the next stage of my tour around Germany was scheduled to take me to the state of Brandenburg, and more specifically to the Uckermark Lakes Nature Park – nine hundred square kilometres of rural gorgeousness in the north of Brandenburg State. I would *have* to stay over in

149

Berlin at some stage of course – not that I particularly wanted to, but it is a state in its own right as we've already established, so I was duty-bound to visit the city according to my 'all-sixteen-states-rule'. In fact, Berlin would be next on my 'to do' list just as soon as I'd finished in Brandenburg. But the Uckermark Lakes Nature Park is not an easy place to get to. Rail connections are scarce, and bus services in this area are few and far between. Having the use of a car during my stay in Uckermark would be a perfect solution – but I'd have to go to Berlin first to collect it. And this seemed to me like an awful lot of faffing about. [22] I'd have to take the train to Berlin to collect the car from Günter Schneider, and then drive all the way back to Uckermark. A day or two later, I would have to drive back to Berlin again – this time to return the car. I shouldn't be complaining, I know. It was very generous of Schneider to offer to lend me his Trabant, so the very least I can do is stop my moaning and try to appear grateful.

So with my graffiti-defaced tent duly dismantled, rolled up snugly into its sheath and strapped to the bottom of my rucksack, I bid *Natur-Camping Usedom* a fond farewell, and headed to the station at Zinnowitz to catch the 10.09 to Berlin. It wasn't a direct service of course – I had to change trains at Züssow for my onward connection. It was a journey of a little over three hours, so it was lunchtime by the time my train finally reached the German capital.

After the peace and serenity of Usedom Island, my arrival in Berlin came as something of a shock to the system. Of all the cities in Europe, Berlin is about as 'in your face' as a city can possibly be. Whereas Usedom Island's spectacular rural beauty wakes you gently, blows fresh

---

[22] *Is that how you spell 'faffing'? I also tried 'phaffing', 'phaphing' and 'faphing' as possible alternatives, but neither my spellchecker nor my dictionary seems terribly impressed with any of them.*

crispy-clean air into your lungs and kisses you softly on your forehead, Berlin picks you up by the lapels of your coat and slaps you brutally across the cheeks. It's a sprawling, vibrant conurbation that flaunts all the excesses of capitalist decadence. There are advertising hoardings, skyscrapers, neon lights – and profligacy by the bucket load. Berlin was bustling in the afternoon sunshine; her streets noisy and congested with a relentless flow of taxis, trucks and vans – and trams rattled and clattered their way through the hullabaloo. I had no intention of staying in Berlin for a moment longer than was absolutely necessary, so armed with a small scrap of paper with Günter Schneider's address scribbled on it and another with a hand-drawn map of Günter's street in relation to its most proximate 'U-Bahn' station, I headed down a seemingly endless flight of steps into the murky subterranean world of Berlin's underground railway network.

I shared a carriage with a party of Japanese tourists, each wearing face masks covering their mouths and noses. I have never fully understood why Japanese tourists insist on wearing face masks everywhere they go. Yet wherever you venture in Europe, be it London, Berlin, Paris, Athens or Rome, the Japanese will be there, capturing snapshots of our iconic landmarks in their state-of-the-art cameras, with their mouths and noses protected from the air around them by those silly little face masks. I've never been able to decide whether I find this practice deeply offensive or highly commendable. If the intention is to protect their delicate little nostrils from having to inhale our putrid, germ-ridden air and run the risk of contracting some hideous and debilitating European disease, then that would indeed be deeply offensive. It would also beg the question why any of them bother coming to Europe at all. It would surely be much safer to stay at home in their highly sanitised, disease-free country where they can converse freely without having to protect themselves – even if it does expose them to each other's halitosis. If, however, the purpose of the face mask is to protect us Europeans from contracting hideous and debilitating oriental diseases which our Japanese friends may themselves be carrying, well, that would be selfless and considerate – so fair play to them.

I found Günter Schneider's home far more easily than I thought I would – nothing to do with the quality of my hand-drawn map, more attributable to a stroke of good fortune. The address I had scribbled on my scrap of paper turned out to be a flat, located within a four-storey apartment block set in an enclosed area on an unprepossessing social housing estate. There was a pathway leading to the main entrance, lined on either side with beds of overgrown honeysuckle, brambles and assorted weeds. And among this unsightly flora was an abandoned refrigerator – unceremoniously dumped in the undergrowth several months or possibly years earlier – and now thick with rust. The pathway led to the main entrance – a large aluminium ranch-style front door painted in a hideous shade of mustard yellow. Mounted on the wall beside the door was a metal casing for ten security buzzers – one for each of the apartments in the block – and many of them labelled with both the occupant's surname as well as a door number. Sure enough, flat number 2 had the word 'Schneider' displayed alongside it – which, I decided, was rather reassuring. I pressed the buzzer and waited.

Nothing.

I pressed the buzzer again.

After a while, a muffled, almost inaudible voice croaked at me through the intercom.

"Ja?"

"I'm Chris," I said – followed by a brief period of silence that was as awkward as it was uncomfortable.

"Ja?"

"I'm here to collect the car."

There followed another period of worrying silence and discomfiture. According to the convention of a normal conversation between two people (even one taking place through an intercom), it should have been Schneider's turn to speak next. But he didn't – so the silence continued. In fact, the gap in our conversation was so big I could have pushed a manatee through it.

"I'm here to borrow the Trabant," I shouted – my mouth moving ever closer to the intercom, albeit rather pointlessly. In much the same way as Ali Baba managed to gain access to the cave of treasures by uttering the obligatory code words '*Open Sesame*', it was the magic word '*Trabant*' that eventually unlocked the mysterious world of the equally enigmatic Günter Schneider. A buzzer sounded and the lock released – so I pushed the door open and stepped inside. I followed a dank and shadowy entrance hall, lit by a single 40-watt light bulb suspended from the ceiling by a short piece of frayed electrical cable, until I stumbled upon the door to what I believed was Schneider's flat. I knocked.

To this day, I can't be certain whether the creature that answered the door was human or not. Whatever it was, it had the characteristics of a sloven: a man lacking in tidiness and order and evincing a significant degree of laxity in his physical appearance.

"Günter Schneider?"

"Ja."

The man standing at the door was, without question, the scruffiest person I have ever met. His thick, wiry hair was matted and unkempt – and his beard equally so. His hair and his comb had clearly had a blazing argument with each other long ago and neither, it seemed, was keen on reconciliation. He wore a pair of ill-fitting grey tracksuit bottoms and a white sleeveless vest – the latter being several sizes too small for him and barely covered his substantial beer belly. I say his vest was white, but in point

153

of fact it wasn't easy to tell – it was decorated with an extensive collection of assorted food stains. At least, I hoped they were food stains. Either he hadn't bothered to wash this vest for several months, or it was something Tracey Emin had created for him as a birthday gift. But by far the most grotesque thing about this man was his smoking habit. It wasn't so much the fact that he smoked (I too was a habitual smoker until relatively recently) – it was the *manner* in which he smoked that bothered me. Schneider stood at the door with a lit cigarette dangling from his lips – tilted downwards at an angle of about 40 degrees from the horizontal. And as it slowly burned away, large lumps of ash would fall into his beard and onto his vest – prevented from falling directly onto the floor by his protruding beer gut. Not once did he attempt to remove the cigarette from his mouth – it remained stuck between his lips even when he was speaking.

"I'm here to borrow the Trabant," I said – for the second time in less than five minutes.

"Yes I know," Schneider replied. "But I've only just woken up – I wasn't expecting you so early in the day."

I looked at my watch – it was half past two in the afternoon.

"Wait one moment," he said.

Schneider stepped back inside his flat to fetch his keys, leaving me standing alone in the corridor. He returned a moment or two later, keys in hand, and ordered me to follow him. I was frogmarched back along the corridor and out through the hideous mustard-coloured front door. Without a word being exchanged between us, Schneider led me along a pathway around the building and eventually to a secluded area at the rear of the apartment block which housed the communal garages. I was gripped with excitement – the anticipation of seeing Günter Schneider's Trabant was almost unbearable. As I waited for him to unlock the garage door, I felt like a contestant on some surreal East German game show from the 1970s, where the curtain was about to be opened to reveal this week's star prize. I kept my fingers crossed hoping I wouldn't be disappointed. So many East German game show contestants have had to conceal their disappointment when presented with the prizes on '*Who Wants to Win Some Nail Clippers?*'

Schneider eventually opened his garage, and there, gleaming like a jewel in the summer sunshine was the star attraction – a 1990 VEB Trabant 1.1 Limousine – looking immaculate in a brilliant-white matt finish – one of the last Trabants to have rolled off the Sachsenring production line. I stepped inside the garage to take a closer look at this truly magnificent specimen. Despite her age, Günter Schneider's car was in pristine condition – having been garage-kept since the day he acquired her. He'd serviced and maintained the car himself and lovingly washed and polished the paintwork every Sunday morning as if it were some sort of religious obligation. It seemed almost inexplicable that someone who cared so passionately about his car could demonstrate such scant regard for his own personal appearance.

"You can borrow this one," he said. "I'll need to use the red one myself over the next couple of days."

"You have *two* Trabants?" I asked, incredulously.

"No, I have three," he replied. "In addition to the vehicle I keep here, I have a red one which is parked outside my girlfriend's flat, and a third Trabant 1.1 that's in pieces in my brother's garage. I keep it for spare parts."

I was astounded by Schneider's revelations, although I'm not sure which of them surprised me more – the fact that he owned *three* Trabants, or the fact that he had a girlfriend. I immediately took pity on the poor woman. I climbed into the driver's seat and, on Schneider's instruction, wound down the window using the manual lever attached to the side of the door. At this point, Schneider poked his head through the window along with his greasy, matted hair and his unruly beard, before launching into a desultory guided tour around the Trabant's primordial dashboard. Schneider pointed out the location of a few of the vehicle's critical levers, knobs and buttons, whilst imparting a brief explanation of how to cajole the machine into action by using just enough choke to start the engine but not too much so as to flood it. It was advice that I'm afraid went in one ear and out the other, but I nonetheless smiled at Schneider politely in the hope of convincing him that I'd understood the instruction clearly. Perhaps then he'd move away from the window and get his revolting beard from out of my face. Having applied what I thought was the optimum level of choke, I turned the ignition key a couple of times and the Trabant's archaic engine coughed and spluttered on both occasions – presumably in protest at having been disturbed from hibernation in the warmth of Schneider's cosy garage. But when Schneider leaned in through the open window and took control of both the choke and the ignition key, the spark plugs fired, the fuel ignited and whatever other mysterious stuff is supposed to happen in the inner sanctum of an internal combustion engine miraculously happened. Suddenly the Trabant leapt into life.

A cloud of thick black smoke blasted from the exhaust, causing two wood pigeons in a nearby tree to cough and reach for the Kleenex. To accompany the smoke, the Trabant's interior filled with petrol fumes, forcing me to lean my head out of the window to ease a temporary feeling of nausea. It was a mistake of course – the air outside was thick with smoke from the exhaust. I realised at once that I should have invested in one of those silly face masks after all – I take back everything I said about Japanese tourists. But after a while the exhaust fumes dispersed and the stench of petrol subsided, and the Trabant's little one-litre engine juddered away excitedly like an impatient puppy waiting at the park gates for its owner to unfasten the leash.

"I'll see you back here in a couple of days," I said, as I tried to jam the primitive gearstick into what I hoped was first gear.

"OK," Schneider replied. "Take good care of her, won't you?"

I assured him I would as I drove this extraordinary contraption out of the garage and onto the street.

It didn't take long to reach the city limits – out of Berlin and across the state boundary into Brandenburg. I can't pretend I wasn't delighted to be out of the city. Berlin, I'm afraid, is one of those places that seem so much nicer when you're looking at them through a rear-view mirror. In that respect, Berlin has much in common with Slough. It took around ninety minutes to drive to the Schorfheide campsite in the Uckermark National Park, which was time enough for me to get acquainted with some of the Trabant's quirky and less conventional features. The gears took bit of getting used to, as indeed did the brakes – the latter seeming to operate using the following mathematical equation:

'Brick Wall + Press Pedal + Short Pause + Another Short Pause = Stop Eventually.'

Twenty minutes after I'd assembled my *Wind-Breaker DeLuxe* tent for what seemed like the umpteenth time on my trip so far, I received the devastating news that I would have to dismantle it again. The news was delivered by a morose-looking man with all the charm of a traffic warden and the personality of a bucket of gravel, who made a beeline towards me just as soon as I'd hammered home the last tent peg.

"The graffiti on the side of your tent is offensive," he said. "The tent will have to be taken down."

I assumed he was referring to the word *'Schwanz'* written in large black letters across one side of the flysheet. I tried to explain that my tent had been defaced by a spotty, tone-deaf oik from Finland, and that in fact, it was *I* who was the victim here. But the man (who I presumed was a member of the campsite staff and was therefore speaking to me in an official capacity) was having none of it.

"It doesn't matter how it happened," he insisted. "This is a family camping site. There are families with small children here as well as children on adventure trips with their schools. You cannot have rude words displayed on the side of your tent – we shall receive complaints!"

He was right of course – a bit pompous and full of his own self-importance perhaps, but his argument was incontestable. Using all my skills in charm and diplomacy I managed to persuade him to allow the tent to remain standing, as long as I promised to remove the offending word. I knew the ink wouldn't wash off, but I figured that if I were to purchase a black marker pen similar to the one used by the bastard who defaced my tent in the first place, then I could cunningly disguise what was written there. By my reckoning, there were a couple of options open to me. I could simply obliterate the word *'Schwanz'* by scribbling all over it until the offending word was no longer decipherable. The resulting splurge of black ink on the side of my tent wouldn't look terribly attractive, I admit – but at least I wouldn't be frightening small children with profanities. My alternative option was to change the word *'Schwanz'* into something else. The word *'Schwänzen'*, for example, could be created by deviously adding an umlaut over the 'a' and inserting 'en' on the end. On the plus side, having the word *'Schwänzen'* written on the side of my tent would be offensive to nobody, as it's a perfectly innocent and harmless German verb with no sexual connotations or double-entendres. On the downside, the verb *'Schwänzen'* means 'to play truant' – i.e. to skip school without parental knowledge or consent. So with hindsight, given that there were children at the Schorfheide Camp who were here on an adventure holiday, it would perhaps be unwise to turn my tent into a billboard encouraging them to bunk off school. After some initial reluctance, the campsite official (I'll call him *that* since I was unable to determine his job title or his exact role), seemed surprisingly agreeable to my proposal – but made it clear that until I had purchased the marker pen and deleted the offending graffiti as we'd agreed, I would have to cover it up using a bed sheet or a towel or something of similar size that could be draped across the tent to provide a veil over the offending word.

Now as it just so happened, my sleeping bag desperately needed a jolly good airing – and since it was another warm and balmy evening I decided to kill two birds with the one stone by spreading it over my tent.

Seemingly satisfied with this as a temporary solution, the campsite official walked off in the direction he came from, stopping momentarily to berate a group of young boys who were kicking a football in a nearly field – presumably for playing too noisily.

The Schorfheide campsite is located in the village of Vietmannsdorf, in the heart of the Uckermark National Park. It's a small site with pitches for around thirty tents, and other than a small toilet and shower block, and a communal barbeque area, there's little else on offer. The campsite's publicity brochure suggested that shops and restaurants were located 'nearby' – so I presumed I would have to cross the periphery of the camp and stroll into the village to find them. Since the Trabant had brought me the sixty kilometres from Berlin without complaining, breaking down or spontaneously combusting, I rewarded her with the chance to sit quietly in the campsite's little car park where she could catch up on some well-earned rest, while I took a stroll into Vietmannsdorf to find the shops and restaurants which the brochure had assured me would be there. I didn't hold out much hope of being able to purchase a black marker pen in Vietmannsdorf. It was, after all, just a tiny rural village – no doubt there'd be a pub and village post office maybe, but I wasn't expecting a multi-storey shopping mall. Not only that, it was now late in the evening and the village post office would have closed its shutters hours earlier. But by my reckoning it didn't really matter. The offending obscenity that had been daubed across the side of my tent would be covered up by my sleeping bag whenever there were children around – and during the night when my sleeping bag was employed in a more conventional capacity, it would be too dark to see the graffiti anyway. So there was no rush to purchase the marker pen. I was planning to drive the Trabant into *Templin* the following day – one of the main towns in the Uckermark district, and I felt sure I'd find a stationery shop there.

My supposition that Vietmannsdorf would offer little more than a pub and a post office turned out to be remarkably accurate – although I did discover a rather attractive village church, complete with a half-timbered clock tower. But there was one other building in Vietmannsdorf that attracted my attention – the *Landhaus Askanien* – a pretty little restaurant located directly opposite the church. There was something quintessentially English about the Landhaus Askanien – which was odd, given that it was built within the boundaries of East Germany and just a stone's throw from the border with Poland. The building resembled one of those charming little houses you find in the Cotswolds – a honey-coloured stone cottage with pink Germania Rhododendrons planted on either side of the main entrance. But there was something else about this enchanting little restaurant that reminded me of home – there was an old-fashioned British telephone box standing on the lawn outside, which I have to say looked resplendent in its fresh coat of bright red paint – and despite its alien geographical location, it didn't look in the least bit out of place. [23] I decided there and then that the Landhaus Askanien would be the perfect place to dine that evening – a decision which I will admit was influenced partially by the presence of the telephone box, but mostly by the fact that, as far as I could determine, it was the only restaurant in Vietmannsdorf.

Despite the restaurant's apparent British influences, the food on offer was unmistakeably East German – in fact, the menu was almost a throwback to the era of communism. The menu included dishes such as *Würzfleisch* – a cheap version of ragout fin with pork instead of expensive veal. I also came across *Ketwurst* and *Grillettas* – two dishes I hadn't previously encountered on my travels, and I felt duty-bound to ask the buxom waitress for a brief explanation of what they were. Despite their inventive names, it appeared that Ketwurst was simply the East German version of a hot dog and a Grilletta, a hamburger. But as 'anglicisms' were strictly outlawed in the former socialist state, the pen-pushers at the Ministry of Gastronomic Bureaucracy came up with more 'appropriate' German names. [24] Ketwursts and Grillettas disappeared from menus in restaurants and canteens after the fall of the Berlin Wall, but in recent times

[23] *Around 1,000 K1 red telephone boxes appeared for the first time on British Streets in 1925 and more were added every year thereafter with the introduction of the K2, K3, K6 and K8 versions. By 1980 there were 73,000 of them in the UK. Sadly though, since we now live in an age where none of us are capable of functioning properly without a mobile phone glued to our ear, the old-style red telephone box has all but disappeared from Britain's streets. Mercifully though, there are still a few remaining, and I'm pleased to report that Malta, Bermuda and Gibraltar have all had the good sense to hang on to most of theirs. Finding one in East Germany was a wonderful surprise.*

[24] *In the government of the former German Democratic Republic, there was no such department as the Ministry of Gastronomic Bureaucracy. I just made that up.*

they appear to be celebrating something of a comeback in many East German restaurants. The Landhaus Askanien was offering both, along with a selection of other socialist culinary classics. After much forethought and deliberation, I finally opted for the Grillettas – with a generous accompaniment of fries, lashings of mayonnaise and a couple of glasses of beer. With dinner over, I loosened my belt by a couple of notches to allow my bulging stomach the space it so clearly craved, and I sauntered slowly back to the campsite.

The following day began well. The weather was good, and I had received a newsy text from my wife during the night – a little note keeping me abreast with her adventures on the high seas. I texted her back with an equally newsy response, hoping I would convince her that I was having as much fun as she was. I had my doubts as to whether that was true. But it was good to hear from her, and receiving her text was a wonderful start to my day.

The Uckermark National Park is a thinly populated region comprising around four hundred lakes, peaceful rivers, forests, moors and meadows. As I'm sure you can imagine it's an area of outstanding natural beauty, its centre point being the biosphere reserve – centuries old, with landscapes ranging from oak forests to swamps and open grasslands. It is home to a diverse community of flora and fauna – a natural habitat for cranes, black storks and eagles – and some of the oak trees here have been standing for over six hundred years. So, with a natural environment as beautiful as Uckermark, with its complex, yet fragile biological ecosystem, I decided to begin my day by committing an act of wanton environmental vandalism, by filling Uckermark's fresh, unsullied air with emissions of carbon monoxide, lead, sulphur dioxide, carbon particles, fine particulate matter and small amounts of aromatic hydrocarbons and dioxins. Yes, I was planning to drive the

Trabant along the twelve-kilometre stretch of country road from the campsite at Schorfheide to the little town of Templin, with carbon dioxide blasting from her exhaust pipe at a rate of 500 grams per kilometre. So with this in mind, I carefully spread my sleeping bag over the tent (so that the eyes of small children were once again protected from the obscenity scribbled on the flysheet), and made my way over to the car park to fire up the Trabant.

Now, you may have noticed that so far during this chapter, I've been less than complimentary about the dear old Trabbi. In fact, my comments about her have been depreciatory to say the least. I've accused her of being...... well, a bit of a crap car. Now, don't get me wrong here, the Trabbi *is* a crap car – there's no doubt about that whatsoever. But for many East Germans, the sight of a Trabant (and particularly one in pristine condition) has a peculiar effect on their general disposition – it fills them with a sense of nostalgia and national pride, and brings them out in goose bumps. It's a bit like the Reliant Robin, I suppose. We all know it's a crap car – poorly designed, badly built – a fibreglass death trap on three wheels. But it's a death trap that we Brits find strangely likeable – a piece of wacky British engineering for which we all feel something of an affinity. It was when I arrived at the campsite car park that I first discovered this extraordinary effect that the Trabant seems to have on the East Germans. There were three of them (East Germans that is, not Trabants), all brawny, muscular men, gathered around the car and gazing with approbation through her windows in search of a closer look at her immaculate interior. I could see them nodding at each other almost in veneration of this magnificent machine. I smiled at them politely as I negotiated my way around them in an effort to reach the car door.

"Is this *your* Trabant?" one of them asked me as I fumbled with the car keys.

"It isn't mine," I replied. "I'm just borrowing it from a ..... *friend*."

Now then, I know Günter Schneider isn't a friend. But this conversation was being conducted in German and the word *'friend'* was the only word I could think of on the spur of the moment. Not only that, it was far easier simply to tell them that I'd borrowed the car from a friend, than to go into a long and loquacious explanation of how I'd actually borrowed the car from a friend of a friend of a friend who cared more about his car than he did his personal hygiene, and who may or may not have received payment for lending it to me anyway – making the car, technically speaking, 'hired' rather than 'borrowed'. I really wasn't in the mood for a conversation about motor cars so early in the morning either – especially one conducted with three burly, bearded men, each with a regional drawl so thick that it was almost unidentifiable as being *German* at all.

"You are English?" he asked.

I'm not sure whether it was my unconvincing accent or my appalling German pronunciation that gave me away, but I nodded anyway.

"Your friend must be very proud of his motor car," said another of the men. At least, I think that's what he said.

"Yes he is," I feebly replied, whilst climbing hurriedly into the driver's seat before any of them could bombard me with more of their irritating questions. As I placed the key into the ignition the three men were still inspecting the car, and I suddenly became conscious of just how humiliating it would be if the Trabant wouldn't start. I decided that a few words of encouragement might be appropriate, even if they were muttered under my breath so that the men outside couldn't hear me talking to myself.

"Please, my sweet little Trabbi – please start first time."

I turned the ignition key, and the Trabant coughed and spluttered as she had done on the previous afternoon.

"Come on sweetheart," I muttered. "Please start for me."

I turned the key again, and again the Trabant's prehistoric engine gasped and stammered. The three men were no longer inspecting the paintwork but were now standing beside me, staring at me through the window.

"For God's sake *START* you useless piece of communist shit!" I muttered, as I turned the engine for the third time, only to be met with the same obstinate response. There was a tap on the window, and I turned around to discover one of the men making a gesture with his hand, which I interpreted as an instruction for me to wind down the window. Either that or he was demonstrating the rinse cycle motion of a washing machine for reasons that I'm not able to explain. I wound the window down and one of the burly, bearded men (the most burly and bearded of them all), stuck his head into the car.

"There's a knack to starting a Trabbi," he said. "It all about using enough choke to start the engine – but not too much so as to flood it."

"Is that right?" I said.

"It is," he replied. "Let me show you."

The man leaned rather awkwardly into the car, taking control of the keys in one hand and the choke lever in the other.

"That will probably do it," he said, after making a few minor adjustments to the choke. The man turned the ignition key – and as if to spite me, the Trabant's engine immediately sprang into life. It was as if a defibrillator had been attached to her chest to restore the natural rhythm of her heart. The man gave me a wry smile as he pulled his head away from the window.

"Enjoy your drive," he said.

"I will," I replied – too embarrassed to think of anything smarter to say. I drove out of the campsite leaving a cloud of thick, toxic, black smoke behind me, and tried my best to ward off that feeling of nausea which was caused, once again, by the stench of petrol fumes that filled the air inside the car.

The smoke and fumes soon subsided as I drove along the L216 towards Templin. It was one of those roads that make driving an almost pleasurable pursuit. It was smooth, well maintained and virtually traffic-free – and the twelve-kilometre stretch of the L216 between Vietmannsdorf and Templin carves its way through a forest of oak trees for much of the route. Templin is a charming little town, typical of many in the state of Brandenburg, and is home to around 17,000 people. Templin's original city walls remain intact, along with three ancient gate towers – the most dramatic of which is the rather imposing *Berliner Tor*. But I hadn't come to Templin to admire the architecture or to browse the shops and market stalls (although I still needed to buy a black marker pen of course). I had come to Templin for an altogether different reason.

Now, I consider myself to be reasonably well travelled, and over the years have journeyed on just about every kind of land transport imaginable. I've sat aboard buses, trains, tractors and trams. I've travelled by car, by bike and even on horseback. There was one occasion when I travelled across a stretch of desert with my arse lodged precariously between the humps of a Bactrian camel. It was a painful experience from which my testicles have never fully recovered. My eyes start to water every time I think about it. But there is one type of land vehicle which, until today, I had never experienced the pleasure of riding on. In fact, until I began my preparation for this decadent trip across Germany, it was a mode of transport I had never even heard of. You see, the town of Templin marks the starting point of a sightseeing tour through Uckermark's wild and rugged landscape – a landscape of lakes created during the Ice Age and set

166

against a backdrop of gently rolling hills. This was a sightseeing tour so popular that I had been advised to pre-book my ticket several months in advance. And today was the day on which my much-coveted ticket was valid. Yes, today, for the first time in my life, I would be travelling through the German countryside on a draisine.

I said this was a mode of transport I had never previously heard of, but in fact, that isn't strictly true. It turns out that I have known exactly what a draisine looks like since I was four years old – it's just I've never realised that '*draisines*' are what these contraptions are called. A draisine is a light auxiliary railway vehicle, designed for use by service personnel for the maintenance of railway infrastructure. Although some draisines may be battery operated or even powered by small engines, the majority are operated manually, in most cases using a hand crank. The cart is pushed to get it started – then the driver jumps on it and starts pushing a central lever forwards and backwards which, in turn, operates the linkages. Some draisines are operated by foot pedals which drive the wheels along the railway track using a chain mechanism – not dissimilar to a pushbike. I was four years old when I first saw a draisine. I was watching the 1966 film 'The Great St. Trinian's Train Robbery' – where two girls in St. Trinian's school uniform were hurtling down a railway track on a pump-action handcar in hot pursuit of Frankie Howerd, Reg Varney, Arthur Mallard et al. who were escaping from the scene of the crime in a steam engine and with the loot safely stashed away in one of the train's carriages.

The name 'draisine' is actually an eponymous term (well, almost), named after its inventor, the German-born 'Baron Karl Christian Ludwig **Drais** von Sauerbronn'. Try fitting that on the back of an FC Borussia Mönchengladbach shirt. Although there are thousands of draisines all over the world carrying out the sort of duties they were designed for, I had never heard of them being used in the leisure industry – being rented out to tourists for sightseeing purposes. But there's a twenty-eight-kilometre stretch of railway track running from Templin to the little village of Fürstenberg which tourists can travel the length of under their own steam, by hiring one of these extraordinary contraptions for the day. And that was exactly what I intended to do – having purchased my ticket several weeks earlier.

The draisines at Templin were pedal-powered and designed to carry four people – two of them pedalling the cart along the track, and the other two sitting regally on a central bench seat, sandwiched between the two poor souls doing all the hard work. Many of the draisines were rented by families or by groups of friends who wanted to explore the beauty of the Uckermark National Park on their own. But since I was a sad and lonely old git who wasn't travelling with anybody, I joined one of the escorted tours, along with a couple of other sad and lonely old gits who found themselves in a similar predicament.

There were four of us in all, including our tour guide, *Griselda* – a thin, sinewy woman in her mid to late fifties, with short, curly ginger hair and a freckled complexion. Despite her age, Griselda appeared to be in pretty good physical condition – the shape of her slim, yet muscular frame was accentuated by her clingy, sleeveless lycra vest and her lycra three-quarter-length cycling shorts. She had, without question, the stature of a woman who had spent a great deal of time pedalling a draisine up and down a twenty-eight-kilometre stretch of railway track. She also had a dragon tattoo on her calf and another slightly larger one on her shoulder blade. I'd like to bet that in her younger days she'd valiantly represented the GDR in an Olympic shot put competition.

The second of my travelling companions was a tiny Japanese man by the name of *Takumi*. Of course, I can't be

168

sure I've spelled that correctly, but I think 'Takumi' is phonetically close enough. Takumi was a terribly scrawny-looking man, almost unhealthily so in my opinion, and was carrying twice his body weight in the form of the largest and heaviest rucksack I have ever seen. Around his neck he wore the mother of all cameras – thousands of pounds' worth of Japanese technology complete with all the accoutrements of modern photography – the functions of which I can't even begin to speculate on.

Last, and by some means least, there was *Chad*. I'm not sure whether 'Chad' was his real name or whether it was short for something else – like *Chadwick*, for example. I'm quite certain that had *I* been christened 'Chadwick', then I would almost certainly abbreviate my name to 'Chad', or better still, change it by deed poll to 'Bob' – or something equally less ridiculous. Chad was an American, hailing from the small town of Benton near Little Rock, Arkansas. I must admit that until I met Chad I hadn't heard of Benton, but any desire I may have had to pay the town a visit some day was soon quashed by Chad's rather disparaging assessment of his hometown.

"It's the most godforsaken hell-hole on the entire goddamn planet," he said. Evidently, he had never been to Milton Keynes.

Like our tour guide, Griselda, Chad was pushing sixty, but whereas Griselda's physical shape made her appear much younger than she was, Chad's haggard features and gaunt expression made him look every bit his age. He was evidently wealthy, certainly very opinionated, and was of short, stocky build. He sported a short, tidy and well-maintained white beard and wore a baseball cap to disguise his receding hairline. Chad, it transpired, was on holiday in Germany with his wife. But whereas *he* had opted for an excursion through the German countryside on a railcar propelled by pedal power, his wife had chosen to go shopping instead. Quite why anyone of sound mind would choose shopping over a ride on a draisine, I really can't imagine. Maybe it's just a 'bloke' thing. Still – whatever floats your boat.

Now, you may have noticed something from my description of this little entourage – none of us (with the exception of our tour guide of course) was a native German. And this, as you may have already guessed, was no coincidence. Our group wasn't simply assembled from a mishmash of sad, lonely old gits who happened to be travelling alone – we were also bound together by a more obvious common denominator. Despite the three of us representing a veritable gallimaufry of nationalities and cultures, we were all English speaking. And Griselda, who among her many talents could speak English fluently, had been assigned to lead today's 'English-Speaking Tour'.

"We shall take it in turns to pedal the draisine," she declared. "I'll start us off, but since two of us can pedal at the same time, I shall need a volunteer to help me."

Takumi's hand shot skywards like an assiduous schoolboy.

"I will," he said, already in the process of clambering into the driver's saddle. Chad and I took our places on the wooden bench seat between Takumi and Griselda, and very soon we were on the move. A fifty-six-kilometre cycle ride from Templin to Fürstenberg and back again could have been easily completed in less than a couple of hours. But under the expert leadership of Griselda, we set out from Templin just before noon, and arrived back again just after 10 o'clock that evening. Now, you may think that spending ten hours riding around the countryside on a railway handcar with three complete strangers sounds like a mind-numbingly tiresome way to spend my day. Well, you'd be wrong. I enjoyed myself so much that I hardly noticed where the time went. The four of us shared the pedalling duties by swapping over every hour or so – Griselda and Takumi in one team and me and Chad in the other. Griselda's knowledge of the Uckermark district was astonishing – her commentary both fascinating and informative. Along the route from Templin to Fürstenberg we would pass all manner of notable landmarks – buildings, canals, bridges, lakes and monuments – and as we reached each one, we'd stop for a well-earned rest while Griselda bombarded us with fascinating facts, figures and statistics.

But the wily Griselda would tell us only half the story. Being the consummate professional, she would be careful to divulge only a smidgen of her boundless knowledge – judiciously saving the remainder for when we reached the same spot again on the return journey. We stopped for lunch in a charming little restaurant at Lychen – roughly halfway between Templin and Fürstenberg, where we filled a cool box with enough ice-cold beers to keep us going during the numerous stops we'd be making en route. As it happened, Takumi was teetotal and had brought his own vacuum flask of Japanese herbal tea to satiate his thirst – and quite frankly, he was welcome to it. The smell alone was enough to make you reach for a bucket. But Griselda surprised us all with her beer-drinking skills. Despite her lean and muscular stature, she could knock them back like a Slovenian deckhand on shore leave, and yet show no physical side effects whatsoever. Not that it would have mattered all that much – I don't believe that being drunk in charge of a draisine would necessarily impair one's ability to operate it. As the rented handcars are restricted to using only a single track, we occasionally met another draisine either heading towards us, or wanting to overtake. Of course, Sod's law dictated that this would always happen when the four of us were taking a few minutes' respite, and were sitting cross-legged on the grass beside the track, drinking beer and tucking into salted pretzels the size of steering wheels. But whenever we did encounter an oncoming car, the solution was simple enough – a draisine can be easily lifted off the rails to allow others to pass, and then be placed back onto the track afterwards. Admittedly it takes a couple of people to lift it – although Griselda did claim to be capable of lifting a draisine off the rails single-handedly but sited a 'dodgy knee' as her reason for being unwilling to demonstrate.

It was dark by the time I arrived back at the car park in Templin where I'd parked the Trabant almost twelve hours earlier. It was also raining – only a fine rain, admittedly, but it was raining nonetheless. I suppose that, on the one hand, I should have been grateful that the rain was starting now, rather than earlier in the day. Riding on a draisine is very much an 'outdoor' activity and the day would have been spoiled had it been wet. But on the other hand, rain of any sort, be it fine rain or otherwise, was about as welcome as a nut cutlet at a cannibal's banquet, seeing as how my sleeping bag was still draped over my tent. But it probably didn't matter all that much. By my reckoning, it would take only twenty minutes to drive back to the Schorfheide campsite, so there would be time enough to shove my sleeping bag in the tumble-dryer before the laundry room closed at midnight. But first, I'd have to get the Trabant's engine started.

Now, I'm afraid I am quite unable to offer any explanation for what was about to happen. All I can assume is that, for whatever reason, the gods must have been in a jovial frame of mind. Despite the odds being stacked against me, I somehow managed to start the Trabant's engine on the first turn of the key. Don't ask me how it happened – it just did. You can imagine how happy I was. The English language is teeming with a multitude of similes: happy as a clam, happy as Larry, happy as a sand boy. Take your pick – any one of these would have summed up my general disposition rather nicely. The thing is, I can't actually

172

remember *what* I did to make this happen. I remember pulling the choke lever out a couple of centimetres before pushing it back in again, but I can't recall whether I did this once, twice or three times before I turned the ignition key – and I definitely can't recall exactly how far I extended the choke lever. But what did it matter? Whatever I did seemed to do the trick – the Trabant's engine was fired up and ready to go.

I drove rather carefully along the L216 back to Schorfheide. It was dark and it was raining, and with such a feeble battery sitting beneath her bonnet, the Trabant's windscreen wipers functioned very slowly when the headlights were on. When I say it was dark – I mean it was eerily dark. Not only was it a moonless night, but also the road wound its way through a dense forest of oak trees with the branches providing a canopy which blocked out light from any source. And with a wet and slippery road surface to contend with, I wasn't prepared to take any chances – even if there weren't any other cars on the road. And perhaps that was just as well.

About ten minutes into my journey I saw something run out into the road in front of me. Nothing very big (we're not talking Tyrannosaurus Rex here), but I'm guessing it must have been a rabbit or a fox, maybe, or perhaps even a wild boar. Whatever it was it scared the bejesus out of me. My natural instinct was to slam my foot on the brake pedal as aggressively as possible. I knew that the Trabant wouldn't stop instantly – I'd become acquainted with her 'leisurely' stopping distances, but I *had* to execute something as close to an emergency stop as one can muster in a Trabant, in order to avoid a collision. As it happened, I *did* manage to stop the car in time, and the rabbit/fox/wild boar (delete as applicable) made it safely to the other side of the road before scurrying into the forest, presumably unharmed.

Unfortunately though, I managed to stall the Trabant's engine.

Now, why is it, do you think, that when you're parked in a car park in a town where there are 17,000 people on hand to help you in times of trouble, you are capable of starting an engine without any problems whatsoever? Yet, when you're stuck in the middle of a narrow country lane, in the middle of the night, in the pissing rain, with not a soul in sight for miles and miles in every conceivable direction, the bastard engine refuses to budge. It's called *'Sod's law'* – an informal, humorous or facetious precept stating that if something can go wrong or turn out to be thoroughly inconvenient, then it bloody well will.

I can't recall exactly how many times I tried to start the engine – but it was a fair few. And every time I did, the engine coughed and wheezed and made all sorts of ugly rasping noises, not dissimilar to those my grandfather used to make while stubbing out his fiftieth cigarette of the day. I decided in the end that it was unwise to continue trying, as there was a danger of draining the battery. And then of course, it occurred to me that leaving the wipers and the headlights on might also have similar consequence. So I stepped out of the car, released the handbrake, and pushed the Trabant over to the side of the road, so that two of her wheels remained firmly on the tarmac whilst the other two rested on the forest floor. I climbed back into the car, switched off the wipers and the headlights, and stared inanely into space whilst contemplating my unfortunate predicament. As the windows misted up and the rain hammered down on the duroplast roof, I tried to come up with a suitable solution. At one point I seriously considered abandoning the car and walking back to the campsite in the pouring rain. But then it occurred to me that by the time I reached the camp, the laundry room would have closed for the night and I'd be left with a soaking wet sleeping bag. It

174

may not have been comfortable sitting in the confines of Günter Schneider's Trabant – but at least it was dry. Not only that, I felt sure the car would have been towed away had I abandoned it – I'd return to the scene the following day only to discover a huge gap in the space that the Trabant had occupied the night before, and I really didn't want to have to explain to Schneider that I'd managed to get his pride and joy impounded. So I simply sat there until I eventually fell asleep.

I suppose I must have slept for five hours, or thereabouts, as I noticed that dawn was in the throes of breaking when I woke up. The rain had stopped too. It wasn't the advent of daybreak that woke me though – it was the burly police officer from the *Brandenburg Landespolizei* who was tapping on the window. He wasn't alone either: there were two of them – both dressed in their immaculately pressed navy blue police uniforms with their deadly Walther P99Qs dangling from their holsters. One was tapping on the window trying to verify whether I was dead or merely sleeping, and the other was about to step out of the shiny seven-series BMW that was parked behind me – its blue lights still flashing. The officer who had tapped on the window was indicating that I should step out of the car, so given the surfeit of firearms that he had strapped around his waist, I thought it best to comply.

"Is this *your* vehicle?" he asked rather severely.

I told him that the car belonged to Günter Schneider and handed him the scrap of paper with Schneider's address written on it (which, mercifully, I still had in the back pocket of my jeans). After I'd finished my almost incoherent explanation of how I came to be sleeping in a car belonging to a complete stranger whilst parked precariously at the side of a narrow country lane, the two police officers took Schneider's details, together with my passport and driver's licence, and strolled back to their patrol car to make

175

enquiries over the police radio. I waited nervously beside the Trabant whilst they made the necessary checks. But after a nail-biting ten minutes, the two officers strolled back to where I was standing, this time looking even more menacing than before and wearing sullen expressions on their faces. I braced myself for some terrible news.

"Is everything OK, officer?" I asked.

One of the officers reached into the car and grabbed the keys, drawing me to the conclusion that the vehicle was about to be impounded. But then, with the ignition key gripped in one hand, the officer grabbed hold of the choke lever with the other.

"There's a knack to starting a Trabbi," he said. "It all about using enough choke to start the engine – but not too much so as to flood it." And with that, he turned the ignition – and believe it or not, that bloody, bastard engine started first time.

"You can be on your way now, Sir," he said. "Have a pleasant morning."

oOo

Dear Diary,
The Beer, Cheese and Tent Report for the State of Brandenburg:
Beer: Raubritter Dunkel*:*

I wasn't quite sure what was going on with this beer. Raubritter is a dark, dry lager with a bitter(ish) aftertaste, and had an aroma of chicory, toffee and black peppers. Raubritter, I've decided, is weird yet strangely compelling.

Cheese: Steppenkäse:

According to the beautiful lady I met in a cheese shop in Templin, this cheese was originally made by German immigrants living on the Russian Steppes. Present day versions are mostly greyish-yellow in colour with regular holes and a piquant, full-bodied flavour.

Tent Stability:

I didn't sleep in my tent last night – I chose instead to sleep at the roadside in a Trabant. I can only assume the tent is standing in the same upright position at Schorfheide Camp as it had been when I last saw it. My sleeping bag will almost certainly be soaking wet.

oOo

Chapter Eight – Under the Lime Trees

I'm sure I've already mentioned how much I dislike Berlin, so I won't labour the point – except to say that I've visited the German capital on several previous occasions, and I've tried very hard to love it. But I'm afraid I simply can't. Sure, it has some iconic landmarks – the Brandenburg Gate; Checkpoint Charlie; the Berlin Wall – and it's a city that is unquestionably imbued with history. But it's not a city with an *intriguing* history like London, or one with a *flamboyant* history like Florence or Venice. It's a *macabre* history that I'm afraid I find terribly depressing. Every landmark, every icon in this bustling metropolis has a chilling tale to tell and stands as an unwelcome reminder of Germany's turbulent past. Whether it's the atrocities of the Nazis or the brutality of communism, there are reminders everywhere you turn – in every square and on every street corner.

I arrived in the city centre at around 8.00am, which I will admit is a ludicrously early time for any sensible person to arrive anywhere. But having been moved on by the Brandenburg State Police in the early hours of the morning, I found myself at a loss for something better to do other than to drive to Berlin.

Three hours earlier, at the side of the L216, I breathed a sigh of relief that the police hadn't opened the Trabant's boot and discovered the gold bullion that (for all I knew), might have been stashed there, and I drove straight to the Schorfheide Camp to set about dismantling my tent and saving my sodden sleeping bag from further rain damage.

Fortunately, Günter Schneider had given me two sets of car keys, so I left one key in the ignition, and locked the car door with the other. So, while I was packing away the tent, I was able to leave the Trabant's engine ticking over. I realise of course that by doing so, I ran the risk of having the car stolen – I suppose that finding an unattended vehicle with the keys in the ignition and the engine running would be an irresistible temptation for any potential car thief. And I suppose also that any competent car thief would regard a locked door as being merely 'inconvenient' rather than prohibitive. But if I'd switched the engine off then there would have been no guarantee that I'd ever get the damned thing started again – and I simply wasn't prepared to go through all that palaver again. Besides, the risk was minimal in my opinion. There was nobody else around. It was 5.30 in the morning and the campers were sound asleep. Not only that, *who* in their right mind would want to steal a Trabant? These extraordinary vehicles may have a special place in the hearts of the people, but even East Germans would concede that a Trabant is a worthless piece of crap.

And so with nothing better to do I headed for the autobahn to join the thousands of commuters who derive so much pleasure from sitting in queues of stationary rush hour traffic they choose to do it day after day after day. I had come to Berlin for two reasons as you are already aware. Firstly, I was obliged to spend at least one night in the capital because the rules of my trip around the German states dictated that I should. Secondly, I had to return the car to its rightful owner, and to be brutally honest, the sooner I could be rid of *that* particular burden, the better. Berlin may be a huge, sprawling metropolis, but it's not completely bereft of open spaces. There are, in fact, several camping sites within the state boundary. But for my overnight stay in Germany's capital city, I decided that tonight, as a special 'one-off' treat, I would check in to a hotel. Now, I know what you're thinking. This is supposed to be a camping holiday – just me, my tent and the miracle of Mother Nature. Staying in a hotel is hardly in keeping with the spirit of the adventure. Well yes, all right, all right – you've made your point. But although this slight deviation from my original itinerary may seem a little self-indulgent, I, for one, could think of three very good reasons that sat firmly in its favour.

Point one: my sleeping bag was soaking wet. I realise that I can sometimes be prone to exaggeration, but when I say it was soaking wet, I mean it truly was *soaking* wet. If I had wrung it out, torrents of water would have come gushing out of it – enough water to supply a hydroelectric power generating plant for a year at least. OK, perhaps I am exaggerating a bit.

Point two: I only had four hours' sleep during the previous night, and I reasoned that spending a night in a hotel would be more conducive to a good night's sleep than spending a night under canvas.

Point three: sleeping in an upright sitting position whilst wedged in the driver's seat of a Trabant isn't terribly good for one's posture – it can play havoc with the vertebral column. To put it simply, my back was killing me.

And so to summarise my two options: I could either spend another night in my tent, lying on a rock-hard floor, wrapped in a soaking wet sleeping bag and running the risk of catching double pneumonia – or I could check into a hotel room with a bouncy mattress on a king-size bed; rest my head on a soft, feathery pillow and snuggle up into a warm, fluffy duvet. I think it's what our American friends might refer to as a 'no-brainer'. But before I could consider seeking suitable hotel accommodation, I decided my first mission of the day would be to return the car to Günter Schneider.

It would take about an hour to drive to his flat in Friedrichshain, which would mean arriving there at around 9.00am. I didn't think for a minute that there would be any

180

possibility of Schneider being awake at such an unearthly hour in the morning, but I was desperate to get rid of the Trabant and I didn't dare turn the engine off. I made the decision that if Schneider didn't answer the door, then I'd press the security buzzer continuously until he damn well did. And if *that* didn't work and I was unable to raise a reply, then I'd simply dump the car outside his garage and post both sets of keys through his letter box.

My estimated time of arrival at Schneider's flat turned out to be spookily accurate – by the time I pulled up beside his garage it was nine o'clock on the dot. I didn't bother with the security buzzer as one of Schneider's neighbours, who was sitting on the doorstep smoking a cigarette, had the door to the apartment block propped open using a ceramic flowerpot. The neighbour made a strange grunting sound as I asked him to move aside to allow me to pass – a sound that reminded me of one of the orcs that guard the gates of Mordor. Once inside the dimly lit corridor, I headed for flat number 2, and knocked. To my surprise the door was opened almost immediately – *not* by the enigmatic Günter Schneider, but by a middle-aged woman wearing red pyjama bottoms and fluffy pink slippers. In contrast to Schneider's rotund physique, the woman was rather skinny – almost painfully so, in my opinion. Actually, I'd prefer to describe her as skeletal – emaciated even, her ribcage clearly visible through a tightly-fitting T-shirt that clung to the contours of her scrawny midriff. The woman had a rutted complexion and scruffy blond hair, almost straw-like in texture, which I guessed from her auburn roots was not her natural hair colour.

"May I speak to Günter?" I asked.

"Nein."

"Is he awake yet?"

"Nein."

"I'm returning his car," I said, dangling two sets of keys in front of her. The woman snatched the keys from me, promising she would give them to Schneider as soon as he surfaced from hibernation.

"Where did you leave the Trabant?" she continued.

"Outside the garage."

"OK – aufwiedersehen," she said, and slammed the door closed.

I took the U-Bahn back to the city centre and began my search for overnight accommodation, stopping en route a couple of times to carry out some essential errands. My first stop was at the 'Alles-Sauber' laundrette, where I dropped my sleeping bag in for a service wash (I couldn't be bothered to sit in a self-service laundrette for an hour watching it spin round and round in a washing machine, and then for another hour watching it do much the same thing in a tumble dryer – it just seemed easier to pay someone to do it for me). Next on the list – a quick detour to a stationer's to purchase that elusive black marker pen that I had been desperately trying to track down for the past couple of days. As I strolled for a while along Berlin's famous Kurfürstendam, I happened upon the three-star Hotel Comet – not a terribly elegant looking building (it had all the charm and charisma of a multi-storey car park), but the reception area looked pleasant enough, and there were cheap rooms available, which made it instantly likeable. I headed straight to my room, kicked off my shoes, threw my rucksack into a corner and lay down on the bed. I was asleep in less than five minutes.

I woke a few hours later feeling thoroughly ashamed of myself. Berlin may not be my favourite European city, but to be here, in Germany's bustling capital surrounded by all its architectural splendour – well, it would have been shameful to spend my time sleeping. That, I decided, was precisely the way that Günter Schneider would be spending his day, and I wasn't prepared to lower myself to his level. So I showered, changed into a clean shirt and a fresh pair of undercrackers, and headed off into the sunshine for a long stroll through the city streets. My hotel on Kurfürstendam was some distance away from the city centre – several kilometres away in fact. But it was a pleasant afternoon – hazy sunshine through a thin layer of cloud, and it was warm enough to stroll through town in a short-sleeved shirt. All in all, the sort of conditions that Michael Fish might have described as 'a spell of quiet weather', whilst presenting the forecast in one of his loud shirts.

My four-hour stroll around Berlin's city centre took me along the *Straße des 17. Juni* (17th June Street) – one of the city's main thoroughfares running east-west through Berlin's famous Tiergarten, a large tract of urban forest / parkland to the west of the city. I joined the street at its western end, at *Ernst-Reuter Platz* in the suburb of Charlottenburg, and followed it all the way to its eastern extremity marked by that most iconic of Berlin's architectural landmarks, the Brandenburg Gate. The street was named *Straße des 17. Juni* to commemorate the uprising of the East Berliners on the 17th June 1953, when the brutal and ruthless GDR 'Volkspolizei' and the positively sadistic Russian Red Army shot and killed a huge number of insurgent industrial workers. Whether that's something worthy of commemorating is decidedly arguable. I would suggest not. But like so many of Berlin's idiosyncrasies, the street name remains – to serve as a reminder of Germany's troubled history – lest the people ever be allowed to put their past behind them and move on. Before 1953, the street was called *Charlottenburger Chaussee* – and was where Adolf Hitler staged his victory parade after his infamous 'inspection' of Paris in 1940. The street would then have been decorated along its entire length with flags bearing the swastika symbol and other assorted Nazi insignia. The Berlin Victory Column or S*iegessäule,* is located about

183

halfway along the main boulevard. But I'm pleased to say that it's not all doom and gloom. Today, the street is often used for major events such as 'Live 8' and the 'Love Parade'. In the summer of 2006 it was used as the '*Fanmeile*' (fan mile) for a period of six weeks during the 2006 Football World Cup – and every year, it serves as the starting point for the Berlin Marathon.

Nowadays, one can stroll freely through the Brandenburg Gate and continue along the boulevard into East Berlin. The street name changes though. As you pass through the gate you'll leave the *Straße des 17. Juni* behind you and continue along the aptly named '*Unter den Linden*', which I'll tell you a little more about in just a moment. But for twenty-eight years, from 1961 until that historic day on the 9th of November 1989, it wasn't possible to walk across this boundary – there was a wall in the way. Well, *two* actually – the wall was double-layered, with row after row of barbed wire in the stretch of 'no-man's-land' that sat between the two layers. This was known as 'the Kill Zone' – protected by GDR border guards who acted on strict instructions to shoot anybody attempting to cross the demarcation line, and were paid cash bonuses if their shots resulted in a fatality. The Berlin Wall was known in the Democratic Republic as the "Anti-Fascist Protective Rampart" (the Communist East remained convinced that Fascism was still alive and well in West Germany long after the wall was constructed). When the wall was built, families were split. East Berliners were cut off from their jobs and deprived of any chance of financial improvement, and of course, West Berlin became an isolated enclave in a hostile land. I found it quite chilling to cross this point – it was sobering to think that between August 13, 1961 and November 9, 1989, 171 people were killed or died whilst attempting to escape over the Berlin Wall.

Nowadays of course, the wall has gone and there are very few places where remnants of it still remain. But there are some: the East Side Gallery is one example, and Potsdamer Platz is another. But I chose to visit neither. It may have been a monument of extraordinary historical significance, but it's only a wall – and I've seen an awful lot of those in my lifetime. And the fact is that, wherever you wander in Berlin, you'll find souvenir shops selling what they claim are pieces of the Berlin Wall. Now, forgive me if I seem a little cynical, but it all sounds a bit like a scam to me. That said of course, if tourists in their thousands are gullible enough to fall for such a palpable con, then I suppose they get no more than they deserve. Did it ever occur to any of those naive fools as they were shelling out millions of euros for their own little piece of history, that the tiny fragment of concrete they now have taking pride of place on their mantelpiece might *not* be an authentic piece of the original Berlin Wall? Did any of them ever consider that maybe – just maybe – they were buying a lump of rock that could once have been a part of any old wall?

The last time the world was taken in by a scam as despicable as this one was during the months leading up to the turn of the 21st century – when the Information Technology (IT) industry managed to convince us all that at midnight on January 1st 2000, the world would come to a dramatic end. I refer of course to the fabled millennium bug – the greatest swindle of them all. Millennium Mug, more like. We were told that all the world's computers would suddenly cease to function and our global infrastructure would go into meltdown. At the stroke of midnight our nuclear power stations would switch off causing dangerous levels of pressure to build in their reactors; our gas and electricity supplies would fail; street lamps would cease to function and aeroplanes would suddenly fall from the sky. In short, the world would be facing Armageddon – total global destruction on an unprecedented scale; the end of the world as we knew it. But luckily for us, help was at hand – all this impending doom could be averted! Yes, there was hope for us all. If all the world's governments and global corporations were to employ the services of an IT expert to visit their headquarters and fiddle about a bit with their computer systems, then we'll all be saved. It would, of course, cost us hundreds of billions of dollars to pay for it all, and it's true to say that thousands of 'consultants' working in the IT industry would become overnight multi-millionaires as a coincidental side effect – but at least global annihilation would be averted and we'd all be saved from certain death. I can't believe we all fell for it. At the time, mankind had the technological capability of launching computer-programmed space probes on missions to other planets. We had the expertise to control them remotely once they landed on alien soil, program them to collect rock samples and bring them back to earth again using technology so advanced it would have rendered poor Albert Einstein completely befuddled. And yet, the IT industry claimed that they had no way of being able to tell what would happen to your electric razor when, at the stroke of midnight, the little electronic microchip inside it failed to understand the concept of a new millennium.

Anyway, I digress. Buying a piece of the Berlin Wall seemed to me to be a very foolhardy venture. Falling for a scam this obvious is, in my opinion at least, utter stupidity – especially if you're buying your bit of concrete from one of the 'unofficial' suppliers. You see, even the 'authentic' souvenirs are not all they claim to be. It is an open secret in Berlin souvenir shops that the coloured spray-paint on most chunks of the Wall is added in *Volker Pawlowski's* workshop – a company located in the city's northern district of Reinickendorf and the supplier of around 90 percent of the Wall pieces sold in Berlin. So you may be surprised when I tell you that, quite suddenly, and in a moment of weakness and of uncharacteristic impulse, I did something that even to this day I am still at a loss to explain. I stepped into one of the souvenir shops that was so brazenly cashing in on the fall of the iron curtain and I purchased a little piece of history of my own. For the princely sum of twelve euros, I bought a lump of concrete, probably picked up off the floor from a building site in Potsdam, spray-painted in Pawlowski's factory in North Berlin, and mounted on Fuzzy Felt in its own Perspex container with the words '*Authentische Berliner Mauer*' engraved on the lid. All of which proves beyond a shadow of doubt that I am just as gullible as the next man, and possibly even more so. I should probably apologise to the IT industry too, following that groundless and inexcusable outburst. We owe our lives to you guys, so on behalf of the whole of mankind and from the bottom of my heart – *thank you*. [25]

And so, I crossed through the Brandenburg Gate and wandered casually along another of Berlin's well-known thoroughfares – 'Unter den Linden' (literally 'Under the Lime Trees') which takes its name from the rows of trees that were first planted there in 1647. They were the brainchild of Duke Friedrich Wilhelm, also known as 'The Great Elector', who, incensed by the city's shabbiness and general squalor, decided to spruce things up a bit by planting long rows of Linden trees along the route between his castle home and the Tiergarten hunting ground – in an effort to make the path shadier and the journey more comfortable whenever he rode along it. Thus his carriage ride would literally take him "Unter den Linden". The lime trees that are lined up along either side of this picturesque avenue today are not the original ones planted by the Duke, of course. Trees have been dug up and replanted on numerous occasions, most recently in the 1950s when they were temporarily removed during

[25] *Tossers.*

construction of a section of the Berlin underground railway. I should also point out that the Duke didn't plant them all personally – I would imagine he had an army of landscape gardeners to do it for him – just in case you were wondering. My stroll 'under the lime trees' took me past a number of Berlin's grandest of edifices, including Humboldt University and the Berlin State Opera, and brought me eventually to the city's ultimate pièce de résistance – the Berliner Dom (Berlin Cathedral) – which has occupied this site in one form or another since the mid fifteenth century.

I stopped momentarily at a fast-food restaurant called '*Schnell*' (as in '*Schnell – fetch me a bucket!*'), where I decided to satiate my hunger pang with what I was led to believe was a burger with French fries. It was a mistake of course. With the benefit of hindsight I should have waited until my return to the Hotel Comet, and dined at the hotel's restaurant. It might have been a tad more expensive but the staff would have been more courteous and the food would have been fit for human consumption. The thing is, I hadn't eaten all day, and the sight of a fast-food restaurant seemed particularly alluring at the time – like a desert oasis, except nothing at all like a desert oasis. I scoffed my cardboard burger a little voraciously, and to slake a raging thirst (I had a few fries with my salt), I washed the whole thing down with a lukewarm coffee, served in a polystyrene cup.

With stomach churning, I continued my saunter around Berlin's bustling city centre until I stumbled by chance upon what is known as the 'Nicolaiviertal' or the Nicolai quarter. It covers a relatively small section of the city, and to be brutally honest is a bit of an oddity, since it appears to be something it isn't. At first glance, the area gives the impression of being a charming and tranquil backwater – a remnant of medieval Berlin that has somehow managed to survive the trials of history and escape the various traumatic events that have scarred the rest of the city so indelibly. But appearances can be deceptive. During the 2nd World War, the Allied bombers wrought their destruction in this part of the city as much as they did elsewhere, leaving much of Berlin in tatters. But whereas other parts were reconstructed to a more contemporary design, here the developers embarked on the recreation of 'Old-Berlin' – with narrow, cobbled alleyways and mock medieval houses. The area is crammed with touristy shops and chic boutiques, and was a pleasant place to stroll through. But the deception wasn't all that convincing in my opinion – it felt to me like something the Disney Corporation might have created.

After calling in at the laundrette to collect my now freshly laundered sleeping bag, I headed back to my hotel, switched on the TV and began pressing all the buttons on the remote control in an effort to find something that might have been remotely watchable. Among the usual diet of quiz shows, music videos and advertisements for motor insurance, I eventually hit upon an episode of *Midsomer Murders* (or '*Inspektor Barnaby*' as it's known in Germany), being aired on the ZDF Channel. It was dubbed into German of course, but that didn't bother me. The fact that I could only vaguely understand what was going on didn't spoil my enjoyment in the least, as it was an episode I'd already seen – the one where Barnaby and Troy dash to the manor to find a woman lying dead beside the swimming pool with a syringe in her stomach. I presume it was the stuff inside the syringe that killed her rather than the syringe itself – otherwise millions of people would be dying in doctors' surgeries and in hospitals every couple of seconds – and I for one wouldn't be visiting a dentist ever again. I left the television switched on with the sound turned down, and set about doing something I had been meaning to do for several days. I spread the flysheet of my *Wind-Breaker DeLuxe* over the small section of floor space between the wall and my bed, and with my black indelible marker pen I drew a box around the word '*Schwanz*', before colouring it in to leave a large, black, oblong-shaped splodge on the side of the canvas. I felt like a five-year-old child practising his colouring-in skills.

I woke early the following morning. I didn't intend to, but there are some mornings when your body clock decides it's time to wake up even through your aching muscles and your weary bones are telling you to stay asleep for a few hours longer. But you know what it's like when you're in that early morning half-conscious state and your brain is working in hyperdrive – you wake up thinking about all kinds of absurd nonsense. And this morning, my brain was giving due consideration to the wonderful world of culinary possibilities that had been opened up by the acquisition of my *Pocket Rocket* camping stove which I had purchased from the camp shop at *Natur-Camping Usedom.* A *Pocket Rocket* wasn't just about being able to make cups of tea or coffee whenever I wanted – it was the key to so much more. I could cook sausages, bacon and eggs. I could heat up tins of baked beans, ravioli or spaghetti hoops. The possibilities were endless – with just a little practice I could even try my hand at rustling up the occasional assiette de cochon de lait, gratin de navet, purée d'oignon et ail. I'd need a couple of pots and pans of course – neither of which would fit into my rucksack. But if it's not beyond the wit of mankind to put a man on the moon, then surely I could find a way of attaching a couple of pans to the side of my backpack using one of the plethora of straps, clips, buckles and toggles – the function of which I hadn't yet been able to decipher.

And so I headed down to the breakfast room to investigate the Hotel Comet's breakfast menu – the usual European spread of bread rolls, cold meats, cheeses, and strong coffee. In the end, I just settled for the Cornflakes. There was a notice on the wall asking guests not to remove food from the breakfast room, but I chose to ignore it – a few bread rolls and some slices of ham and cheese would be the perfect thing to take on the long train journey ahead of me. And so, with my ill-gotten gains wrapped in a paper napkin, I left the breakfast room and prepared to check out of the Hotel Comet.

oOo

Dear Diary,

The Beer, Cheese and Tent Report for the State of Berlin:

Beer: Berliner Bürgerbräu Rotkehlchen:

Bürgerbräu Rotkehlchen has a cloudy, light red colour and a generous head, which peters out to nothing as you reach the bottom of the glass. Not my favourite brew, I'll admit – it had a sweet, rather intense taste and was lacking in flavour.

Cheese: Rotschmierkäse:

Literally translated as 'red mould cheese', I was alarmed to learn that this particular Berlin delicacy hails from a family of cheeses often referred to as the 'the stickies and the smellies'. No doubt you can guess why – it has an overpowering aroma and a sticky texture. Don't be put off by the mould on the surface of Rotschmierkäse though. It may look utterly repugnant, but the taste is sublime.

Tent Stability:

I've nothing to report here, as I spent the night in a hotel and left the Wind-Breaker DeLuxe rolled up and discarded in a corner of my hotel room. However, I can report that the word 'Schwanz' is no longer visible beneath the splodge of black ink now plastered across the face of the flysheet – thanks to my astonishing creativity and ingenuity.

oOo

Chapter Nine – Coins and Thieves and Inveterate Escapees

"The Castle Aaaagh! Our quest is at an end! God be praised!"
King Arthur (Graham Chapman) – (to the sound of ethereal music) as he and the Knights of Camelot finally reach the Castle of Aaaagh in the 1974 film 'Monty Python and the Holy Grail'

As if German political geography isn't complicated enough, there are three (yes, three!) German states with the word *'Saxony'* in their name. To begin with, there's *Lower Saxony* – the first state I encountered on my tour around Germany and represented, as you'll recall, by my visit to Borkum Island. Next is *Saxony-Anhalt* – a former East German state of around two-and-a-half million people; famous for nothing that I can think of other than being home to the Harz Mountains. I would be heading there in a few days' time. Finally, there's just plain old *Saxony* – a small, triangular-shaped state to the far east of Germany, bordering both Poland and the Czech Republic.

There are three major cities within Saxony's borders: *Dresden* – famous for being virtually obliterated by incessant Allied bombing during the Second World War; *Chemnitz* – famous for not being called 'Chemnitz' for 37 years during its recent history (it was named *Karl Marx Stadt* between 1953

---

[26] *Actually, my statement about Leipzig being worth a lot of points in a game of Scrabble isn't true. Although the letter 'z' is worth 10 points in a game of Scrabble, the remaining letters are all relatively low-scoring, so 'Leipzig' would be worth only 19 points. As it happens, in the German version of the game, 'Leipzig' would be worth only 14 points, partly because the letter 'z' (more common in the German language than it is in English) scores only 4 points. Fervent Scrabble aficionados will have realised that this is all rather academic, given that the word 'Leipzig' (being a proper noun) wouldn't be acceptable under Scrabble rules anyway.*

and 1990 – after the founder of modern communism, of course. But the city had the good sense to revert to its original name once the iron curtain was taken down to allow a bit of sunshine back into the room); and *Leipzig*, famous for.....well, having a 'z' in its name and being worth lots of points in a game of Scrabble. [26]

But after my overnighter in Berlin, I had no intention of visiting a city, and although my stay at the Hotel Comet had been both pleasant and relaxing, I was eager to get back to the bucolic tranquillity of the countryside and the rustic simplicity of camping. So my destination this morning was the *Campingplatz am Waldbad* – a small campsite close to the Mulde River in the very heart of Saxony. My plan over the next couple of days was to visit a few castles – and one in particular which I'll reveal later. Now if, like me, you're a bit of an avid castle enthusiast, then Saxony is the place to come – the state is home to around 140 of them. And although forty years of communism resulted in many of the Democratic Republic's buildings falling into a state of disrepair, almost all her stately castles, palaces and fortresses have been generally well cared for. My chosen campsite was in the heart of '*Schlösserland Sachsen' (The Land of Castles in Saxony)* – and the perfect base for me to visit a few of them. Saxony may not be home to the country's most iconic castle (that accolade, I suspect, probably belongs to Bavaria's '*Schloss Neuschwanstein'* – the inspiration for Walt Disney's faux castle used on their corporate logo), but it does have some of the most fascinating and historically significant.

The nearest railway station to the Campingplatz am Waldbad is at *Grimma* – a small, unassuming little town about 35 kilometres east of Leipzig – although still a thirty-minute bus ride away from the campsite. So I set off early from the Hotel Comet and headed for Berlin's Hauptbahnhof – where my train, hopefully, would be waiting. It should have been a straightforward journey – a seventy-five-minute ride from Berlin to Leipzig; then a forty-minute hop from Leipzig to Grimma; culminating in a thirty-minute bus ride to the campsite. All in all, a journey from A to B in a little less than three hours, including waiting times for connecting trains and buses. But it wasn't, of course – it took considerably longer than that. The first part of the journey went swimmingly well – it was one of those 'ICE' trains – those sumptuous Inter-City Expresses that zip you from one place to the next in opulent comfort. But sadly, it was the second stage of the journey when everything went pear-shaped. Due to a late-running train from Leipzig, I missed my bus connection – resulting in a three-hour wait at Grimma. Those nice people at *Deutsche Bahn* were profusely apologetic of course – their apology delivered with all the remorse and sincerity that the recorded announcement could muster. But I'm afraid to say that Grimma isn't the sort of town you'd choose to linger in for any prolonged period of time – it's about as exciting as having your ears stapled to a tree. It's a town with a perfectly apt name – I can't remember visiting anywhere grimmer. So, with the prospect of spending the next three hours just simply killing time, I left Grimma's quaint little station and walked along Karl-Marx-Straße towards the river.

Across the whole of the former East Germany, most of the propagandist monuments to communism have been dismantled and subsequently destroyed. But there are a few that have managed to survive, intact, and I stumbled upon one such example during my stroll through Grimma. Mounted on a stone plinth in a small pedestrian square at the side of Leipziger-Straße is the *'Denkmal für die Opfer des Faschismus'* – (the 'Monument to the Victims of Fascism'). I felt it necessary to take a couple of snapshots on my camera before continuing on my way. As I strolled down the footpath that ran along the bank of the River Mulde, I came upon what I'm going to describe as a village hall – for no reason other than that it bore an uncanny resemblance to the village hall in my hometown. On the pavement outside was a free-standing blackboard – upon which the words '*Münzsammlung Auktion*' (coin collector's auction) had been hastily scribbled in white chalk. It didn't appear to be a private event – I couldn't see any notices suggesting that ordinary members of the public were barred from entering. So, satisfied that the doors of the village hall were open to any Tom, Dick, Harry, Fritz or Wolfgang, I wandered inside.

I should tell you here and now that at no point during my lifetime have I ever been a collector of coins – but for reasons that I am about to explain, I do have a scintilla of knowledge on the subject. My father, you see, was a numismatist. Now, before you conjure an image in your mind's eye of an elderly man wearing a white surgical coat, wheeling some complex-looking piece of medical equipment along a hospital corridor – I should point out that the word 'numismatist' has nothing whatsoever to do with the medical profession. It's just that whenever I've referred to my late father as being a numismatist, some people have simply made the assumption that he was some sort of doctor specialising in a particular discipline – so please forgive me if I've insulted your intelligence by suggesting that you may have made a similar supposition. In fact, *'numismatist'* is a rather sesquipedalian word meaning 'a collector of coins' – and my father was a particularly dedicated one. It was only after my father's death just a few years ago that I suddenly developed a cursory interest in the subject – an interest of a rather ephemeral nature, I admit (my brush with the bizarre world of numismatics was surprisingly short-lived). But following his death, I was faced with the task of disposing of his collection – an undertaking that would involve identifying every individual coin against its description or illustration in a catalogue, and determining its approximate value. And almost by accident, I couldn't help but pick up a little bit of numismatic knowledge along the way. So although my interest in coin collecting faded almost immediately after my father's collection went under the hammer, I decided I would revive it for an hour or so by wandering into the village hall and viewing the collection of coins and box sets that made up the lots and the multi-lots in today's auction. Of course, temporarily renewing my interest in numismatics that morning also came with one or two other added benefits: bidders could help themselves to as much free coffee as they could drink (and there was nobody there who was wise to the fact that I had no intention of bidding), and it helped to kill another hour or so whilst I waited for my bus.

My bus to the campsite pulled up outside Grimma railway station at the precise moment the timetable said it would, and the doors swung open, making the same pneumatic shushing noise as the automatic doors connecting the bridge to the engineering room corridor on the Starship Enterprise. [27] The bus was surprisingly empty, just me and one other passenger – an elderly lady with a tartan shopping trolley and an unfeasibly large amount of facial hair. She was mumbling to herself like a demented witch. I decided to sit as far away from her as I could, hoping that a few other passengers might board the bus before the driver closed the doors and pulled away from the bus stop. Nobody did – so I spent the entire thirty-minute journey staring inanely through the window and praying that the demented witch wouldn't make any attempt to engage me in conversation. So, I arrived at the Campingplatz am Waldbad much later than I'd originally intended thanks to Deutsche Bahn's inability to keep to their published timetable. But it

[27] *For those who have never seen an episode of Star Trek and are therefore oblivious to the noise made by the Starship's automatic doors – just imagine unscrewing the lid on a previously unopened bottle of tonic water, but prolonging the resulting sound for approximately three seconds.*

didn't matter. After my night at a hotel in the hustle and bustle of the city, it felt good to be camping once again in Germany's beautiful rural countryside. And there was something of a treat in store for me at the Campingplatz am Waldbad – a little camping shop selling everything the serious camper could wish for – including a fine selection of pots and saucepans. The saucepan I eventually settled on was a dinky little thing – ingeniously designed, with a nifty, detachable handle that retracted into the side of the pan after use. It was lightweight, had a slit in the handle so that I could attach it to the straps on my backpack, and it performed rather efficiently (as I was soon to discover) as a handy device for swatting wasps. Of course, it also performed rather well as a saucepan – as I discovered when I used it to heat up the *Knackwurst* which I also bought from the campsite shop. Knackwurst, by the way, is a short, plump, spicy sausage, commonly sold pre-cooked in hermetically sealed plastic packaging, and can be heated up by boiling in a saucepan of water. They're made from pork. At least I think it's pork. Actually, I dread to think what they might actually be made of, so let's just skip over that bit.

As my knackwurst gently simmered in the pan, I assembled my tent on a suitable patch of grass beneath the shade of a willow tree, before taking a few steps backwards to admire my handiwork. My *Wind-Breaker DeLuxe* looked magnificent as she stood there in the summer sunshine – like a photograph from a camping magazine. She leaned a bit, I admit (one of the central support poles was a tiny bit warped, causing my tent to list slightly to one side). Oh, and the tape I had used to cover the holes was beginning to come unstuck, so the tears in the canvas were visible once again. If anything, the rip in the canvas appeared to have widened since I last used the tent – and I noticed a couple of other patches further along the support pole where the canvas looked a little frayed and threadbare. And then, of course, there was this huge, unsightly oblong-shaped splodge painted on the side of my tent with a black marker pen, which didn't look terribly attractive at all. But other than those few trifling details, my tent was in pretty good shape. It was no oil painting, I'll admit, but she looked remarkably stable to me – and as a scrawny seventeen-year-old tent salesman with a ruddy complexion once told me – one should never underestimate the importance of tent stability.

The knackwurst went down very well with a couple of the bread rolls I still had left over from those I'd stolen from the breakfast room at the Hotel Comet. I suppose with hindsight it was foolish of me to heat all six sausages – so I ate a couple, and left the rest in the pan, which I tucked inside the tent away from the wasps and the flies and out of harm's way.

I mentioned earlier that during my brief stopover in the state of Saxony I intended to visit a few castles. Well, within easy reach of the Campingplatz am Waldbad there are *three* castles worthy of exploration. Two of them – Kriebstein Fortress and Rochlitz Castle – are a bus-ride away – so in view of the amount of travelling I had already done that day, I decided to leave them both until the following morning. But the third castle was just a short walk from the campsite.

Less than a kilometre from the Campingplatz am Waldbad lies a quaint and charming little hamlet, built on the banks of the River Mulde. It's quiet, unassuming and has a population of just five thousand. Yet it's a town that is known throughout the world – mainly because of the castle that has sat on top of a neighbouring hill, casting its shadow over the town since the early thirteenth century. The name of this town is *Colditz.*

The castle overlooking the town of Colditz has a 900-year-old history, and since it was originally constructed, has been burnt down, abandoned, bequeathed and twice rebuilt. The castle's function over the years has been remarkably varied – it's been used as a stately home, a hospital, an asylum for the mentally ill, a workhouse for the indigent and destitute, and in more recent years – a youth hostel. But Colditz Castle's most notorious function was, without doubt, its role during the Second World War, when it served as one of the Third Reich's most notorious prisoner of war camps. There were 172 'Stalag' and 'Oflag' camps holding prisoners of war in Germany and Poland during WW2, but Colditz Castle was generally regarded as the mother of them all.[28] Colditz, you see, was no ordinary POW camp, because the prisoners it housed were no ordinary prisoners. Colditz Castle was designed to accommodate what the Nazis referred to as 'incorrigible' prisoners – inveterate escapees. In other words, it housed allied officers who had repeatedly escaped from other camps and were therefore becoming something of an embarrassment for the Germans – a thorn in their side, so to speak. Colditz had another unique feature too – it housed POWs of different nationalities – not common practice in other POW camps. Polish officers were the first residents, followed by British, Canadian, Australian, New Zealander, Dutch, Belgian, and French. American officers were also imprisoned here towards the end of the war although in relatively small numbers. And the reason these 'incorrigible' prisoners were sent to Colditz as opposed to any other POW camp was perfectly simple – Colditz Castle was impregnable. Its hilltop location and its solid 'fortress' construction made it so. An abundance of armed guards on 24-hour surveillance duty made it doubly so. The perimeter walls, the watchtowers, the barbed wire and a whole host of other infallible security measures made it trebly so. There

[28] The term 'Stalag' was an abbreviation for 'Stammlager' (base camp) which housed enlisted personnel. 'Oflag' stood for 'Offizier-Lager' or Officer-Camp, as these were POW camps specifically for officers. The term 'Stalag-Luft' was applied to those POW camps housing Allied air crews, and were administered by the German Air Force (Luftwaffe).

was absolutely no point in trying to escape from Colditz – its walls were utterly impenetrable. Even Field Marshal Hermann Göring once declared that Colditz was "utterly escape-proof". It was a claim that turned out to be both audacious as well as alarmingly inaccurate. Between 1941 and 1944, 32 prisoners managed to achieve what the Nazis claimed was impossible – they all managed to escape from Colditz, and many of them made it all the way home.

The bravery and sheer ingenuity of the men who managed to escape is well documented, and I suppose is the reason why Colditz is renowned the world over. There have been more than one hundred books on the subject, published in a multitude of languages and distributed throughout the world – arguably the most famous of which is 'The Colditz Story' by Major Pat Reid – the celebrated British Colditz escapee. But if, like me, you haven't read any of the books, then I'm guessing you've probably seen something 'Colditz-related' on the telly. The BBC made a drama series in the early 1970s which, coincidently, employed the services of Major Reid as a technical consultant. If you're old enough to be able to cast your memory back that far, then you may recall the programme starring Robert Wagner and David McCullum (the original man from U.N.C.L.E.), along with a veritable 'Who's Who?' of thespian heavyweights. Two series of the programme were made, with 28 episodes aired on our TV screens over a two-year period. But if you're way too young to remember the 1970s, then perhaps you'll recall the Channel 4 three-part drama series 'Escape from Colditz', aired in 2006. It starred Damian Lewis and Timothy West and was made into a film shortly after its premier on national television. I remember watching this film – it seemed to go on longer than World War II.

But my favourite tribute to those brave and daring young men who managed to escape while incarcerated at this most infamous of POW camps, has to be 'Escape from

Colditz' – the board game! Yes, there was a board game. It was manufactured by *Parker Games* and if my memory serves was first produced in the 1970s and featured a swastika on the lid of the box. I'll say that again – there was a swastika on the lid of the box. I think there might have been an illustration of Colditz Castle too, but one's attention was very much drawn to the swastika. In later editions of the game, Parker Games replaced the swastika with the German 'eagle' emblem, which was deemed as being more politically acceptable. The thing is, we didn't have political correctness in the 1970s – we just said what we thought and did what we wanted – without giving a moment's consideration as to whether we were causing any offence. I remember playing 'Escape from Colditz' with my friends when I was a child. One player took the part of the German guard, whilst the others played 'Escape Officers' – responsible for organizing escape attempts by their team of prisoners. The escaping officers had 'opportunity' cards to help them on their way – which gave them access to a key, a rope and a wire cutter. But I always preferred being the German guard. Their 'security' cards were far more menacing – they enabled you to detect tunnels or arrest anyone you found hiding under the floorboards. You could even *'shoot to kill'!* What could possibly be more exciting than that? 'Escape from Colditz' was so politically incorrect, I'm surprised there wasn't an 'opportunity' card bearing the instruction 'Shoot a German – go forward three spaces'. You can't buy 'Escape from Colditz' any more – not even a version *without* a swastika on the lid. I can't imagine why not.

Anyway, enough of this babble. I had a tour of a castle to cross off my 'to do' list and time was pressing on. The castle was the first thing I spotted when I reached Colditz. This imposing fortress dominates the skyline and is visible from every vantage point in the town. It's painted in a sickly off-white colour which makes it rather eye-catching if not a little sinister. In view of the substantial size of Colditz Castle – its numerous rooms, its bewildering labyrinth of corridors – I decided not to explore the castle on my own, but chose instead to pay a few extra euros for the English-speaking tour, and be whisked around the building by the beautiful and vivacious Steffi. Steffi was, without doubt, the consummate professional – one of the most knowledgeable and enthusiastic tour guides I have ever had the pleasure of following around a castle. Her English was impeccable, her historical knowledge seemingly boundless, and she had an extraordinary ability to wander off-script at a moment's notice whenever circumstances demanded that she should.

I visited the famous Neuschwanstein Castle in Bavaria a few years ago, and was disappointed by the official castle tour. It was hurried and decidedly unedifying – I was rushed in and out in twenty minutes flat. Not so here at Colditz. Steffi took us to every part of the building – around every room and into every nook and cranny – recounting tales of prison life, the camaraderie among the inmates and the German guards, and providing animated accounts of the most audacious and inventive escape attempts imaginable. Some of them were so ingenious they simply defied belief. She talked us through many of the castle's artefacts; she showed us the tunnels that the prisoners constructed (a network so elaborate they could feasibly have been used as part of the Leipzig U-Bahn system), the copied maps, the forged papers, even the partially-constructed glider in a remote corner of the castle which a group of the more resourceful prisoners began building during the latter stages of WW2. The glider was never used in any fanciful escape attempt – the war came to an end and Colditz Castle was liberated by American troops before the glider's construction was completed. But in addition to her many affable qualities, Steffi also had the patience of a saint. Now, I fully accept that everybody, myself included, has the right to ask a stupid question every once in a while. But there was one member of our tour party (a short, fat Australian tourist with sideburns that haven't been fashionable since the 1950s) who was seriously abusing the privilege. Some of the questions he asked Steffi were ridiculous, some completely absurd, and others just downright bizarre. *'Did the German Guards and the British Officers use the same toilets?' 'Were prisoners issued with their own mugs?'* But the steadfast Steffi retained her stoicism admirably, and simply answered his questions as best she could. I was impressed that she was able to maintain her civility and her professionalism – there were others in the tour group who were noticeably irritated by the man's ceaseless, nonsensical questions.

It was dusk by the time I returned to the campsite. I'd lingered a little longer in Colditz Castle than I'd originally planned to – largely due to Steffi's fascinating and informative interpretation of the castle's historical heritage. I'd also stopped at a quaint little restaurant in Colditz town – the *Schlosscafé* – to satiate another of those hunger pangs and to sample a couple of glasses of *Radeberger Bier* – brewed in Dresden and served at the Schlosscafé both ice-cold and on draught. As I approached the spot where my tent was pitched I discovered I was not alone. Sniffing around my tent was a fox, which I later discovered was a European red fox, apparently the largest of the *vulpes vulpes* family and officially one of the 'world's 100 worst invasive species'. (That particular snippet of enlightenment was provided by Klaus – but we'll come back to him in just a moment.) Of course I didn't know *that* at the time – it was just a shadowy figure skulking around in the half-light. I didn't even realise it was a fox. And when I did eventually recognise it as such, I certainly wouldn't have been able to identify the species.

Now as far as I'm aware, foxes are generally of a timorous disposition and rather fearful of humans. They usually run away if they spot somebody approaching. But the smell of sausages, it would seem, can change the course of nature – it can, at a stroke, alter the inherent equilibrium in the planet's ecological system, effectively altering the intrinsic behavioural pattern of an entire animal species. This particular fox had a fondness for knackwurst and wasn't about to let my presence deter him from getting what he came for. With just a couple of metres between us, I stood perfectly still and stared into the fox's eyes. The fox stood perfectly still too and stared back. For what seemed like an eternity (although was probably no more than a few seconds in reality) the two of us were locked in an intense staring competition – both of us resolutely determined not to be the first to blink. I won of course – the fox bottled out when he realised how fierce his competition was. The creature turned his back on me and walked away nonchalantly, in a manner that was both offhand and blasé. It was the vulpine equivalent of sticking two fingers up at me as he wandered off into the nearby woods.

Klaus, as you may have guessed, was a fellow camper who approached me almost as soon as the fox had disappeared from view. He turned out to be something of an expert on foxes (anybody more knowledgeable than I on any given subject makes them an expert, in my book), as was evidenced from his opening gambit.

"That was a European red fox," he said. Actually, he said it in German, but reverted to English just as soon as he became aware that I wasn't a native German speaker.

"Did you know that the European red is the largest of the family of foxes, and is officially listed as one of the world's 100 worst invasive species?" he asked. I didn't of course, but I feigned interest rather convincingly.

"I'm Klaus," he said, offering me a handshake.

"Chris," I replied.

"Well Chris, I've been watching the fox sniffing around the campsite for the last half-an-hour or so. He seemed particularly interested in *your* tent. Is there some food inside perhaps?"

"Yes – I have some knackwurst in a pan. I suppose the fox must have smelled them."

"Of course," replied Klaus rather matter-of-factly. "Foxes have a very acute sense of smell – and knackwurst has a particularly pungent aroma. If you're not going to eat your sausages then you should throw them away."

I didn't like the way Klaus said that – it sounded rather dogmatic and dictatorial. Who the heck did he think he was, telling me what I should or shouldn't do with my sausages? As it happened, I fully intended to eat them. But not right now – I had been planning to heat them up again on my return from visiting the castles at Kriebstein and Rochlitz the following day. I certainly had no intention of throwing them away. With millions of children in the world on the brink of starvation, consigning my uneaten knackwurst into a bin would have been wholly indefensible.

"I'll bear that in mind," I said.

As soon as Klaus had gone, I carefully placed my four remaining sausages back into their original plastic packaging, wrapped the whole thing up in aluminium foil, and, for good measure, placed the resulting silver package into a Lidl carrier bag. Triple protection against foraging foxes or any other scavengers with a nose for knackwurst.

I woke the following morning to the gratifying sound of birdsong, a turquoise sky and a grassy campsite covered with a delicate sprinkling of early-morning dew. It was one of those mornings that make you feel glad to be alive. So I filled up the kettle with water from the nearest supply tap, fired up the *Pocket Rocket* and set about making the tea. The wonderful thing about travelling is that there are always new things waiting to be discovered. I made two discoveries that morning. Firstly, I discovered that the lavatories in the toilet block at Campingplatz am Waldbad flushed in E-flat. I discovered this in much the same way as Vespucci discovered the Americas – it was all rather accidental. As I stood in one of the toilet cubicles shaking hands with the president, I began humming Ian Dury's *Billericay Dickie,* for no reason other than I woke up with that particular tune in my head. And as I pulled the handle to flush, the sound that resonated from the toilet cistern was attuned perfectly with the note I just happened to be humming. Yes, the toilet cistern and I were humming *Blockheads'* songs together in perfect harmony.

My second discovery (which happened just moments after the revelation of finding a toilet that flushed in E-flat) was that the showers in the campsite shower block didn't work. When I say they didn't work, I should perhaps offer a little more clarity. There was nothing wrong with the functionality of the shower as such – when you turned the tap on, water came gushing from the shower rose in torrents. But the water was cold – freezing cold – colder than an ice-maiden's tits in a brass brassiere. And despite my efforts to twist every knob and fiddle with every dial, I couldn't get the water to run hot. I suppose it was the campsite's way of discouraging campers from spending too long in the showers. Still, it was invigorating if nothing else.

My plan for the day was a complex affair – I would visit the castles at Kriebstein and Rochlitz – another two of the 'must-see' recommendations in my *Schlösserland Sachsen* guidebook. Now, under normal circumstances, visiting a couple of castles wouldn't be a complicated matter. But here's the thing: the town of Rochlitz lies about 12 kilometres to the south of Colditz, and Kriebstein around 24 kilometres to the south-east. There are no trains connecting any of these places so I would be relying on local bus services to take me from Colditz to Kriebstein, then on to Rochlitz, and finally from Rochlitz back to Colditz – all in all, a journey of around 56 kilometres. Now, I appreciate that 56 kilometres doesn't sound like an awfully long journey (one could cover such a distance in around thirty minutes in a Ford Mondeo on a UK motorway without breaking any national speed limits, or in a little under eleven minutes going flat-out in a Porsche 911-Turbo on a German autobahn – also without breaking any national speed limits). But the roads in *Schlösserland Sachsen* are not motorways – not by any stretch of the imagination. They are little narrow country lanes that provide lifelines for small rural communities living in chocolate-box villages. The villages are served by a network of local bus services that operate 'infrequently' to put it mildly. Travelling just a few kilometres from one sleepy little village to the next may involve changing buses more than once and having to wait an eternity for a connecting conveyance. My circular route from Colditz via Kriebstein and Rochlitz would involve spending the best part of six hours either travelling on a bus or waiting for one to come along. But that didn't bother me – travelling was all part of the adventure, and besides, the journey would be broken every couple of hours by a pleasant stroll around a medieval castle. And so, with a feeling of renewed vigour, fully refreshed after my cold shower and still humming *Billericay Dickie*, I left the Campingplatz am Waldbad and headed back into Colditz town to wait for the first of many buses.

The castle at Kriebstein (or Burg Kriebstein, as it's called in German) has a history dating back to 1384 and is generally regarded as one of Saxony's best preserved palaces. Whereas other historic buildings have been ransacked and pillaged over the centuries, Burg Kriebstein has somehow managed to stay out of the firing line, which I guess is why it appears in such pristine condition today. The castle is located on a high cliff and so dominates the surrounding area from its elevated position. There's a basement chapel here which my guidebook particularly recommended. The chapel houses a collection of elaborate and ornate frescoes which have been preserved perfectly over the centuries. I toured the castle for a couple of hours, exploring as much of it as my time here would allow. But it was one of those days where my freedom to do as I pleased was impeded by my travelling arrangements. My day was governed by timetables and connection times – and although I would have preferred to stay at Kriebstein a while longer, there was a bus waiting outside the castle gates that wouldn't be waiting very much longer.

Schloss Rochlitz – my next port of call – is located high above the valley of the Mulde River, and was first mentioned in documents dating back to 995. The palace has served as the residence of Saxon royalty on numerous occasions over the centuries, and is an impressive piece of medieval structural design – presenting a host of architectural surprises. The building is flanked by two huge towers known as 'Jupen', which house a number of rooms including the now reconstructed warder's rooms. I paid just €2,50 to enter Rochlitz Castle – a bargain given everything there is to see here and the sheer number of exhibits on display. There's a torture chamber, with iron bars and racks still fixed to the wall. Also on display is the 'Dark Hole' – an underground chamber where prisoners were denied access to natural daylight. Food and water were simply lowered into the recess beneath the stone floor using a rope. Other than its function as a royal palace, the castle has been used more recently as a prison, a Third Reich stronghold and, under the DDR government, even a kindergarten. I'm not sure how comfortable I would have been sending my kids to a state-run kindergarten that had a dungeon, a torture chamber and its very own 'dark hole'. But in my opinion, the best bit about Rochlitz Castle is the spectacular panoramic vista of the surrounding countryside. I stood for a while on top of one of the castle's towers just simply admiring the view – the perfect tonic to prepare oneself for the two-hour bus journey back to Colditz.

When I returned to the campsite in the early evening I discovered that my tent had been virtually destroyed. Tent poles designed to stand perpendicular in support of the main frame were lying horizontally on the ground. Others were buckled and misshapen. The canvas was spread across the grass like a used parachute, and tent pegs with the guide ropes still fastened to them, had been ripped out of the ground. It was as if an armour-plated military assault vehicle had ridden roughshod over my *Wind-Breaker DeLuxe* – more or less destroying it in the process and leaving carnage in its wake. I was staring at the detritus of a small war. Scattered around the debris (and blowing around in the breeze) were small shreds of polythene bag and strips of aluminium foil. As I stood there staring incredulously at the carnage, Klaus crept up behind me and tapped me on the shoulder, scaring me half to death.

"You had another visit from the fox," he said – a statement of the blindingly obvious, in my opinion.

"Yes," I replied "It would appear so. Just look at the mess it's left behind!"

Klaus nodded in agreement as he surveyed the chaos around him.

"Yes I know," he said eventually. "I saw the fox sniffing around your tent again and I watched him tear it to pieces."

For a moment I was dumbstruck. Had Klaus just said that he *watched* the fox tear my tent to pieces? Or had his phraseology simply been lost in translation? If Klaus really had stood by and watched idly as a fox destroyed my tent, then that would have been 'unhelpful' of him – to say the very least.

"Sorry – did you say you *watched* the fox destroy my tent?" I asked.

"Yes."

"And you didn't scare him away or do anything to prevent him from wrecking it?"

"No. Why would I do *that*?"

"Well, because....." I was completely nonplussed. So incensed, I couldn't even finish the sentence.

"The fox was merely doing what foxes instinctively do," he continued rather emphatically. "He was scavenging for food and he found some in your tent. One cannot, indeed *should not* interfere with the natural cycle of nature. Besides, you said you were going to throw the knackwursts away."

"I *didn't* say that!" I expostulated. "I wrapped them up in aluminium foil."

Klaus shook his head slowly and despairingly.

"Wrapping them in foil is no deterrent for a fox," he said. "A fox has a heightened sense of smell and it can rip through packaging with its razor-sharp teeth very easily. Aluminium foil doesn't make a fox's fillings tingle, you know."

I recognised the sarcasm immediately although I didn't appreciate it. Unhelpful *and* sarcastic? That's borderline criminal in my book. Klaus walked away, leaving me to rebuild my tent as best I could from the tousled remains – and trust me, it isn't easy trying to reassemble a tent using components that have been gnarled and contorted by a pack of ferocious wolves. OK, so they weren't wolves – they were foxes – and there wasn't a pack of them either – there was only the one. And yes, OK, so it wasn't all that ferocious either – in fact it was actually rather placid. But to say that my tent had been destroyed by a pack of ferocious wolves sounds so much more dramatic than 'my tent had been destroyed by a placid fox'. So, I've decided that my next paragraph will open with the phrase: '*After reassembling my tent following its destruction by a pack of ferocious wolves*' –

in the interests of dramatic effect and regardless of what the truth may be.

After reassembling my tent following its destruction by a pack of ferocious wolves, I studied its profile very carefully – and I think it would be fair to say that it was a complete and utter mess. It had never been a terribly attractive-looking tent – I already knew *that* – I'd learned to live with its ugliness some time ago. The poles were bent, the canvas torn and the sticky tape was gradually peeling away. And then there was that hideous black ink splodge of course. All of these things contributed to the tent's general unsightliness, but until now, none had bothered me. But for the first time on the trip so far, I was suddenly beginning to question her ability to function properly as a tent. The truth of the matter was that she simply didn't look all that stable. There, I said it. I found it painful to admit that. It wasn't that I was in denial – I knew my tent was a wreck and I'd become increasingly aware of this ever since I bought it. The reason I found it so painful to admit was because by doing so, I had been forced to concede that Gary might have been right all along. And *that* didn't sit comfortably with me at all. In my mind's eye I could picture Gary standing in the camping shop, dressed in his garish tangerine-coloured overalls and wearing his ridiculous girly ponytail – lecturing me about the folly of buying a cheap, lightweight tent that would more than likely blow away if I were to experience anything stronger than a gentle breeze during my trip around Germany. And I remember how I sneered when he advised me to spend three hundred quid on something more durable; baulked at the very suggestion that 'strength and stability' were more important than 'lightweight and portable'. Well, it turns out he may well have been right. That scrawny, acne-ridden, rude, obnoxious little upstart, with his wispy stubble and piercings through his ears and eyebrows – may have been bloody well right! Maybe he wasn't the dickhead I'd thought he was.

But then again......

As I stood there, perusing the damage to my *Wind-Breaker DeLuxe,* it occurred to me that perhaps her wounds weren't all that serious after all. Maybe the damage was relatively superficial. There were holes in the canvas, I admit – some of them recent contributions made by the local wildlife. But holes could be patched up couldn't they? I could buy another roll of waterproof duct tape to replace the pieces that were peeling away, and use the rest to cover the gaps and strengthen the seams where the material was fraying or threadbare. As for the bent tent poles, well, surely they were repairable. That's the great thing about cheap tent poles: they're made of light, pliable materials. Yes, they bend out of shape fairly easily. But there's a well known proverb that states *'tent poles that bend out of shape fairly easily can be bent back into shape again with the minimum of effort'.*[29] In fact, I'm fairly certain that Obi-Wan Kenobi imparted exactly that advice to Luke Skywalker, just before Luke set off to fight his battles against the Galactic Empire. [30]

And so I made a resolution. The following day – as soon as I arrived at the campsite at *Domäne Stiege,* I would dedicate some of my time to repairing the tent. I'd sleep in it tonight in its present condition, but tomorrow night, following comprehensive repairs and servicing, my *Wind-Breaker DeLuxe* would be every bit as good as a brand new tent. So yes, Gary – you *are* still a dickhead.

oOo

[29] *Well known only in parts of the small village of Oue'a Tadjoura in Djibouti.*

[30] *I may be wrong about that.*

Dear Diary,

The Beer, Cheese and Tent Report for the State of Saxony:

Beer: Radeberger:

Radeberger is a crystal-clear pilsner beer with a white, foamy cap. It has a moderate bitterness that was ever present although never overpowering. It has a very nice texture and is easy to drink.

Cheese: Altenburger Ziegenkäse (PDO):

Ziegenkäse translates literally as 'goat's cheese', but actually, it's made from a combination of goats' and cows' milk. Ziegenkäse has a Protected Designation of Origin (PDO), and as such, can only be produced at two dairies in Saxony, although during the time of the German Democratic Republic (former East Germany), very little of this type of cheese was produced at either of these locations. Since reunification, this once rare cheese is now available all over the country.

Tent Stability:

After a brief moment of despondency – when I began to lose faith in my Wind-Breaker DeLuxe following an incident involving a pack of ferocious wolves – I am delighted to report that my faithful tent will be undergoing some essential repairs during the next 24 hours and I fully expect her to look and feel like a new tent thereafter. She's looking a little rough around the edges at the moment though – as indeed am I.

oOo

Chapter Ten – Cowboys and Camembert

"A cowboy is a man with guts and a horse."
William James 1842 – 1910 (American philosopher and
psychologist, leader of the philosophical movement of
pragmatism)

Along with hundreds of other spectators, I stood at the side of the street and waited. It was another of those blistering hot days, so I'd taken appropriate precautions to protect the top of my head from the damaging effects of the sunshine – by donning a white baseball cap with the words *'Ich liebe Berlin'* emblazoned across the brim. Naturally, this hadn't been my preferred choice of headwear – particularly as *'Ich liebe Berlin'* was hardly a factual statement. But the man in the kiosk who was selling the sunhats was doing a roaring trade in the sweltering heat of the midday sun, and this hat was the best of what was left of his rapidly-depleting stock. It was either *that* or a green confederate slouch hat with a pink ribbon trailing around the rim. The man in the kiosk said the slouch hat suited me better than the baseball cap – it made me look dignified and venerable. But with a price tag of €40 he *would* say that, wouldn't he? So I settled on the baseball cap – and regardless of the fact that I didn't love Berlin – not even just a tiny bit – the hat did at least serve a useful purpose protecting me from sunstroke – so naturally, the ever-widening bald patch on the top of my head was suitably appreciative.

The street itself was unusual – bereft of traffic, and paved with sawdust and the occasional smattering of horse dung. There were no cars of course. How could there be? We were supposed to be 1875 and development of the internal combustion engine would still have been in its infancy. But the dung and the water troughs provided suitable clues as to the nature of the four-legged transportation employed by the citizenry of this extraordinary place – and that lingering horsy smell that filled the air was also something of a giveaway.

Lining both sides of the street were rows of buildings – constructed mainly from timber and, in my opinion, looking distinctly shabby – rather hurriedly and crudely assembled. I glanced along the row of buildings on the opposite side of the street – there was a barber's shop offering a 'gentleman's shave' for just two cents, an undertaker's parlour and a 'Wild West' saloon with its inevitable veranda, its hitching posts for tethering horses and its obligatory slatted wooden swing doors. Further along the street – the Sheriff's office, which doubled up as the county jail – and it was on *this* building in particular that most of the spectators' eyes were focused. Right on cue, the door of the jailhouse swung open and the Sheriff with his posse of lawmen came swaggering out. There were nine in all – each one squinting as they emerged from the shadowy interior of the faux jailhouse and into the blinding sunshine outside. Dressed in their cowboy apparel – the chequered rodeo shirts, the denim jeans, waist holsters, leather boots and Stetsons – they sauntered along the road towards the saloon, to the spot where most of us expectant observers had gathered. With his badge glistening in the summer sunshine, the Sheriff stopped dead in his tracks and, along with the others in his posse, fixed his gaze towards the far end of the dusty road – awaiting the imminent arrival of 'Wild' Willy Smith.

'Wild' Willy Smith, it transpired, was the most hunted outlaw in the Wild West. There were 'wanted' posters of his ugly mug everywhere – some offering a $10 reward for information leading to his arrest. Smith and his band of desperados were wanted by the County Sheriff on charges of gun slinging, cattle rustling and robbing a stagecoach at gunpoint. Through a series of strategically located loud speakers, the commentator told the excited crowd that Smith

216

and his men had 'moseyed' into town on the previous day and had 'caused mayhem during a raucous evening of whisky drinking, cheating in poker games and molesting dancing girls'. And now (and I suppose, understandably so), the townsfolk wanted them gone. It was the Sheriff's job to make sure that happened. Yes, the crowds had gathered here to witness a showdown – a staged performance which would inevitably result in good triumphing over evil – a little piece of theatre where 'Wild' Willy Smith would be thrown into jail and his band of villainous associates driven out of town.

From a point somewhere in the distance came the sound of horses' hooves. At first we saw just red dust kicked up by the horses from the unpaved surface of the road – then the silhouettes of 'Wild' Willy Smith and his two associates came into view – all three on horseback and looking dapper in their cowboy finery. Their horses slowed to a canter before stopping a few metres short of where the Sheriff and his men were waiting. 'Wild' Willy Smith turned towards the crowd and sneered. The crowd booed in response – many of the younger children rather enthusiastically.

I was hoping to witness a gunfight – but I knew such a thing wasn't going to happen. Not here. Not in Pullman City. *Nobody* gets shot in Pullman City – there was a notice at the main entrance making *that* perfectly clear. The Pullman City 'Wild West' theme park doesn't advocate violence of any kind. So the guns remained in the cowboys' holsters and 'Wild' Willy Smith – outnumbered by the Sheriff's posse to the tune of three to one – gave himself up following a momentary stand-off and a brief exchange of words with the Sheriff. Smith's duo of henchmen was driven out of town without a single shot being fired. The crowd applauded – well, most of them did. Personally, I was disappointed that

217

nobody had been shot, and, judging from the expressions on the faces of some of the children, I wasn't the only one.

Pullman City Harz is Germany's only 'Wild West' theme park – set in 100,000 square metres of woodland in the heart of the eastern Harz Mountains National Park in the state of Saxony-Anhalt. Pullman City is the self-proclaimed 'Home of Cowboys and Country Music' – according to its publicity brochures anyway. That's a fallacious claim in my opinion – I would have thought that Nashville, Tennessee has a more cogent argument, at least in its claim to be the true home of country music. But I am clearly misguided, or so it would seem. Pullman City Harz is *indeed* the ancestral home of cowboys *and* country music and that's that – there's another sign above the main entrance to the park to prove it.

On the face of it, a Wild West theme park seems like a very laudable concept, and this one appeared to be a popular venue, particularly with families with younger children. It's true to say that Pullman City has much on offer that will draw the crowds and keep the children entertained. There's Buffalo Bill's 'Wild West' show, starring around 50 participating performers from the theme park's 'cast'. The hour-long show tells the story of Buffalo Bill Cody; how the first 'Wild West' settlers lived and the great cattle treks across America's 'dusty plains'. There are cowboys and Indians riding through the streets and there's a bizarre re-enactment of the Civil War where nobody gets killed or wounded. There are stagecoach rides for the kids, horse riding lessons, demonstrations of Native American handicrafts and a museum offering an insight into the history of American colonisation. There's even an exhibit called the '*Klondike Camp Gold Rush*' – where families can wade knee-deep in mud whilst panning for gold.

But despite all its attractions, I found Pullman City Harz to be really rather twee – and more worrying still – there was something about it that, for me, simply didn't work. The park's anti-violence policy was estimable, I suppose – I guess it makes sense not to advocate violence with so many younger children watching the stage shows. But this is a 'Wild West' theme park – and life in the Wild West in the 1870s was fraught with danger, wasn't it? How is it possible to perform an authentic re-enactment of the American Civil War without any firearms being discharged? How is it feasible to stage a credible or convincing re-enactment of a stagecoach being ambushed by a Red Indian tribe without a single arrow being fired? The most wanted outlaw in the land wouldn't have simply turned himself in to the Sheriff – there would surely have been a gunfight first – a battle of nerve between two arch-enemies to establish who was quicker on the draw. And isn't *that* what kids *really* want to see? The authenticity was further tarnished by the fact that at least two of the Red Indian tribesmen were wearing Seiko wristwatches, and I spotted another two smoking Marlboro cigarettes behind the Pullman City General Stores during one of the breaks between performances. The restaurant didn't impress me either. '*Authentische Wild-West Küche*', the menu declared (authentic Wild West cuisine). Now, I don't claim to be an expert in the culinary preferences of cowboys back in the mid nineteenth century, but I'm pretty sure that Currywurst, Pretzel and Sauerkraut wouldn't have featured predominantly in their day-to-day diet. But then again, what do I know? If the marketing bods at Pullman City Harz say it was so, then who am I to argue?

I can't pretend to have been particularly enamoured with Pullman City. It was an interesting concept, I admit – and to its credit it *did* represent good value for money. For just €13 I could have stayed in the park all day if I'd had either the will or the stamina to do so. Of course whether anyone would really *want* to stay in Pullman City for an entire day is a thumping good question. The thought of having to listen to that 'Pullman City' signature tune blasting through the public address system over and over again is enough to justify cutting your visit short.

I hadn't planned to visit a Wild West theme park you understand – I didn't even know it was there. I simply stumbled upon it when I arrived in the Harz Mountains and decided that it might provide an entertaining way to while away the rest of the afternoon. I'd left the campsite at Colditz at around eight o'clock that morning and began the arduous six-hour journey to the Harz Mountains National Park – a journey that took me out of Saxony and into state number nine – the neighbouring province of Saxony-Anhalt. Like all my journeys through the former Democratic Republic, this one was fragmented and multifaceted – a combination once again of buses, trains, and long periods of waiting around for onward connections. So much so, that during a lengthy wait for a train connection from Halle to Nordhausen, I had enough time to explore Halle's main shopping centre – and it was here that I made a lucky discovery.

There was a small camping shop in Halle – suppliers of everything imaginable for the discerning camper. I must admit I was sorely tempted to add to my growing complement of kitchen equipment. I already had a pocket-sized stove, a tin mug, a kettle and a saucepan – but for just a handful of euros, I could have been the proud owner of a Highlander folding toaster and a non-stick frying pan. I resisted temptation despite the efforts of the little pocket-sized devil that was sitting on my shoulder and shouting in my ear '*buy them you idiot – you could be having fried eggs on toast in the morning!*' I did make a few purchases though. As promised, I bought a replacement tent pole kit, a new set of alloy tent pegs, a twelve-metre length of luminous green

---

[31] *A wonderful piece of alliterative verse is that – hats off to the marketing chaps for naming their product 'McNett Seamsure Seam Sealer'. Try repeating that over and over after a couple of Jäger-bombs.*

guy line (I opted for luminous green to prevent me from tripping over it again during a mission to find the toilets in the middle of the night), a roll of waterproof duct tape and a 60-millilitre bottle of 'McNett Seamsure Seam Sealer'. [31] Major repairs to my *Wind-Breaker DeLuxe* would begin the moment I reached the campsite at *Domäne Stiege*, I decided. Of course, it didn't quite work out that way. As soon as I arrived at the station at *Hasselfeld* in the Harz Mountains National Park, I stumbled upon the Pullman City Wild West theme park – so restoring my tent to its former glory was subject to an unforeseen delay. It was the final stage of my journey that was the most memorable. The ninety-minute hop from *Nordhausen* to *Hasselfeld* was incorporated into the price of the DB rail fare, but ran along railway tracks not officially part of the Deutsche Bahn network. The route is part of the *Harzer Schmalspurbahn (the Harz Narrow Gauge Railway)* – and is operated by locomotives powered by steam.

By the time I reached the campsite at *Domäne Stiege* it was getting late. I'd spent the best part of six hours sitting on buses and trains and my impromptu detour to Pullman City had eaten away another three or four hours of the day. So when I eventually arrived at the campsite, I was exhausted. I had promised myself earlier in the day that I'd make the necessary repairs to my *Wind-Breaker DeLuxe* as soon as I reached the camp, but to be brutally honest, that flame of enthusiasm was beginning to flicker a little. But the job urgently needed doing, and since that beautiful clear blue sky from earlier had now given way to some rather ominous cloud cover, I decided that these essential repairs couldn't be postponed any longer. So I set about the task with as much gusto as my energy levels would permit. I threw away the old guy lines and replaced them with the luminous green ones that were twice the thickness and considerably stronger. Any poles that were buckled or warped were also consigned to the bin and substituted for nice shiny new ones. I tore off those pieces of sticky tape too – the ones that were peeling away, and I patched up the rips and the tears using my new roll of waterproof duct tape. I even treated the frayed seams in the canvas with my newly acquired tube of *McNett Seamsure Seam Sealer* – although I have no idea whether I applied it correctly, given that the instructions for use were in Lithuanian. Repairs were halted temporarily at the halfway stage – I desperately needed a pee. But I also took the opportunity to nip into the campsite shop and purchase a few ice-cold cans of *Lüdde Pils* to see me through the second half.

The ground at *Domäne Stiege* was 'firm', to say the least, and I had a spot of trouble driving some of the tent pegs all the way home. But as luck would have it, one of the German lads in a neighbouring tent saw me struggling with my pathetic little rubber-coated mallet, and lent me a heavy industrial club-hammer, designed for light demolition work or, as the German lad worryingly suggested, for bludgeoning one's victim to death. It made light work of the tent pegs though – so I gave him one of my beers, partly by way of a 'thank you' for lending me his hammer, but largely as an insurance against being clubbed to death in my tent by the infamous *Domäne Stiege Hammer Murderer.* But once the repairs had been completed and my *Wind-Breaker DeLuxe* fully assembled, the difference was immediately apparent. I had what appeared to be a brand new tent! She still looked a mess of course (splodges of black marker pen and pieces of duct tape plastered all over the place were never going to enhance her overall beauty), but for the first time since the beginning of my trip, she looked stable. In fact, she looked as solid as a rock. If Hurricane Hugo were to sweep through the campsite during the night, uprooting trees, deracinating plants and bushes and leaving in her wake carnage and destruction on a biblical scale – then I would be prepared to wager every euro in my wallet that my *Wind-Breaker DeLuxe* would still be standing in the morning. To me, she looked completely indestructible. So, feeling as smug as the cat that got the cream, I drank another can of *Lüdde Pils* and settled down for the night – with that dreadful Pullman City signature tune still resonating in my brain.

Now then, here's a question for you. What do the following people have in common: the classical German playwright and all-round polymath *Johann Wolfgang von Goethe*; pioneering American heavy metal rock band *Coven;* and an eighty-year-old fitness fanatic by the name of *Benno Schmidt?* The answer is *Brocken Mountain,* but I'm afraid you'll have to wait a while for an explanation.

At 1,141 metres above sea level, Brocken Mountain is the highest peak in the Harz Mountains National Park, indeed the highest in Northern Germany – and my plan for the following day was to climb to the top of it. Brocken Mountain (not to be confused with *Brokeback Mountain* which was a film about gay cowboys), is set among a range of lush, grassy hills – also described, perhaps rather incongruously, as 'mountains'. There is, of course, that age-old debate about how high a hill has to be before it can officially become a 'mountain' – and although I've researched the subject to death in order to find the definitive answer, I'm afraid my efforts have been wholly futile. There are a multitude of suggested definitions, and for every one of them there are thousands of mountains, hills, knolls, peaks, fells, crags and tors that stand as exceptions to the rule. There was a film made in 1995 called '*The Englishman Who Went Up a Hill But Came Down a Mountain*' which suggested a figure of 1,000 feet (304.8m) as the definitive height at which a 'hill' becomes a 'mountain'. It seems an unlikely number to me though – I have molehills in my garden that are bigger than that. You may remember this film. It was famous for being the only film in history where

223

the entire one-hour-forty-minute plot, in all its nauseating detail, was summarised in the title. It starred Hugh Grant and Tara Fitzgerald – with Grant playing the role of the bumbling, floppy-haired English twat – which coincidently, is the exact same role he's played in every film he's ever appeared in.

But Brocken is indisputably a 'mountain' by anybody's definition – its summit is above the treeline, it's usually shrouded in mist or hidden in the clouds and is snow-covered for up to 300 days of the year. And since it's located in one of the most beautiful and picturesque regions in the whole of Germany, I intended to spend the day climbing it.

Anyway, I promised you an answer to the question I posed earlier – and I think I've kept you waiting on tenterhooks for long enough. Goethe had Brocken Mountain as the setting for his classical play *Faust* – first published in 1808 and generally regarded as Goethe's 'magnum opus' and one of the greatest works of German literature. Brocken Mountain is where the witches gather for a night of revelry on the eve of St. Walpurga's Day. There are two rock formations on the path leading up to Brocken's summit known as the '*Teufelskanzel*' (Devil's Pulpit) and the *Hexenaltar* (Witches' Altar) – and it's not beyond reason to believe that Goethe may have taken some of his inspiration from them. By the way, the path leading up to the summit, which I would be negotiating later that day, is known as the '*Goethe Trail*'.

Psychedelic American rock band Coven's 1969 debut album '*Witchcraft Destroys Minds & Reaps Souls*' featured a track called 'Black Sabbath' – a rather dark and sinister ditty that opened with the lyric:

'They journeyed far to Brocken Mountain pinnacle; A gathering of dread, an awesome spectacle.'

Admittedly, 'pinnacle' and 'spectacle' don't rhyme all that well, but pioneering heavy metal rock bands will always be forgiven for minor lyrical transgressions as far as I'm concerned. No such forgiveness for Chris de Burgh though. Anyone who tries to rhyme 'chance' with 'romance' and expects to get away with it deserves imprisonment.

And finally, there's young Benno Schmidt. At 80 years old, *'Brocken Benno of Wernigerode'* as he's affectionately known, is the oldest man to bear an official *'Badge of honour'* from the state of Saxony-Anhalt – a distinction he has unquestionably earned, having climbed to the summit of Brocken Mountain on more than 6,000 separate occasions. His extraordinary feat has been registered in the Guinness Book of World Records, and rightly so in my opinion. Some say he's an octogenarian fitness phenomenon – but I reckon *'as mad as a barrel full of monkeys'* is probably nearer the mark. Still, if Benno Schmidt can conquer Brocken more than 6,000 times, then I was pretty sure I could manage it just the once.

I should point out that climbing up Brocken Mountain under one's own steam isn't the only means of reaching the summit – there's an alternative method also involving 'steam' of a more literal nature. The *Harzer Schmalspurbahn,* which brought me from the small town of *Nordhausen* to my campsite at *Hasselfeld,* has several spurs and branch lines covering much of the Harz Mountains National Park. It connects all of the region's principal towns with about 140 kilometres of track – much of which is fabulously picturesque and steeply graded. And there is *one* section (the *Brockenbahn*), which follows the contours of Brocken Mountain, gently winding its way up to a quaint little railway station located at the summit. Actually, that's not strictly true – the railway doesn't make it quite that far. The station is located at 1,125 metres – about 16 metres short of the pinnacle – so travellers conquering Brocken Mountain on a steam train will have to walk the rest of the way. But I had absolutely no intention of taking a train to Brocken's summit. Pah! Steam trains are for wimps.

My mission for today was to take a leaf out of Benno Schmidt's book – and trek to the top of Brocken Mountain following the Goethe Trail. I've had a bit of previous experience with this uphill hiking malarkey, and if there's one thing that experience has taught me it's this: trekking up a hill is a lot less arduous when you're walking with a stick. Now, that may seem like a statement of the blatantly obvious to some people and to others – well, perhaps not. But if you're planning a long walk – especially one that involves trekking uphill, then you shouldn't underestimate the importance of a good old-fashioned walking stick. It will help provide a rhythm to your pace and will offer you added support. On steep slopes, a stick will provide useful lateral stability and even help to reduce knee and back pain. The Goethe Trail leading to the summit of Brocken Mountain was paved, I admit, but on less certain terrain you can even use your stick as an aid to climbing rocks or to probe the depth of mud or water to facilitate a crossing. Naturally, hiking sticks (or poles) come in all sorts of sizes and varieties – and you can, if you want to, spend a small fortune. The manufacturers will do their best to bamboozle you with technical terms or attempt to bemuse you with product features that, according to them, you cannot possibly do without. When you're choosing your hiking pole you'll read a great deal about on-off shock mechanisms, lightweight alloy tubular frames, steel carbide tips, rubber ferrules and ergonomic cork hiking grip handles. But my advice would simply be this: an ordinary wooden walking stick will do perfectly well – so long as it's strong, cut to a length that suits your frame, and has a handle that won't rub an enormous blister on the palm of your hand. And at the little village of *Schierke* at the foot of Brocken Mountain, I found the perfect stick in a little village shop and got change out of a five-euro note.

Before my arrival here, I had read a great deal about Brocken Mountain – and in particular, about the weather. Brocken, you see, is a place of extreme weather conditions. Due to its exposed location in the north of Germany the area has its own micro-climate, similar to that of an alpine location. It's all to do with the short summers and very long winters and with the many months of continuous snow cover, strong storms and low temperatures. To give you some idea of how cold it can get up there, Brocken's average annual temperature is a chilly 3°C. That's the *average* remember! You can imagine how cold it gets in the winter. Even though it was a balmy 26°C down here in Schierke on this beautiful June morning, it was only 8°C on top of the mountain. And as for rain – well, Brocken has the highest precipitation of any point in northern central Europe, with an average of around 180 centimetres a year. And, as I was reliably informed by a party of German tourists who had just completed the descent, it was raining up there today.

"It's not *pouring* down," one of the party reassuringly told me. "It's that fine, light rain that settles on the top of your hair and gets you wetter than you realise."

I wasn't quite sure what he meant by that. But it did make me realise one thing. I had ventured out today on a mission to climb to the summit of Brocken Mountain completely unprepared. The beautiful clear turquoise sky and the soaring summer temperatures I had woken up to that morning had led me into a false sense of security. Without a moment's thought for how the weather might turn as I began my ascent up the mountain, I had set off towards the little village of Schierke wearing my sunglasses, a pair of knee-length shorts and my favourite '*Pink Floyd – Dark Side of the Moon Tour 1972*' T-shirt. All of which were wholly inappropriate for the weather conditions up there on Brocken Mountain. So although I may have saved a great deal of money by investing in a reasonably-priced walking stick, I ended up spending a small fortune on a woolly fleece and a cagoule – both of which were items of clothing I already possessed, but had foolishly left behind in my tent at the campsite at *Domäne Stiege.*

My twelve-kilometre ascent of Brocken Mountain began in Schierke, and followed the *Goetheweg (Goethe Trail)* all the way to the summit. For the most part, the Goetheweg is paved and maintained to a high standard – although I noticed along some stretches of the path that the paving was showing signs of fatigue, crumbling away and leaving hikers to negotiate large sections of mud. As the man I'd met in Schierke had quite rightly forewarned, the weather began to deteriorate as soon as I began the ascent. It was what the Irish might call a 'soft' sort of day – a little bit of mist in the air and a light, barely discernible drizzle, best described, perhaps, as that fine, light rain that settles on the top of your hair and gets you wetter than you realise. But the air smelled sweet with the scent of the spruce trees that lined the pathway on the lower levels, and every now and then, through the occasional clearing in the woods, I'd catch a glimpse of the spectacular scenery across the foothills of the Brocken and the valleys in between. The panorama was both dramatic and strikingly beautiful, but sadly only visible at the lower levels. The higher I climbed, the mistier it became.

I wasn't alone of course. Around two million visitors flock to the Harz Mountains every year and many of them choose to climb Brocken via the Goetheweg. In fact, when I joined the path at Schierke, I was accompanied by dozens of fellow walkers – most of them far more suitably equipped than I was – with their hiking poles, trekking boots and waterproof clothing. But as I began to settle into a comfortable pace, the crowds began to disperse – with those choosing a more leisurely gait falling behind and the more serious walkers racing ahead. And although I'd be overtaken every now and then, there were times during my ascent of Brocken Mountain when I'd have the entire Goetheweg pretty much to myself. I'd meet the occasional person making the descent of course – and as we passed each other there'd be the friendly nod, the exchanges of *'Guten Morgen'* or *'Guten Tag'* and of course a gracious and friendly smile. The smile seemed to be a sort of unwritten rule – a surreptitious code of conduct between fellow members of the exclusive *'I've-climbed-Brocken-Mountain-via-the-Goetheweg'* Club.

But despite Brocken Mountain's indubitable beauty, there was something rather spooky about the Goetheweg. The Mountain has always played a role in legends as a hunting ground for goblins, witches and other creatures in the pagan pantheon. Goethe, of course, took up this theme in *Faust* as I've already mentioned. But there's a strange occurrence that takes place in the Harz Mountains that, although not unique to Brocken, has created a legend from which this extraordinary phenomenon takes its name. It's a spectacle known as the *'Brockengespenst' or 'the Brocken Spectre'.* The 'spectre' appears when the sun shines from behind you if you're looking down from a ridge into the mist, and the light projects your shadow in a strange triangular shape. Just imagine seeing the sun's rays shining through a mist and casting your shadow in the gloomy half-light in a giant stick-man shape. It's quite a spine-chilling phenomenon, believe me – no wonder Goethe was so inspired by Brocken Mountain.

The mountain's harsh climate makes Brocken's flora and fauna rather unique too – it's a habitat for a number of rare species. Between the rocks on Brocken's higher ground I found hawkweeds, Iceland moss and pasque flower – rarely if ever found elsewhere in northern Germany and usually more at home in Alpine terrain or in the colder climes of Scandinavia. There's some interesting wildlife too. I spotted a viviparous lizard – which occurs on Brocken in a unique, dark-coloured variant – and a couple of capercaillies nesting in the lichen. I'm reliably informed that the Eurasian lynx was reintroduced to the Harz Mountains and can be found here in fairly large numbers. I didn't spot one during my visit though – which was a pity.

Climbing up Brocken Mountain was no walk in the park. Well actually, given that the Harz region *is* officially a national park and I was here on a walking expedition, I suppose it *was* a walk in the park, literally speaking. But I was quoting an idiom. What I meant to say was that climbing Brocken Mountain wasn't easy. Quite the opposite in fact – I found it rather arduous. I sweated and toiled, and by the time I eventually reached the top I had muscles aching in places where I didn't realise I had muscles. But it was worth the effort – the view from the observation tower at the summit was simply sublime. It was just as well that Brocken's peak afforded such a spectacular view – because anyone hoping to be rewarded with something interesting to look at may find themselves bitterly disappointed. There's a small museum and botanical gardens up there, and an array of satellite dishes and TV masts. Oh – and a weather station. But that's about it. Actually, I suppose I should have felt honoured to be here – climbing Brocken Mountain was a pleasure denied to everybody in the communist years between 1961 and 1989. The '*Stasi*' (East Germany's detested secret police) used the old tower on Brocken Mountain for surveillance and espionage purposes. Two powerful listening posts were erected here which were used for all sorts of sneaky, clandestine operations. To seal the area, the entire Brocken plateau was surrounded by a huge concrete wall. The posts and the wall have been dismantled long since, thank goodness, and the mountain is open once again for all to enjoy.

I decided not to linger for too long on the summit of Brocken Mountain. The rain had stopped and the mist had cleared, giving way to the spectacular vista – but even in my fleece and cagoule I felt a tad chilly. And since the little museum didn't really appeal, I decided to make my way back down again. To be honest, I didn't relish the prospect of walking all the way back to the foot of Brocken Mountain. It had taken me what seemed like an eternity to get to the top, and as I've already mentioned (but will mention again in the vain hope that it might attract a modicum of sympathy), the muscles in my upper thighs were aching like crazy.

Now, I'm no medical expert, I admit – nor do I claim to have any particular expertise in the field of human anatomy. But I do know that walking downhill doesn't have quite the same impact on one's poor aching muscles as walking uphill does. *Descending* the mountain would be more likely to affect my calf muscles and would, with a bit of luck, take some of the pressure off my quadriceps. That was *my* theory at any rate – for what it's worth. So I joined the Goetheweg at the summit of Brocken Mountain and retraced my steps back down again along the same pathway.

At a point roughly halfway down the mountain, I slipped on a patch of mud and fell over. I can't recall *exactly* how it happened. I remember noticing a small patch of mud and some loose rocks on the pathway ahead of me, but I think I must have overconfidently concluded that the thick rubber soles of my trekking boots would make me surefooted enough to cope with a little bit of mud. I was wrong. As I stepped onto one of the loose rocks, my foot slipped from underneath me and I fell backwards onto the stony path. But that wasn't the end of it. When you fall over on a steep incline, the laws of gravity kick in from the moment you hit the ground – and I suddenly found myself rolling down the hill for some considerable distance, before the impact of my body slamming into the trunk of a spruce tree prevented me from rolling any further. For a moment I just lay there, splayed across the pathway like a cartoon cat flattened by a juggernaut.

The good news is that, generally speaking, people tend to exhibit a kindly nature in situations such as this – a crisis tends to bring out the best in people and mountain hikers are certainly no exception. There was no shortage of fellow climbers rallying around me, insisting on helping me to my feet, enquiring after my well being, or offering me plenty of tea and sympathy. (I mean that literally, as one elderly lady kindly offered to pour me a hot beverage from her vacuum flask, to help me recover from the shock of my fall.) Of course, I tried stoically to reassure the dozens of well-wishers gathered around me that I was perfectly OK – but as a stocky man in a purple windcheater lifted me to my feet, I suddenly realised that it wasn't just my pride and my humility that had sustained some serious damage. There was something wrong with my ankle – and I was in some considerable pain. My ribcage was a little sore too, from where I'd slammed into the side of a tree. But the pain in my side wasn't half as bad as the pain in my foot. In fact, it was so intense that the stocky man in the purple windcheater had to sit me back down again after it became evident that I wasn't able to stand on my own two feet. As I sat there momentarily, not knowing quite what to do next, I became acutely aware that the number of people gathered around me had dramatically increased. I had become something of a tourist attraction, it appeared. Like the *Devil's Pulpit* and the *Witches' Altar,* I had suddenly morphed into another of Brocken's static exhibits – something else for inquisitive onlookers to gawp at – '*Man on Ground Unable to Get Up Due to Injured Foot'.*

"We should call the rescue services," one of the spectators insisted. It was a thoughtful suggestion, but not one I was willing to agree to. Not just yet, anyway. The

Goetheweg was certainly not designed for vehicular traffic and the rescue services would have had considerable difficulty in reaching me. So despite a plethora of volunteers offering to call an ambulance on their mobile telephones, I urged them to hold fire until I was sure that all alternative options had been exhausted. If only there was some way I could hobble the rest of the way down Brocken Mountain. It would be uncomfortable, I know – I was prepared for that. But if I could possibly make it back down to the valley, I'd be able to seek medical assistance once I reached civilisation. Once again I tried to stand up, but it was no use – my right foot simply couldn't withstand my body weight and I immediately collapsed to the ground.

But just as I was about to concede defeat, along came the breakthrough I had been hoping for. It came in the shape of Jérôme – the stocky man in the purple windcheater who had so obligingly helped to lift me onto my feet – twice – and failed on both occasions. Jérôme was a Frenchman as it happened – Grenoble born and bred, and luckily for me, was here in the Harz Mountains National Park on a week-long hiking holiday. Jérôme realised intuitively that the only way I would be able to walk by myself would be with the aid of *two* walking sticks. One stick would be no use at all as I would still have to apply my full body weight to both my left and right feet. But with the aid of *two* sticks, my left foot could do all the hard work while my damaged right foot could remain suspended above the ground without having any pressure applied to it. Of course, I didn't have *two* walking sticks. But Jérôme did.

My newly found Gallic companion turned out to be something of a Good Samaritan. Not only did he offer me both his walking sticks like a latter-day Simon of Cyrene, but he also held on to my arm and accompanied me all the way to the foot of Brocken Mountain – even though his pace was slowed to a fraction of what it would have been had he not

233

been nursing an invalid. And as if that wasn't enough, Jérôme turned out to be the most affable of gentlemen – one of the most likeable chaps I have ever had the good fortune of bumping into on a mountain trail. And since his inability to speak German was matched only by my complete ignorance of French, we both settled on English as our common tongue – and enjoyed the most congenial of conversations as we made our way down Brocken Mountain.

To call the town of Schierke a 'town' would, I think, be somewhat overstating its grandeur. Although it may be classed as a town officially, Schierke had an element of 'somnolent little village' about it – and was lacking the amenities one would expect to find in a town of comparative size. But I did manage to spot the local *'Apotheke'* just across the main street – immediately distinguishable in a small parade of shops by the luminous flashing neon sign of a cross in two-tone green that seems to have become the established and universally recognised symbol for pharmacies and drugstores throughout Europe. Jérôme helped me to cross the road like a dutiful cub scout collecting another of his 'good deed' badges, and he held open the door of the chemist's shop for me as I clumsily hobbled in.

The pharmacist seemed delighted to see me – so much so, he could barely contain his excitement. He watched me carefully as I struggled to negotiate my way along the narrow aisle separating the shampoos from the condoms. But in a quiet little chemist's shop in the sleepy little town of Schierke, the sudden arrival of an Englishman with a suspected broken ankle was the most exciting event to have happened in a long, long while. It was, in fact, such a notable event that it would replace as the major subject of local tittle-tattle, the tale of when Mrs. Müller swallowed half a dozen laxatives in the mistaken belief they were vitamin pills. The pharmacist turned to his young assistant and ordered her to fetch a chair from the back. This she dutifully did, returning just a moment later with a large Wassily chair, which she clearly had some difficulty carrying. I removed my shoe and sock, and sat in excruciating agony as the pharmacist gently rotated my swollen foot – first clockwise, then anticlockwise, until I could tolerate the pain no longer. Then I squealed like a silly schoolgirl who had found a spider in her shoe – and the pharmacist immediately stopped. Once again, the chemist barked instructions at his pretty young assistant who obediently ran off to fetch an aerosol spray-can from one of the shelves.

"This will help to reduce the swelling," he said, spraying a foul-smelling liquid mist over my distended ankle. The pharmacist grinned at me inanely, in the manner of a mad scientist and wiped a bead of sweat from his forehead with a tissue from his pocket.

"I don't believe it's broken," he said. "Just a sprain I think – but you should have it x-rayed just to be certain. Are you going anywhere in a hurry?"

"No," I said, uncertain whether the pharmacist was being deliberately sarcastic or attempting to be humorous.

"Then I shall telephone the clinic and arrange an appointment for you. If you're lucky they may be able to squeeze you in this afternoon. Oh – and you owe me €7,50 for the foot spray."

The pharmacist disappeared into a back room to make his telephone call, leaving me to put my shoe back on. Jérôme, who, until now, had been waiting patiently beside me and had demonstrated the most compassionate of bedside manners, was suddenly starting to show signs of restiveness.

"I won't be able to accompany you to the clinic," he said. "I'm afraid I have an engagement I need to attend."

I didn't believe him of course – he was on holiday for pity's sake. His time was surely his own. That's the beauty of being on vacation – holidaymakers don't have engagements they need to attend. But of course I didn't question him. He had done his good deed for the day – indeed, he had already done far more for me than I could ever have expected of him. Jérôme had been the ultimate Good Samaritan. He had allowed me the use of his hiking poles for support; he had helped me down the mountain by holding on to my arm and had walked alongside me at a snail's pace. But above all else, he had stood by me in the chemist's shop while the pharmacist cruelly twisted my foot around in circles in his resolve to inflict as much pain as possible. But now, poor Jérôme wanted his life back, and it seemed only fair that I should allow him his liberty. But just as I was thanking Jérôme for his kindness and generosity, the pharmacist returned with a grin even more inane than before.

"Some good news," he declared, "The clinic can see you in half an hour."

Jérôme held on to my arm once again and the two of us made our way outside – to a small public square surrounded along its perimeter by a number of wooden park benches.

"We could sit here for half an hour until it's time for your appointment with the clinic," Jérôme suggested. "Are you hungry?"

It was at that point that I suddenly realised I was. The pain of spraining my ankle had taken my mind off the fact that I hadn't eaten anything since breakfast – other than a few energy sweets which I took with me on my ascent of Brocken Mountain. Jérôme produced a lunch box from his backpack and insisted that we both shared its contents – little brioche rolls, crudité vegetables with wedges of fennel, and slices of creamy camembert – a veritable French *pique-nique* wrapped in silver foil and crammed into a little boîte de Tupperware. There was scarcely enough for two – he clearly hadn't expected to be sharing his lunch with anyone and had therefore set the catering arrangements accordingly. But

Jérôme's kindness knew no bounds, it seemed. He was generous to the hilt and insisted that I shared everything he had.

"It's not *French* camembert," he said, as I munched my way through my second brioche roll. I could sense his profound disapproval as he said this. "It's *German* – I bought it from a delicatessen in Halle. I believe camembert is widely produced throughout Germany, but is particularly popular in Saxony-Anhalt."

"Is that right?" I said.

"Yes. But it doesn't taste anywhere near as good as the camembert we have in France. The Germans shouldn't tinker with things they know nothing about. I mean – the French don't pretend to know anything about Frankfurters or Sauerkraut do we? Of course we don't! And have you ever tasted German wine?"

"Well, yes as a ma...."

"I tried a glass of German pinot meunier the other day. *German* pinot meunier! Can you believe it? Whatever next? The Germans should stick with what they know best."

When it was time for my appointment at the clinic, Jérôme's tirade eventually ended.

oOo

Dear Diary,

The Beer, Cheese and Tent Report for the State of Saxony-Anhalt:

Beer: Lüdde Pils:

I must admit I rather liked Lüdde Pils. A product of Saxony-Anhalt's own Lüdde Brauerei, this beer has a hazy yellow tinge and a nice citric aroma. The flavour is a bizarre combination of malt and apricots.

Cheese: German Camembert:

Despite Jérôme's obvious disapproval, German Camembert wasn't too bad. Rich and creamy and with a texture making it adaptable for permanently sealing cracks in brickwork, Camembert is widely available in Saxony-Anhalt.

Tent Stability:

Well, what can I say? I have a brand new tent! New guide ropes, new tent poles and the holes in the canvas have been patched up beautifully. She's still no oil painting, I admit – but practicality is more important than aesthetics in my book.

oOo

Chapter Eleven – One Giant Leap

"I think we ought to do all we can to make these creatures friendly. It might turn out to be well worth the trouble."
Richard Adams – from the novel 'Watership Down'

I woke with a start the following morning, having suddenly emerged from another of those bizarre dreams that seem to haunt me with increasing frequency. As always, the dream featured Ronnie Corbett and Ant and Dec, but this time included a guest appearance by that woman who used to play *Penny* in '*Just Good Friends*' – whose name, I'm afraid, momentarily escapes me. [32] All five of us were standing on the surface of the moon and were about to board a spacecraft. We were wearing spacesuits, I think, and although I cannot remember the dream in all its illogical detail, I seem to recall that Corbett's suit had dinner-plate-sized comedy buttons on the front of it. My dreams seem to be getting more extraordinary by the day. Perhaps I should refrain from eating so much cheese.

Anyway, there were two pieces of good news to report that morning. Firstly, the x-ray I had at the clinic on the previous afternoon confirmed that my foot wasn't broken (thank goodness) and that it was, in fact, merely a sprain – just as the pharmacist had predicted. And, according to the gorgeous consultant who carried out the x-ray, if I were to continue using the foot spray I had been hoodwinked into purchasing, then the swelling would start to reduce a little and the pain would gradually ease. The second piece of good news was that, after continuing to use the foot spray I had been hoodwinked into purchasing, the swelling had reduced a little and the pain was gradually starting to ease –

---

[32] *I've just remembered – it was Jan Francis.*

so much so that I was able to walk on it that morning without the aid of *both* sticks. The consultant clearly knew what she was talking about. I now had *two* walking sticks – one that I purchased from the shop in Schierke for a little less than five euros, and another that the clinic very kindly made for me by sawing the end off a plain wooden stick to match the length of the one I already had, and attaching a rubber grip-ferrule to the base. My two sticks weren't an exact colour match admittedly, but I was hardly in a position to complain. Anyway, the point is, I now had *two* walking sticks, and although I felt reluctant to throw either of them away I knew that I would be perfectly able to walk using only one, and so the other was probably surplus to requirements.

I had a few things I needed to do before I could leave the campsite at *Domäne Stiege.* I had to dismantle the tent of course, but I also needed to spend a couple of hours in the laundry room – catching up on washing a few items of clothing. (The clean socks and undercrackers situation was becoming critical.) Also, I needed to repack my rucksack. I had gained one or two new acquisitions over the last day or two, and I wasn't sure whether my already bulging rucksack would be able to cope. Since I last packed it, I had gained a few additional tent poles, a fleece, a cagoule, and of course, a couple of walking sticks. As luck would have it, I somehow managed to squeeze everything in. It took a bit of arranging and rearranging, but it all fitted eventually. But sadly, not the spare walking stick – I'm afraid I had to discard that by leaning it against a fence while nobody was watching. So by the time I was packed and ready to leave, it was very nearly lunchtime.

It was day sixteen of my adventure across Germany – the halfway point – and so far I had covered nine of the sixteen states. Next on the list was *Freistaat Thüringen* – the 'Free State of Thuringia' – a territory of around 16,170 square kilometres that lies, for the most part, within the watershed of the River Saale. Since the late 19th century the state of Thuringia has been known as *'the Green Heart of Germany'* on account of the dense forest that covers much of the terrain. Thuringia was also the sixth (and final) state that once formed part of the German Democratic Republic – and would therefore be my final taste of the former communist east.

When I was a child of maybe eleven or twelve, I was a fervent plane-spotter. Now, that may sound a little geeky, but let me assure you that in the early 1970s pretty much every child in the country who lived within commutable distance from a major airport was every bit as committed to the pursuit of plane-spotting as I was. At the time, it was a fad – one of those fashionable crazes that come into vogue for a short period of time and then disappear into oblivion. In my parents' day it was the Hula-Hoop; when my children were growing up it was collecting milk caps and *Pokemon* cards. Well, for eleven-year-old kids in the early 1970s – it was plane-spotting. My friend Colin and I would spend every day of the school holidays dedicated to spotting aeroplanes. We would set off on our bikes to Heathrow Airport and stand by the perimeter fence, along with hundreds of other like-minded souls, with our binoculars poking through the gaps in the wire mesh fencing. And there we would stay pretty much all day, come rain or shine – watching aeroplanes landing one after the other and jotting down their civil registration markings in our little red notebooks. On those occasions when Colin and I had earned a bit of extra pocket money by

[33] *Sadly, there is no viewing gallery in the central area at Heathrow Airport any more, so families today are unable to experience the wonders of a major international airport. Unfortunately, having spectators standing on the roof gawping at aeroplanes is not deemed to be commercially viable by the airport operators and is also considered a security risk. Stand by the perimeter fence at Heathrow Airport with a pair of binoculars today, and you're liable to be arrested. It's a terribly sad world we live in.*

helping the milkman complete his rounds, we'd treat ourselves to a day in the opulent surroundings of the Queen's Building – Heathrow's spectator viewing platform that once spanned the roof of Terminal 2. The Queen's Building was, without a shadow of a doubt, the eighth wonder of the modern world. [33]

So why am I telling you this? Well, for Colin and me, spotting aeroplanes was more than just a hobby – it had become something of an obsession. So much so, that the two of us decided that if we were going to stand on the top of airport viewing galleries recording the registrations of civil aircraft then we really ought to invest in a decent pair of binoculars. Both Colin and I helped with a milk round during most weekends and for nine hours of toil on a Saturday and another five hours on a Sunday, the pair of us earned the princely sum of £3 each. Now as it just so happened, my grandmother was an agent for the *Trafford's* mail order catalogue and my parents were regular customers. Credit wasn't easy to obtain in the 1970s, but there were a number of mail-order catalogues like *John Noble, Trafford's* and *Great Universal* that gave consumers access to thousands of everyday items and allowed them to pay for them through fixed weekly instalments. So you can imagine my delight when, flicking through my granny's catalogue one Saturday morning, I stumbled upon the perfect pair of binoculars in their very own carry-case for just £1.50 per week for 26 weeks. How fantastic was that? I could pay for them with my hard earned milk round money and still have enough cash left over to stuff my face in the school tuck shop on a Monday morning. Of course, *I* couldn't legitimately buy them – there was some absurd legal clause stating that a credit agreement couldn't be entered into by an eleven-year-old (which I regarded at the time as being the most ridiculous load of autocratic nonsense I had ever heard), so I had to persuade my father to sign up on my behalf. When the package arrived in the post a few days later, I was beside myself with excitement and I opened it with the exhilaration of child locked in a sweet shop. It was the most beautiful thing I had ever seen and I decided at once that my new binoculars needed to be tested. I ripped them out of their carry-case and spent the remainder of the day sitting at my bedroom window – spying on the bedroom windows of the neighbouring houses across the street, and on the woman next door who was sunbathing on the lawn in her '*Hawaiian Beauty*' bikini – also available in the Trafford's catalogue through ten weekly instalments at fifty pence per week. Don't ask me how I know that – let's just say that as an eleven-year-old boy I had fumbled through every page of that Trafford's catalogue a dozen times over, with special attention paid to the lingerie and lady's beachwear sections.

My new binoculars were made by *Carl Zeiss* of *Jena* – a fact I was absolutely certain of, since the manufacturer's name and stamp were engraved on the front of the bridge. I remember being particularly impressed by this. After all, as far as I was concerned 'Carl Zeiss' was the coolest name I had ever heard. I mean, just *imagine* being called 'Carl Zeiss' – is that a cool name or what? – even cooler than being called Buzz Aldrin or Mark Spitz – which until that point in my life had been two of the coolest names imaginable – until my discovery of Carl Zeiss, that is. But then my dad added a contribution of his own, and suddenly my excitement almost reached boiling point.

"Mmm," he said. "Carl Zeiss eh? That's interesting."

"What's interesting, dad?" I said, almost wetting myself with anticipation. My father adopted that tone of voice that he usually reserved for those rare occasions when he had something quite profound to declare.

"Carl Zeiss is generally regarded as the world's leading manufacturer of lenses and optical equipment. The name is synonymous with quality. What you have here, son, is the

Rolls-Royce of binoculars – I'd take good care of them if I were you."

Wow – the Rolls-Royce of binoculars eh? Manufactured by someone with the world's coolest name? Colin was going to be green with envy. But my dad hadn't quite finished his story – there was more.

"These binoculars were manufactured in Jena," he continued.

"That's in the German Democratic Republic. They're all commies in the GDR you know."

Of course, I had no idea what he was talking about – I didn't know what a 'commie' was. I knew it had something to do with politics, so naturally I wasn't in the least bit interested. I'd never heard of Jena or the GDR either. But if my father had told me that Jena was in the Democratic Republic of Bonga-Bongoland, I would have accepted his word without question. He was my dad after all – the font of all knowledge – the fount of all wisdom.

Anyway, again I digress. What this flashback to my childhood is leading to, is that the next port of call on my whistle-stop tour of Germany was the campsite '*Unter dem Jenzig'*, just a stone's throw from the little Thuringian town of Jena – home of the world famous *Carl Zeiss Optics Corporation.* I didn't choose to visit Jena specifically because of its association with Carl Zeiss, you understand – there are several major towns in the state of Thuringia that are equally worthy of exploration. There's Erfurt for example, the state capital – home to over 200,000 people and to the oldest synagogue in Europe; and there's the historic city of Weimar – where Germany's first democratic constitution was signed after the First World War, giving its name to that period in German politics between 1918 and 1933, known as 'the Weimar Republic'. But I chose Jena – a small university town built on the banks of the River Saale and the location

244

for the most extraordinary sporting event one could possibly imagine. But I'll tell you more about that later in the chapter.

Jena's function as a university town is immediately apparent from the moment you step out from the concourse of the railway station and into the town's vibrant centre. There's a veritable cornucopia of young people milling around in every part of the town. There was something about Jena that reminded me of Cambridge. Aside from the town's youthful population, there were bicycles chained to every available railing, an abundance of specialist academic bookshops and more pavement cafés and coffee shops than you can shake a stick at – many of them tucked away down narrow cobbled alleyways.

I had arrived in Jena on what was probably the warmest day of my trip so far – a sweltering 30 degrees Celsius (or *centigrade* as I'd prefer to call it), and a day when most of the town's student population were lying on the grass in the *Paradiespark*, basking in the sunshine in varying degrees of undress. There were couples sitting on park benches – some reading, some chatting, some simply sitting in meditative silence. In one corner of the park, a rally was underway. There were students gathered in disappointingly small numbers, some carrying crudely-made placards expressing their anger over what appeared to be a local issue – the proposed closure of a library. One of the students, a tall, scrawny man wearing a knitted beanie hat (which seemed to me to be wholly inappropriate in the searing summer temperatures), delivered a coruscating speech which, once finished, prompted a thunderclap of applause from the dozen or so students who had gathered around him like disciples of a latter-day divinity. Most people however, simply walked past the protestors – ignoring them completely or paying precious little attention to their cause.

I desperately wanted to sit down on one of the park benches, just to rest for a few minutes, take the weight off my feet and watch the world go by. With the burden of my rucksack on my shoulders and the burning heat of the afternoon, I had beads of sweat dripping from my forehead – and my 'Ich Liebe Berlin' baseball cap which I wore to protect my bald patch from the blistering sunshine was adding to the problem rather than contributing to the solution. My foot was sore too. Although I had sprayed it several times during my journey to Jena and the swelling was slowly diminishing, I was still in some considerable pain. But vacant seats were a scarce commodity in the Paradiespark – every square centimetre of bench space appeared to be occupied by somebody's backside. But as luck would have it – as I was passing a bench conveniently situated in the shade of a weeping willow, two of its three occupants stood up and walked away, leaving a couple of vacant spaces. I wasn't the only person to spot this. A woman with a pushchair also noticed that a couple of seats had suddenly become available, as did a pair of tattooed students, who until that moment had been leaning against the trunk of the willow, smooching and cuddling with their tongues down each other's throats. But I just happened to be in the right place at the right time, and I bagsied my space on the wooden bench, placing my rucksack on the seat in the middle between me and the elderly gentleman sitting at the far end, before anybody else could steal the space away from me.

The elderly man glared at me contemptuously as I made myself comfortable. He said nothing, but the look of derision in his eyes suggested that he wasn't enamoured by my presence. I immediately removed my rucksack from the space it was occupying, and placed it on the ground in front of me with it resting against my knees. I thought, perhaps, that he was silently rebuking me for putting it on the bench and therefore depriving some little old lady of a place to sit down. And I suppose, if that were the case, then he probably had a point. He then stared disapprovingly at the small group of students waving their home-made banners in protest at the closure of the library, and shook his head in antipathy for those involved and in condemnation of their cause.

"Damned students," he said – his embittered voice crackling as he spoke. "In my day we had no right to protest. The Stasi would have had us all arrested. And now that these youngsters *have* the right to protest, they choose to waste that right on matters of utter trivia. Just *think* of all the important things they could be protesting about: the dreadful state of our social housing; the plight of pensioners in the East. Yet, here they are, whinging and whining about the closure of a stupid library."

I didn't answer him – I'm afraid I didn't know how to. I knew nothing about the state of social housing or the plight of pensioners in the East, or, for that matter, whether it was a library worth fighting for. I didn't know whether to concur with his point of view or to argue against it – so I chose instead to simply respect it – and I said nothing. With his rant over, the elderly man picked up the newspaper that had been resting on the bench beside him, stood up and walked off.

The two vacant spaces resulting from the old man's departure were occupied within a flash by the two amorous tattooed students who had missed their chance to sit down once already, and were clearly determined not to miss the opportunity again. I nudged along a little to allow them enough space to sit together (they were both a little on the 'chubby' side). For a few moments they just sat in silence, gazing at each other with lascivious eyes. And then, as if I wasn't there at all, they held each other in a passionate embrace, and the snogging resumed. I decided it was time to move on. I didn't want to, obviously. I wanted to sit in the park in the shade of that willow tree for the remainder of the day – soaking up the last of the late afternoon sunshine and watching the whole of humanity simply walking through the Paradiespark. But I couldn't – it was too embarrassing having to share a park bench with *Licentious Lena* and *Promiscuous Pieter* – both of whom deserved to have a bucket of water thrown over them.

So I repaired to a small waterside café with tables spilling out onto a footpath that ran along the bank of the River Saale. Like the Paradiespark, the café was heaving – it was full to overflowing with hungry and irritable customers. There were dozens of waiters milling about, dressed as penguins in their white shirts, black waistcoats and matching bow ties and all scuttling feverishly around like whirling dervishes. I loitered outside on the footpath for a while until I spotted a man and a woman settling their bill before leaving their table. As swiftly as a shadow, I marched purposefully into the café and took my seat at the table which the couple had recently vacated. The service was slow, but that didn't bother me. The waiters were rushed off their feet and many of them seemed harassed or hopelessly confused. They clearly hadn't been expecting the café to be quite this busy – orders were being forgotten or served to the wrong tables. But as far as I was concerned, the longer I was here the better. It was an excellent place to rest my foot, the perfect vantage point for watching the world passing by, and a chance to enjoy the sunshine with a large glass of ice-cold beer. A careworn waiter with dishevelled hair eventually arrived at the table.

"Ein grosses Bier, bitte," I said – the four most important words in the German language and the only phrase you'll need to know should you choose to visit this wonderful country.

Now, it's a well-known fact that students the world over have the same common characteristics. To begin with, they all seem to be strapped for cash most of the time – many of them don't have a penny to their name. So, impecunious scholars are always seeking ingenious ways of making ends meet, and some of them are so inventive, their audaciousness deserves a standing ovation. In Jena, as in most of Europe's towns and cities, there is an abundance of street performers (or buskers as they used to be called). I saw several of them in the town square as I walked from the park to the café, engaged in performances of every imaginable genre. Some students were singing; others dancing – and some were performing magic tricks to amuse the crowds. I even saw one young woman re-enacting the Japanese attack on Pearl Harbour through the medium of mime. At least, I *think* that was what she was doing. They were all students of course, and many of them were clearly very talented. There was one young woman in particular who had the voice of an angel. She was a full lyric soprano with a vocal range of maybe three octaves. [34] I spotted her singing her heart out in Jena's town square to raise a few extra euros to help finance her studies, much to the delight of the crowds of people who had gathered around her. I'm pretty confident that one day she'll make it as a world-famous opera singer. At least, I hope she does – she certainly deserves to. Less impressive however, was the over-abundance of street 'entertainers' who were dressed in various costumes – their hands and faces coated in silver spray-paint and standing perfectly still for hours on end pretending to be statues. Apparently it's art.

But the indisputable winner of the '*Most-Ingenious-Student-Money-Making-Venture-of-the-Day*' award was a young man called Ebner – who, as I sat there in the café supping on my beer and minding my own business, suddenly burst into my life as if a live hand grenade had

[34] *A three-octave vocal range is not a piece of kitchen equipment – in case you were wondering.*

fallen from the sky and landed in my lap. He brazenly sat down at my table – in the chair directly opposite me. The thing is, I didn't see him sit down. I had my head buried in a large map of Jena at the time. I was trying to work out the best route from the town centre to the campsite *'Unter dem Jenzig'* – where I was planning to set up camp for the next two nights. There was a small illustration entitled *'How to find us'* on the back of the campsite's glossy publicity brochure, but it was of particularly poor quality – far easier, I thought, to work out the route myself. I happened to peer momentarily over the top of my map to see if a waiter was anywhere nearby, and I immediately spotted Ebner sitting there staring at me. He was grinning at me like a village idiot. I was so startled to see him – I almost fell off my chair.

"Hello," he said with the enthusiasm and sincerity of a man who was clearly trying to sell me something. "My name is Ebner, and I'm here to help you today."

"Well, I don't need any help, thank you," I said, rather glibly.

"You're going to the campsite *'Unter dem Jenzig'* – am I right?"

For a moment, I wondered how he could possibly have known that. After all, I could have been staying anywhere in Jena – in a hotel; a guesthouse; a hostel – the possibilities were endless. And yet, rather worryingly, Ebner knew exactly where I was planning to stay. But then it occurred to me that if somebody has a tent strapped to the side of their rucksack, and is holding one of the campsite's brochures in his hand (I was guilty on both counts), then it wouldn't take a genius to conclude that he was probably here on a camping holiday.

"Yes, I am," I replied tartly.

"And how will you get there?"

The question irritated me. Actually, Ebner was beginning to irritate me. I had come to the café for a little peace and quiet, when suddenly, and without invitation, this contemptible little pipsqueak joins me at my table and starts to quiz me about my travel arrangements. How dare he? I thought – the impertinent little bastard.

"Well, not that it's any of your business," I replied brusquely, "but I haven't yet decided. I shall either take the bus or, since it's only a couple of kilometres away, I'll walk."

"Or I could take you in my boat," he replied.

For a moment I was nonplussed. I stared at him for a while, not quite sure whether I'd heard him correctly.

"I have a rowing boat," he continued. "The campsite *'Unter dem Jenzig'* is about two-and-a-half kilometres upstream on the east bank of the Saale. You can relax in the boat and admire the sights along the way while I do all the hard work. I'll even give you a guided tour and explain the history of some of the landmarks we'll pass along the way. And because you seem like a very nice man, I'll only charge you thirty euros."

"Well, I'm not sure whether......."

"There's no better way to get to your campsite on a beautiful day like today than on the river. It's so tranquil. Are you a nature lover, sir?"

"Well, yes I suppose I......."

"The Saale is alive with dragonflies and coots and moorhens and stuff. The bus will be hot and sticky and I'm sure you'd prefer not to walk – what with your bad leg."
He nodded towards the walking stick that was resting against my rucksack.

I said, "It's my foot actually, not my leg."

"Whatever," he replied insolently. "It would still be better for you to travel by boat than to walk. Why don't you have a think about it while you're finishing your beer – and let me know when you're ready? I'll either be *in* the café or just outside – and if you decide to go ahead within the next five minutes, I'll knock it down to twenty-five euros."

251

And with that, Ebner left my table and sat down at another. The next victims of his sales patter were a young couple – both in their late twenties, I'd say. *He* had a stubbly beard and wore designer spectacles; *she* wore false eyelashes and had lips that were burnished with a shocking red lipstick. They were smiling adoringly at each other whilst sipping from champagne flutes, and were understandably taken aback when Ebner presumptuously pulled up a chair and parked himself between the two of them.

"Hello, my name is Ebner, and I'm here to help you today," I heard him say.

I decided not to accept Ebner's offer of a boat ride to the campsite, despite his last-ditch effort to persuade me otherwise (he reduced his price yet again – this time to a 'mere' twenty euros). But it wasn't a decision I made lightly – in fact, it was a decision I really rather regret. It's not that I would have relished Ebner's company, you understand – he didn't seem to be a particularly affable chap – too cocky and conceited for my liking. And I can't imagine either that his commentary would have been terribly insightful. But he was right about one thing: it *was* a perfect day for a ride in a boat. Although it was now heading towards the early evening, there was still plenty of warmth in the sunshine, and the sky was a perfect blue – with just a few wispy clouds floating like dreams across the azure. And it would have been nice to get up close to nature on the Saale and watch the dragonflies and coots and moorhens and 'stuff'.

That night, the heavens opened. I was woken just after 3.00am by the most torrential rainfall I think I have ever witnessed – a monsoon, almost. The rest of the campsite woke up too – there were dogs barking, babies crying and children screaming. The rain battered my tent unremittingly as if on a mission to destroy it. There were lightning strikes and claps of thunder loud enough almost to perforate the eardrums. There was nothing I could do other than remain in my sleeping bag and listen to the hostilities outside – hoping against hope that the repairs I'd made to my tent would survive the battering they were having to endure. And then, as if the gods had simply run out of steam, the storm passed. The lightning became less frequent until it ceased altogether; the thunder became ever more distant; and the leaden sky finally retreated – replaced almost at once by a clear, star-spangled heaven.

I woke a few hours later to a fresh, crisp summer morning – the sunshine already doing its best to soak up what remained of the dampness in the air. Any evidence that a storm had passed through the campsite during the night had been completely erased. It was as if nothing had happened.

There were two items on my agenda for today. Firstly, I intended to pay a visit to the Carl Zeiss optical factory – a sort of tribute to my childhood, if you will. Then in the afternoon, a special treat – an extraordinary sporting event which is becoming increasingly popular throughout the whole of Europe, although not widely followed in the UK. I'm not prepared to reveal just yet the nature of this bizarre sporting experience – suffice to say that from a spectator's viewpoint it was probably the most entertaining activity I've ever witnessed – and if you happen to be in Jena during the summer, I would implore you attend a 'race meeting' if the town happens to be hosting one.

I spent about an hour in the Optical Museum. Had I been there a minute longer I'm afraid I would have been forced to tie a noose around my neck and hang myself from one of the oak beams in the ceiling. I wouldn't say the museum was boring, but if I were to make a list (in order of preference) of all the things I'd rather have spent an hour of my life doing, then being stuck in a lift with a claustrophobic gorilla would have been higher up the list than a visit to the Optical Museum. Actually, that's a little unfair. The museum does have an extensive collection of exhibits from the world of microscopy and photography. There are telescopes, camera lenses, peep shows and magic lanterns – and a huge collection of ophthalmological instruments. And of course, there's an entire section dedicated exclusively to the life and work of Carl Zeiss. So, if you happen to be one of those people with a fervent interest in telescopes from antiquity, then the Optical Museum in Jena might just be your cup of tea. It's easy to find, open every day except Sunday, and it cost me only €6 to get in. More importantly, it also houses a little basement café which serves a splendid cappuccino and a damn fine apple strudel. And thank goodness for that.

Anyway, let's not dwell on my visit to the Optical Museum any longer than is strictly necessary. I'd prefer to move on to the main event of the day – an event that dominated most of my afternoon and from which I derived several hours of unrestrained joy and pleasure – and I didn't have to take my clothes off. Every year, the town of Jena plays host to a sporting event that brings competitors together from across the whole of Europe. It's a sport you may not be familiar with – I'm pretty sure that *Sky Sports* have not yet signed any 'exclusivity' deals with this sport's governing body. That said, I have my serious doubts whether this particular sport *has* a governing body. The event in question is the annual *'Jena Kaninhop'* – the most important fixture in the rabbit show jumping calendar.

Kaninhop was invented in Sweden in the early 1980s and involves bunnies leaping their way around specially designed courses comprising several small hurdles of varying height and levels of difficulty. Rabbit enthusiasts throughout Europe have harnessed their bunnies' natural jumping skills to create this extraordinary new spectator sport – and through a quirk of fate, I just happened to be in town on the day the *Jena Kaninhop* event was taking place.

Along with hundreds of fellow spectators, I made my way to a corner of the Paradiespark, where a giant marquee had been erected to stage the first of the qualifying rounds. I was handed a *'programme of proceedings'* – and was intrigued to discover that as a prelude to the main rabbit show jumping event, there would be a short opening ceremony where the '*Stadt Bürgermeister'* (the Mayor of Jena) would be making a short speech to welcome the contenders and to declare the event officially open. This would be followed by a brief musical performance by the *'Friedrich Schiller University Woodwind Ensemble'*. You can imagine how excited the crowd was becoming – the tension had almost reached fever pitch. I guessed that the mayor and his entourage had already arrived – there was a fleet of black CL-Class Mercedes-Benz executive saloons parked beside the marquee – but with just a minute to go before the mayor was scheduled to deliver his opening oration, there was no sign of him anywhere.

A makeshift stage had been assembled near the main entrance to the marquee. It was decked with a crimson carpet, had a microphone stand at the front and a row of seats along the back – presumably where the various dignitaries would be sitting whilst the *Friedrich Schiller University Woodwind Ensemble* bored them all half to death with their banal renditions of *'Bright Eyes'* and *'Run Rabbit Run'*. There were two flagpoles positioned on either side of the stage with a flag flying from each of them. Actually – to describe these two flags as *'flying'* is a little erroneous. It was a warm afternoon and there was no wind – not even the gentlest of breezes – so the two flags hung from their respective poles, limp and lifeless. This didn't go unnoticed either. A rotund and smartly-dressed woman who I assumed had some official function in the day's events, marched purposefully over to one of the flagpoles and tugged on the halyard in an effort to goad the recalcitrant piece of cloth into

255

a respectable tautness. It was a fruitless exercise of course – the flag remained flaccid despite her valiant efforts. The flag to the left of the stage I recognised immediately – it was the German flag: the national tricolour – black, red and gold in horizontal bands from hoist to fly. But the flag on the right had me flummoxed – two horizontal stripes of equal width – the upper band white and the lower band red. I recognised it as being the national flag of Poland, but I couldn't understand the significance of flying a Polish ensign alongside Germany's own national flag. I checked my programme for the list of countries participating in this year's *Kaninhop*. There were contestants from Germany, Denmark, Sweden, Norway and Austria – but not Poland. So why the flag? I thought.

And then the mayor stepped onto the stage, tapped the microphone a couple of times with the tips of his fingers to ensure it was switched on – and began his opening address against a momentary screech of feedback which had the audience pressing their hands to their ears.

"*Meine Damen und Herren,*" it began – as all good German speeches generally do. I'll translate the next bit:

"*I am proud to be standing here this afternoon, with the German national flag on my right, and the flag of the Free State of Thuringia to my left.........*"

I'm afraid I can't remember anything else the mayor said in his speech that afternoon – I switched off completely as soon as he'd helped me to solve the mystery of the red and white flag. Once the *Friedrich Schiller University Woodwind Ensemble* had completed their short repertoire, the audience applauded appreciatively – mainly, I suspect, in appreciation of its brevity – and I, along with my fellow spectators, were ushered inside the marquee and invited to take our seats in the 'grandstand' – an ensemble of temporary, demountable plastic seats, tiered on ten levels and arranged in a semi-circle.

I took my position in row 10, seat 23 – which I soon discovered was on the upper tier at the rear of the grandstand – it had a perfect, unrestricted view of the 'racetrack'. I should, perhaps, explain a few of the rules of rabbit show jumping rather than leave you to conjure up your own version of events in your mind's eye. To begin with, all the participating bunnies are accompanied by their trainers at all times – the trainer holds on to a leash which is fastened to a collar around the rabbit's neck. Now, you may think that attaching a collar and a leash to a rabbit seems a wee bit cruel – especially when the poor little thing is being forced to run along a race track and leap over a succession of fences. Indeed, the practice has been censured by various animal rights groups who have even accused trainers of using the tethers to pull uncooperative bunnies over the obstacles. But there are two things one should appreciate here. Firstly, if you line up a few rabbits at the starting blocks on a racetrack and you fire a starting gun, you shouldn't expect them to spring into action and begin sprinting down the course or leaping over any obstacles that they happen to encounter along the way. Greyhounds, maybe – rabbits, definitely not. Sprinting along a racecourse and leaping over fences is not part of a rabbit's instinctive or innate behaviour. The reality is that unless the rabbit's trainer is running alongside the track holding on to a leash that's attached to a collar around the bunny's neck, there's little point in firing a starting gun at all – it would be unlikely to have any impact on a rabbit whatsoever – other than frightening the wretched creature half to death.

Secondly (and this, I think, is a more crucial consideration) – if you allow a large number of bucks and does to wander about in a confined space unharnessed, then they will naturally choose to partake in the one activity that rabbits are renowned for – and the annual *Jena Kaninhop* will become not so much a wholesome fun-filled

257

event for all the family to enjoy – but more of an *'orgia leporidae'* – a scene of unbridled indulgence in rabbit passion, depravity and debauchery.

The sawdust track was only sixteen metres long, but in today's competition the competing rabbits were required to jump a series of seven fences – each one spaced at two-metre intervals and progressively increasing in height. I'm told that competition rules around Europe tend to vary from country to country, but in the *Jena Kaninhop* the more jumps a rabbit clears the higher its score – with additional points awarded for the time taken to complete the course. The fences resembled those you'd find in any equestrian show jumping event, but on a much smaller scale, obviously. The height of the first fence was set at a relatively undemanding 10cms – which proved to be a straightforward proposition for all 35 of the fluffy, floppy-eared contenders. But at each consecutive fence the bar was raised by an additional 10cms – with the final fence set at a rather challenging 70cms (about three times the height of the average competitor) – and all 35 of them managed to send several of the tubular-shaped balsa wood poles crashing to the ground as they attempted to clear it. The world height record for a rabbit jump currently stands at 99.5cms – but it was evident from the standards set in the qualifying rounds that the record wasn't going to be broken that afternoon.

The most impressive performance was that of a black and white Beveren doe called *Zucken* (which I think may be the German verb *'to twitch'* – an entirely apposite name for a bunny if you ask me). Zucken managed to clear the first six fences with relative ease – and, on the seventh, knocked only four of the balsa wood poles off, giving her the honour of having achieved the highest jump of the competition – a staggering 66 centimetres. That, coupled with a course completion time above the average set by the other competitors gave Zucken the accolade of overall competition winner. It was Zucken's trainer – a lanky, bespectacled woman by the name of Helena Weiss who collected the trophy on Zucken's behalf – and once the formalities were over (there were medallions for the runners-up and for some reason it was necessary for all the trainers to shake hands with the mayor and the other dignitaries), Weiss held the trophy aloft to the sound of tumultuous applause, with an air of smug satisfaction – as if it were *she* and not Zucken who had battled against the exigencies of the Kaninhop racecourse.

On my way back to the campsite I called in at the same riverside café where I'd stopped the previous afternoon. Quite coincidently, I sat at the same table as before – not because I wanted to sit at that particular table – it just happened to be available. So I made myself comfortable and raised my hand in the air in an effort to attract the attention of one of the penguins. My motivation for stopping at the café was two-fold. Firstly, I rather fancied a beer. Well, it was another warm day after all (although the temperatures weren't quite as searing as they had been the day before), and I had been deprived of alcoholic refreshment for most of the afternoon. For reasons unclear, the organisers of the Kaninhop had missed a trick by failing to sell anything stronger than coffee. Secondly (and I guess this was my primary motivation), I was hoping to bump into Ebner.

Now, I fully accept that my relationship with Ebner started off on the wrong foot – I wasn't enamoured by his sales technique, to say the least. Indeed, I believe that 'cocky', 'conceited' and 'impertinent' were among the adjectives I used to describe this irksome little man. But the truth was, I'd had a change of heart. He was, after all, only trying to make a few euros to see him through college and we've all been there – even though for me it was hundreds of years ago. And I had, over the past twenty-four hours, rather warmed to the idea of relaxing on a boat, being at one with nature and enjoying the peace and serenity of the river. So I decided to call into the café for a couple of beers and if I happened to bump into Ebner, then perhaps I'd sign up for a slow boat back to the campsite. Two hours and four large glasses of beer later, I staggered merrily to the bus stop and waited for a bus to the camp. There had been no sign of Ebner.

oOo

Dear Diary,

The Beer, Cheese and Tent Report for the State of Thuringia:

Beer: Thuringia Radler:

Thuringia Radler is a pale, golden pilsner with a flavour best described as 'lemony'. But beware – it's a bit moreish. Once you've finished one bottle you're mysteriously overcome by a compulsion to order another.

Cheese: Butterkäse:

The name Butterkäse comes from its buttery taste and colour – it's a deep yellow – an almost unnatural colour for a cheese. Apparently, this cheese is sometimes referred to as "Damenkäse" (or Lady's Cheese) for reasons that I'm afraid I'm unable to explain or willing to speculate on.

Tent Stability:

Well, I'm delighted to report that my Wind-Breaker DeLuxe seems to have come through remarkably unscathed, despite a ferocious storm during one of the nights I stayed at the campsite 'Unter dem Jenzig'. I'm interpreting this as a good omen.

oOo

Chapter Twelve – Battles in Bathtubs

"There's big boats and wee boats and all kinds of craft;
Puffers and keel boats and some with no raft."
From the song 'Messing About on the River' – Tony
Hatch & Les Reed

Sometime during the late 1960s (I'm sorry if that sounds a little vague but I'm afraid I can't be any more specific), I asked my father what a 'buster' was. I suppose at the time I must have been six or seven years old – and to me, it seemed like a perfectly reasonable question, seeing as how the subject of 'busters' had been cropping up with alarming regularity over recent days during conversations between a number of my school friends – conversations I felt unable to contribute to, given that I had no idea what a 'buster' was. But there were a couple of things I *did* know. Firstly, 'busters' were always talked about as if there were an awful lot of them – it was always 'busters' in the plural and never 'buster' in the singular. Secondly (and this was the piece of the jigsaw I found most perplexing), they were always referred to rather derogatively. 'Busters', whatever they were, must have been irksome little critters as they were always prefixed by the pejorative epithet 'damn'.

"Did you see the damn busters?" my friends would ask. "I really enjoyed the damn busters!" I just shook my head and walked away – I didn't want to let on that I had no idea who or what these 'damn' busters were. But my father, being the font of all knowledge, somehow managed to decipher my blithering and concluded that my friends had, in fact, been referring to *'The Dam Busters'* – that celebrated British Second World War movie, made in black and white in 1955, starring Michael Redgrave and Richard Todd – a film which had been aired for the umpteenth time on ITV just a few nights earlier. All my friends had watched it of course –

which is why it had become the primary topic of conversation. I think I must have been the only child in my class who had watched *Z-Cars* instead. All around the school there were pockets of pupils huddled together in small groups – recounting tales of bouncing bombs and the genius of that 'bloke' who invented them, whose name none of them could remember. The film was based on a true story of course – and although the British film industry has never been disinclined to allow poetic licence for the sake of its art, I'm pleased to report that '*The Dam Busters*' screenplay stayed pretty loyal to the facts.

Now, if there happens to be anybody out there who isn't familiar with the Dam Busters' story, here's a potted version which, I hope, covers the most salient bits. On 16th May 1943, 617 Squadron of the Royal Air Force launched the '*Dam Busters Raid*' – or '*Operation Chastise*' as it was officially codenamed. Their mission was to fly nineteen Lancaster bombers into enemy territory and destroy three key targets in the Ruhr Valley – namely the Möhne, Sorpe and Edersee Dams. It was hoped that the raid would result in the loss of hydroelectric power and the supply of water to nearby towns and cities. But destroying a dam called for precision bombing of extraordinary technical accuracy. Simply dropping bombs indiscriminately from an aircraft was too haphazard – the guided missile technology that is used in modern warfare wasn't around in the 1940s. But thanks to the ingenuity of the British scientist, engineer and inventor Barnes Wallis (or Sir Barnes Neville Wallis, CBE, FRS, RDI, FRAeS, as I think one should respectfully refer to him), a purpose-built, cylindrical-shaped bomb was developed – which, if spinning at 500 revolutions per minute and dropped from a height of sixty feet into the face of its target from an aircraft travelling at precisely 240 miles per hour – would bounce along the surface of the water and hit the wall of the dam head on – blowing a bloody big hole through the middle of it.

Any manner of things could potentially have gone wrong on a mission as intricate and as complex as this, but nevertheless, both the Möhne and the Edersee Dams were breached – and, in the case of the Möhne, around 330 million tons of water were sent cascading into the valleys of the Western Ruhr resulting in devastating floods and the loss of hundreds of lives. Although damage to the Sorpe Dam was relatively superficial by comparison, Operation Chastise was hailed a rip-roaring success.

Anyway, if you're wondering where this impromptu lesson in 20th century history is leading... well, the Edersee Dam was my next port of call. It's approximately 250 kilometres from Jena to the Edersee and once again it was a journey fraught with complications – another circuitous hotchpotch of trains, buses and seemingly endless periods of waiting around on station platforms and in gloomy bus depots. The gloomiest of them all was located in the historical town of Kassel – a town more than 35 kilometres away from the Edersee Dam and yet virtually destroyed during the Second World War, in part by the floodwaters of the Edersee following the "success" of Operation Chastise. I had almost an hour to wait at Kassel's bus station – a gruesome monstrosity made from an unsightly mixture of concrete and steel pillars supporting a roof of corrugated sheet metal – a pustule on the face of what was otherwise a seemingly elegant town. The local authorities didn't believe that passengers who are forced to wait for over an hour at Kassel's bus and tram station might want to sit down while they are waiting – and therefore didn't consider it necessary to provide any seating. And so, using my rucksack as a makeshift stool, I perched precariously with my backside resting on my bag and my back leaning against a wall, and with time to kill I started on another of my paperbacks – one of Dave Gorman's travelogues this time (I needed something light-hearted after Deaver's *The Empty Chair*).

I was only halfway through reading the opening paragraph when a pigeon shat on me. I'd noticed the pigeon earlier – flapping around in the corrugated roof of the bus depot, but I'd chosen to ignore it. The bird's aim was perfect – hitting its target with precision accuracy. But this was no ordinary dollop of pigeon shit – this one had been brewing for quite some time, almost as if this bloody creature had been saving it all up especially for me. Very nearly a dessertspoonful of pigeon shit landed on my shoulder as I sat there reading my paperback.

"You bastard!" I muttered under my breath, as I gazed upwards to where the bird was nesting. The pigeon cooed back at me as if to say "that's what you get for destroying the Edersee Dam in 1943 – you cruel English bastard."

"It wasn't me," I silently replied. "I wasn't even *alive* in the 1940s."

"Maybe not," the pigeon cooed, "but I bet you watched that bloody Dam Busters film when you were a kid – didn't you?"

"I didn't," I protested "I watched Z-Cars!"

I think I must have muttered that last bit rather more audibly than I had intended, because a small child who was waiting at the bus stop with her mother turned her head around and gawped at me.

"Lisa," said her mother in a calm, mellifluous voice, "komm hier, mein liebchen" (*come here Lisa, my darling*). I think what she really meant to say was '*Don't stand too close to the weirdo, Lisa my darling – he's clearly off his trolley. And don't stare at his shoulder either – it's covered in pigeon shit.*'

The six-hour journey from Jena to the Edersee took me out of Thuringia and into the state of *Hesse* – the province bordering Thuringia to the west which covers an area of a little over 21,000 km². Hesse's largest city is Frankfurt am Main – a huge, sprawling metropolis and home to around 2.4 million people. [35] Although the southern half of the state is dominated by a vast expanse of urban sprawl, Hesse holds the official accolade of being the 'greenest' state in Germany, with around 42% of its total land area covered by forest. And that fact alone was precisely the reason for my visit. I didn't embark on such a gruelling journey just to see the Edersee Dam, by the way (although the dam's intriguing history has given it something of an iconic status as a major tourist attraction). I decided on the Edersee as my next port of call for a whole truckload of reasons – so many in fact, that it's difficult to know where to start.

So I'll begin, if I may, with the Edersee itself – the body of water on which the dam is built. The lake is set in the heart of the *Kellerwald* – an area of stunning natural beauty and another of Germany's numerous officially designated national parks. The whole area is a major tourist attraction – 5,700 hectares of lush green rolling hills, and one of the last large, unbroken stretches of deciduous forests in central Europe. The surrounding hills are covered with blankets of beech trees, mountain elms and thousand-year-old oaks, and there are crystal-clear streams that carve their way through damp gullies lined with orchids and knapweed. If you stare out across the glistening expanse of water from the shores of the Edersee, it's difficult not to marvel at the splendour of it all – this haven of peace and serenity – this wondrous example of God's magnificent handiwork. Except it isn't.

You may be surprised to learn that God played no part in the shaping of the Edersee. The lake is man-made – built

[35] *Despite being the largest city in Hesse, Frankfurt, perhaps surprisingly, is not the state capital. That acclaim goes to the city of Wiesbaden, considerably less populous than Frankfurt with just 276,000 inhabitants plus around 10,000 United States citizens associated with the US military.*

between 1908 and 1914 to provide hydroelectric power and water supplies to nearby towns and cities. I'm told that, at low water during the late summers of drier years, it's possible to see the remnants of three villages (*Asel, Berich* and *Bringhausen*), that were submerged when the lake was filled in 1914. And, rather spookily, descendants of people buried in the now submerged cemeteries still come to the banks of the Edersee to visit the graves of their ancestors. The lake itself is pretty large. It contains almost 200,000 cubic metres of water and is the third largest reservoir in Germany. But aside from its more practical function of supplying the surrounding population with electricity and water, the Edersee is also a major summertime recreational facility, hosting a variety of water-sports ranging from fishing, waterskiing and sailing, to some lesser-known sporting pursuits which can only be described as 'downright bizarre'. And the event I had come to the Edersee to witness over the coming weekend was without doubt one of the most extraordinary of them all. So bizarre, I think, it made competitive rabbit showjumping seem like a very ordinary activity.

Over the following two days (which happened to be a Saturday and a Sunday), a large, cordoned section of the Edersee and the surrounding woodland would become the setting for the annual '*Edersee Blue Festival*' – the highlight of the calendar year for hundreds of oddballs and eccentrics from all over Germany. It would be a weekend of music and dancing – a festival of cultural Hessen traditions – a country fair, a flea market and a spectacular display of pyrotechnics. Oh, and a bathtub race.

Now, I wouldn't wish to insult anybody's intelligence by explaining what a bathtub race is – there's a clue, I believe, in the title. But I'm going to anyway – if only for the sake of clarity. A bathtub race, quite simply, is where a bunch of fruitcakes race one another from one side of a lake to the

267

other in suitably converted bathtubs – bathtubs which they have spent the previous 363 days of the year modifying and adapting specifically for the purposes of racing. The event would include separate races for each of the different 'classes' of bathtub. Some tubs were motorised and some manually propelled by a bloke with a beard and a paddle. (The beard was purely coincidental by the way, not a condition of entry – it's just that I happened to notice that it seemed nearly all the men in the *'male single-person manual paddling class'* races had either goatee or chin-curtain beards.) There were races for men only, races just for women and even races exclusively for the under 14s. But the jollity of the Edersee Blue Festival wasn't scheduled to kick off until the Saturday, so there was still plenty of time for me to kill.

I arrived at the *DKV Campingplatz Edersee* late on the Friday afternoon, but after a gruelling day of travel I was very nearly exhausted by the time I arrived. My foot wasn't quite back to normal either. The swelling had gone completely, thank goodness, but it was still a little sore and I found it uncomfortable to remain standing for any prolonged period. I could tolerate standing for about twenty minutes at the most – after which it became necessary for me to sit down and stretch my leg out in front of me to relax my ankle.

The campsite was jam-packed – more so than any of the camps I had stayed at during my travels through Germany. There are several campsites located in the Kellerwald – a few of which, like the one I had chosen, are located along the shores of the Edersee. But the *DKV Campingplatz* was the closest to the festival site – a fact which was clearly an influencing factor in my decision to stay here. I should have realised of course that everybody else would choose it too – for precisely the same reason. Unfortunately, a busy campsite can spoil the whole camping experience. Camping should be a quiet, leisurely and relaxed affair – but none of those things applies when your campsite is packed to the rafters. Pitches were so close together that campers found themselves jostling for space – hammering tent pegs into the ground just a matter of centimetres away from neighbouring tents. It was noisy too – with hundreds of families having descended on the campsite with their boisterous and unruly offspring in tow – all of them whipped into a frenzy of overexcitement at the prospect of the forthcoming bathtub races. And the sheer number of people staying here put a severe strain on the campsite's facilities, which were proving wholly inadequate at a time of heightened demand. I waited in a queue for almost fifteen minutes just to use the toilet. I stood for over an hour in another queue with my toiletries wrapped in my rolled-up towel, waiting patiently for a shower cubicle to become available. And as for the queue at the laundrette, well... in the end I decided not to bother – my socks would just have to stay dirty. There were five washing machines and three dryers – all of them in use, with at least thirty people waiting for their turn to use them – each one of them queuing patiently and clutching a laundry basket overflowing with enough clothes to dress every one of the hundreds of band members of *Earth, Wind and Fire*. So I abandoned hope and looked for a suitable spot to pitch my tent.

After an exhaustive search I chose to assemble it on a small patch of grass sandwiched tightly between a large two-person dome tent on the left, and an enormous family-sized multi-bedroom frame tent on the right. The dome tent, in a garish two-tone pink, belonged to a couple of young women – in their late teens I'd imagine, who, in time-honoured rock festival tradition, were sitting cross-legged on the grass beside their tent, smoking a roll-your-own cigarette and drinking beer from a can. Only one of each, you understand – there was one cigarette and one can of beer, both being passed backwards and forwards between the two girls. So, whilst one of them knocked back a swig of beer, the other dragged on the cigarette as if her life depended on inhaling as much smoke as her lungs could reasonably be expected to cope with. One of the girls had brightly coloured hair – a shocking shade of pink which was an almost perfect colour match with her tent. The other was strawberry blond – with occasional streaks of black. Both girls sat there in silence staring at me intensely as I assembled my tent. They seemed almost mesmerised by what I was doing – as if I were creating an intricate ice sculpture of a swan or constructing a replica model of the Taj Mahal from lolly sticks.

The large frame tent to my right belonged to a German family. Mum and dad were sitting in deckchairs positioned athwart the main entrance to the tent, whilst their army of children (I counted six, I think) were kicking a football to each other whilst simultaneously attempting to break the world record for screaming loudly and annoyingly. Kicking the ball around couldn't have been easy for them, as the space they had available to do it in was 'confined' to say the least. I can only assume that before my arrival the children had been utilising the space between their tent and the two-tone pink dome tent to kick their football around in – space that I had now stolen from them by pitching my *Wind-Breaker DeLuxe*. No wonder then that mum and dad were staring at me so contemptuously. But hey, it wasn't my fault. I didn't feel terribly happy with my chosen pitch either – sandwiched between two teenage weirdos with their unconventional hairdos and the family from hell. The fact was – there simply weren't any other available spaces – I could either pitch my tent here or walk six kilometres to the next campsite without a prior reservation, and run the risk of finding no space available there either.

When my tent was finally assembled, one of the teenage girls leaned towards the other and whispered something in her ear. Both of them began sniggering – but not for very long. After a couple of minutes the sniggering turned into uncontrollable giggling and eventually into hysterical laughter. Neither of them seemed able to suppress it – as soon as one of them started the other joined in – until eventually, the two of them were laughing so hysterically they had tears rolling down their pale cheeks and black mascara streaks dribbling down the sides of their noses. The mother and the father from the family-frame tent, still seated in their deckchairs, glanced over to see what all the commotion was about – and they too were trying their level best to suppress their laughter.

And then, suddenly – like a bolt from the blue, I found myself unexpectedly being slapped across the face by a major reality check. At that very moment, I found myself confronted by a most uncomfortable truth.

They were laughing at my tent.

You see, I had rather assumed that the recent repairs I'd made to my *Windbreaker-DeLuxe* – the new tent poles, the application of duct tape and seam sealer – would have been enough to solve her problems once and for all. But I realised at that moment – I was wrong. I had been in denial all this time. The truth was that the storm I had experienced a couple of nights earlier during my stay at Jena had taken its toll on my poor old tent. The duct tape was peeling again; the seam sealer was barely strong enough to prevent the canvas from further wear and tear. Yes, my *Wind-Breaker DeLuxe* was a mess. So much so, that it now appeared to be something of a laughing stock – just to add insult to injury. The damage was so severe, her appearance so unsightly, that she was barely serviceable as a tent at all. 'Not fit for purpose', I believe is the rather clichéd phrase that seems to be in vogue nowadays. I suppose that deep down in my heart of hearts I already knew that my tent's days were numbered – it's just that I hadn't been prepared to admit it –

until now. The fact of the matter was that my *Wind-Breaker DeLuxe* needed replacing. Throwing what was left of her into a dustbin and replacing her with a brand spanking new one would of course be the most sensible thing to do.

It's a bit like having an ugly girlfriend, or an ugly boyfriend (depending, I suppose, on either your gender or sexual inclination). Ugly girlfriends or boyfriends serve a useful purpose, don't they? They're friendly, dependable, they'll dance to Abba songs with you at the school disco, they'll accompany you to the pictures on a Saturday morning and share their packet of *Love Hearts* with you. [36] But behind your back your friends are sniggering – and deep down, you know that sooner or later your ugly girlfriend/boyfriend (delete as applicable) will have to be unceremoniously dumped. The truth is that, whether I was prepared to admit it or not, ugly boyfriends rarely become ugly husbands and ugly girlfriends rarely become ugly wives. Relationships between a beauty and a beast simply don't last very long – unless the beast miraculously turns into a handsome prince or a gorgeous princess – which of course never happens in real life. And so, with the sound of mocking laughter still ringing in my ears, I crawled inside my tent to shut myself away from the nasty, malevolent world outside, and I waited for night to fall.

But as I lay there, I began to wonder when I might get an opportunity to purchase a new tent. After all, there wouldn't be time this weekend – I'd be witnessing bathtub racing at the Edersee Blue Festival this Saturday and Sunday, and besides, I was in the Kellerwald National Park – about a million miles away from a shop selling tents. I

[36] *I suppose this is a sign of the changing times, but what has become of 'Love Hearts'? When I was a kid they had syrupy messages on them like 'Tease Me' and 'Be Kind'. I was offered a Love Heart the other day with 'Piss off You Smelly Bastard' written on it. (Although I suspect the person who gave it to me had written it herself using a fine grade felt-tip pen.)*

probably wouldn't get a chance to buy a new tent immediately after the weekend either. My plan for Monday morning was to continue my journey westwards, out of Hesse and into the state of Rhineland-Palatinate. I'd be heading for the little town of Wittlich, where I would be staying on a farm with my friend Jan Henke and his family for a few days. I wouldn't need my tent there – Jan's farmhouse has almost as many guest bedrooms as Kensington Palace. And by the time I moved on from there, well....I would have ticked off twelve of the sixteen states of Germany. There'd be just four more states remaining – my tent and I were nearly at the finishing line! It would be such a pity, I thought, to have to replace my tent at this late stage. If only she could manage to hold out for just a few more days – ten days at the most. It was a huge gamble, I admit. I'd be relying on ten days of dry weather – one more rain shower would undoubtedly trigger a few leakage problems and another storm would finish her off completely. But surely it was worth the risk?

It wasn't that I was being tight-fisted. I knew a brand new tent would set me back around only thirty or forty euros – hardly a king's ransom. No, it had now become a matter of personal pride. Those silly, giggling girls with their ridiculous hair and their penchant for swilling beer and smoking fags could mock me if they wanted to. They could laugh at my tent if it made them feel good. But they had underestimated our resolve – my tent and I were made of stronger stuff. I might be rapidly turning into a middle-aged, miserable and cantankerous old git, and my tent might well be falling apart at the seams – but by golly, when it comes to survival you'll never meet a more hardy and resilient pair of troopers than me and my *Wind-Breaker DeLuxe.* So go ahead – laugh at us if you want to, I thought – just see if we care. I think at that point I must have fallen asleep.

273

Mercifully, there was no rain during the night, and when I woke on Saturday morning I was greeted by a clear blue sky and radiant sunshine. I stepped out of the tent and breathed in the fresh, unsullied air before making my way, with towel and toiletries in hand, to the nearest shower block. I was in fine form that morning – calm and sanguine, and in a positive frame of mind. I even began to whistle rather cheerfully as I marched purposefully towards the shower block and I think I may have exchanged a *'guten Morgen'* with some miserable-looking individual whom I encountered along the way – I felt he needed cheering up. I had risen early that morning – deliberately so, for I had devised what I considered to be a rather cunning plan. My strategy, quite simply, was to wake up early enough to secure a shower cubicle before any other bugger could get there before me. A judicious plan indeed, but sadly flawed – I'm afraid I hadn't anticipated that everybody else on the campsite would have forged a similar plan of their own. By the time I reached the shower block, the queue was almost as long as it had been on the previous afternoon.

Generally speaking, I've always been a fairly easy-going kind of guy. I tend not to allow myself to become riled by the absurdities of the modern world (and there are an awful lot of them to potentially get riled about). But when you're heading towards the age of 50, changes begin to take place in your brain. Character traits like *'patience in challenging situations'* and *'tolerance of the behaviour of others'* are generally considered virtuous of course – and for that reason they're bolted into place within one's personality profile (a small nook within the thalamus of the brain) by little tiny stainless steel rivets which keep them a safe distance away from your less desirable character traits – like *bigotry* and *narrow-mindedness*. When you reach your late forties these little rivets start to become loose. This process continues over the next couple of years until eventually, on

274

or around your fiftieth birthday, they drop out completely and the virtuous bits of your personality profile break free – allowing them the freedom to mix with the undesirable traits and become influenced by their pessimism and negativity. The metamorphosis is now complete – you have successfully changed from '*an easy-going kind of guy*' to an '*irritable and tetchy old bastard*' in the space of a few months.

As I stood in the queue, the chap standing in front of me turned around and called out to another man who had been standing further down the line.

"Gert!" he shouted, as he beckoned him to the front of the queue using a summoning hand gesture. Within seconds, Gert had pushed his way to the head of the queue and had assumed a position a couple of places ahead of me. The man who had invited Gert to jump the queue was an odd-looking individual – a youngish man with a blond porcupine-style hairdo and a hooked nose – which was thin, sharply contoured and had a bend in the middle – a bit like a hawk's beak. Now, queue jumping, in my opinion anyway, is audacious at best and at worst downright rude – and so naturally I was angered by this bout of unruly behaviour. But I think what incensed me more was the fact that nobody else in the queue seemed to care. Nobody said anything – nobody even so much as tutted. What was the matter with these people? Surely they too were victims of these lads' impudence? Well, I thought, this sort of civil disobedience might be acceptable to Johnny Foreigner, but it certainly wasn't the British way. If everybody else in the queue wanted to ignore the injustice of queue-jumping, well that was their prerogative – but I wasn't prepared to simply let it go.

"Excuse me," I ventured, in my best German, naturally. "There is a queue of people waiting to use the shower."

The man with the hooked nose whose name wasn't Gert scrutinised the queue of people as if he was seeking evidence that a queue even existed. [37]

"Yes, I know," he said eventually. "My friend was in this position in the queue earlier – but he had to disappear for a while to have his breakfast. I was merely saving his place."

"You can't save somebody's place in a queue while they go for their breakfast," I replied indignantly.

"Why not?"

"Why not? Well, because..." I hesitated. "Because it's not fair on everybody else!"

"Nobody else seems to mind," he said – and I must admit, he was right on that score.

"OK then – will you and your friend kindly save my place in the queue while I go for my breakfast?"

The man whose name wasn't Gert seemed baffled by my logic and for a moment was unable to think of a suitable response.

"No," he said – eventually.

It was Saturday of course – day one of the two-day 'Edersee Blue Festival' and there was a mass exodus from the camp as virtually everybody made their way to the festival site. The bathtub races – the main event which everybody had come here to witness – weren't scheduled to start until after lunch, so rather than spend the morning perusing the stalls in the flea market or examining the competitors' bathtubs, as everybody else seemed impetuously determined to do, I chose instead to visit the Edersee Dam – to see for myself one of the targets of

---

[37] *Of course I don't have any evidence that his name wasn't Gert. I'm only referring to him as 'the man whose name wasn't Gert' because I never found out his name. All I knew was that his friend* **was** *called Gert. Of course, they could both have been called Gert, I suppose, but that would simply have added unnecessary complication to a pretty mundane storyline.*

Operation Chastise, and to pay my respects to those poor souls who lost their lives in the madness of it all.

The dam looked rather magnificent – much larger than I had anticipated, and since tourists are invited to walk the length of it along a raised pedestrian walkway, I decided it would have been rude not to accept the invitation. When I eventually reached the other side of the Edersee I immediately did a full 180° turn and retraced my steps back again – for the simple reason that the forest enclosure where the festival was being held was on the other side of the Edersee – and unless I had been prepared to embark on a ten-kilometre detour around the perimeter of the lake (which I most emphatically wasn't), then marching back across the dam was the only viable option.

The Edersee dam was rebuilt remarkably quickly following the battering it sustained during Operation Chastise. The damage was repaired within a matter of a few months thanks to an army of forced labour – deployed from nearby labour camps to carry out the reconstruction work. But if you look closely enough, evidence of the damage is still visible today – the stones used to build the 'newer' parts of the dam are a slightly different shade of grey from the originals, and the sluice holes which are a uniform feature along the length of the dam are noticeably missing from the repaired section.

And so, just after noon, I made my way to the festival enclosure to join the thousands of spectators who had flocked here from every corner of the country to witness the lunacy known as bathtub racing. My ticket was valid for both the Saturday and the Sunday, and as I handed it to the woman at the entrance for inspection, she dutifully offered me a 'programme of events' – which seemed like a fair exchange. Although the bathtub races seemed a little anarchic, I'm reliably informed that there are stringent rules and regulations governing this 'sport' – regulations that are rigorously applied, and woe be unto anyone who fails to comply.

So here are just a few of them:

1) *Competing vessels must be built from a conventional household bathtub – and must be recognisable as such.*

Of course, most of the competitors have a tendency to tart up their bathtubs rather flamboyantly – by painting them in vibrant colour schemes or by adding logos, flags or painted caricatures. Others go one step further, by making elaborate structural modifications to their bathtub. Some have additional hulls added – effectively converting their tubs into catamarans. Some have added sails, or have attached fibreglass fins to the keel for added stability. I even spotted one bathtub with a tiered platform made from polyester resin which supported an armchair. Yes, an armchair! Whilst a bearded man paddled the bathtub with beads of sweat rolling down his forehead, a woman (who I presume was his wife) sat in the armchair wearing a bikini, a life jacket and a pair of Ray-Ban sun shades and was soaking up the sunshine. Judging by the sheer creativity of some of the designs on display here, it was clear to me that bathtub racing is a 'sport' which some competitors take very seriously indeed.

2) *Competing vessels must be painted using materials that are water resistant and environmentally safe.*

Although some of the bathtub designs were highly creative, I think the prize for the most artistic of them all (had there been such a prize) should have been awarded to the two silver-haired brothers in their seventies, who, as a tribute to their late father (a submarine commander in the Second World War), designed their bathtub to resemble a German U-Boat. It came complete with hull, propeller shaft, tower and periscope, was painted in traditional military grey and was made from plywood (I think).

3) Crew members must wear life jackets and appropriate safety headwear.

And for very good reason. You see, this may sound like a statement of the blatantly obvious to sensible people like you and me, but a bathtub isn't designed to be used as a seafaring vessel – particularly when being used for competitive racing in choppy water. It's a bit like attaching a pair of wings to a bicycle and entering it in a flying competition. The chances of you successfully completing the course unscathed lie somewhere between slim and zero. And it seemed to me from my general observations that the more time and energy a competitor had spent working on his bathtub – and the more ornate or elaborate its design – the greater the likelihood of the vessel either capsizing or sinking to the bottom of the Edersee. There seemed to be an inexplicable inverse correlation between creativity and seaworthiness. Of the two hundred or so bathtubs that entered the races, only a handful of them made it to the finish line. Most of them capsized, sank or took on so much water their crews simply abandoned ship. Some didn't even make it beyond the starting line. Even the U-Boat disappeared beneath the surface of the Edersee – and there's an irony in that somewhere. But safety was of paramount importance at the Edersee bathtub races. Rescue launches were on hand to help out those in need – and at the end of 'day one' there had been no significant injuries other than a few superficial cuts and bruises – and the emotional injury of a ten-year-old child who bawled his eyes out after witnessing his father's bathtub spring a leak just yards from the finishing line. I'm told also that sunken vessels are retrieved from the bottom of the lake at the end of the festival and returned to their rightful owners.

When the racing was over, we were treated to an open-air rock concert and light show, courtesy of the amateur rock-band '*Lazydaisy*'. Despite their absurd name, *Lazydaisy* weren't bad at all. They performed for a couple of hours, churning out a mixture of covers of classic rock tunes as well as some original material of their own. The evening ended with what the programme described as *'Fantastisches Feuerwerk'* – but I decided to skip the firework display. I chose instead to head back to the campsite – get a head start before my fellow campers returned en masse (as they inevitably would about half an hour later), once the firework display had finished.

When I returned to my tent, the two teenage girls were sitting in their usual spot and, as had now become something of a regular ritual, were passing a single can of beer and a cigarette back and forth between them. The girl with the blond hair with black streaks grinned at me inanely and nodded her head towards my *Wind-Breaker DeLuxe.*

"Schönes Zelt," (*nice tent*) she said.

"Schöne Farbe," (*nice colour*) I replied, nodding my head towards her hideous pink dome-tent. Two can play the sarcasm game.

As I lay there in my tent, snugly wrapped in my sleeping bag listening to a cacophony of screaming children and giggling pink-haired teenagers, I made what *I* thought was a very brave decision – I would temporarily abandon my travel schedule. Now, *you* may not consider that deviating from my pre-planned travel itinerary constitutes a particularly *'brave decision'. You* may take the view that one of the advantages of backpacking across Germany is the freedom it allows you to go wherever you want to go, whenever the fancy takes you. But the thing is this: I'm not really what you might call a 'spontaneous' sort of person. Spontaneity isn't in my genes. Everything in my life has to be ordered – pre-planned – and in nauseating detail. That, I believe, is the only way of guaranteeing any element of certainty – it keeps the risk factor to an absolute minimum. If I needed a haircut, for example, I'd have my visit to the hairdresser pre-booked at least a week in advance. The appointment would be with a specific individual whose hairdressing skills were already a known commodity – proven through previous experience. I'd know exactly how I wanted it cut – the length; the shape; the style. My wife, by stark contrast, is far more impulsive. She could be walking past a hair salon having previously had no intention whatsoever of having her hair cut, but on the spur of the moment will make a decision to step inside and get a herself a new hairdo.

"How would you like it styled today?" the hairdresser will ask.

"Well, I think I might try something different," she'll reply.

And if you were to ask my wife after the event why she made such an arbitrary and spontaneous decision to get her hair restyled, she'll bamboozle you with the sort of logic that only a woman could possibly understand.

"Because it wasn't necessary to book an appointment," she'll say.

Anyway, I digress yet again. The point is this: according to my well-planned itinerary, I should be spending the following day (Sunday) back at the Edersee for 'Day Two' of the Blue Festival – the finals of the bathtub races. That would be followed by another night at the DKV Campingplatz, before I'd be setting off on Monday morning to visit my friend Jan and his family in Wittlich. But I really didn't want to prolong my stay at the Edersee. Yes, I had a very expensive two-day ticket for the festival, I admit – but if I were to miss the second day it wouldn't be that much of a disappointment. After all, the programme of events scheduled for Sunday wasn't vastly dissimilar from today's – a couple of marching bands, an awards ceremony, and more bathtub racing. And let's be brutally honest here – once you've seen one garishly-painted bathtub sink to the bottom of the Edersee, then all subsequent ones seem mundane by comparison. But my main reason for wanting to cut my visit short was the campsite I was staying at. Now, don't misunderstand me here – there was nothing wrong with the *DKV Campingplatz Edersee* per se. Actually as camping sites go, it was really rather splendid – a fine, well-equipped site with clean, well-maintained facilities in an area of outstanding natural beauty – and I'd chosen it from a selection of alternative possibilities for all of those reasons. But it was just too damned busy. I hated having to wait fifteen minutes to use the toilet; I hated having to queue up for an hour for the privilege of being able to take a shower; and above all, I hated having to run the gauntlet of being laughed at by two silly giggly teenagers every time I crawled in and out of my tent. And the best bit of all was that my plans for the next few days allowed me the opportunity to be a little more flexible. I didn't have to arrive at another campsite at a specific time on a specific day which I'd pre-booked more than three months earlier. For the next stop on my tour of Germany I'd be staying on a farm with an old friend of mine – where there would be no schedules; no timetables. I appreciate, of course, that Jan wasn't expecting me to arrive until late on the Monday afternoon – but as I've said, he is an old friend of mine, and I felt sure that if I turned up twenty-four hours earlier than scheduled he'd be equally as delighted to see me as I would be to see him.

So that was that – my decision was made. I'd give Jan a call after breakfast the following morning to let him know the changes to my itinerary. While everybody else on the campsite would be making their way back to the Edersee for 'day two' of the bathtub races, I'd be heading off on my seven-hour journey to Wittlich.

I woke ridiculously early the following morning, excited at the prospect of another day of travel. There was a spit of rain in the air which, if anything, cemented my determination to move on. It was so early that there was no queue at all for the toilets, and only one other person was waiting outside the shower block for a cubicle to become available. By the time I'd showered and shaved (I didn't want to arrive at Jan's house looking like one of the guitarists from *ZZ-Top*), and I'd polished off a breakfast of jam croissants and strong coffee, I was itching to get going. It was still only eight o'clock but I had a colossal journey ahead of me – four trains this time. The first would take me from Kassel to Frankfurt, followed by another from Frankfurt to Mainz. From there I'd be catching a fast train as far as Koblenz; and after changing platforms, a final thirty-minute hop on the Mosel Valley line into Wittlich. But despite its apparent complexity, the journey by rail didn't worry me in the slightest – it was my journey from the campsite to the station at Kassel that was my main concern. Kassel is 35 kilometres from the Edersee and I'd be relying on a bus to take me there. The bus service wasn't exactly 'frequent' even on weekdays – but on Sundays it was considerably less so. There was a bus scheduled at 8.30 which would get me to the station at Kassel in time to catch the ten o'clock train to Frankfurt. But if I were to miss it – well, I might as well start walking, as I'd be facing a four-hour wait for the next one. So you see, missing my bus simply wasn't an option – I'd have to be on it and that was that.

As I stood at the bus stop in the drizzling rain I thought about giving Jan a call on my mobile phone. After all, my journey to Jan's farmhouse had already begun, a full twenty-four hours ahead of schedule, but I hadn't yet had the courtesy to let the poor man know I was coming. I looked at my watch. It was 8.25 – far too early, I decided, to telephone Jan. It was a Sunday morning after all, and I felt sure that Jan and his wife, Stella, would be treating themselves to a well-deserved lie in. Knowing Jan, he'd be planning to stay in bed until lunchtime. So I decided not to call him just yet. Instead, I'd wait until I arrived in Frankfurt and call him then – midday is a far more civilised hour to wake somebody from their slumber, I thought. And if I know Jan as well as I think I do, then I'd probably manage to catch him just before he and Stella set off to the local pub for their Sunday lunch.

At just after noon, as my train pulled into Frankfurt, I telephoned Jan on his mobile. His phone just rang and rang. Nobody answered. Half an hour later, as my connecting train arrived at Mainz, I called again but there was still no reply. I tried again, this time at around two o'clock as I waited for my connection at Koblenz. But since all I could hear was a perpetual ringing tone, I was starting to become a little anxious.

At precisely seventeen minutes past three on that Sunday afternoon, I arrived at the station in Wittlich – Jan's home town. The train had reached Wittlich at exactly the time the DB timetable said it would – yet another triumph for German reliability and efficiency. You know, somehow – even though East and West were reunified more than twenty years ago, you can still tell the difference between travelling in the former GDR and travelling in the former Federal Republic. Things somehow seemed a little more efficient now that I was back in the West.

I stood outside Wittlich station and telephoned Jan. There was still no reply. I must admit that, by this stage, my anxiety had almost reached boiling point. The original plan was for Jan to meet me here at Wittlich station – but not until Monday afternoon, of course. I had arrived here twenty-four hours too early and the seemingly elusive Jan had no idea I was here. The number I was dialling was the only number I had for Jan. It was his cellphone number, and I knew it to be correct as I'd spoken to him about two weeks earlier using the same number. And that had been our most recent communication – it was the same number I'd used to speak to him on what must have been a billion previous occasions. So why wasn't he answering? Jan *always* had his cellphone with him everywhere he went. He even answered a call I made to him once while he was taking a shower.

Unfortunately for me, although I'd visited Jan's farmhouse on a couple of previous occasions, I had absolutely no idea how to get there. I knew it wasn't in Wittlich itself. It was a few miles out of town in the rural countryside beyond Wittlich's town boundaries. On both my previous visits, Jan had picked me up from the railway station and driven me back to the farm. I hadn't paid much attention to his route though – we had both been too full of chatter for me to notice which direction we were heading. All I could remember was that the main roads suddenly turned into minor roads and the minor roads eventually became nothing more than dirt tracks, and eventually Jan would pull up in his 'S-Class' Mercedes saloon outside the most delightful farmhouse imaginable, with its elegant picket fence and wisteria-covered whitewashed walls. To be honest, I couldn't even remember whether Jan had turned left or right when he drove out of the station car park. So, here I was. I had no idea what to do for the best. What *could* I do? My only option was to wander around Wittlich and telephone Jan every fifteen minutes or so in the vain hope that he would answer my call eventually.

The town of Wittlich is very pretty – that much I'm prepared to concede. But it's also very peaceful – there's precious little for visitors to do. On Sunday afternoons it's exceptionally peaceful, and on rainy Sunday afternoons it's so peaceful, you'd be forgiven for thinking the population had been wiped out my a mysterious virus – an unexpected epidemic of bubonic plague, perhaps. The shops were all closed and the doors of the cafés and restaurants all firmly bolted. The High Street was reminiscent of the *Mary Celeste* – just as Captain Moorhouse had found it in 1872 – eerily deserted, although not bobbing up and down in the Straits of Gibraltar, obviously. Believe me, if there's somewhere you really don't want to be on a wet and windy Sunday afternoon, then the sleepy little town of Wittlich is a very strong contender.

After two hours of wandering aimlessly around, and after several more fruitless calls to Jan's cellphone, I sought refuge on a leather sofa in the reception area of the *Hotel Wittlicher Hof*. The weather had deteriorated since my arrival in Wittlich – the wind had increased in strength and the rain was falling more heavily. So I sought sanctuary in the hotel and ordered a large cappuccino with a thick cream topping, nuggets of marshmallow and a sprinkling of cocoa powder. It was all rather decadent. As I sat there slurping uncouthly on my drink, it occurred to me that there was a strong likelihood that I would have to stay in the hotel overnight. Rooms at the Wittlicher Hof weren't cheap by any stretch of the imagination, and staying here would have been something of an unnecessary expense – particularly as I could have stayed another night at the campsite at the Edersee for less than ten euros. But as I resigned myself to the fact that my choices were distinctly limited, something rather miraculous happened. My telephone rang.

"Hi Chris, it's Jan here – how are you matey? I thought I'd just give you a quick call to check what time you'll be arriving in Wittlich tomorrow afternoon."

You can imagine how pleased I was to hear from him.

"I've been trying to contact you all day," I said. "You must have at least a dozen 'missed calls' from me."

"On my old phone maybe," Jan replied. "I lost my old phone a couple of days back – I dropped the damned thing – it fell through one of the gaps in a drain cover, so I had to buy a new one. It's one of these new hi-tech phones – it's got the internet, a touch-screen and all sorts of bells and whistles. I'll show it to you when I see you tomorrow. Anyway, I have a new phone number now – you might want to make a note of it."

"Well, the thing is, Jan," I said, "There's been a slight change of plan. I decided I would bring my visit forward a bit."

"Sure," Jan replied. "You can come over whenever you want. I can pick you up from the station tomorrow a bit earlier than we had originally planned – it won't be a problem. Where are you now?"

"I'm in Wittlich. I'm drinking a coffee in the Hotel Wittlicher Hof."

There was a portentous pause that seemed to last an eternity. I could almost hear the cogs in Jan's brain whirring around as he tried to decipher the significance of what I had just told him.

"You're in Wittlich?"

"Yes."

"What, now?"

"Yes."

Another pause.

"Then stay right where you are and finish your coffee, old chap," he eventually replied. "I'll be with you in twenty minutes."

oOo

287

Dear Diary,

The Beer, Cheese and Tent Report for the State of Hesse:

Beer: Alsfelder Schwarzbier:

Despite the name 'Schwarzbier' (Black Beer), this lively brew has a reddish-brown shine and is topped with a beige-coloured, frothy head. Every sip creates a fizzy sensation in your mouth and leaves a delicate taste of coffee on your taste buds.

Cheese: Odenwälder Frühstückskäse:

Frühstückskäse literally translates as 'breakfast cheese' and this particular variety can be found on breakfast tables throughout the state of Hesse. The cheese has been awarded a PDO and can only be produced in the Hessian Odenwald region.

Tent Stability:

My tent has become an object of ridicule. Yes, she's in such a sorry state that people are now laughing at her. I've drawn the conclusion that we live in a cruel and callous world – a world where poverty, despair and tent-mockery have become inexorable facts of life.

oOo

Chapter Thirteen – Six Things You Should Know About My Friend, Jan

"No man is an island."
John Donne (1572 – 1631) – from Meditation XVII - 1624

1) Tardiness

If you've read my account of my adventure '*From Hammerfest to Syracuse*' then you'll already be acquainted with my friend Jan Henke. If not, then I'll offer you the following by way of explanation. A couple of years ago I embarked on a five-thousand-kilometre journey from the northernmost point in mainland Europe to the southern tip of Sicily – a journey which began in the chilly climes of northern Norway before taking me south through Denmark, Germany, Austria and finally Italy. Jan had planned to join me for a couple of days during the Roman leg of my journey – a chance for two sad old gits to visit the city sights, drink copious volumes of alcohol and talk utter drivel for an entire weekend. I think I've already mentioned that this star-crossed trip to Rome didn't have a particularly happy ending. Our excursion was cut short when Jan 'tasted' a little too much wine at a wine tasting event, and fell down a flight of steps onto a stone cellar floor – breaking a bone in his forearm in the process. But what I haven't yet mentioned was that the trip didn't get off to a particularly auspicious start either.

Jan was booked on an early morning flight from his local airport at Hahn. Well, reasonably local – Hahn is almost fifty kilometres from Wittlich and about an hour's drive away. Admittedly ten-past six in the morning is a ridiculously early departure time – but I shouldn't be making excuses for him. The point is – he missed his flight. He overslept, and that was the long and the short of it. Jan was forced to wait at the airport for almost fourteen hours before being allowed to board the next available flight – which was scheduled at around 8.00pm that evening. But of course, missing the flight wasn't Jan's fault. Nothing could possibly be *Jan's* fault. If Jan can find somebody or something to blame for his own shortcomings then he undoubtedly will. And that night in Rome, when he and I finally met up over a late evening dinner, Jan was on a mission. He blamed just about everyone you can imagine for having missed his flight – the pilot; the ground crew; his wife; his children. At one point I seem to remember him mentioning his chickens, although I can't remember the context in which they had been responsible for Jan's tardiness. Of course I did point out to Jan that the reason he missed his flight was because he arrived at the airport an hour late, and that he was, in fact, the architect of his own misfortune. But Jan didn't seem either willing or able to entertain *that* even as a remote possibility.

When I worked with him in the mid 1990s, Jan would always stroll into the office at least twenty minutes late. Sometimes he'd go for broke and not bother turning up at all. But it was the excuses that he made for his tardiness that never ceased to amaze me – many of them were 'inventive' to say the least; but most of them were downright egregious. All incidents of 'unpunctuality' (as the management called it) had to be noted in what the firm's employees sarcastically referred to as 'the naughty book' – a ledger which recorded details such as name, date, reason for lateness etc. It was a document that employees who arrived late for work were required to self-complete. Needless to say, Jan was responsible for a significant number of entries in the 'naughty book'. So much so, that eventually it was renamed '*The Henke Book*' in honour of the man who made the greatest use of it. On one occasion, Jan cited '*incident involving seagulls*' under the 'reason for lateness' column and on another – '*series of problems with teeth*'. So when

Jan told me on the telephone to "*stay right where you are and finish your coffee – I'll be with you in twenty minutes*" (and I'm pretty sure those were his exact words), my expectations weren't high.

Needless to say, twenty minutes came and went and still there was no sign of Jan. I called him on his cellphone a couple of times (using his new number, naturally, which had been captured automatically on my own mobile phone through the wizardry of modern technology), but my calls went straight to his voicemail. After thirty-five minutes I ordered another cappuccino – not that I wanted one you understand; the cream and the marshmallow made them taste rather sickly. Not only that, each cup contained over twelve billion calories and they were a staggering five euros a shot. But the man at the reception desk was looking at me disdainfully – giving me the evil eye, so to speak. It was a look that said 'either you order another coffee or you leave. This is a hotel – not a refuge for wayward strays.' So I forced my way reluctantly through another cappuccino and waited for what I hoped would be Jan's imminent arrival.

One hour after our telephone conversation (almost to the second), Jan burst his way clumsily through the revolving door and sat down in the armchair beside me. He was flustered and breathless.

"I didn't expect you to be *here,*" he said.

"But I told you I was here," I replied. "I told you on the phone that I was waiting at the Hotel Wittlicher Hof."

"Yes, I know you did. But I didn't realise *this* was the Hotel Wittlicher Hof. I thought the Wittlicher Hof was the one near the railway station. When I couldn't find you in there I went to another hotel round the back of the station that I also thought might have been the Wittlicher Hof. But *this* hotel isn't near the station – it's near the bridge! Why didn't you tell me that? If you had told me that you were waiting at the

291

hotel near the bridge, then I would have known exactly where you were!"

Having established that Jan's inability to navigate his way around his home town was somehow my fault, Jan slumped into the armchair and summoned the receptionist over to where we were sitting.

"Two cappuccinos please – with cream and marshmallows."

The receptionist nodded in acknowledgement and walked away before I had a chance to say anything.

"I don't want another cappuccino, Jan," I said. "I've had two already."

"Well, it's too late now," he declared indignantly. "Why didn't you tell me that before I ordered them?"

2) *Oenophilia*

On Sunday evening, Stella served the most delicious chicken and mushroom pie I have ever tasted – with potatoes, carrots and red cabbage dug from the soil just a couple of hours earlier on Jan's twelve-acre tract of farmland. It prompted a discussion at the dinner table about life on the farm and I ventured to ask how many chickens they kept.

"We have almost two hundred chickens," Stella declared. "But their numbers have decreased since this morning."

"Why have their numbers decreased since this morning?" I asked rather naively, as I chomped my way through Stella's delicious chicken and mushroom pie. After dinner, and until it was time for them to go to bed, I played *Ker-Plunk* with Jan and Stella's two seven-year-old boys – the twins Oskar and Markus. They are what are known as *monozygotic* twins, which simply translated means 'of one egg'. I suppose the more common term would be 'identical twins' – but that's a term Stella and Jan believe is a misnomer and one they prefer not to use. After all, 'identical' twins, as Stella rightly pointed out, can never be truly identical and should not therefore be labelled as such. And she has a fair point. Simply by looking at them, I have always found it impossible to tell Oskar and Markus apart. They look exactly the same, and Stella and Jan have a tendency to dress them in matching clothing which only adds to the confusion. But when it comes to their quirky little character traits, Oskar and Markus are as different from each other as night and day. Oskar is the playful, rather mischievous sibling – with a Cheshire cat grin and an infectious, wheezy snigger – a bit like *Mutley* from the *Wacky Races*. Markus however is more meditative – lost in thought much of the time. He has a minor speech impediment – a slight but noticeable lisp, and is the proud owner of a toothy grin and a smile that could illuminate a football stadium. The two of them have a tendency to bicker and squabble – which I suppose is normal behaviour for most seven-year-olds. But there was one issue on which they were both unanimously agreed – having to go to bed at eight o'clock was totally *'ungerecht'* – an absolute travesty of justice.

"Never mind it being unfair," said Stella authoritatively, as she ushered them towards the stairs. "You can play Ker-Plunk again after school tomorrow. Now say goodnight to daddy and to Chris."

I gave both the boys a hug before Stella marched them out of the living room and escorted them up the stairs. With the children in bed, Stella and I slumped into our respective armchairs, while Jan went down to the cellar to fetch a selection of his favourite wines.

Among his many passions and leisure interests, my friend Jan is something of a wine connoisseur (or at least he likes to think he is). He's one of these self-taught oenophiles who once attended a twelve-week wine appreciation course and then spent a small fortune building a modest collection of fine wines in his cellar. Jan, you see, is one of those people with more time on their hands and more money in the bank than they truly know what to do with. He bought a yacht once, which he still has moored along the Rhine somewhere near Koblenz. Having spent the best part of 150,000 euros on this sleek and curvaceous piece of nautical engineering in brilliant white fibreglass, Jan took it out for a 'spin' with a few of his chums before returning it to its moorings a week or so later. That was several years ago. I don't think he has been out on it since. But in fairness to Jan, his appreciation of fine wines seems to be more than just a fad. Personally, I couldn't tell the difference between a *Chateau d' Yquem Sauternes* and a bottle of Blue Nun. But Jan can – and I confess to being just a tiny bit envious of his skills in this regard. Jan returned a while later carrying three large goblet-style wine glasses and three bottles of *Spätburgunder* (a locally-produced German Pinot Noir) – a choice which seemed to meet with Stella's approval.

"I reckon you will love this one, Chris," she said – speaking from her previous experience. (I'm guessing she had drunk gallons of the stuff over the years.) As it turned out, it was a veracious prediction. Jan uncorked one of the bottles and poured its entire contents into the three glasses, filling each of them to the brim. He passed one of the glasses to Stella and another to me.

"Now then," Jan declared in the manner of a college lecturer, as he raised his glass in front of him. "For your first lesson in wine tasting – remember the five '*S*' words'."

"Sorry, Jan – did you say 'the five '*S*' words'?"

"Yes. They are *see, swirl, sniff, sip* and *savour.*"

I could see Stella mouthing each of the words as he said them – they were both clearly well-practised.

"Start with what you see," Jan continued. "Study the colour – you can see the colours more vividly if you hold the

294

glass against a white background or tip the glass slightly at an angle."

Stella suddenly leaped to a heightened state of animation.

"Don't tip the glass at an angle, Jan," she said. "I don't want red wine all over my carpet again, thank you very much!"

"Good point," Jan continued, as he shrewdly revised his instructions. "Without spilling wine all over Stella's carpet – swirl the glass to aerate the wine and release the aromas. Then, stick your nose in and take a good sniff to allow the bouquet to drift through your nasal chemoreceptors."

I looked at Stella and took some comfort from the fact that she clearly didn't know what he was talking about either. But I could see Stella following the motions as Jan demonstrated the wine tasting process, so I indulged them both by doing the same. I must confess though – all I really wanted to do at this stage was drink it. But as Jan had told me on several occasions in the past – you can't rush a good wine. And besides, this wine tasting malarkey was rather fun.

"Then take a sip," he said, "whilst simultaneously sucking in air through your mouth."

The three of us sat there making ridiculous slurping noises.

"And finally – savour!" Jan looked pensive as the wine saturated his taste buds.

"I'm getting flavours of dark chocolate, spices and red berries," he announced.

"And I'm getting red berries too – and roasted almonds," added Stella.

"I'm just getting pissed," I said. "At least, that's my plan. Cheers, you two!"

3) *Compassion*

295

We polished off all three bottles of the *Spätburgunder*, which at the risk of insulting your intelligence works out at roughly a bottle each – and believe me, it was potent stuff. I woke up the following morning with a bit of a headache – not a full-blown *Katzenjammer,* admittedly, but I did feel a little delicate. The two boys wanted to say goodbye to me before they went to school, which on reflection was rather sweet of them – so they were understandably disappointed after they'd barged into the spare bedroom to discover me still sound asleep. Oskar decided to wake me gently from my slumber by smacking me over the head with one of his toy

[38] *Hangovers should, in my opinion at least, be measured on some sort of official internationally recognised scale, in much the same way as earthquake strength is measured. So, I would suggest that the 'Hangover Intensity' (HI) scale might be appropriate for this purpose – a scale ranging from 0 to 5 where the following hangover symptoms apply:*

Level 1 – No pain or feeling of nausea, but your hands are shaking and your mouth is dry. No matter how many glasses of water you drink, your thirst remains stubbornly unquenchable.

Level 2 – No pain, but something is definitely not right. You feel a little nauseous, and you have the attention span of a goldfish. If you're planning to go into work with a level 2 hangover, then you may want to restrict yourself to light duties. Consider spending the day just sending junk e-mails maybe.

Level 3 – You have a headache and your stomach is decidedly unsettled. Going to work today may be ill-advised as you'll be unproductive and are likely to gag whenever you catch a whiff of that pungent new perfume the fat woman from the accounts department insists on wearing.

Level 4 – Your head is throbbing and you are incapable of any (even slight) head movements. Any attempt at verbal communication would be inadvisable, as it may result in you accidentally vomiting. You'll need to take the day off work as your boss is likely to send you home anyway – or lambast you for reeking of booze.

Level 5 – The throbbing in your head is so loud it's actually disturbing people around you. Alcohol vapours are seeping through every pore of your skin, and your mouth has lost the ability to generate saliva. If you don't lie still in a darkened room, your tongue will eventually suffocate you.

Of course, hangovers don't have to be measured using whole numbers on the HI scale – each level can be sub-divided into decimal places. For example, my hangover that morning rated as a 1.9.

dinosaurs – made from toughened, moulded rubber. It was then that I realised I had a headache. Both Stella and Jan, who had clearly consumed so much *Spätburgunder* over the years that their systems had developed immunity, were up and dressed and going about their morning routine as if the previous evening had been one of absolute sobriety. Stella was doing her best to coerce the twins into the back of her Range Rover, whilst Jan was busy preparing breakfast in the kitchen. The alluring aromas of coffee and fried bacon rashers were wafting through the house and were competing for the attention of my nasal chemoreceptors – which I'm pleased to report hadn't been damaged in any way by my overexerting them the previous evening.

Now, as I've said before, there's nothing on this earth that compares with the superlative qualities of a bacon sandwich: its inimitable smell; its unique taste; its uncanny ability to cure a hangover regardless of its intensity rating on the HI scale.[38] But when a bacon sandwich is accompanied by a cup of hot, strong coffee, you have a divine combination – an ambrosial *ménage à deux* worthy of the gods. So I prized myself out of bed, showered, dressed, and made my way downstairs to Jan and Stella's spacious kitchen – the centrepiece of which was an enormous pine breakfast table large enough to accommodate a regal banquet. At the precise moment that Jan began plating three mouth-watering breakfasts of grilled bacon, poached eggs (freshly laid from the farm), and German rye bread, Stella returned home from the school run. I suspect that this impeccable timing was no coincidence – it was a routine that Jan and Stella had perfected after a great deal of practice.

As the three of us sat at the table gorging ourselves on a hearty breakfast, Stella asked me about my plans for the next couple of days.

"Is there anywhere you'd like us to take you?" she asked. "Or anything specifically you'd like to see?"

It was a perfectly reasonable question, but one that took me a little by surprise. You see, until that moment, I hadn't given the subject a great deal of thought. Every day of my trip so far had been planned in meticulous detail. My diary had been filled with details of train schedules, campsite check-in times, and comprehensive notes on places I needed to be and the times I needed to be there. It was draisine riding on this day, rabbit showjumping on that day and bathtub racing on another. It was all pre-planned in punctilious military detail – in most cases many months beforehand. But my diary entries for the next couple of days had simply read 'staying with Jan and Stella'. I hadn't given any thought at all as to how my time might be spent. There was certainly no shortage of things to do here. The little town of Wittlich is both picturesque and historical – it can trace its roots back to the third millennium BC. Wittlich sits snugly in the valleys of the Eifel region, and is surrounded by lush green rolling hills and lakes carved from ancient volcanic activity. Around 110 square kilometres of the Eifel is protected as a national park and nature reserve. As I'm sure you can imagine the Eifel is an area of outstanding natural beauty – a little haven of peace and solitude. Yet despite its indubitable splendour, the area is virtually unknown – especially to tourists.

Not far away from Jan's farm is the Mosel Valley – Germany's 'Wine Valley'. It stretches along eighty kilometres from Trier to Koblenz, and is arguably one of the most beautiful valleys in the world. Along the route and on every bend of the meandering river, there are tiny wine-producing towns, attractive hillside vineyards, Roman ruins and Baroque castles tucked away on the steep valley walls. River cruises operate along the Mosel, and no matter what time of the year you choose to visit, at least one of the Mosel Valley towns will be holding its annual wine festival. There were a thousand things I could potentially do with my time here – from river cruising to cross-country cycling; or from hot-air ballooning to motor racing at the nearby *Nürburgring*. But I'd come here primarily to visit Jan and Stella (and their two boys of course), and I was perfectly happy for them to dictate the agenda. If they were planning to go nowhere at all over the next couple of days – just simply stay at home, sitting on their backsides and guzzling *Spätburgunder* in voluminous quantities, well, that would have suited me just fine. But as I was soon to discover, idleness did not feature in Jan's plans for me.

"We're taking Chris into *Trier* today – to walk around the town and see the sights," he said – which was news to both Stella and me. The conversation that followed was conducted in my absence. Actually, that isn't true. I was sitting at the kitchen table with my congenial hosts – but anyone listening in on the banter between Jan and Stella could be forgiven for thinking that I wasn't there at all.

"And supposing Chris doesn't want to go to Trier?" Stella said.

"He does."

"How do you know he does? Have you asked him?"

"There's no need to ask him."

"Well, I'll ask him then," said Stella, turning towards me. "Would you like a trip into Trier today, Chris?"

"Well......" I spluttered, before being immediately interrupted.

"Of course he'd like a trip into Trier," said Jan.

This bout of infantile, self-indulgent bickering continued as we raced along the E14 towards Trier in Jan's 'S-Class' Mercedes – with its plush leather seating and its 258-brake horsepower engine that was barely audible in the comfort of the vehicle's swanky sound-proofed interior. The argument this time however, was not over whether we'd be going to Trier or not (that, quite clearly, was already a done deal), but whether we'd be spending the greater part of the day wandering around Trier's ancient town centre visiting the town's numerous places of interest; or whether we'd be spending sufficient time relaxing in coffee shops. It was Stella who favoured the latter, as she wasn't able to walk for any prolonged period of time on account of her "*Schwielen*". Despite their ability to speak English fluently, neither Stella nor Jan knew the equivalent English term, and since I was unfamiliar with the word '*Schwielen*', I was unable to offer an accurate translation. I knew from Stella's general explanation that "*Schwielen*" was some sort of skin condition affecting the feet – so I made the assumption that she was suffering from verrucas or calluses of some form or another. After scanning the internet on whatever complicated gadgetry he had built in to the dashboard of his Mercedes, Jan revealed that *Schwielen* were in fact, *corns*. So, the two of them eventually agreed on a compromise – we would visit a few of the town's attractions – interspersed with regular stops for liquid refreshments and a chance for Stella to take the weight off her feet.

The town of Trier is tucked away in a deep Mosel River valley in the far west of Germany, less than ten kilometres from Germany's border with Luxembourg and only fifty kilometres from Luxembourg City centre. The town serves as a gateway along the Mosel from Germany to Luxembourg and the Alsace-Lorraine regions of France – and the surrounding area is mainly rural with the valley sporting a number of vineyards, woods and forests. If you're an architecture buff, Trier is something of a Mecca. It is, officially, Germany's oldest town – founded in 16BC as part of the Roman Empire – and for four hundred years served as an imperial residence. There are many Roman-era buildings and ruins still in evidence here, despite the battering the town endured during the Second World War. There's baroque and renaissance architecture in Trier too – as I was to discover during the course of my day here.

As soon as we reached Trier's lively town centre, Jan parked the car and marched Stella and me through the town's *Hauptmarkt* – as if he were a man on a mission. I noticed as I hurried past them that many of the shop fronts were painted in bright pastel colours – some sporting colourful, ornate frescoes. But there was no time to stop or study the intricacy of the murals on display – Jan was determined to hurry us through the town as quickly as he possibly could. We were heading towards the *Porta Nigra* (*Black Gate*) – Trier's only remaining Roman city gate (the Romans originally built four, but whereas the other three have long since disappeared, this one remains in remarkably good condition). When we reached the monument, Jan suddenly assumed the role of our official town tour guide – a responsibility he embraced with a degree of vivacity. In fact, Jan took on this role with such enthusiasm that I'm surprised he didn't don a uniform and a peaked cap with the words 'Tour Guide' inscribed across the rim.

"It's called the Porta Nigra because of the darkened colour of the stone," Jan explained. "It's the largest Roman city gate north of the Alps."

Jan escorted Stella and me around many of Trier's landmarks. We visited the town's two main squares: the cathedral of St. Peter that dominates the *Domplatz;* and the beautiful *Kurfürstliches Palais (Electoral Palace)* – a rather fine rococo palace built in 1756 – distinctive on account of it being painted in a rather discerning shade of pink.

"I really need to sit down somewhere," Stella protested, despite Jan's determination to usher us both to the next landmark on his 'to do' list. "My feet really are hurting me."

Now, my friend Jan may be many things, and like all of us he has his faults. But he certainly isn't lacking in compassion, and the expression on his face at that moment was one of total sympathy and understanding.

"There's a little pavement café across the square, sweetheart," he said, gently stroking his wife's arm in an effort to comfort her.

"Shall we stop for coffee?"

Needless to say, neither I nor Stella raised any objections, and so the three of us sat down at one of the tables that spilled out from the café's shadowy interior onto the sun-drenched pavement outside. After ordering our coffee, Stella kicked off her shoes, put her feet up on the chair opposite and lit up a cigarette.

"There's still a lot to see in Trier," Jan said. "There's a Roman baths just a few minutes' walk from here – and there's a rather well-preserved Roman amphitheatre. We'll take a stroll over there as soon as we've finished our coffee."

"There's no rush!" Stella interjected rather abruptly before settling into her chair and taking another drag from her cigarette.

We did eventually visit the Roman baths – and the amphitheatre, although our pace had slowed considerably. Stella was clearly in some discomfort and was struggling to keep up. But, as the saying goes, all good things must come to an end – and by 3.00pm it was time for us to head back to Wittlich, stopping en route to pick up Oskar and Markus from the *Grundschule Wengerohr*.

4) Congeniality

That evening was almost a carbon copy of the night before. Stella rustled up another fabulous evening meal – a fish pie this time, with a side of farm-grown broccoli and cauliflower. The pie was another triumph of culinary excellence, and I could almost hear the chickens in their coop outside in the yard breathing a sigh of relief. After dinner, and once the twins had gone to bed, Stella and I retired once again to the comfort of the living room while Jan headed for his wine cellar in search of further supplies of

Spätburgunder. But this time, Jan returned with only two bottles. I had opted for a wine-free evening, choosing beer as my poison of preference instead. Not that my decision presented a problem for my gracious hosts, you understand. There were several refrigerators scattered around this capacious farmhouse – at least two in the kitchen, one in the garage and another in the closet under the stairs. There were several outhouses on the farm too, and I'm sure I saw a couple of fridges there also. As it turned out, Jan had one particular refrigerator which he used exclusively for storing bottles of beer, so as you might well imagine, my choices were illimitable. I decided after a great deal of contemplation to go for the *Bitburger Pils* – mainly because of the label on the bottle, which unlike many of the other brands was plain and unfussy.

"A wise choice," said Jan reassuringly. "It's brewed in *Bitburg* – only about half an hour's drive from Wittlich – so you'll be supporting the local economy by drinking it."

Jan, Stella and I burned the midnight oil that evening. We chewed the fat and we put the world to rights. I was disappointed when it was time to go to bed. I could have sat there all night in the company of my two generous, warm and congenial hosts.

5) Entrepreneurship

The Henkes had a few things to do on Tuesday morning, so there were no special treats or excursions on today's agenda. Jan was planning to visit a local farmer's mart where he'd be selling a few of his eggs – and he asked me if I wanted to accompany him. I'd never been to a farmer's mart before, but the prospect of attending one sparked my curiosity, so naturally I agreed to tag along. Stella had things to do too. After dropping the twins off at school, she had an appointment with her chiropodist (the poor woman had spent much of the previous evening complaining bitterly about the discomfort she was suffering). So, as Stella bundled the twins into the back of her Range Rover, Jan and I climbed into the luxury interior of his executive Mercedes with its delicate cargo of chickens' eggs stacked carefully in the boot.

"I hope the chiropodist can do something for Stella," I said, as Jan very gently negotiated a couple of speed humps at the bottom of the lane.

"I bloody hope so," Jan replied – somewhat hard-heartedly, I thought. "She's done nothing but grumble and moan for the last two weeks."

"Well," I said, rather quick-wittedly in my opinion, "as the old saying goes: hell hath no fury like a woman's corns."

Jan stared at me blankly – he was evidently bemused.

"I don't understand," he said with archetypal German solemnity. "What do you mean by that?"

I didn't bother to explain. The moment had gone – I think any further explanation would have been lost in translation.

The farmer's mart was an interesting event – the combination of an agricultural trade fair and a farmer's market. On one side of the field livestock auctions were under way, with crowds of bidders gathered around pens full of cattle, pigs, sheep and chickens; with auctioneers bellowing their strange language of rapid-fire rhythmic chanting which would still have been incomprehensible to me even if it hadn't been in German. On the opposite side of the field, a farmer's market – where local farmers had set up a variety of booths, tables and stands to sell their produce to the general public. There was everything imaginable on display here – cuts of meat, cheeses, fruits and vegetables, sausages, pies, jams and home-baked bread. Jan drove his car across the field and parked it next to an empty stall which was sandwiched between a tall, bearded man selling olives by the half-kilogram in sealable plastic tubs, and a rotund woman in a white pinafore selling pies. Judging by the size of her, I was surprised she had any pies left to sell. She must surely have eaten most of them.

Jan's stall wasn't what you might call an elaborate affair. It was nothing more than a wallpaper pasting table, covered in plastic, waterproof sheeting. Jan produced a couple of portable fold-up camping stools from the boot of his car and set them up behind the table.

"Will you give me a hand to fetch the eggs from the car, matey?" Jan asked. Naturally, I obliged.

Jan explained that although the farmer's market was open every day, he set up stall on only three days per week. With only 200 of them, Jan's chickens couldn't produce enough eggs to justify the stall being open any more frequently than that. But if he set up stall any less frequently, he wouldn't be legally entitled to advertise his produce as 'freshly laid'. So, with a stock of around four hundred eggs on each occasion, Jan attended the stall on Tuesdays, Stella on Thursdays and, for a remuneration of ten euros, employed a teenager from the local village to attend the stall on Saturdays.

"You stingy git!" I said. "Only ten euros?"

"Ten euros is actually a very generous wage." Jan insisted. "Do you have any idea how long it takes to sell four hundred eggs?"

"No. But I'm guessing four or five hours, maybe?"

"The whole lot will be sold in twenty minutes."

And Jan was right. Our stock started selling from the moment I began to unload the cardboard trays from the boot of the car – and in less than half an hour every single egg was gone.

Armed with more than €150 from the sale of his eggs, Jan and I browsed the market stalls in search of the ingredients for the evening meal. It was Jan's turn to cook that night, and he was planning to rustle up one of his specialities – authentic *Wienerschnitzel* and champignon sauce, with sautéed potatoes and red cabbage. So, while Jan went in search of a prime cut of veal, I bought a selection of cheeses and a tub of olives for afters. And then we drove home again – the car's boot fully laden with epicurean delicacies.

6) Presumptuousness

"Chris and I are going to a nightclub tonight," said Jan, as we sat at the dining table enjoying a veal schnitzel that was so tender, it almost melted in the mouth.

"And supposing Chris doesn't want to go to a nightclub?" Stella said.

"He does."

"How do you know he does? Have you asked him?"

"There's no need to ask him."

"Well, I'll ask him then," said Stella, turning towards me. "Would you like to go with Jan to a nightclub this evening, Chris?"

"Well......" I spluttered, before being immediately interrupted.

"Of course he'd like to come with me to a nightclub," said Jan.

But the truth of the matter was that I really *didn't* want to go to a nightclub at all. In fact, if Jan had suggested that we spend the evening severing each other's limbs using a blunt, rusty scythe it would have been a preferable alternative. Let's be honest here, Jan and I are both far too old to go to nightclubs. Jazz clubs – maybe, bingo clubs – certainly; but when one reaches a certain age, nightclubs are, or at least *should* be, completely out of the question.

"Which club are you going to?" Stella asked.

"The *Palais am Dom*."

Stella frowned momentarily before replying, "mmm, that'll be nice" – a comment which I sensed was loaded more with sarcasm than sincerity. In a desperate bid for a get-out clause, I suddenly had what I considered to be a fabulous idea – the perfect solution to my dilemma and an impressive example of quick-thinking on my part.

"Why don't you two go?" I said. "I can stay here and babysit the twins, and you two can get your dancing shoes on and enjoy a well-deserved night out together."

"What? Go to a nightclub with *her*? – you must be joking!" Jan said.

"You're expecting me to go to a nightclub with *him*? No way! Besides, how can I go dancing with *these* feet?" Stella added. I assumed she was referring to her corns rather than her lack of dancing prowess, but I guess I shall never know for sure. Their response to my suggestion seemed fairly conclusive – it looked very much as if I was going to a nightclub with Jan whether I wanted to or not. I couldn't refuse to go, could I? After all, Jan was my friend. He had welcomed me into his home; allowed me to share his food, his wine and his beer. He had even granted me the honour of being whacked over the head with a moulded-rubber dinosaur by a seven-year-old. And in exchange for his generous and bountiful hospitality, Jan had asked for nothing. So how could I say no? Whatever flights of whimsical fantasy Jan proposed during my stay at his home – I felt obliged to indulge him. *That* was the deal. So although my heart was reluctant to agree to accompany him to a nightclub, I felt compelled to feign a small degree of enthusiasm.

Jan ordered a taxi to take us there, so I knew a boozy night was on the cards. And when the driver asked where we were going and Jan replied "The Palais am Dom", he looked at Jan and me rather inquisitively – the sort of facial expression that said, "Really? Are you sure?"

The Palais am Dom was even more dreadful than I'd concluded it would be long before our arrival. In typical nightclub style, its doors were guarded by a couple of brawny bouncers – their corpulent frames designed for standing statue-like in one spot rather than moving anywhere quickly. They both wore ill-fitting suits, had shaven heads and both had eyebrows that met in the middle. From their general appearance, these two Neanderthals could easily have been brothers – except that one of them was black and the other wasn't. The club was virtually empty. There were a handful of people standing at the bar and another small group skulking in one shadowy corner of the dance hall. They were all women, I think. It was difficult to tell as their faces were camouflaged by strobe lighting of constantly changing colours. There was nobody at all on the dance floor – which must have been rather disconcerting for the DJ.

The music, so my daughter has subsequently informed me, was *'garage'* – a syncopated 4/4 percussion rhythm with beat-skipping kick drums and shuffling hi-hat sounds, which was being played at an ear-splitting volume – so loud, that it was impossible for Jan and me to conduct a conversation without shouting in each other's ears. And so, unable to communicate with Jan in the conventional manner, I stood watching *'DJ Sponge'* demonstrating his skills in the subtle arts of beat-juggling, needle-dropping and phase-shifting (these phrases were all supplied by my daughter, so best not to ask), and I could feel most of my internal organs vibrating to the resonance of the bass.

"Let's neglect a stink," Jan shouted in my ear. At least, I think that's what he said.

We were both alarmed to discover that the club bar served nothing other than cocktails. There was no beer or wine on sale – such beverages apparently weren't favoured by the clubs usual clientele, and the barman seemed almost offended that Jan had been audacious enough to ask. And so, faced with no other choice, we both ordered a cocktail – two drinks for a staggering €27, which I paid for. (Jan had already forked out an astonishing €50 for entry into the club.) Jan decided on the rather unimaginatively named '*Fizzy Apple Cocktail*' – a sickly blend of apple vodka, lemonade and apple juice. It was the cheaper of the two drinks – a snip at only €12, but it was little more than a mixer drink – a tiny splash of alcohol diluted with so much lemonade that the flavour of the vodka was barely detectable. I opted for a *Pink Squirrel*. It was €15 admittedly, which on reflection was an absurd amount of money to pay for a drink. But I decided that if I was destined to get ripped off by forking out a small fortune for a sickly, overpriced cocktail, then I'd at least get one with a quirky sounding name. Made from a stomach-churning mélange of crème de noyaux, crème de cacao and single cream, my Pink Squirrel was truly disgusting – so much so that I managed to drink only half of it.

As I stood there with my cocktail in hand, mesmerised by flashing strobe lighting, having my eardrums pounded by the deafening din of '*two-step garage*', I suddenly felt very old, very fat and horribly self-conscious. I was a fish out of water – an old man in a young person's environment – and a most unwelcome intruder. I think Jan may have sensed my discomfort.

"You're not really enjoying this, are you?" Jan shouted in my ear.

"Not really. Are you?"

"Not even slightly," Jan replied. "Shall we find a nice quiet pub somewhere matey, and put the world to rights over a beer?"

Jan smiled and patted me on the shoulder. He already knew my answer.

oOo

Dear Diary,

The Beer, Cheese and Tent Report for the State of Rhineland-Palatinate:

Beer: Bitburger Pils:

Bitburger is Germany's premier draught beer and for very good reason. The stuff has been brewed in Bitburg for more than 200 years and has a crispy-clean, dry, hoppy taste. Bitburger is decidedly flavoursome and if the manufacturers want to send me several crates of free samples as my reward for saying so, then I wouldn't want to discourage them.

Cheese: Weinkäse:

The name 'Weinkäse' (Wine Cheese) was invented by German cheese-makers specifically as an accompaniment to the fruity wines of the Moselle and Rhine Rivers. It's a mild, creamy cheese that goes perfectly with a slice of rye bread. I bought an unfeasibly large quantity of the stuff from a stall at the farmer's market.

Tent Stability:

I'm giving my Wind-Breaker DeLuxe a well-deserved rest while I'm in Rhineland-Palatinate – she's resting in one of the outhouses on Jan's farm whilst I'm enjoying the comfort of a proper bed.

oOo

Chapter Fourteen – A Little Piece of France

"Every man has two countries, his own and France."
Henri, vicomte de Bornier – French poet and dramatist
1825 – 1901

"So, where are you heading to next?" Stella asked, as the three of us sat around the kitchen table on Wednesday morning enjoying another of Jan's egg and bacon breakfasts.

"Well, I've already been to twelve of Germany's states – so there's only four left for me to visit. Next on the list is Saarland. I'll be heading there later today."

"The state line between Rhineland-Palatinate and Saarland is only a few kilometres south of Trier," Stella said. "Whereabouts in Saarland will you be staying?"

"I'll be camping for two nights in the *Saar-Hunsrück National Park*. There's a beer-tasting festival in a little village called Losheim near to my campsite, but I was also planning to hire a bike when I'm there – to explore a bit of the countryside."

"Saar-Hunsrück is beautiful," Stella said. "I used to visit the park when I was a child – my parents would take me there regularly."

"Yes, it sounds great," Jan interjected. "Nice scenery, fresh air, a beer-tasting festival *and* a bit of cycling. What could be better than that? I shall come with you."

For a moment, there was silence. Stella and I stared at Jan in disbelief – our mouths wide open with astonishment.

"What do you mean – you'll go with him?" said Stella indignantly. "You can't just invite yourself! This is Chris's adventure – not yours. Chris likes to travel alone."

"Chris won't mind me tagging along, will you Chris? It's only for a couple of nights. I'll be back on Friday. We could take a couple of my bikes on the train as far as Trier and cycle to Losheim from there. I'm pretty sure it's only about forty kilometres from Trier to Losheim and it's a pretty good road – we could cycle *that* easily! Just think, Chris – you and me on a camping expedition! How does that sound to you? It'll be great fun – don't you think?"

Jan turned to his wife and smiled at her inanely.

"You don't mind do you, love?"

"It's not a question of whether I mind or not!" Stella replied. "As it happens I'd be quite happy to have you out of my hair for a couple of days. But that's hardly the point, is it?"

"Well, what *is* the point?"

"The point is, my darling husband, you've never been camping in your life. You don't even own a tent!"

"I can share Chris's."

It was at that point that I felt it necessary to intervene in Jan and Stella's conversation. There was a vital piece of information that Jan urgently needed to be aware of.

"You won't be able to share with me," I said. "I've only got a one-man tent, and there's barely enough room in it for me."

"Then I'll buy one," said Jan. "There's a camping shop in Wittlich. I'll drive into town after breakfast and buy myself a tent."

"A waste of money!" Stella ranted. "Another of your fads! When you get home on Friday you'll throw the tent in the cellar and it will never see the light of day again."

"You never know, Stella – I might *love* camping. This little excursion might give me a taste for the outdoor life. Who says I'll never use the tent again?"

"You *won't* enjoy camping, Jan. You enjoy your luxuries too much."

Now, in my opinion, Stella had made a valid point. She was absolutely right: my friend Jan *did* enjoy his luxuries – he certainly wasn't accustomed to 'slumming it'. It seemed to me that spending a couple of nights in a tent would be Jan's idea of hell. It was rather like asking the Queen and the Duke of Edinburgh to abandon their holiday on the Royal Yacht Britannia, and spend a week in a caravan in Skegness instead. Jan was a five-star hotel man. If he wanted a cup of coffee, he'd expect room service to bring him one. The prospect of trekking to the nearest supply tap to fill a kettle with water and then boil it on a portable butane gas stove? Well, Jan would regard the whole ordeal abhorrent. But if Jan makes his mind up about something, then there's precious little anybody can do or say to make him reconsider. Jan is the most obdurate, stubborn, pig-headed individual one could ever meet, and quite frankly, that's what I love about him.

As I think we've already established, I'm not really one for spontaneity – the thought of making spur of the moment decisions that haven't been meticulously pre-planned months and months in advance is enough to bring me out in a cold sweat. But there was something about *this* particular 'off the cuff' decision that I found rather appealing. I was delighted that Jan wanted to accompany me on the next leg of my trip. He was right – it *would* be great fun.

Unbeknown to me, at the time anyway, Jan was the proud owner of three (yes, three!) terribly expensive road bikes. It was another of his fads, according to Stella. He acquired all three of them a few years ago following a chance conversation with a man he'd met in a pub. But within a few weeks of purchasing his new toys, and with his usual caprice, Jan alternated between having a zest for cycling one minute, and a languor for it the next – and then he lost interest altogether. So, for the past three years, all three of Jan's bikes have been stored in one of the outhouses, neglected and unloved, waiting for the day when some compassionate soul might throw aside their dustsheets and give them a new lease of life. Well, for two of them at least, that day had finally come. And I must admit, I was rather looking forward to a forty-kilometre cycle ride. There's nothing quite as invigorating or as effective in brushing away the cobwebs and getting the heart pumping.

This rather sudden and impulsive change of plan would require a few small amendments to my itinerary. Once my adventures in Losheim were over, my original plan had been to travel from the state of Saarland directly to the state of Baden-Württemberg. But now, with Jan's bike needing to be returned to the farmhouse, I would have to accompany Jan back to Wittlich on Friday morning before heading to Baden-Württemberg from there. I hadn't worked out a route, or checked the times of the buses and trains, or even given any thought as to whether a public conveyance even existed. But I didn't care. Three days in the relaxed, carefree company of Jan and Stella had clearly rubbed off on me. To hell with the itinerary! It was 'day one' of the 'new me' – I would approach life with gay abandon from here on in.

With breakfast over, Jan took the car into Wittlich and I helped Stella with a few of the daily chores. After washing up the breakfast things, Stella and I fed the chickens and the pigs, and I dug up a few potatoes to replenish the dwindling stocks in Stella's larder.

"Don't dig up too many," Stella shouted. "Jan won't be here for the next couple of days, so we only need enough for me and the boys."

I was enjoying doing 'farm chores' – so much so that I lost track of time. Jan had been gone for more than two hours, and when he eventually returned, he marched straight into the kitchen with a package in his hand and was grinning like a bushel basketful of possum heads. Jan summoned Stella and me into the kitchen and like an excitable schoolchild he placed the package on the kitchen table.

"I've bought a tent!" he said excitedly.

314

I stared at the tent Jan had bought in utter disbelief. My eyes widened; my mouth opened; I was momentarily so astounded that I found myself unable to speak. What *was* this strange emotion I was feeling? Was it surprise? Or anger, perhaps? Or was I feeling just a small tinge of envy? I decided it was time to break my silence.

"That's a *Vaude Power Tokee Ultra-Light!*" I said.

"Yes it is," Jan replied. "Isn't she a beauty?"

"But it's probably the most expensive one-man tent you can get. How much did you pay for it, Jan?"

"I got change out of four hundred euros."

"*Four hundred euros?*" Stella shouted despairingly.

There was genuine anger in her eyes. Jan seemed surprised by his wife's reaction.

"I don't understand what all the fuss is about," he said. "I didn't say it *was* four hundred euros. I said I got *change* out of four hundred euros!"

"Well how much was it then?"

"Three hundred and ninety-nine – but it's only money, Stella. If I was spending the next two nights in a hotel it would cost at least that. Plus I'd have nothing to show for it afterwards. At least I'll be coming home on Friday with my very own tent."

"Which, no doubt, you'll shove in the cellar and never use again!"

"Look," said Jan, in an effort, I suspect, to convince himself as well as Stella and me. "If you want something decent, you have to spend a bit of money. There's nothing to be gained from buying something cheap and cheerful. The sales person at the camping shop said the Power Tokee was the best on the market – it offers maximum stability and it weighs only 800 grams."

"Let me guess," I said. "He was a scrawny-looking seventeen-year-old with a pimply face, wispy stubble on his

315

chin, piercings in his ears and eyebrows, and a ponytail in his hair."

Jan appeared somewhat baffled by my outburst.

"No," he said, in a calm and passive tone. "Actually *she* was a very attractive young lady with blond hair and a pair of rather sexy spectacles. Why do you ask?"

"No reason," I said. "I think I may have met her brother once."

By mid afternoon, Jan and I were ready to make a move, and it was time for me to say goodbye to Stella. It was a moment I had been dreading – after all, parting is such sweet sorrow, as some particularly clever old bugger once penned. I'd already said goodbye to the twins before they'd set off for school that morning, and I'd given them both a little present that I'd bought from a toyshop in Trier the previous day. It wasn't a terribly imaginative gift I'm afraid – a selection of toy dinosaurs to add to the ones they already had. But the kids seemed happy enough. Jan fetched a couple of his bikes from the outhouse and made some adjustments to the height of the saddle and the handlebars, until both were attuned to accommodate my short legs and my portly frame. And that was that. We were ready to hit the open road.

Jan and I rode our bikes as far as Wittlich station where we boarded a commuter train to Trier. Unable to find a space designed specifically for the purpose, we had no option other than to prop our bicycles against a row of retractable seats – and since they were balanced so precariously, it was necessary for Jan and me to stand for the duration of the journey, holding on to the handlebars to prevent the bikes from toppling over with the movement of the train. But, mercifully, our carriage was virtually empty – and since the bikes weren't depriving any frail, elderly ladies of their right to sit down, nor appeared to be causing any obvious obstruction, we left them in that position until we reached Trier and spent the thirty-minute journey simply chatting to each other about everything and anything that happened to crop up in conversation.

With our panniers laden with bottles of mineral water and our worldly belongings tucked safely in the rucksacks we had strapped to our backs, Jan and I left the station at Trier, mounted our bikes and headed south along the B268 – the least busy of the roads connecting Trier with Saarbrücken (the state capital of the Saarland), but by far the most picturesque. About halfway between Trier and Saarbrücken lies the charming little village of *Losheim am See,* located in the heart of the *Saar-Hunsrück National Park* – and it was there, at a lakeside camping site close to Losheim village, that Jan and I would be staying for the next two nights. Jan had estimated the distance between Trier and the campsite to be around 40 kilometres, and had also predicted a journey time of around two-and-a-half hours assuming a leisurely cycling speed. He was right about the distance – well, almost. According to the rather snazzy, if not gratuitous, piece of electronic gadgetry Jan had attached to the handlebars of his bicycle, there were 37.9 kilometres between Trier and Losheim. Jan, by the way, is very much an 'electronic gadget' kind of guy. He was wrong about the time it would take us to cycle there though – his original two-and-a-half-hour estimate didn't allow for an impromptu hour-long stopover at the village of *Obermenning*, where a poster advertising *Bitburger Pils*, placed strategically outside an enchanting little village inn, succeeded in luring us (against our will, naturally) into the beer garden. That's the trouble with unscrupulous advertisers and their confounded poster boards – they lead people astray, inveigling them into doing things they shouldn't. It's tantamount to entrapment if you ask me. But the beer went down well, and as we sat there in the summer sunshine we were able to continue chatting whilst keeping an eye on our bikes which we'd tied to a set

317

of wrought-iron railings. The journey time was protracted too by the undulating nature of the terrain. It was uphill one minute and downhill the next; and I must confess that I found some of the uphill stretches a tad strenuous. That's what happens when you're middle-aged and out of shape. Jan, by stark contrast, seemed to take it all in his stride, and cycled to the pinnacle of even the steepest of inclines without so much as breaking into a sweat.

Eventually we reached a signpost displaying the Saarland state flag with the words *'Willkommen im Saarland'* printed beneath it in gilded lettering. We had reached the state border – the state of Rhineland-Palatinate was now behind us. With only six kilometres of our journey remaining, we dismounted once again and wheeled our bicycles into a clearing in the woods.

"Watch my bike for a moment, will you matey?" Jan shouted. "I desperately need a piss." And with that he ran into the woods leaving me to babysit his bike.

The state of Saarland lies in the far west of Germany and shares borders with Luxembourg to the west and France (*département de Moselle*) to the south and west. It is named after the River Saar – a tributary of the Mosel (itself a tributary of the Rhine), which snakes its way through the state from the south to the northwest. Aside from the three city states of Berlin, Hamburg and Bremen, the Saarland is the smallest of Germany's *Flächenländer* or *area states,* occupying an area of just 2,570 km². With just a fraction more than one million people living within its boundaries, Saarland is the least populous of all the German states, with most of its inhabitants living in a city agglomeration on the French border surrounding the state capital, Saarbrücken.

I had been particularly looking forward to visiting the Saarland. The state's publicity brochures promised a great deal, and I'd heard straight from the mouths of previous visitors to the Saar region what a delightful and fascinating place it was. When we arrived at the campsite at *Losheim am See*, we checked in at reception before cycling around the park in search of a suitable patch of ground to pitch our tents. It didn't take us long to find the perfect spot – a small area of grassland in a shady dell surrounded by willow trees and with a perfect view of the lake. It was an idyllic little spot, picturesque and peaceful – a tad isolated perhaps, but there was room enough for both our tents and Jan seemed happy with his surroundings. And if it was good enough for Jan, then it was certainly good enough for me. We chained the bikes to the trunk of a tree and set about assembling our respective tents. Jan was clearly having problems getting to grips with the assembly instructions, and I wasn't in the least bit surprised when he asked me to help him.

"Let me assemble my tent first, Jan – then I'll help you with yours afterwards."

"Thanks matey. I'm just nipping off to find the toilet. I'll be back in five minutes."

I didn't expect Jan to be back in five minutes. Given his record on tardiness I expected him to be gone for a bit longer than that. In the event, he was gone for over half an hour.

"Where the hell have you been?" I asked when he finally found his way back. "I was about to send out a search party."

"I couldn't find the toilet block," he replied. "I walked the entire circumference of the campsite looking for it."

"It's over there!" I pointed to a large brick building just thirty metres away and clearly visible from where the two of us were standing.

"Yes, I know," he replied. "I found it eventually."

Whilst Jan had been wandering around the campsite in search of the toilet, not only had I managed to assemble my *Wind-Breaker DeLuxe*, but I'd also made a start on Jan's *Power Tokee*. Not much of a start, admittedly. I had only got

319

as far as tipping the various components out of their bag and spreading them across the grass in order to identify each of them by their illustrations and colour codes as shown in the assembly instructions – but Jan seemed pleased with my progress. It was at that point that Jan suddenly noticed *my* tent, fully assembled in all its resplendence. He stood there, staring at it with incredulity – evidently both shocked and speechless.

"What the fuck is *that*?" he said eventually – which surprised me somewhat, as generally speaking Jan was not a proponent of such earthy language.

"It's my *Wind-Breaker DeLuxe*," I said, proudly. "What do you think of her?"

"What do *I* think? It's a disaster! Please don't tell me you've travelled around Germany with this........." He paused for a moment, whilst racking his brain for an appropriate noun to finish his sentence with. I waited in anticipation for him to come up with something deeply profound, but when he did finally think of something, I'm afraid it was a terrible disappointment.

"........pile of shit," he said.

"It's not pretty, I agree."

"Not pretty? Chris, it isn't even a proper tent! The poles are bent; the whole thing is leaning over to one side; the canvas has tears in it; there are splits in the seams; it's covered with an unsightly black ink splodge; it's being held together with pieces of masking tape – and most of that is peeling off! For God's sake, Chris – it's a heap of junk – the most dreadful-looking tent I've ever seen!"

"But it's perfectly practical," I protested, perhaps rather unconvincingly. "It doesn't matter what it looks like, does it? Captain Robert Scott and his team didn't worry about what their tents looked like when they set out to conquer the South Pole! They intended to sleep in them – not enter them in a beauty pageant. As long as it keeps the rain out then it's perfectly practical."

"And *does* it keep the rain out?"

"It isn't raining, so the question is entirely academic."

"But if it *was* raining – would it keep the rain out?"

"Probably not."

Once Jan and I had managed to decipher the assembly instructions, we put *his* tent together before stepping a few paces backwards to inspect our handiwork. As the two of us stood there staring with admiration at Jan's *Vaude Power Tokee Ultra-Light* tent, I was overcome by the same emotion I'd experienced a few hours earlier – when Jan had placed his newly-purchased tent on the kitchen table and summoned me and Stella into the kitchen to see it. Except this time, there was no doubt in my mind as to what that feeling was. I am ashamed to say that it was envy.

Now, as emotions go, envy is neither subtle nor kind, but it is definitely complex, encompassing feelings such as fear of abandonment, rage, humiliation and coveting thy neighbour's *Power Tokee*. It certainly isn't an emotion that one should be proud of. I think that Jan may have sensed my envy too – there are times when he can be annoyingly perceptive. Jan put his hand on my shoulder.

"Fancy a beer and something to eat, old chap?" he said, in a kindly, though ever so slightly patronising way.

It was at that moment that I realised how hungry I was – neither of us had eaten anything substantial since breakfast and a forty-kilometre cycle ride had burned off an awful lot of calories that urgently needed replenishing. [39] Both of us, it seemed, had a rapacious appetite.

---

[39] *Calories are those tiny little creatures that crawl around in your wardrobe during the night and mischievously sew your shirts and trousers, making them feel tighter around your waist.*

"Let's see what the campsite shop has to offer," I said. "They may have a tin of something that we can heat up on the stove."

Jan stared at me in astonishment, as if I had suddenly sprouted an extra head.

"What are you talking about?" he said, rather tersely in my view. "We're not eating something out of a tin! We're in France – the home of gastronomic excellence! You and I are going to the finest restaurant we can find – to gorge ourselves on a five-star slap-up dinner fit for royalty – and I'm paying."

At the risk of stating the blatantly obvious, I told Jan that we *weren't* in France, but in fact, we were in the Saarland – a part of Germany – although of course he already knew that. But as Jan explained, the Saarland might be part of Germany both geographically and politically, but in terms of its culture the region is as much a part of France as the neighbouring *Région de Lorraine*. French culture, it seems, has a long tradition and a special standing in Saarland, not least because of the fact that, shortly after the Second World War, France sought to incorporate the region into the French state. The Saarland has been part of the French Republic off and on for the past five hundred years – even as recently as the 20th Century. Between 1920 and 1935, for example, the Saarland was administered by France under a League of Nations mandate. Even the language spoken in the Saarland (a dialect of German known as *Moselle Franconian*) has a subtle yet distinct Gallic cadence. But as I was about to discover, the most persuasive evidence of French influence in the Saarland is in the food.

Within an hour of arriving at the campsite, Jan and I mounted our bikes once again and cycled along a narrow country lane for a little over six kilometres until we reached the tiny village of *Rappweiler*. For it was here, in this tiny little hamlet, in what appeared to be the middle of nowhere, that Jan and I discovered '*La Provence*' – a charming, rustic restaurant with pretty pink table cloths and matching napkins, specialising in classic French cuisine. Actually, that isn't strictly true – we didn't exactly '*discover*' it by happenstance. It really would have been a stroke of good fortune had we simply *stumbled* upon it. The truth was Jan had used his recently-purchased mobile phone to '*Google*' details of the nearest authentic French restaurant to Losheim-am-See. So we knew *La Provence* existed – it was simply a question of finding it.

Our meal, generously paid for by Jan, was quite simply superb. After our 'ouverture' of 'Soupe du Jour' (I can't remember what the soup of the day was, but I think it may have been Wednesday) it was a toss-up between the Muscovy duck breast with elderberry and the braised lamb shank with couscous. In the end the duck breast won the day, but it was a close call. Jan and I settled for the '*Sélection de Fromages'* rather than dessert – to accompany the bottle of *Château de Stony* that Jan had insisted on ordering. Not that my stomach had any spare capacity to accommodate cheese and dessert-wine after such a substantial dinner, but Jan was paying – so my stomach's opinion on the subject was therefore irrelevant.

"Mmm, that's beautiful," said Jan as he took a sip from his wine glass. "There's a persistent aroma of apricots, vanilla, acacia and honey. It has a fresh taste on the palate with a lingering finish of peaches and hazelnuts."

"You really are full of shit, my friend," I said, drawing a final conclusion on the matter. "But here's to your good health, old chap. Cheers!"

I am pretty sure that after such a scrumptious dinner and a few glasses of fine wine, Jan would have much preferred to take a cab back to a five-star luxury hotel suite, snuggle up beneath a fifteen-tog duvet and fart and snore for the rest of the night in the privacy of his own room. But Jan had chosen to come camping with me – and, as yet another old saying goes, 'as you make your bed, so must you lie in it.' The pair of us cycled the six kilometres back to the campsite in the pitch dark along the same unlit country lane. Fortunately we had the foresight to attach lights to our bikes before we set out, but the journey back was slow and arduous, and Jan did nothing but complain until we'd made it back to our tents. And Jan's grumbling didn't end there – it continued throughout the night. On several occasions I could hear Jan mumbling under his breath, and every now and then a salvo of expletives would emanate from within his tent. I think I can safely say that Jan and camping do not make happy bedfellows – spending a night sleeping under canvas was not Jan's idea of fun.

"How did you sleep last night?" I made the foolish mistake of asking him the following morning, as I boiled a kettle of water to make us both a cup of coffee. I immediately wished I hadn't asked.

"Not very well," he said. Actually that's not what he said at all, but after censoring all the profanities and vulgarities, that's a potted summary of what was left.

"I hate having to get up in the night and walk a thousand kilometres to the nearest toilet. There are bats out there! And the toilets are filthy and full of moths and spiders. And sleeping on the ground was really uncomfortable. I was cold too – and your snoring kept me awake."

I decided to treat Mr. Grumpy with kid gloves – tread on eggshells for a while until he calmed down.

"Would you like some coffee, Jan?"

"Yes," he snapped.

Our plan for today was to visit the Losheim-am-See beer festival which was due to start at 11.00am. I was hoping that the prospect of spending an entire day sampling beers from dozens of local breweries would cheer the miserable old bugger up a bit. And I was right. As we strolled into Losheim village (we wisely decided to leave the bikes behind) Jan stopped grumbling about how much he hated camping, and actually managed a smile.

Now, if you've ever visited a German beer festival, such as Munich's famous Oktoberfest or Stuttgart's Cannstatter Volksfest for example, then you'll know that the Germans know a thing or two about hosting these sorts of event. You'll find giant marquees – several of them usually, each sponsored by different breweries. Each of the marquees will be filled to capacity with hundreds of jocular revellers sitting elbow to elbow at long wooden trestle tables and guzzling beer from pewter '*Bierkrugen*'. There'll be music too – supplied, more often than not, by members of the brewery's resident 'oom-pah' band – its members identically dressed in their white, sharply-creased trousers and matching dinner jackets, churning out a string of traditional drinking ditties which the crowds will feel compelled to sing along to – even though there won't be a single person among them who will be familiar with either the lyrics or the tune. Oozing out from the marquees is an unruly cacophony of boisterous conversation, raucous laughter and dissonant singing fuelled by alcohol and high spirits. And there'll be lots going on outside the marquees too. There'll be fairground rides – dodgem cars, carousels and roller coasters. You'll find traditional stalls selling candy floss, mulled wine, grilled sausages, pretzels, gingerbread, crepes and marzipan sweets. A German beer festival is more than just a beer-tasting event – it's a phenomenon – an experience that should hold a primary position on everybody's list of 'stuff to do before you die'.

Of course, I knew long before I arrived at Losheim that its beer festival wouldn't be in the same league as the Munich Oktoberfest. Losheim was a tiny village after all, and the only space available to accommodate such an event was the tiny village green. So in comparison with any of

Germany's premier-league beer festivals, this one wouldn't be on quite the same scale or have quite the same degree of panache. When Jan and I reached the village, the marquee was the first thing we spotted, largely, I think, because it wasn't quite what either of us had been expecting. It wasn't so much a marquee, more a makeshift gazebo – a large polythene sheet held aloft by a number of vertical supporting poles – somewhere for people to seek shelter in the event of rain. The weather forecast for this morning certainly hadn't mentioned rain – far from it, in fact. Today's outlook had been one of unbroken sunshine – with temperatures in the high twenties. We hoped the weathermen hadn't made a mistake – this morning's newspaper had predicted 'warm and dry' and Jan and I had dressed in anticipation of exactly that – me in my three-quarter-length trousers, white canvas shirt and sunshades, and Jan in his blue cotton pique T-shirt with the slogan '*I may be schizophrenic, but at least I have each other*' emblazoned across the chest. [40]

We wandered around the green for a while, browsing the assortment of delicacies on sale at the various market stalls – but there wasn't a great deal to see. It was still early in the day, and although the beer festival had officially been open for an hour or so, many of the stallholders were still in the throes of setting up their pitches, with much of their stock still packed away in wooden crates in the backs of tradesmen's vans. The surge of revellers the organisers had presumably been expecting had yet to materialise too – it seemed eerily quiet, almost as if Jan and

---

[40] *My friend Jan is the proud owner of several T-shirts bearing comical slogans. During my three-night stay at his farmhouse he modelled a few humorous designs that made me chuckle, including 'All the tastiest animals are made out of meat'; '668 – The neighbour of the beast'; and my particular favourite 'My wife says I never listen to anything she says (or something like that)'.*

I had arrived several hours before the event was due to start – or perhaps, several hours after the event had ended.

"Let's come back in an hour or so," Jan suggested.

"I think that might be wise," I agreed.

For at least an hour, the two of us roamed around on our own guided tour of Losheim-am-See – with Jan assuming the role of chief tour guide, naturally. Actually, it wouldn't have mattered whether it had been Jan or I who had assumed this role. Neither of us had visited Losheim before, so we were both equally ignorant of what the village had to offer.

The *Park der Vierjahrezeiten* (Park of the Four Seasons) was our first port of call – a 50,000-square-kilometre landscaped garden with a diversity of plants, shrubs, grasses and trees, managed and maintained by *NABU* – Germany's leading society for nature conservation. I picked up a glossy publicity brochure at the main entrance which contained photographs of flower beds awash with colour, and a narrative overflowing with superlatives. But in reality, this 'wonderland of floral displays'; this 'paradise for garden lovers' didn't quite live up to expectations. There was a great deal of construction work underway during our visit, and the sporadic din of mechanical drilling rather spoiled the tranquillity of it all. And many of the bedding-plant displays seemed a little bland, in my opinion. But I suppose in fairness, many of the plants had been newly-planted and not all of them would have been in bloom during the summer anyway – this was the 'park of the *four* seasons' after all. But on a brighter note, the gardens *did* offer a fabulous panorama of the lake and the bistro served a cracking cappuccino – and since Jan had generously paid the entrance fees to the gardens for both of us – I had no justifiable reason to grumble.

Another of Losheim's notable tourist attractions is its railway museum, part of which includes a passenger train

327

service along a fourteen-kilometre stretch of track from Losheim to the neighbouring town of Merzig – a service that is operated, perhaps unsurprisingly, by steam locomotive. This was once a part of the now defunct *Merzig-Büschfeld line* which closed in 1962. It was market forces that closed many branch lines in Germany in the post-war years – the simple mechanics of supply and demand. Britain, of course, relied on Dr. Richard Beeching to destroy its railway network – his report on the reshaping of Britain's railways in the early 1960s led to the axing of 7,000 (mainly) rural stations and the closure of 7,000 miles of railway tracks. It was a wholly short-sighted act of shameless butchery in my opinion, but I digress. The *Merzig-Büschfeld line* remained derelict for twenty years until a small section of it was resurrected by a group of volunteers – all of them dedicated railway enthusiasts, naturally. The museum, I'm reliably informed, tells the history of the Merzig-Büschfeld line through a collection of photographs, paintings and videos and also houses a number of exhibits from the railway's heyday. But Jan and I chose not to visit the museum, nor did we elect to take a ride on the steam train. I'm pretty sure that, had I been touring Losheim on my own (as was my original plan, of course), I probably *would* have visited the museum. Not that I have any particular interest in railway history or a fervent bent for steam locomotives – but I would have paid the museum a visit simply because it's there. It's a part of the village's heritage – and without the support of visitors like me and Jan, attractions like this would simply close down, and another small piece of history would be lost forever. Sadly though, Jan took an entirely different view. For Jan, a walk around a musty museum browsing a collection of railway artefacts simply didn't float his boat – and a pointless hour-long trip on a crowded steam train was just an inexcusable waste of valuable drinking time.

By the time we arrived back at the village green some two hours later, things had livened up at the Losheim beer festival. The roads around the village green had livened up too. Losheim's main thoroughfare had been virtually empty when we walked along it earlier, but it was now at a standstill as huge crowds of festival-goers descended upon this usually somnolent little town, snarling up the roads and creating gridlock. But the organisers seemed to have everything under control. Hastily-scribbled directional signposts had been stapled to the trunks of every roadside tree; plastic bollards had been strategically placed around the green to prevent unlawful parking; and two morose-looking men in yellow, high-visibility tabards had been hired to direct drivers onto a nearby field – now functioning as a temporary overflow car park. [41] Most of the stalls were now fully operational and for many, trade was brisk. There was one stall in particular that Jan and I seemed strangely drawn to – we were lured by the sounds and smells of sausages and onions barbecuing on an open grill. The main beer tent had also undergone a major transformation – its status having changed from 'gazebo' to 'marquee' in the space of a couple of hours. Tarpaulin side-panels and several doors had been added to the bare frame, and it was now recognisable as a beer tent.

We noticed too, as we strolled around the village green inspecting the various stalls, sideshows and fairground rides, that everybody appeared to have their own beer tankard.

[41] *I suppose that strictly speaking the organisers didn't hire two morose-looking men in yellow, high-visibility tabards. I suspect that, in reality, they hired the men first then issued them with the tabards afterwards. Their morose disposition, I suspect, was merely coincidental. I could be wrong of course. For all I know, the festival organisers could have placed an advert in the local paper which read: 'Two morose-looking men wanted for directing traffic into overflow car park. One day's work only – must have own yellow, high-visibility tabard.'*

Well, maybe not *everybody* – there were still hundreds of people using the plastic beer glasses that came free with every beer ordered, but they appeared to be in the minority. And there seemed to be something of a stigma attached to drinking beer from a plastic glass. Revellers, it seemed, were divided into two separate camps – those with their own ornate, elaborate and terribly expensive beer tankards occupying one row of trestle-tables, and the plebeians who were drinking from substandard receptacles, occupying another. Now, as far as I was concerned, it didn't matter to me one way or the other what type of receptacle my beer was served in. If the barman had handed me beer in a cardboard bucket, then, quite frankly, I would have been perfectly contented. But for Jan, observing a division between the 'haves' and the 'have-nots', was like a red rag to a bull.

"We have to buy a couple of tankards," he said.

"We don't, Jan," I said. "We can drink from plastic cups."

"No chance. It's clearly the convention at these events to bring one's own beer tankard, and I'm not going to be seen as the dickhead who failed to bring one. And if I'm going to spend the afternoon drinking with you, then you'll need your own tankard too. I can't be seen drinking with a heathen."

Jan dragged me over to a market stall with a huge variety of beer tankards on display and asked me to choose one. I protested of course – firstly on the basis that even the most basic designs were shockingly expensive, and secondly on the grounds that I couldn't carry one around with me on the final leg of my trip through Germany, as most of these tankards were cumbersome and heavy, and I didn't have room in my rucksack. But there is another trait in Jan's character that I'd forgotten to mention – he has an answer for everything. Actually, it's the one quality in Jan's personality profile that I found most appealing back in the 1990s, when we first met as work colleagues. Jan has what's known in *corporate speak* as a 'can-do' attitude. He has always hated negativity. Throw the word *'can't'* at him, and he'll bat it back at you like Shane Warne striking a cricket ball with the power of an Exocet missile.

"The cost of the tankard doesn't matter, because *I'm* buying them. *You're* not paying," he said.

"But you've paid for everything on this trip so f......."

"It's not negotiable – so stop moaning. When we get back to Wittlich tomorrow, I'll wrap your tankard up in bubble wrap and I'll post it to the UK. It'll be there waiting for you by the time you get home, so you won't have to carry it around with you."

I had no choice but to agree.

Beer tankards are a serious business in Germany – many are ornately decorated and are highly collectable. Often referred to as a *Stein* or a *Krug,* a traditional German beer tankard may be made from stoneware, pewter, porcelain, wood, or even silver or crystal-glass. Some have lids with a thumb lever, believed to have originated during the 14th century in the age of the *Black Death* – when lids were added to prevent diseased flies from falling into the beer. They come in a variety of sizes too, generally a third or a half-litre measure, although a larger tankard, known as a *Maßkrug* [42] (or 'full-measure tankard') will accommodate a full one litre. Jan rejected my first choice of tankard as it was made from tin and was the cheapest one on the stall. So he forced me to choose another. In the end I settled for a

---

[42] *There are 30 letters in the German alphabet – comprising the 26 standard modern Latin letters A to Z; three diacritic vowels Ä, Ö and Ü (the Umlauts effectively change the A sound to Ae, the O to Oe and the U to Ue), and one ligature known as 'eszett' or 'scharfes-S' – represented by the symbol ß, often used as a substitute for a double s (ss). The word 'Maß' meaning 'measure' may also be written as 'Mass', for example.*

tankard that I rather liked which also met with Jan's approval – a simple, stoneware jug with *'Hochwälder Brau'* written on the side in black and gold lettering. Hochwälder, by the way, is one of the local Saarland Breweries which, as I was to discover during the course of the afternoon, produce a wide variety of rather excellent beers of which the *Stammwürze* is the most excellent of them all (in my opinion, of course).

So Jan and I spent what must have been the best part of eight hours wandering from one brewery stall to the next, sampling as many beers as our respective metabolisms could be reasonably expected to cope with. I am quite certain that, had Jan been at the Losheim beer festival alone, he would have introduced himself to every single person on the green and made a thousand new friends in the process. But since I was there with him, Jan was remarkably restrained. We spent the entire day chatting, playing each other at chess, comparing notes whilst sampling various different brews, and generally talking the sort of banal, prosaic nonsense that Jan and I have always been terribly proficient at.

There was one point during the proceedings when Jan made a sterling effort to chat up two young ladies who were sitting at the far end of our table. But his efforts were doomed to failure from the outset. He was old enough to have fathered both of them for a start. But as Jan swaggered nonchalantly towards them, silently practising his opening gambit – his tankard in one hand and a cigar in the other, he somehow managed to trip on a raised clump of grass and fell awkwardly onto the ground. He wasn't hurt thank goodness, at least not physically – but his pride had taken a battering. When Jan was back on his feet, I noticed his T-shirt was covered in mud and grass stains and he had managed to spill most of his beer down the front of his jeans. Since the two young ladies seemed unable to control their hysterical laughter, Jan decided not to pursue his original plan of 'chatting them up', but suggested instead that we should consider moving to another table. Apparently, the table across the other side of the green was in a far shadier position than the one we were currently occupying, so the sun wouldn't be shining directly into our faces.

At around 10.00pm that evening, Jan and I staggered back to the campsite. At least, I think we did, but to my shame I couldn't remember making the journey back, and neither could Jan. But clearly, we must have done, because we both woke the following morning inside our respective tents, and not in a ditch at the side of a road.

As my eyes adjusted to the sunlight, I realised I had the mother of all headaches. I didn't feel nauseous, which was something to be thankful for, but I had a raging thirst and a pounding head – a Katzenjammer measuring a full 4.5 on the HI scale. Jan wasn't feeling that great either – it was he who was the first to break open a fresh packet of paracetamols. Once again, I made the mistake of asking Jan if he'd slept well and once again he responded with the now customary torrent of profanities.

"I hate camping," he said. "I just don't see how anybody can derive any pleasure from it. Having to sleep in a tent has spoiled what has otherwise been a fabulous couple of days. I've really enjoyed the cycling and the beer festival and all, but sleeping in a tent has taken the shine off it. Next time you and I go on a trip together, matey, we're staying at a five-star hotel – my treat!"

By lunchtime, once the painkillers had kicked in and the soreness in my forehead had begun to wane, the pair of us packed away our tents, mounted our bicycles and set off on the 37.9-kilometre journey back to Trier. The route seemed somehow shorter this time – and we completed it in record time. There were more downhill stretches on the return journey and we had the advantage of a tail wind with us for most of the way. When we reached the little village of

Obermenning, we managed to resist the temptation to call in at the enchanting little village inn. Somehow, the poster advertising *Bitburger Pils* didn't seem quite so alluring this time. When we finally arrived back at Jan's farmhouse in the outskirts of Wittlich, Stella was waiting at the gate to greet us.

"I expect you're both hungry," she said.

She was right – we *were* hungry – starving, actually. So you can imagine our delight when Stella ushered us into the kitchen and served up three huge platefuls of chicken stew with fresh, home-baked bread.

"So, how did you enjoy *camping*?" Stella asked.

"Don't ask," Jan replied. "Sleeping in a tent is a nightmare. We'll be booking a hotel next time."

Stella stared at her husband with a self-satisfied smirk on her face. It was a look I'd witnessed before – a sort of 'told you so' smugness that was one of Stella's trademarks.

"So I suppose the tent is going in the cellar – never to see the light of day again!"

"Actually, no – that's not what will happen, Stella," Jan replied. "I shall donate my tent to a worthy cause. I'm going to give it to Chris, as a replacement for that pile of shit he's been carrying around with him for the past three weeks."

"But I can't take your tent," I protested. "It cost you four hundred euros!"

"No, it *didn't!*" he snapped. "If I'd have spent four hundred euros on a tent I certainly wouldn't be giving it away! It was only three hundred and ninety-nine euros, as well you know!"

Stella's smirk had turned into a warm smile. She leaned over to her husband and kissed him gently on the cheek.

"Well, I think giving your tent to Chris is a wonderful idea," she said.

oOo

Dear Diary,

The Beer, Cheese and Tent Report for the State of Saarland:

Beer: Hochwälder Brau – Erzbräu:

Jan and I sampled a whole stack of beers at the Losheim Bierfest, but the Erzbrau was unquestionably my favourite. There were two varieties available: the 'helles' (light beer) – an amber beer brewed with soft water which had a light, fruity flavour, and the 'Dunkel' (dark beer), which was much smoother and had a malty kick to it.

Cheese: Edelpilzkäse:

Translated literally, Edelpilzkäse means "Noble Mould Cheese", and is a high quality variety of mature blue cheese. It's crumbly rather than creamy, has a pungent aroma and a distinctively sharp edge to its flavour.

Tent Stability:

My Wind-Breaker DeLuxe is literally falling apart at the seams and looks feeble and pathetic next to Jan's Power Tokee UL. Yes, I'll admit it – I'm profoundly envious. There, I said it.

oOo

Chapter Fifteen – Church Bells and Chocolate Cake

"Cake is happiness! If you know the way of the cake, you know the way of happiness! If you have a cake in front of you, you should not look any further for joy."
C. JoyBell C.- U.S writer and poet

For the first time on my 'grand tour' of Germany I had fallen behind schedule. Not that falling behind schedule should have mattered that much – after all, this was meant to be the 'new me' – the new, carefree, live-life-for-the-moment me. And the 'new me' shouldn't be worrying about schedules. But old habits die hard, don't they? The thing is – I'd spent weeks planning this trip. Night after night I'd burned the midnight oil sifting through mountains of guidebooks; scrutinising railway and bus timetables; analysing Alan Rogers' excellent guides to European campsites – I'd planned every part of this journey in meticulous detail. And it seemed to me that when you've worked that hard; when you've spent that much time planning, preparing, calculating, researching – doing all you can to ensure everything runs like a military operation – well, falling behind schedule simply undermined all my hard work – it made my precision planning seem utterly futile – a pointless waste of time. Yes, the 'old me' was back again.

According to my original plan, I should have left Losheim on Friday morning and journeyed on to state number fourteen – the Swabian state of Baden-Württemberg. But in the company of my good friend Jan, I spent the Friday afternoon cycling almost 40 kilometres back to his farmhouse in Wittlich – with the pair of us still suffering the remnants of our respective hangovers. And when we finally made it back to the ranch, we were presented almost immediately with a huge plateful of mouth-watering chicken

336

stew which Jan and I demolished with almost uncontrollable voracity, like a couple of barbarous savages who hadn't eaten a decent meal in months. So, after a long cycle ride and with my stomach now replete with chicken stew, I didn't really feel like travelling anywhere else that afternoon. Jan, perceptive as always, sensed this feeling of lethargy on my part, and suggested I stay at the farmhouse for one more night. That way, I could get a good night's rest in a comfortable bed and wake up on Saturday morning filled with renewed vitality and dynamism – ready to hit the road once again. I must admit, I didn't take much persuading.

Of course, there were a couple of other expedient advantages to staying an extra night at the farmhouse. In addition to a good night's sleep in a comfy bed, Stella very obligingly did my laundry for me. She washed, dried and ironed every single item of clothing I had, including the clothes I was wearing. (I borrowed a pair of Jan's tracksuit bottoms and one of his T-shirts, in case you've assumed I was wandering around the farmhouse in a state of undress.) I didn't *ask* her to do my washing for me, but she insisted – and although a part of me was extremely grateful (heaven knows my togs needed freshening up a bit), there was also a part of me that rather wished she hadn't. I found it a little embarrassing having Stella rummaging through my dirty undercrackers – especially the ones with the Wile E. Coyote motif which Markus and Oskar regarded as a source of great amusement.

The next stage of my journey through Germany would take me to the state of Baden-Württemberg, and more specifically, to a tiny village by the name of *Münstertal*. Now, I cannot imagine for a moment that there are many people out there who will have heard of Münstertal – there's no reason I can think of why they should. It's a small, unassuming little village in the far south-west corner of Germany, close to her borders with France and Switzerland.

There's nothing particularly remarkable about it, I admit, but like all the villages in this little corner of the country, it has a neat, clean appearance and the usual enticing array of shops and restaurants. It's a village that exudes an air of tranquillity – which I suppose is a polite way of saying that there isn't a great deal going on. So if you're wondering why I chose Münstertal as my next port of call – I shall explain.

There were two reasons actually. Firstly, Münstertal is home to one of the best-equipped camping facilities in the whole of Europe. The site here has just about everything one can possibly imagine: thermal baths, a sauna, an indoor heated swimming pool, an *outdoor* heated swimming pool, entertainment for adults and children, a plethora of sporting facilities and a ski lift to take you up into the mountains that surround the site. They're not huge mountains; the highest peak is the *Feldberg* with an elevation of 1,493 metres – not exactly of Himalayan proportion I'll admit, but the peak is above the tree line and is snow-capped in the winter (perfect for skiing and snowboarding) and is green and lush in the summertime – perfect for leisurely hiking. I knew all this to be true, not solely through my extensive research, but also from my own personal experience.

You see – twelve or thirteen years ago I visited the campsite at Münstertal on one of our many family camping holidays. I drove all the way across Europe with my wife and children in tow – the kids asking *'are we there yet?'* at regular ten-minute intervals. Tucked safely in the boot of my car was the *Paradox 1900*, our trusty family frame tent with assembly instructions that required a degree in mechanical engineering to decipher. It was one of our more successful family camping holidays as I recall, memorable for a whole variety of reasons – and since I had such fond memories of it, Münstertal seemed the perfect place to represent Baden-Württemberg on my whistle-stop tour around the German states. But there was another reason why I chose to visit

Münstertal which has more to do with its location. The village is set in another of Germany's national parks – another area of outstanding natural beauty. However, I'm prepared to go one step further than that. The area in which the village of Münstertal is situated cannot simply be described as 'beautiful' – that would be grossly understating it – a bit like saying that Shakespeare was quite good at writing plays. Münstertal lies in what, I believe, is one of the most stunningly beautiful regions in the whole of Europe – *The Black Forest*, or the *Schwarzwald*, as it's known over here.

Now, I'm quite sure that 'The Black Forest' is a name that most of us will be familiar with – but I suspect that remarkably few would be able to pinpoint its exact location on a European map. It's one of those places that we've all heard about – because it happens to be famous for something – but we have no idea where it is. There are lots of places in Europe that fall into this category – Transylvania is another good example. Of course, the reason we've all heard of Transylvania is because of the area's association with Bram Stoker's 1897 gothic horror novel *Dracula*. [43] It's through this and other works of modern fiction that the area has become more commonly associated (at least, in the English-speaking world), with vampires. But how many of us know where Transylvania is exactly? I must admit – I always thought that it was fictitious – a figment of a classical author's imagination. They'll be telling me next that Narnia exists.

We're all familiar with the Black Forest as I've said, but mainly, I suspect, because of the region's association with a particularly delicious cherry and cream gâteau, known as '*Schwarzwälder Kirschtorte*' in German. But that's a subject I

[43] *Transylvania is in central Romania, bounded on the east and south by the Carpathian mountain range – and since the fall of communism, the area is becoming increasingly popular as a tourist destination.*

shall return to a little later in the story. So, as you might well imagine, I was particularly looking forward to revisiting the Black Forest. Aside from the scenery, the rolling hills and knolls, the dense forests of pines, firs and conifers, the winding rivers and natural lakes carved by glaciers – it is a landscape rich in fairy tale mythology – said to be haunted by werewolves, witches, sorcerers and the devil himself – in a number of differing guises. So it was a good thing that Stella had freshened up my undercrackers.

I set out from Jan and Stella's farmhouse on Saturday morning after yet another of Jan's bespoke bacon and egg breakfasts, and embarked on another circuitous five-hour train journey. Jan very obligingly gave me a lift to Wittlich station in his Mercedes, where I caught the first of four trains via Koblenz, Freiburg in Breisgau and Bad Krozingen – eventually arriving in Münstertal shortly after 3.00pm. Actually the journey was far less arduous than it might sound. The trains were comfortable and punctual, and the connection times relatively short. But above all, the charming little railway station at Münstertal is conveniently located alongside the perimeter of the campsite – a walk of less than two minutes.

It felt good to be on the move again. It felt good to be alone too. No disrespect to Jan and Stella – I love them both dearly. They were the most congenial of hosts and I enjoyed having Jan with me on our adventures in the Saarland. But there's something about travelling alone that somehow feels right. It's the epitome of freedom – there's nobody you have to please other than yourself. If you want to stop for coffee, you can stop for coffee; if you want to go to bed early, you can go to bed early; and if you want to stand on the top of a mountain, take all your clothes off and practise your yodelling, well, the Germans are a very tolerant and broad-minded race.

And so, on my own once again and happy to be so, I negotiated the one-hundred-metre walk from the station to the campsite and registered my presence at reception. I was greeted by a middle-aged lady with grey roots, a beetroot-red, sun-blasted complexion and a pair of thick-lens spectacles, who seemed pleasant enough if a little fretful.

"We were expecting you yesterday, Herr Lown," she said, in a wavering voice and a hint of genuine concern. The woman seemed so upset that I expected her to burst into tears at any moment.

"We were worried when you didn't turn up," she continued. "Is everything OK, my dear?"

I explained about staying the extra night with Jan – not that it was any of her business of course. But having a conversation with this woman was like having to explain to an uncompromising headmistress why I was late for school. For some inexplicable reason I found myself justifying my tardiness with a detailed account of my movements over the previous twenty-four hours. Anyway, my explanation seemed to placate her.

The campsite at Münstertal was expensive compared to many of the others I'd stayed at, but as the old saying goes, you get what you pay for – and at Münstertal, you get an awful lot. The facilities, as I've said, are excellent – and I expected to pay a premium rate. Having found the perfect spot beneath the shade of a conifer tree, I set about the now well-rehearsed ritual of assembling my tent. Except this time, things were different. There were *two* tents attached to the side of my rucksack – my *Wind-Breaker DeLuxe* and Jan's *Vaude Power Tokee Ultra-Light.* I say '*Jan's*' Power Tokee, but in point of fact that was no longer the case. Jan, as you'll recall, had given me his tent as a gift; donated it to what he had described as 'a worthy cause'. So I suppose that, strictly speaking, it wasn't *Jan's Power Tokee* at all – it was mine. I sat on the grass beneath the conifer tree for a while and

341

contemplated what, for me, was something of a worrying dilemma. I obviously didn't need two tents – but I'd have to make a decision as to which of them I would assemble. Now, I know what you're thinking, and you're probably right – it was another of those 'no-brainer' situations. It made no practical sense at all to assemble my old tent. My *Wind-Breaker DeLuxe* was on its last legs. It was, quite literally, falling apart at the seams. The poles were buckled; the canvas was torn; the flysheet was held together with pieces of duct tape. It looked unsightly with its ugly black ink mark, and there were streaks of solidified 'seam sealer' that had dribbled down the side of the flysheet. Its general appearance aside, my old tent wasn't terribly functional either. In wet weather, the tears in the canvas allowed droplets of rainwater to penetrate the fabric, trickle along the length of the support pole above me, and drip on top of my head. And as rainwater dripped from above, small holes in the groundsheet simultaneously allowed moisture to seep in from below. Not wishing to put too fine a point on it – my *Wind-Breaker DeLuxe* was a mess. The entire structure leaned at an angle of around ten degrees out of plumb, and I'm pretty sure that just one medium-strength gust of wind would have ripped her from her moorings and destroyed her completely.

The *Power Tokee*, by stark contrast, was a fine-looking specimen. With its more or less indestructible reinforced tubular frame and its super-resilient silicon-coated fabric, it was, without a shadow of a doubt, the toughest, most robust piece of kit money could buy. The Tokee was designed to remain stable even in the most extreme weather conditions – so no matter what meteorological misery the Black Forest could throw at me, I'd be safe and secure inside my *Power Tokee*. She looked pretty handsome too, with her sleek, curvaceous lines and her lustrous patina of chartreuse green. If I were to assemble my newly-acquired *Vaude*

Power-Tokee Ultra-Light tent, then instantly she would have become the talk of the campsite – fellow campers would have gathered round her – to stare in awe and admiration. I suspect that much the same thing would have happened had I assembled my *Wind-Breaker DeLuxe* (except she may have become the talk of the campsite for rather different reasons and you may need to substitute '*awe and admiration*' for '*ridicule and derision*'). So, having listened attentively to my own opening arguments; having conducted both direct and cross-examinations of my own opinion; and after sifting through the evidence, giving due consideration to my own closing summation, I finally reached a decision. I placed the *Vaude Power Tokee UL* back into my rucksack, and, as I had done on so many previous occasions, I assembled my *Wind-Breaker DeLuxe*.

OK, I am fully aware that, as decisions go, this was one of monumental stupidity. Discarding the finest single-person tent on the market in favour of the *Wind-Breaker* was illogical, irrational and completely anomalous – but I'm afraid I simply couldn't have made any other decision without it playing on my conscience. My *Wind-Breaker DeLuxe*, despite her obvious inadequacies, had been with me through thick and thin since this journey began. How could I forsake an old friend? I couldn't. And that was the end of the matter.

I'd planned to stay in the Black Forest for two nights, but as you are aware, I arrived here a day later than I originally intended. So, I had two options open to me – I could either stay here for one night only and stick with my original departure date, or I could go ahead with a two-night stay as planned and extend my expedition through Germany by an additional twenty-four hours. I chose the latter – and for one simple reason. Of all the places I had visited on my trek around Germany, the Black Forest was probably the finest example of bucolic gorgeousness – it is spectacularly beautiful and remarkably serene – the perfect place to relax, unwind and forget about the troubles of the world. So, if you're going to cut short a trip to anywhere on this planet of ours, then the Black Forest isn't the place to be doing it. And relaxation was exactly what I intended during my stay here. Of course, the Black Forest does open up a wealth of possibilities for the intrepid explorer – if adventure is what you're looking for. Every corner of it is worth exploring. The region is criss-crossed by a spider's web of well signposted trails that allow hikers to reach vistas that are often inaccessible by car, including hidden waterfalls and the ruins of ancient castles. Bicycle touring is popular here too. Signposted cycle routes, many of considerable length, snake their way through the mountain valleys. There are some which cross the borders into Switzerland and others crossing into the French region of Alsace.

But I had come to the Black Forest simply to relax. I was staying on a campsite which boasts some of the best facilities in the whole of Europe and it would have been foolish of me not to make the most of what was on offer. And if that meant staying within the confines of the campsite's perimeter walls until it was time for me to leave, well, that would suit me perfectly. I could unwind in the spa; take a dip in either of the pools (or in both the pools if the fancy took me); or catch up on some reading whilst relaxing on a sunlounger – the possibilities were endless.

With my tent assembled, I spent an hour or so wandering around the campsite checking out the amenities – an investigative reconnoitre of my surroundings, if you will – and it wasn't long before I stumbled upon the campsite's restaurant with its outdoor seating area known as the 'Garten-Terrasse'. It was another beautiful summer afternoon, so I took a seat at a vacant table beneath a giant parasol and pondered both the menu and the assortment of laminated flyers advertising the restaurant's various 'special offers'. One flyer in particular caught my attention – it advertised a special promotion on *'afternoon cappuccino and a slice of authentic Schwarzwälder Kirschtorte'* – a chance for me to sample real Black Forest gâteau in the region where it originated.

Or so I thought.

It was the word 'authentic' that I found most appealing. I've sampled Black Forest gâteau before, as I suspect most people have – but to be brutally honest I'm not a huge fan – it's a bit too tart and sickly for my taste. But I suppose, in fairness, I've probably not given it a fair hearing – the Black Forest gâteaux I've eaten have all been shop-bought – covered in sickly-sweet glacé cherries at a factory on the Slough Industrial Estate and transported by refrigerated juggernaut to the freezer cabinet in my local supermarket. Needless to say, I was expecting 'authentic' to be a considerable improvement on my previous experiences. So, when a young and pretty waitress in a pristine white pinafore arrived at my table with her pencil and notebook poised in readiness, I eagerly ordered the *'afternoon cappuccino and a slice of authentic Schwarzwälder Kirschtorte'* whilst pointing at the photograph on the laminated flyer – just in case she wasn't aware of the restaurant's special €7,50 deal.

Now, you may assume, as I did, that Black Forest gâteau is so called because it originated in the Black Forest. After all, that would be the most plausible explanation. But you'd be wrong – for two reasons. Firstly, Black Forest gâteau was (allegedly) invented 500 kilometres north of the Black Forest, in a suburb of Bonn known as Bad Godesberg – a town which I'm sure can't be nearly as bad as its name suggests. For it was here in 1915, in the then prominent Café Agner, that the confectioner, *Josef Keller* created the first *Schwarzwälder Kirschtorte.* I use the word *'allegedly'* intentionally – as this was Keller's own assertion, and I don't believe his claim has ever been substantiated. But if Josef Keller, the soi-disant inventor of Black Forest gâteau says it was so, then who am I to argue? But the second reason is definitely not shrouded in uncertainty. Black Forest gâteau is not named after the region from which it originates, but from one of its critical ingredients – Black Forest cherry liqueur (or *Schwarzwälder Kirschwasser)* which is distilled from tart cherries. It's a cherry schnapps which originated in the Black Forest, but for decades (or possibly even centuries) has been available throughout the whole of Germany. It is *this* ingredient, with its distinctive cherry flavour and its high alcoholic content that gives the cake its inimitable and unmistakable taste. And it's this ingredient too that defines the product itself – since German law dictates that unless the cake contains the liqueur, it cannot legally be marketed as a 'Black Forest' gâteau.

When the waitress eventually returned with my cake and placed it on the table in front of me, I spent a few seconds simply staring at it. This wasn't just a cake – it was a piece of culinary art – a tour de force of artistic creativity sculpted from edible materials. It consisted of several layers of chocolate sponge with whipped cream and cherries between each layer, and was decorated with butter cream, chocolate shavings and maraschino cherries – which unlike glacé cherries, weren't candied in sickly sugar syrup. It was, quite simply, sublime. I enjoyed it so much, I generously allowed the pretty young waitress to keep the change from a €10 note. And to top it all, the cappuccino at the campsite restaurant was the best I'd ever tasted. I had a feeling that over the next day or two I'd be returning to the *Garten-Terrasse* a number of times.

I woke on Sunday morning feeling unusually chirpy. For someone as miserable and cantankerous as I generally am, waking up feeling chirpy is something of a rarity – so I decided to savour the moment while it lasted. I don't believe my abnormally cheerful disposition could be attributed to any one issue in particular – but a combination of all sorts of things that were going on around me that morning. My tent had survived the night for a start – which was a blessing. But it wasn't just that. I lay there for a while with my eyes tightly shut, hoping this would sharpen my senses of hearing and smell. In the distance I could hear the sound of church bells. They were the bells of *St. Trudpert's Abbey* – a former Benedictine monastery built on a hill overlooking the town, which can trace its roots back to the first half of the 7th century.

There's something rather therapeutic about the sound of church bells calling the faithful to worship on Sunday mornings. They produce no recognizable tunes, yet they are rung in sequences as disciplined and as orderly as any piece of music. However, the bell of St. Trudpert's had a more melancholy tone. It was a tolling bell – a single note chiming at two-second intervals – ringing out across the valley like a carillon intoning the sadness of a funeral. The sound was haunting and yet beautiful to listen to. There's something about the sound of church bells that gives you the feeling that everything is right with the world. They are a metaphor for life itself – a reminder that however grave your troubles, however weighty your woes, life will simply carry on regardless. The monks of St. Trudpert's had been ringing this bell every Sunday morning since 640AD – and will continue to do so for centuries to come. [44]

There was another sound that I also found rather soothing – the sound of a train. Now, I'm prepared to concede that there aren't many people who would find the sound of a train particularly calming. I know of one elderly

---

[44] *Probably not the same monks though. I suspect it unlikely that any of the monks at St. Trudpert's are over 1,350 years old – even those who have lived their entire lives in the restorative environment of the Black Forest.*

gentleman who swears and curses every time an express train rattles past his home – it causes every volume of the Encyclopaedia Britannica to topple off the bookshelf with the consequent vibration. But if you remember correctly, Münstertal station is just a stone's throw from the campsite, and the railway track runs just the other side of the camp's perimeter fence. This is a sleepy little branch line. There are no intercity expresses rattling through at breakneck speed – just dawdling commuter trains comprising one, maybe two carriages, staggering slowly into the station like prey-laden monsters into their lair. Every half-hour, I would hear the wheezing of pneumatic brakes as a train pulled into the station, followed a minute or two later by the mellow, soporific whirr of an electric motor as the train pulled away again. It was a sound I could have set my watch to – the westbound train at precisely one minute past the hour, and the eastbound at thirty-six minutes past. It was regular and reliable – like a tolling church bell. There's something about the sound of a train that makes you feel that everything is right with the world. Trains are a metaphor for life itself. [45] There was something else happening around me that morning which contributed to my general sanguinity. Not a *sound* this time, but a *smell* – the sweet and unmistakable smell of chocolate. This rich, syrupy aroma was emanating from a small factory located in the neighbouring town of *Staufen*. The factory was more than three kilometres away, yet the bouquet from the factory's production line had caught the westerly breezes and had wafted towards the campsite. Chocolate has a distinct aroma of course, and is proven by cerebral academics to stimulate the pleasure-anticipating neurons in the brain. So, along with the comforting sounds of trains and church bells, I savoured the moment while it

[45] *I can't offer any explanation why, so the statement is probably not accurate.*

lasted, before the breeze changed direction and the smell was diverted towards the neighbouring villages.

My routine that morning was no different from that of any other morning. After a shower and a shave, I donned my purple flip-flops and took a short stroll to the nearest water tap to fill the kettle – my metabolism being incapable of functioning properly until I'd fired up the *Pocket Rocket* and made myself a brew. But this morning, all of these activities were conducted at a far more leisurely pace than usual – I was going through the motions of my morning chores in *slowmo*. Normally, these things would be rushed – I'd be zipping through my morning routine like a fart in a colander; unable to think straight – my head filled with train schedules and bus timetables; my brain churning through thoughts of '*must-be-here-at-this-time*' and '*must-be-there-at-that-time*'. But that morning, thanks to the sound of trains and church bells and the alluring smell of chocolate, my mind and body had slipped into a general state of torpor – and that was pretty much the blueprint for the rest of my day. I tried to indulge only in activities that necessitated either sitting down or lying flat on my back. I'd promised myself a day of sluggishness and sloth and I didn't want to ruin it by engaging in anything unnecessary energetic. Only the lure of an 'afternoon cappuccino and a slice of authentic Schwarzwälder Kirschtorte' at the Garten-Terrasse could shake me from this feeling of lassitude. It was another €7,50 well spent – and once again I told the waitress to keep the change from a €10 note. The fresh country air was clearly having a positive impact on my generosity.

In the evening I headed for the campsite bar – which was busy, atmospheric, and very noisy. My intention was to stay only briefly – long enough to enjoy a beer and to finish reading the remaining two chapters of my book. (I couldn't wait to find out whether it was the butler or the maid who put the poison in the old lady's tea. My money was on the butler.) But I found myself strangely enticed by the sound of chinking glasses and raucous laughter – the sort of noises that are synonymous with a bunch of happy people having a good time. But there was something else going on in the campsite bar that evening – something a little mysterious and therefore rather intriguing. A large section of the bar had been set aside for what appeared to be a card game tournament. There were several tables within the partitioned area, decked with purple baize covers and with seats to accommodate four people at each table. Almost every seat was occupied when I arrived and several games were already underway. Now, I'm familiar with an awful lot of card games, but this, I'll admit, wasn't one of them. Whatever it was, the rules seemed unnecessarily complicated. There were no signs of any money changing hands, so I assumed the participants were competing simply to win rather than to liberate their opponents of their hard-earned cash. But even without any money at stake, this mystery card game was clearly a very serious matter – which is why I'd concluded this was a competitive tournament rather than a leisurely diversion among friends. The expression on the faces of the players was sombre to say the least – a furrowed brow, a scrunched forehead and a neutral frown were evidently 'de rigueur'. After carrying out some extensive investigations (I asked a bald-headed man sitting opposite me), I discovered that the game being played at the campsite bar that evening was called 'Skat' – Germany's national card game, invented in the early 19th century in the Thuringian town of Altenburg. I couldn't have known at the time of course, but the bald-headed man sitting opposite me was something of a celebrity in the murky world of competitive Skat. He was the current regional Skat champion for the district of Lörrach – and he was in Münstertal that evening to defend his title. There were a few qualifying heats to be played first before the main event – heats which the bald-headed man was exempt from participating in on account of his status as the incumbent regional champion. So he and I used the time we had together to enjoy a beer and have a good old chin wag about the minutiae and subtleties of Skat. (Well, *he* did most of the chatting – I just sat there listening and wishing I hadn't asked.) [46]

Now, if you were expecting to be enlightened on the intricacies of the game Skat, then I'm afraid that what I'm about to tell you may come as something of a bitter disappointment. There were two problems, you see. Firstly, my hairless new friend spoke German with a thick, almost glutinous Swabian accent, which made it very difficult for me to understand what he was talking about. That, coupled with his irritating ability to rattle through sentences at a rate of 10,000 words per minute, made much of what he was saying completely unfathomable. But more importantly, the rules of Skat are terribly complex – so much so that when the bald-headed man was relaying his brief synopsis, he might just as well have been lecturing me on quantum mechanics or sub-atomic particle physics. Apparently, not even seasoned Skat players understand *all* the rules. Sometimes, games result in fierce disputes which have to be referred to the *Skat Tribunal* for adjudication. Yes, there really *is* an official *Skat Tribunal* – it was founded in Altenburg in 1963, specifically to provide elucidation on the game's complex and multifarious rules. Everything about the game of *Skat* is complicated – even the cards themselves. Whereas most card games in

[46] *I apologise for continually referring to my new acquaintance as 'the bald-headed man'. Unfortunately, during our hour-long conversation, he neglected to tell me his name, and I neglected to ask him what it was. Since the lighting in the bar was rather dim and gloomy, his bald head was the only distinguishing feature that I can remember noticing. Actually, it's probably just as well that I didn't find out his name. He was, without question, the most boring person I have ever had the misfortune in engaging in conversation – and I fear that had I been able to name him in this book, he'd now be suing me for defamation of character.*

the Western world are played using a traditional 'French standard' 52-card deck, with 13 cards in each of the four suits (clubs, spades, diamonds and hearts), the game of Skat is played in time-honoured tradition using a 'German standard' deck. [47] Although the 'German standard' also comprises 52 cards, only 32 of them are used in Skat. (The five lower value cards in each suit are removed before play can begin.) There are still four suits, but instead of clubs, spades, diamonds and hearts, there are 'leaves' (sometimes referred to as 'grass' or 'green'), 'hearts' (sometimes referred to simply as 'red'), 'acorns' (also known as 'old men' for reasons I am unable to explain) and finally, 'bells' (not known as anything other than 'bells' as far as I'm aware). According to my bald-headed friend, Skat is a game designed specifically for three players, which seemed a little strange to me for a number of reasons. Firstly, 32 is not a number equally divisible by three, which must make things terribly awkward in a game using 32 cards. Stupidly, I made the mistake of pointing this out.

"It's all very simple," said the bald-headed man mordantly, as if it were blatantly obvious to anybody with just a smidgen of intellect. "Two of the players – the *rear-hand* and the *middle-hand* players – play with eleven cards each, and the *fore-hand* player plays with only ten."

"So why are there *four* players at each table?" I asked.

"The fourth player deals the cards and referees the game. He's the *Skatmeister* – and he has a very important role to play. He's responsible for making sure that score multipliers have been correctly calculated; he ensures that auctions have been carried out fairly by the declarer; he supervises the players as they count up their Matadors; and

---

[47] *The 'German standard' deck of cards is still commonly used in parts of southern Germany and in Switzerland, but is a dying tradition elsewhere in Germany.*

he makes certain that the rules are correctly followed whenever '*Solo*' or *'Tournee'* is declared."

"Oh, I see," I lied.

Eventually, the bald-headed man was summoned to one of the tables to play the first of several games of Skat in defence of his title – which was my excuse to slip away. As soon as he was gone, I guzzled down the last drop of beer in my glass and made a hasty retreat towards the exit, before anybody else could take his place beside me and bore me to death for another couple of hours bleating on about the merits of the world's most ridiculous card game. I went back to my tent and spent the rest of the evening reading the last two chapters of my book.

On Monday morning I woke up early, feeling bitterly disappointed. I would be leaving the Black Forest later that day – packing my tent away once again and saying goodbye to one of the most beautiful and picturesque places in the whole of Germany. But that wasn't the only reason for my disappointment – there was something else that had been bothering me. It turned out that neither the butler nor the maid had been responsible for poisoning the old lady's tea. The dastardly deed had been perpetrated by Tim, the gardener – a character the author had discreetly and rather sneakily introduced in an earlier chapter and whose ephemeral employment at the manor had, in my opinion, been entirely incidental to the storyline. The fact that the butler was the only person in the house on the night of the murder; the fact that it was *he* who was responsible for making the old lady her cup of tea and personally delivering it to her room; and the fact that he had, on several occasions, declared within earshot of the entire domestic staff that he would '*one day put poison in the old cow's tea'*, was all, apparently, purely coincidental. I felt cheated. I made a note of the author's name and vowed never to read any more of her books – assuming of course, she'd written any. I don't know who this *Agatha Christie* woman thinks she is, but in my opinion, crime stories really aren't her forte.

But substandard plots notwithstanding, I confess that my mood of disappointment that morning was due largely to my impending departure from the Black Forest. I had enjoyed myself here. I hadn't really done very much – but *that*, I think, was what made my stay so thoroughly agreeable. But time and tide wait for no man, or so they say, and since I was a day behind my original schedule I needed to be on the move again – I still had two of the sixteen German states left to visit – and time was pressing on.

Next on my 'to do' list was a trip to the mountains – more specifically, to the little Alpine town of *Garmisch-Partenkirchen.* I made a decision many weeks ago that, rather than take the train, I would *drive* the 340 kilometres from Münstertal to Garmisch-Partenkirchen in a rental car. Now, that may sound like an unnecessary expense, particularly for someone who was in possession of a *Deutsche-Bahn* rail pass – and I will confess that my decision to rent a car wasn't one I made lightly. However, there was method in my reasoning, which I shall explain later. I had arranged to collect the car at around noon from the rental company's offices in Freiburg in Breisgau – a forty-minute rail journey from Münstertal.

Now, here's a thing: although deep down I didn't want to leave the Black Forest at all, there was something in my system that was itching to get going. It's a strange phenomenon, but one I'm sure we've all experienced. You've got to go whether you want to or not – so you may as well hurry up and get it over with. And so, having risen early, showered, shaved, dismantled my tent and packed everything away in my rucksack, I was ready to hit the road. There was just one small snag – my train wasn't due for another ninety minutes. And so with time to kill, I did what any sensible person would have done in the circumstances

– I repaired to the Garten-Terrasse at the campsite restaurant and ordered a 'cappuccino and a slice of authentic Schwarzwälder Kirschtorte'. It was, after all, my last chance to sample the most delicious-tasting coffee on the planet. And once I'd reduced the cake to a plateful of crumbs and the coffee to a few remaining dregs at the bottom of the cup, I asked the pretty young waitress in her pristine white pinafore to fetch me the bill.

"That'll be ten euros," she said.

I stared incredulously at the bill for a few moments.

"Ten euros? But I only usually pay €7,50!"

I picked up the laminated card advertising the special €7.50 offer on coffee and cake and thrust it at her rather rudely.

"There," I said, reading from the flyer. "Special offer: 'Afternoon cappuccino and a slice of authentic Schwarzwälder Kirschtorte' – only €7.50!"

"Yes," she replied. "But it isn't the afternoon! Our special offer is only valid after 12 o'clock – it's now only half-past ten, so that'll be €6,50 for the cake and €3,50 for the cappuccino. That's €10 in total."

I decided not to make a big issue of it. After all, there's no point in getting stressed over the price of a hot beverage and a slice of chocolate cake – it's hardly a matter of life or death. [48] So I handed the waitress a €10 note. If she thought she was getting a tip, then she could whistle for it.

oOo

[48] *Although Pink Floyd fans will concur that, according to Roger Waters, 'for want of the price of tea and a slice, the old man died.' So perhaps I should have made more of an issue of it.*

Dear Diary,
The Beer, Cheese and Tent Report for the State of Baden-Württemberg:

Beer: Gaggenau Rauchbier:

Brewed in Baden-Württemberg by the Christoph-Bräu in Gaggenau, this 'rauchbier' (smoked beer) is similar to the famous smoked beers brewed in Bamburg. It has a distinctive smoky flavour, imparted by drying malted barley over an open flame. It is manna from heaven.

Cheese: Räucherkäse:

This was indeed a lucky find. Räucherkäse is traditionally made using Bavarian Emmentaler which is processed and then smoked. The Räucherkäse I found on the cheese counter at a Münstertal delicatessen was laced with chopped ham.

Tent Stability:

It's now just a matter of time before my tent falls apart completely, but I have my fingers and toes crossed in the hope that she'll manage to hang on for just a few more days.

oOo

Chapter Sixteen – The Demise of a Loyal Friend

"The stars are not wanted now; put out every one.
Pack up the moon and dismantle the sun.
Pour away the ocean and sweep up the wood.
For nothing now can come to any good."
From the poem 'Stop the Clocks' by W. H. Auden (1907 –
1973) – published in 1938

State number fifteen, the penultimate constituent state in my whistle-stop tour of the German *Länder,* was Bavaria (Bayern), or 'Freistaat Bayern' to give it its proper title. It is Germany's oldest political entity with a history going back to at least the 6th century. Bavaria is by far the largest of the German states and arguably the best known. It covers an area of more than 70,000 km² (that's about one fifth of the entire country), and is home to almost 12.5 million people. The state of Bavaria stretches for more than 400 kilometres from its most northerly to its southernmost point – from the rolling Franconian hills in the north, to the rugged, mountainous terrain of the German Alps in the south. It shares international borders with the Czech Republic in the east (the Bavarian Forest and the Bohemian Forest form the vast majority of the frontier), and with Austria in the south. The State also shares a short stretch of borderline with Switzerland, across Lake Constance. It's the Bavarian Alps that define Germany's border with Austria and within the range is the *Zugspitze* – the highest peak in Germany and just a stone's throw from my next port of call – the little alpine town of Garmisch-Partenkirchen.

Now, I believe I've already mentioned that I'd planned to travel the next leg of my journey in a hire car. I believe also that I promised you an explanation as to why I'd decided to abandon the speed, efficiency and comfort of the

German railways in favour of a gas-guzzling rented vehicle – which I suppose, is hardly in keeping with the 'spirit of adventure' that this whole journey was supposed to be about. Well, here's the thing: the distance by road between Münstertal in the Black Forest and Garmisch-Partenkirchen in the Bavarian Alps is approximately 340 kilometres. It's not a fast road, admittedly, but even at a leisurely speed, it's a journey one can complete in around five hours. Virtually bereft of traffic for much of the time, the road follows a relatively direct route through some of southern Germany's most stunning and dramatic terrain. It passes through the heart of the Black Forest and skirts across the northern edge of Lake Constance. It passes through the beautiful lakeside towns of Friedrichshafen and Lindau, before continuing into the mountains – through the 700-year-old town of Füssen at the southern end of the Romantic Road, and past the castle at Neuschwanstein – one of the most imposing palaces ever built. So although, potentially, the journey *could* be completed in around five hours or so, I had no intention of rushing. My plan was to take my time – to stop en route as many times as the fancy took me. At every point of interest along the way I intended to find an appropriate spot to park the car and head off in search of the ideal vantage point to capture a few perfect snapshots in my camera. Perhaps I might stop for lunch somewhere idyllic, without having to worry about train times and rail connections.

By stark contrast (and I must admit, somewhat surprisingly), the train route between Münstertal and Garmisch-Partenkirchen is much less scenic, absurdly circuitous and about as exciting as watching bats sleep. The rail route adds another 200 kilometres to the journey, takes seven hours to complete and involves four separate connections at Freiburg in Breisgau, Karlsruhe, Stuttgart and Munich. Although it pains me to say so, this was the one part of my journey where travelling by car was by far the most sensible option.

Still smarting from having to pay €10 for a cappuccino and a slice of Schwarzwälder Kirschtorte, I gathered my belongings together and headed for Münstertal's quaint little railway station, where the 11.01 to Freiburg in Breisgau pulled in at 11.01 on the dot – and by midday I found myself waiting in a queue at the Freiburg offices of a well-known international car rental company.

The vehicle the rental company had selected for me was a two-year-old *Renault Twingo Pzaz* in what the 'customer service agent' described as *'capsicum red'* (or what I would have described simply as 'red'). She was an elegant looking contraption with two doors and a 1.2-litre engine (the car, that is, not the customer service agent) – a bit smaller than I had anticipated and a little cramped too, but the rental company let me have it at a specially discounted rate, so I had no cause for complaint. But more importantly, when you've spent a couple of days driving around in a Trabant, as I have, driving a 1.2-litre Renault Twingo Pzaz is like driving a Roll-Royce whilst simultaneously having your shoulders gently massaged by a naked, blond masseuse with soothing hands and breasts the size of the Zugspitze. And so, happily cocooned inside my poky little Renault Twingo, I drove out of the compound of the car rental office and headed towards the B31 – the *'Schwarzwaldstraße'* – the forest road that took me along the first 150-kilometre stretch of my journey – to the university city of Friedrichshafen, on the shores of Lake Constance.

By the time I had reached Friedrichshafen I had been driving for just over two hours – high time, I decided, to stop and stretch my legs. Almost four hours had passed since I'd gorged myself on a slice of overpriced chocolate cake, so I wandered through the streets of Friedrichshafen in search of something to eat. Almost immediately, I happened upon a 'quick snack' kiosk (or *'Schnell-Imbiss'* as they're commonly known) where I purchased a ham and cheese toasted sandwich and a bottle of mineral water. It was too hot to sit inside, so with lunchtime snack in hand I headed for the *Schlosspark* – an idyllic little recreational area sandwiched between the *'Castle Church' (Schlosskirche)* and the lake, where I sat on a wooden park bench and ate my toasted sandwich. All around me I could hear the haunting cry of seagulls – a sound I find strangely reassuring for some reason. I hadn't heard the shrieking of seagulls since Usedom Island, which, inconceivably, was almost three weeks ago.

Lake Constance (or the *Bodensee* as the Germans call it) looked magnificent from where I was sitting – its shimmering surface glistening in the summer sunshine. As I sat there on the bench, I stared out across the lake in every direction, surveying the multitude of vessels dotted around on the surface – some so small and distant they were barely recognisable as boats at all. From my elevated position I felt a strange sense of pre-eminence and superiority – a degree of arrogance almost, like a latter-day King Canute. Before I arrived here, I hadn't realised just how big Lake Constance was. It's huge! The main body of the lake is 63 kilometres long, nearly 14 kilometres at its widest point, and it covers an area of approximately 571 km^2 Constance acts as a natural frontier between three sovereign states – Germany, Austria and Switzerland and is the third largest freshwater lake in Europe. [49] From this vantage point, I could see both Austria and Switzerland in the distance.

But with time pressing on and my appetite now sated by a ham and cheese toastie, I dragged myself reluctantly away

[49] *The three largest lakes in Europe are all surprisingly similar in both size and shape. Lake Balaton in Hungary is the largest at 592 km2. Next is Lake Geneva (bordering Switzerland and France) at 580 km2, and finally Constance at 571 km2*

from the glamour of Lake Constance and retraced my steps back to the car park – where the Renault Twingo was dutifully waiting. Another 120 kilometres later and I had reached the alpine town of Füssen – a charming little town of historic buildings intricately decorated with the most beautiful, ornate frescoes and painted in a variety of bright pastel shades. It's a typical Bavarian town is Füssen – the sort you'll find on picture postcards or adorning the lids of chocolate boxes. But there's another attraction that lures tourists to the town from every corner of the globe – the magnificent Neuschwanstein Castle. Built in 1869 at the behest of King Ludwig II (or *Mad* King Ludwig II to give him his full title), the castle sits on a rugged hilltop above the village of Hohenschwangau, just a couple of miles from Füssen. It looks like a castle straight from a fairy tale, with its pale white façade and imposing spires – so much so that it provided the Disney Corporation with their inspiration for Sleeping Beauty's castle (the Disney Magic Kingdom) which features on the Disney corporate logo.

At the foot of the hill upon which the castle appears to be so precariously perched is a car and coach park – and having driven round it several times I eventually managed to find a vacant space to park the Twingo.

The area was swarming with tourists (mainly of the Japanese and American variety), and was lined around its perimeter by a number of restaurants and gift shops (mainly of the tacky and rip-off variety). I could see the spires of the castle high above me, although the main body of the building was partially concealed from view behind trees. However, I decided *not* to join the queue for the 'castle tour' – for two very good reasons. Firstly, the queue was horrendously long. It snaked its way around a maze of *'Tensa'* barriers – the sort you find at theme parks or used to control the queues at airport security. It would have taken at least an hour to reach the front of the long line of people waiting to

361

purchase tickets, and I was conscious of the fact that I still had a ninety-minute journey ahead of me. But the main reason for my not wanting to join the queue was simply this – I'd seen it all before. During a previous visit a few years ago, I visited Neuschwanstein Castle where I waited patiently in line for the castle tour. After a lengthy wait, I handed over my entrance fee in exchange for a piece of hand-held electronic equipment – a listening device providing 'live' commentary as you wander around the rooms perusing the castle's many treasures and artefacts. But the tour was something of a disappointment, in my view. The tours were operated at ten-minute intervals in order to accommodate as many people as possible, but I couldn't help feeling I was being rushed. The hand-held commentary device dictated the speed and the order in which the rooms were to be viewed. I spent around three or four minutes in the first room before the listening device ushered me out and into another room for my next three minutes' worth. By the time I had completed the tour at the pace dictated by my electronic tour guide, I felt as if I had run a marathon.

The final leg of the journey (from Füssen to Garmisch-Partenkirchen) was a little over seventy kilometres, and as I had so accurately predicted, took around ninety minutes. This final section was by far the most scenic as the verdant and gently undulating alpine foothills suddenly gave way to a much harsher landscape. The road wound its way through a majestic mountain terrain and carved its way through tunnels in the rock. At one point I crossed the border into Austria – but it was short-lived. Just a few kilometres further on, I found myself crossing back into Germany again. The landscape didn't change of course. I wouldn't have known that I'd travelled through a small section of Austria had it not been for a signpost at the side of the road bearing the Austrian national flag and the words '*Wilkommen in Österreich*'. That, and the fact that the centre markings in the road suddenly changed colour – they changed to yellow as I entered Austria before changing back to white again a few kilometres later when I passed another signpost saying *'Wilkommen in Deutschland'*.

By the time I reached Garmisch-Partenkirchen it was early evening. The sun had disappeared behind a layer of ominous grey cloud and the temperature had dropped a few degrees. It wasn't raining, thank goodness – not yet anyway – but I was conscious of the fact that the heavens might open at any moment, and so decided not to waste any time in finding my campsite. The sooner I could get the *Wind-Breaker DeLuxe* assembled, the better – as I knew from previous experience that assembling my tent in the pouring rain was about as much fun as undergoing a rectal examination. Yes, I'd decided once again that my old friend the *Wind-Breaker DeLuxe* would be my accommodation of choice. And yes, I am fully aware that I had a brand new *Power Tokee* strapped to the side of my rucksack – but I had no intention of sleeping in it – not while there was life still in the old *Wind-Breaker*. My old tent still had a pulse – only a faint one admittedly, but a pulse nonetheless.

I found the campsite eventually, having followed some directions I'd scribbled on a scrap of paper before leaving Münstertal. I'd made a call to the camp's proprietor earlier in the day, and he'd given me directions over the telephone. The proprietor, a man by the name of Hans Eider, was a chatty sort of chap, well, to be brutally honest, 'irritatingly garrulous' would be a more accurate summation. Our telephone conversation continued for ten minutes – far longer than was necessary to relay a few simple directions. But Herr Eider had a lot more to tell me other than how to find his camping site. I realise that ten minutes may not seem all that long, but it felt like an eternity to me. I had no option other than to sit with my mobile telephone pressed against my ear, listening to the campsite proprietor's prosaic conversation and his blinkered opinions on a whole range of mundane topics.

I knew the site wasn't going to be the best I'd stayed at. Firstly, it was cheap – very cheap. So cheap in fact that I had to ask Herr Eider to repeat himself after he'd quoted me the price of a single-tent pitch. I thought maybe I'd misheard him. Secondly, my book '*Where to Camp in Germany*' described this site as 'rudimentary' – which I suppose was a pretty good clue. Well, '*rudimentary*' was indeed an apt description. It wasn't what I would describe as a 'camping site' as such – it was more a patch of grassland – a small field situated at the rear of the proprietor's farmhouse. There were no facilities to speak of, save for a small brick-built shed that housed a single toilet and a shower cubicle – only the one, mind – unisex of course. There was none of this *separate-male-and-female-shower-blocks* nonsense that you get at more conventional camping sites. It was a small site too – room for only half a dozen small tents at most, and there were already three other tents assembled when I arrived.

I must admit, I didn't feel entirely comfortable about having to spend the night in a field with only three other fellow campers. For all I knew, one of them could have been a psychopathic serial killer – a lunatic on the run after escaping from a secure mental institution. I suppose one could argue that you run *that* risk when camping anywhere – even at the largest and best equipped of camping sites. But there's safety in numbers, isn't there? The campsite at Garmisch-Partenkirchen did have one rather endearing feature though – it was located next to a meadow. The campsite and the meadow were separated by only the flimsiest of wire fences. There was a herd of cows grazing there, each wearing '*Treicheln*' – alpine cowbells attached to their necks by pretty decorative leather straps with colourful fringing. These cowbells are worn as standard by alpine cattle when they're left to graze in alpine meadows, and they make a distinctive clanging sound which enables herdsmen to locate any animals that may have wandered off in search of greener pastures. I liked the sound the cowbells made – there was something strangely comforting and reassuring about it. I shall add 'cowbells' to my list of favourite things, along with church bells and trains. Perhaps Julie Andrews could sing a song about them.

I assembled my tent as quickly as I could in case the weather deteriorated, and in desperate need of a brew, I fired up the *Pocket Rocket*. I wandered around the campsite in search of a water supply tap, but there didn't appear to be one – so I filled my kettle from what was left in the bottle of mineral water I'd purchased in Friedrichshafen. Mercifully, the weather didn't deteriorate all that much. As the evening went on the temperature fell a few notches further and by the time I climbed into my sleeping bag there was a distinct chill in the air. I'd noticed a few spots of rain earlier in the evening too, but they came to nothing. I fell asleep that night with my fingers crossed – hoping against hope that the rain would hold off.

The following morning I woke with a strong feeling of confidence and a renewed optimism. It hadn't rained during the night – which was marvellous; nor had I been hacked to death by a deranged psychopath – which was equally marvellous, if not more so. I'd already used the last drop of water in my kettle, so making myself a cup of tea or coffee was sadly not an option – and since the campsite was lacking in even basic facilities, like a café or a shop, rustling up a decent breakfast didn't appear to be an option either. I emptied the contents of my rucksack onto the grass and sifted through my clothes in search of a clean shirt and a fresh pair of undercrackers. I found neither. It had been a while since Stella had done my laundry for me, so I found myself having to settle for 'the least dirty' rather than anything clean. I took a freezing cold shower, dressed into the cleanest clothes I could find, and stuffed the rest into a large plastic carrier bag.

Now, it just so happened that there was a self-service laundrette on the main road between the campsite and the town centre. It was almost two kilometres away from the camp admittedly, but it was located more or less adjacent to a charming little café specialising in coffee and a breakfast Panino. [50] So I devised an ingenious plan – I would treat myself to a hearty breakfast while my clothes were spinning around in the washing machine at the laundrette.

It was easier said than done. I am convinced that the manufacturers of washing machines take deliberate steps to discourage men from using their products – by making the instructions for use as complicated and as convoluted as possible. Having inserted three €2 coins, I found myself confronted by a bewildering series of options – none of which made any sense at all. They were all completely meaningless – so much so, they may as well have been written in Vedic Sanskrit. 'Select one of the following wash programmes' the electronic display told me. 'Pre-wash cycle; normal wash cycle; cottons cycle; linens cycle; easy-care cycle; synthetics cycle; delicates cycle; hand-wash cycle; rinse-wash cycle; reduced load cycle; duvet cycle; rinse-hold cycle; reduced ironing cycle; and a partridge-in-a-pear-tree cycle.' In the absence of a 'dirty undercrackers cycle' I pressed one of the buttons at random (I can't remember which one) and as the confounded contraption sprung into motion, I took refuge in the comparative safety of the café.

Garmisch-Partenkirchen is a mountain resort town, and when you're visiting in the summertime, as I was, it is difficult

---

[50] *I feel duty-bound to point out that the Italian word 'panini' is, in fact, a plural. The singular is 'panino', although the English-speaking world appears to be completely oblivious to this fact.*

to imagine how different the vibe must be during the winter. Garmisch-Partenkirchen is a ski resort – in fact it's Germany's *premier* ski resort, and the town is at its liveliest during the winter months. Of course, that doesn't mean that Garmisch-Partenkirchen isn't busy during the summer – it's still a bustling, vibrant little metropolis. Everything one could possibly want is available in the town's shops, from leatherwear and glass items at vendors' stalls, to the most luxurious of fashion goods in the chic boutiques. There are sports shops specialising in ski equipment and snowboarding accessories; cake shops selling local specialities, and of course the big names in designer fashion.

The name '*Garmisch-Partenkirchen*' is actually a relatively recent phenomenon. For centuries, the twin towns of '*Garmisch*' and '*Partenkirchen*' were two separate entities – and even today still maintain quite individual identities. It is noticeable, for example, that the western side of town (what used to be Garmisch) has a relatively modern feel, whereas the eastern side (the former district of Partenkirchen), with its frescoes and its cobblestoned streets, offers something of a glimpse into times gone by. However, in 1935, the towns' respective mayors were instructed to combine the two market towns in preparation for the 1936 Winter Olympic Games – which were to be held in the newly-created town of Garmisch-Partenkirchen. The instruction to combine the two towns came from the chancellor himself – a certain Mr. Adolf Hitler. Germany had already hosted the Summer Olympics two years earlier. The Berlin Olympic Games of 1934 had been a showcase for the newly-elected National Socialist party – a triumphant piece of propaganda for the German government and Chancellor Hitler was determined that the 1936 winter games in Garmisch-Partenkirchen would be equally successful. But nowadays, the name 'Garmisch-Partenkirchen' is considered by many to be a bit long-winded, and quite often this united town with its delightful hyphenated name is casually (although incorrectly) referred to simply as *'Garmisch'* – much to the annoyance and dismay of the residents of Partenkirchen.

The thing that attracts many tourists to the area, of course, is the *Zugspitze* – Germany's highest mountain at 2,962 metres (that's a little over 9,700 feet). The mountain straddles the border between Germany and Austria, so it's possible to reach the summit from either the German or the Austrian side, and even in mid-summer you'll still find snow on the peak. I had been told by a number of reliable sources that the view from the summit is particularly spectacular. Apparently, on a clear day, it's possible to see all the way to Italy. And that, I think, was my primary motivation for visiting Garmisch-Partenkirchen – to take in a view across Italy from the summit of Germany's highest mountain. But the weather today wasn't exactly conducive to panoramic vistas. It was grey and misty and the Zugspitze's peak was concealed within a layer of cloud. I had my serious doubts as to whether I'd be able to see anything at all. But, as I sat in the café gorging myself on a breakfast panino and eavesdropping into the conversation of the young couple who were sitting at an adjacent table, I overheard one of them utter the following pearl of wisdom – which was, in my opinion, one of the most insightful, astute and intuitive observations I have ever heard.

"By the time we get to the summit, the weather might have brightened up a bit," she said.

Now, there are two ways of reaching the summit of the Zugspitze. Well, *three* actually – if you include the option of hiking up there. Hiking is a possibility of course, and there are a number of well-charted trails for hikers to use. But climbing to the summit on foot was an option I had emphatically ruled out. The last time I attempted to *walk* to the summit of a mountain was just two weeks earlier in the

Harz Mountain range. It was during my descent of Brocken Mountain along the Goethe Trail that I lost my footing and fell over, spraining my ankle in the process. Brocken is only 1,141 metres high – the Zugspitze is 2,962 and the terrain far more challenging – even for the most experienced of hikers. So, with hiking discounted, I was left with two possible ways of getting to the summit of the Zugspitze – the cable car or the cog railway. Now I must confess that I'm not a big fan of cable cars. There's something about being cocooned inside a tiny glass capsule and suspended above a mountain by a spindly piece of wire that I find a little unsettling – it gives one a feeling of vulnerability and defencelessness. So I chose the cog railway (*the Zugspitzbahn*) – not that I particularly wanted to, but it was the lesser of two evils. I reasoned that, if I were to fall out of one of the carriages of the cog railway, then I'd only fall a couple of feet before hitting the ground. If however, I were to fall out of the cable-car, I'd experience at least 20 metres of free-fall before colliding rather violently with terra firma. That strong feeling of confidence and renewed optimism I had woken up with was clearly beginning to wear off – replaced rather suddenly by anxiety and a feeling of impending doom. Why else would I be worrying about falling out of a cable car?

The Zugspitzbahn station is some distance from the town centre, so I drove there in the Renault Twingo. I still had a couple of hours' rental time remaining before the vehicle had to be returned, so I decided I'd get my money's worth. Not only that, I still had a drop of fuel left that needed using up. After all, the tank was empty when I collected the car at Freiburg and I was determined to make certain it would be empty again on its return to the rental offices at Garmisch-Partenkirchen. I saw no reason why I should donate any petrol to the next punter who rented the Twingo – gasoline is simply too valuable a commodity to give away.

Not only was the cog railway expensive, it also fell short of taking me all the way to the top of the Zugspitze. The line actually stops at the *Schneeferner Glacier* – a little shy of the summit. There's a chapel at this level – the *Maria Heimsuchung Chapel* – which has the accolade of being the highest place of worship in Germany. It was sanctified in 1981 by the German Archbishop Cardinal Josef Ratzinger. He's moved up in the world since then – he's now Pope Benedict XVI. I fell into a state of utter consternation when I discovered that the only way of reaching the summit from here was by cable car. So I decided not to bother. A 'view as far as Italy' was out of the question anyway. It was a murky day still, and the cloud cover showed no sign of relenting. In fact, it was all terribly disappointing. I'd hoped to be revelling in the beauty of this wonderful mountain, marvelling in the astonishing views it afforded and the entrancing thoughts it inspired. But I wasn't. I was standing on (not quite) the top of Germany, shivering in a damp mist – unable to see anything further than ten metres in front of me. So I drank a coffee at the little chapel café before heading back down the mountain on the same train that had brought me up here.

When I arrived back at the station at the foot of the Zugspitze I decided it was time to return the hire car. The car rental company's offices were located in the outskirts of Garmisch-Partenkirchen, in a little village at the foot of a mountain called '*Wank*'. Now, being an Englishman, I find it very difficult to write about a mountain called Wank without sniggering like a naughty schoolboy. The word is pronounced '*vunk*' in German and obviously doesn't have the same connotations as it does in English. But nevertheless, I couldn't help getting a huge amount of puerile gratification from driving past the '*Wank Haus*' and the '*Wank Garage*' or (and this really did make me chuckle) seeing a sign for the '*1,780-metre Wank*'. I shall apologise in advance for what I am about to say – it is the most inexcusable example of puerility imaginable, but I simply can't resist the temptation to say it. But, in much the same way that residents of Berlin are called 'Berliners', and the citizens of Hamburg are 'Hamburgers', it stands to reason that the good people of Wank are burdened with a most unfortunate collective term. Nowhere else on earth other than right here in the outskirts of Garmisch-Partenkirchen will you find a larger gathering of Wankers.

That evening, my wife telephoned me. She was back from her trip around the Caribbean – in fact she'd arrived home several days earlier and I told her how much I was looking forward to hearing all about her trip away.

"A package arrived for you in the morning post," she said. "Whatever it is, it's very heavy."

"That will be the pewter beer tankard that Jan bought for me," I explained. "He promised he would post it back to the UK to save me having to carry it around in my backpack."

"Oh, I see," she replied. "When will you be home?"

"Friday, probably."

"Friday morning or Friday afternoon?"

Her question seemed a little odd, I thought. Under normal circumstances my wife wouldn't have wanted to know what time I'd be home – it wouldn't have mattered to her one way or the other. But here she was, pressing me for a specific time of arrival. I sensed immediately that my dear wife may have had an ulterior motive for calling. I had a sneaky feeling that the arrival of a package in the post was merely a ruse – the perfect excuse to pick up the phone and call me.

"I don't know exactly what time I'll be home on Friday," I said. "Does it matter?"

"Well, you see, the thing is....."

"Yes?"

371

"Well, I don't have to go of course, but, well, you see, the thing is...."

"Yes?"

"Joanna has booked a weekend away at a health spa in the Cotswolds and she's asked me if I'd like to go with her."

"I see."

"I've been reading through the brochure – it looks wonderful! They do all sorts of interesting treatments as well as the usual body massages – and there's a sauna too!"

"Well yes, I'm sure there is but....."

"I could have a paraffin wax bath or a physiotherm or some hypnotherapy or even Chinese body therapy. I know I haven't seen you for five weeks, but I'll be home again on Monday! You can tell me all about your trip when I get back!"

And she was right of course. We hadn't seen each other for almost five weeks – but that was entirely *my* fault rather than hers. I couldn't possibly begrudge her spending a weekend at a health spa in the Cotswolds with her best friend – after all, I had spent the best part of five weeks gallivanting around Germany. I desperately wanted to get home and spend some time with her after us being so long apart, but I suppose, in the grand scheme of things, another few days wouldn't make a great deal of difference. After all, as the great Bard of Avon once observed, "Absence doth sharpen love, presence strengthens it; the one brings fuel, the other blows it till it burns clear" – and such sentiment couldn't be expressed more eloquently than that.

As I settled down under the canvas that night listening to the dulcet tones of Bryan Adams on my iPod and thinking about my wife and how wonderful it would be to see her again, little did I know that, within a matter of a few hours, my whole world would come crashing down on top of me – literally. Nothing could possibly have prepared me for what was about to happen.

In the small hours of the following morning, my tent collapsed. Two of the main supporting poles buckled, one of them snapped completely – and the entire structure fell down, momentarily trapping me inside. It was like being cocooned in several layers of cling film. As the pole snapped, its jagged edges pierced the already tattered flysheet and sliced through the canvas like a pair of scissors cutting through a sheet of wrapping paper. As it so happened, I was already awake when disaster struck – I had been awake for at least an hour listening to the inclement weather – the toe-curling sounds of one of the most violent storms I have ever experienced.

It was raining. Actually, that statement doesn't even come close to describing what was really going on out there. It was raining harder than I have ever witnessed it rain before – falling with ire on an almost biblical scale. Hailstones, the size of golf balls, were crashing onto car roofs leaving cavernous dents in their wake. The noise was deafening; the pavements had turned into mini rivers; the campsite field and the adjacent meadow had transformed into a swamp. Storms of this ferocity, it seems, are common in the summertime in southern Bavaria – something to do with hot Mediterranean air making its way northwards before clashing with the colder air over the Alps. If only I'd listened more attentively during geography lessons at school, I might have been able to offer you a more educated explanation. All I could hear was the rain pounding against my tent, the hailstones slamming against the flysheet like tiny cannonballs. This was a conflict my tent was simply not destined to survive. She had been wounded in battle on so many previous occasions that she simply had no fight left in her.

With the tent on top of me, I fumbled around in the darkness in search of my shoes and a pair of jeans. I grabbed my rucksack and my sleeping bag before somehow managing to unzip what used to be the entrance flap. Eventually, whilst crawling around on all fours, I managed to find my way out. Having freed myself from the tangled mess that was once my *Wind-Breaker DeLuxe*, I started running across the rain-soaked grass as fast as I possibly could – clutching my rucksack and my sleeping bag as if my life depended on it. I was drenched by the pelting rain; bombarded by merciless hailstones – but I kept on running until eventually I reached the comparative safety of the campsite toilet block. And it was there, in that dank and musty brick-built outhouse that I stayed for the remainder of the night. I sat on the cold stone floor, propped my back against the wall and covered myself as best I could with my damp sleeping bag. It was by far the bleakest, dreariest and most miserable hole I have ever had the misfortune of spending a night in [51] – but it was shelter from the storm and for that reason alone, it would just have to do. And there I sat until daybreak, by which time the mother of all storms had finally abated.

I didn't sleep very well that night, as you can probably imagine. I suppose it's not surprising when you've spent the night on the floor with your back propped against the wall of a toilet block. But I must have dozed off on a couple of occasions if only for relatively short periods of time. I woke from the last of my catnaps feeling groggy and slightly disorientated – and the muscles in my back were aching, presumably the result of such awkward and unnatural body posture. So I decided I would take a shower – get myself washed and dressed and ready to face whatever the day had in store for me. Once again, there was no hot water. The shower was icy-cold, as it had been on the previous day. Needless to say, I didn't hang about – there's no point lingering in a freezing cold shower, unless you're some sort

[51] *Actually, I stayed at a hotel in Lille a few years ago that comes a very close second.*

of deranged masochist. I dressed, rolled up my sleeping bag, grabbed my rucksack with all my worldly possessions therein, and braced myself for what lay ahead. In the aftermath of last night's storm, it was time to inspect the damage.

I think it is probably fair to say that the damage to my tent was nothing short of catastrophic. I know I've always had a tendency to play down the state of my *Wind-Breaker DeLuxe* – she'd been a loyal friend and I'd always seen the good in her, even though the inconvenient truth was staring at me in the face. But this time, there was no denying the reality of the situation – even *I* would have to concede that the damage was way beyond any possibility of repair. Yes, my *Wind-Breaker DeLuxe* was dead. To quote the immortal words of a legendary comic genius, my tent had passed on. 'It was no more. It had ceased to be.' I scraped up what remained of it from the grass – the strips of canvas, the broken tent pegs, the distorted aluminium poles – and I carried its mortal remains over to a line of wheelie bins which were propped against the wall at the side of the toilet block. There were four in all – a green one for metals, half-filled with tins and empty beer cans; a yellow one for glass – again half full with empty bottles of various colours and sizes (although most of them were beer bottles in their former lives); a blue one for newspapers and magazines; and finally, a black one for 'general waste'. The latter was piled high with rubbish way beyond the brim – so much so that the lid wouldn't shut. It was filled mainly with carrier bags containing rotting food waste – many of which had fallen out or had simply been placed on the ground deliberately, since the bin had reached its capacity. There was a pungent, rather obnoxious stench emanating from the black wheelie bin, and the whole area was swarming with flies and wasps.

In my opinion, my *Wind-Breaker DeLuxe* deserved a more dignified funeral than this. After everything we had

375

been through together, it seemed inappropriate that my tent should end its days among a pile of stinking, rotting food waste. She had served me well and it seemed only right that her component parts should be recycled – turned into something else so that she could bring as much pleasure to other people as she had brought me in her previous life. And so I dismantled the wreckage piece by piece. I placed the aluminium poles and tent pegs into the green wheelie bin along with the tins and the empty beer cans, and I folded up what remained of the canvas flysheet before placing it into the blue bin along with the piles of sodden newspapers and magazines. OK, I know the blue bin was supposed to be for paper, but it all goes the same way in the end, doesn't it? And besides, if there had been a purple wheelie bin specifically for recycling fabrics as there jolly well should have been, then I wouldn't have been forced to consign my tent's canvas flysheet into the wrong receptacle.

Despite the stench, and the flies, and the wasps, I stood in reverence for a minute or so – my head bowed in respect for tents recently departed. Yes, I know it was only a tent and my actions may seem a little eccentric – but I had been fond of my *Wind-Breaker DeLuxe*. She was an old pal, and I was saddened by her sudden and untimely demise. My journey, after all, wasn't over just yet. I still had one more German state to visit before I could head back home, and it was a shame, I thought, that my poor old *Wind-Breaker* wouldn't be there with me when I eventually crossed the finish line.

"May she rest in peace," I said, before picking up my rucksack and walking away.

As I wandered through the camp, past the line of other people's tents (which, unlike mine, appeared to have survived the storm completely unscathed), one of my fellow campers stepped out from his tent just at the moment I was passing. He stared at me momentarily before nodding to acknowledge my presence. I nodded back, politely. The man was wearing navy blue pyjamas beneath a matching dressing gown; his hair was unkempt and he was carrying a wash bag. Tucked underneath his arm was a rolled up bath towel.

"Good morning," he said. "That was quite a storm we had last night. I hope it didn't keep you awake. I managed to sleep through most of it."

He chuckled in the manner of a mad scientist, clearly under the misapprehension that he'd said something funny.

"No, it didn't keep me awake," I lied. It was the only response I could think of at the time. What I really wanted to do was punch him squarely on the nose.

"Oh well," he continued, "I'm off for a shower."

His words were music to my ears. 'Good – a freezing cold shower', I thought. 'That'll teach him for being so smug and self-righteous'.

"Well good luck with that," I quipped. "The water in that shower block is freezing cold again!"

The man gave me a puzzled stare, as if I'd said something completely incomprehensible.

"I shan't be using the shower block," he said. "There's no hot water in the shower block! I shall use the one in Hans' farmhouse. It's a lovely shower – quite luxurious. Anyone who camps in the field here is entitled to use all of the facilities in the farmhouse, you know. You can use the kitchen if you wish – to cook yourself a breakfast or make a cup of coffee. There's a washing machine too if you've any laundry to do. Herr Eider only charges two euros to use the washing machine. Apparently, there's a laundrette just along the road towards the town centre, but I'm told it's much more expensive – far better to use the washing machine in the farmhouse, I think."

He paused for a while, presumably in anticipation of a response of some kind. He didn't get one.

"Well anyway, it was nice to meet you," he said – and with that, he nodded at me again and headed off towards the farmhouse in his dressing gown – walking gingerly along the pathway to avoid stepping in a puddle and ruining his slippers.

I strolled along the road towards the town centre feeling more than a little despondent, and once again I stopped at the café where I ordered another breakfast Panino and a cup of coffee. And there I sat – at the same table that I'd sat at on the previous morning. But whereas before I'd been full of optimism and high-spirits, this morning I was feeling decidedly down in the dumps. I had spoken to Hans Eider, the proprietor of the campsite on two separate occasions – once on the telephone, when he'd given me comprehensive and nauseatingly detailed directions on how to get to the site, and again (face to face this time) at the campsite reception desk – where he'd charged me the pitching fee and given me instructions on where I should pitch my tent. And during these multiple conversations of ours, the proprietor and I had talked about all sorts of stuff – mundane nonsense, most of it. We'd discussed the merits of a Renault Twingo in comparison to other cars of similar size; we'd talked about how beautiful the Zugspitze was, particularly at this time of year; we'd pondered the advantages of travelling with a good quality rucksack as opposed to some of the lower-priced examples that were all too often lacking in sturdiness and durability; and we had mulled over that all-important question of whether the German people were better off in the days of the Deutschmark than they are currently, now that they're stuck with the euro. And yet, during all of this vacuous claptrap, not once did he bother to mention that I could use the farmhouse shower instead of having to tolerate that freezing cold plumbing antiquity that was housed in the brick-built shed! Not once did he explain to me that I could boil a kettle in the farmhouse kitchen

378

instead of trying to light a portable stove in the pissing rain and the howling wind! And not once did that gormless moron consider it appropriate to inform me that I could shove my dirty undercrackers in the farmhouse washing machine instead of having to walk almost two kilometres, carrier bag in hand, to a laundrette in the town centre!

And as if that wasn't bad enough, I'd had all those high hopes for my visit to Garmisch-Partenkirchen dashed. It's a sweet little town – the grand old dame of ski resorts. It offers a charming mélange of history and modernism and is set among some of Germany's most spectacular scenery. And yet, Garmisch-Partenkirchen had brought me nothing but bad luck. I had been looking forward to climbing to the summit of the Zugspitze to witness the most spectacular of panoramic vistas. But I chose to go on a day of thick fog – when visibility was down to just a few metres. And then, of course, I had to endure the biggest blow of all.

They say that everyone can remember where they were and what they were doing on the day John F. Kennedy was assassinated. Well, for the rest of my days I shall always remember where I was and what I was doing on the night my *Wind-Breaker DeLuxe* finally gave up the ghost. I was in Garmisch-Partenkirchen – lying on the cold, stone floor of a public toilet, with a wet sleeping bag wrapped around my shivering torso. The only thing missing was the intervention of a kindly Samaritan from the Salvation Army – on hand to provide me with a nourishing bowl of hot soup. As soon as I get home I shall make a very generous donation to a charity that cares for those poor unfortunate souls whose homelessness forces them to sleep in shop doorways. I now feel a sense of affiliation towards them.

oOo

Dear Diary,

The Beer, Cheese and Tent Report for the State of Bavaria:

Beer: Mittenwald Brau - König Ludwig Dunkel:

König Ludwig Dunkel has a dark red chestnut hue – a colour not dissimilar to wood varnish. Its flavour is coarse and slightly acidic – a taste not dissimilar to wood varnish.

Cheese: Allgäuer Emmentaler:

You're probably already aware of Allgäuer Emmentaler. It's a classic hard cheese with a mild, nutty flavour. It's best known for its distinctive round, cherry-sized holes.

Tent Stability:

Well, what else is there left to say? My Wind-Breaker DeLuxe is no more.

oOo

Chapter Seventeen – Bonn Voyage

"Then close your eyes; tap your heels together three times and think to yourself; there's no place like home." Glinda's (the Good Witch of the South) advice to Dorothy at the finale of the 1939 film 'The Wizard of Oz'

You may have noticed that, as I have zigzagged my way across this vast country, dipping my toes in and out of each of the German states, there is one state I have so far managed to bypass. Since the outset of this adventure, I have travelled from the windswept flatlands in the north, to the rugged, majestic alpine terrain in Germany's far south, yet I've ticked off only fifteen states along the way. The state I have managed to circumvent completely is *North Rhine Westphalia*, situated in the west of the country bordering Belgium and the Netherlands. The truth is, I could easily have visited North Rhine Westphalia a couple of weeks earlier – in fact, the campsite I stayed at near the Edersee Dam was a mere 35 kilometres or so from the Westphalia state border. But as you'll recall, I travelled from the Edersee directly to the town of Wittlich in the state of Rhineland-Palatinate, where I stayed with my friend Jan and his wife Stella, delighting in the pleasure of their hospitality and experiencing the incomparable joy of being woken in the morning by two mischievous children bashing me over the head with a plastic dinosaur.

My decision to bypass the state of North Rhine Westphalia during *that* stage of my journey was intentional of course – a premeditated decision on my part, and one which, to the casual observer, may seem a little puzzling. But the thing is this – if I had squeezed a brief stopover in the state of North Rhine Westphalia into my outbound journey; sandwiched it somewhere between my visit to the Edersee and my stay at Jan and Stella's, well, that would mean my journey would have ended here – in Garmisch-Partenkirchen. Bavaria would have been the sixteenth and final state on my German tour – and with all sixteen states crossed off the checklist, I'd have nothing else left to do other than begin the homeward journey back to west London.

The trouble is, Garmisch-Partenkirchen is a long way from west London – it's about 1,200 kilometres actually, a journey which, by my reckoning, would take around eighteen hours to complete, allowing for the rail connections at Munich, Stuttgart and Paris – not forgetting the ferry connection at Calais. And even the most enthusiastic of travel aficionados will have to concede that a journey of eighteen hours is an awfully long stretch to complete in one fell swoop. And so, I reasoned that splitting the journey would be far easier on my weary soul. I could travel the first 600 kilometres or so and make an overnight stop at the halfway mark, before completing the remainder of the journey after a good night's rest. And, as it just so happens, sitting snugly at the halfway point between Garmisch-Partenkirchen in southern Bavaria and my home in west London, is the beautiful cathedral city of Cologne *(Köln)* in the state of North Rhine Westphalia.

It was only eight o'clock in the morning as I sat there in the café – but I'd already made the decision to leave Garmisch-Partenkirchen just as soon as I could polish off the last few crumbs of my breakfast panino. My original plan had been to spend another day here and catch a later train – join one of the walking tours of the town perhaps, or do some shopping in the market. But I decided against it. Instead, I would catch an early train to Munich – the first leg of my onward journey to Cologne. There was no sign of the previous night's storm thank goodness – the rain had finally relented and the wind had calmed considerably, but the skies were still dull and overcast and there was an unseasonable chill in the air. And like the grey skies above me, I too was feeling a little gloomy and despondent.

But my temporary state of melancholy didn't last. As the train rattled towards Munich, a sudden break in the clouds afforded a welcome glimpse of turquoise sky, and a ray of sunshine suddenly penetrated the gloom. And as the weather improved, so did my general disposition. With the sunlight now streaming in through the window, I sat back in my seat, jammed the tiny speakers of my iPod into my ears and closed my eyes. It was an eighty-minute journey to Munich, a chance for me to snooze a while – no more than I deserved after my sleep deprivation of the previous night. But just as I began to experience that warm and satisfying sensation of drifting out of consciousness, my mobile phone rang. I didn't hear it of course – my ears were filled with the mellow tones of Joss Stone at the time, but I had the ringtone feature set to 'vibrate' – which it did. It damn near scared the living daylights out of me. I hastily yanked the speakers out from my eardrums, almost ripping my ears off in the process, and answered the call. It was Jan.

"Chris," he said with his customary cheerfulness and exuberance. "Is it *today* that you're planning to travel to Cologne?"

"Yes – in fact I'm already on my way."

"Fantastic! Cologne is only ninety minutes by train from Wittlich – you can stay at the farmhouse with me and Stella again tonight."

"Well, that's a very kind offer, Jan – and under normal circumstances I would gladly take you up on it. But I'm afraid on this occasion I won't be able to stay with you."

"Why not?"

"Well, it's a matter of principle, you see. The rules of my jolly around Germany dictate that I have to stay for at least one night in each one of the sixteen German states. There's only one state left on my list – that's North Rhine

Westphalia. I know your farm in Wittlich isn't all that far from Cologne, but it's not in North Rhine Westphalia – it's in Rhineland-Palatinate."

My explanation must have seemed more than a little pompous and there was a portentous pause as Jan tried to fathom the logic of my argument. I didn't expect him to understand though. Jan wasn't the sort of man who allowed his life to be dictated by rules – especially rules that were self-imposed and were being adhered to simply on 'a matter of principle'. But for all his shortcomings, Jan was a patient fellow – tolerant of other people's quirks and peculiarities.

"Well, if the mountain won't come to Muhammad," he said rather cryptically, "then I suppose Muhammad must go to the mountain. I'll join you in Cologne if I may. I'll meet you outside the station at around eight o'clock this evening. There's a fantastic jazz club in the city centre that stays open until the early hours of the morning."

"Is there?"

"Yes – you'll love it. I'm sure I can get us in for free – I know the manager you see – he's a good friend of mine."

"Is he? Well, I....."

"I will stay in Cologne with you tonight and then make my way back home tomorrow morning."

"Well, that sounds like a good idea Jan, but I'm afraid there's a flaw in your plan."

"What flaw?"

"Well, I only have one tent. I still have the *Power Tokee* you very kindly gave me, but I'm afraid my old tent finally bit the dust during a storm in the early hours of this morning. I had to administer the last rites before consigning what was left of it to a wheelie bin."

"A tent? Jan exclaimed indignantly. "Who said anything about staying in a tent? I'm booking us both a room at the Hyatt Regency Hotel. It's a fabulous five-star hotel overlooking the river. You'll love it there!"

"You really don't have to go to all that expense, Jan," I said. "I can just as easily stay at the campsite."

"You'll do no such thing. I'm booking two rooms at the Hyatt and that's the end of the discussion! Besides, it won't be anywhere near as expensive as you think. I will wangle a discount."

"How?"

"I know the manager there. He's a good friend of mine."

Now, previous experience has taught me that refusing one of Jan's generous offers is never a good idea. His offers are always of a generous nature – so munificent sometimes that I often feel slightly uncomfortable accepting them. But although Jan is a kind-hearted fellow – philanthropic by his very nature – he doesn't take kindly to rejection – he would regard refusal as an affront. And let's be honest here, I could either spend another night huddled up inside my sleeping bag, protected from the elements by a flimsy layer of waterproof canvas – or I could snuggle beneath a duvet in a comfy king-sized bed in a luxury five-star hotel that somebody else was paying for. As my dear old mother always used to say, 'one should never look a gift-horse in the mouth.' [52]

"OK, Jan," I said. "I shall see you outside the train station at eight o'clock. I shall look forward to it."

I made my rail connection at Munich and was soon rattling towards the city of Cologne at breakneck speed in the comfort of one of Deutsche Bahn's Intercity-Express

---

[52] *My 'dear old mum' used to come up with all sorts of curious proverbs and intriguing adages. Most of them made perfect sense in the context she used them – but there were many that seemed to make no sense at all. Here are some examples: 'A fish always rots from the head down'; 'Parsley seed goes nine times to the devil' and the most illogical of them all: 'A swarm in May is worth a load of hay.' To this day I have absolutely no idea what any of them mean and I remain convinced that she made them up simply to confuse me.*

(ICE) high-speed trains. At almost 280 kilometres per hour, this was the fastest I had travelled during my trip so far, by some considerable margin – and in comparison to most of the other trains I had travelled on it was the epitome of luxury. The view through the window was a little disappointing though. The railway tracks run along deep cuttings carved through the countryside like unsightly surgical scars – so only the sides of the embankments were visible through the train's windows. And whenever something of any interest came into view, the train sped past it at such velocity that there wasn't time to focus long enough to determine what it was. So I adjusted my seat to the 'full recline' position and promptly fell asleep.

It was mid afternoon by the time my train purred effortlessly into Cologne's main station, and as I stepped out from the concourse of the *Hauptbahnhof* and into the city's bustling streets, I sensed almost immediately that I had arrived somewhere rather special. Cologne's most iconic landmark is of course the prodigious cathedral which dominates the skyline and is visible from almost everywhere in the city. Known the world over simply as 'Cologne Cathedral', this magnificent monument of German catholicism and Gothic architecture is officially '*Cologne High Cathedral of St. Peter and St. Mary*'. It is the largest Gothic church in northern Europe; it has the largest façade of any church in the world; it is an official UNESCO World Heritage Site; and as if that wasn't enough, it holds the title of being Germany's most visited landmark, with an average of 20,000 visitors every single day. That's a pretty impressive accolade, especially when you consider the strength of the competition – this extraordinary edifice attracts more visitors than the Berlin Wall, the Brandenburg Gate, or the hilltop castle of Neuschwanstein. The original foundations were laid in 1248 and it's fair to say that the original medieval designs for Cologne's extraordinary cathedral were overwhelming in their ambition. So much so that it took more than 600 years for the building to finally be completed. For more than seven centuries, successive builders found inspiration from the catholic faith and adopted a spirit of absolute fidelity to the original plans. It's a building that testifies to the enduring strength of European Christianity.

I spent much of the afternoon strolling around Cologne cathedral. Visitors are permitted to climb the 509 stone steps of the spiral staircase to a viewing platform about 98 metres above the ground, and since I had time on my hands that afternoon, I decided to join the hundreds of people who had opted to make the slow and tiring ascent to the top. My efforts were rewarded with a magnificent view of the city and, directly below me, a perfect 'bird's eye' view of the river Rhine.

I've always rather fancied a Rhine river cruise. Cologne is a major port of call for most of the Rhine cruise operators, and from my elevated position on the platform I could see a plethora of cruise vessels moored along the quayside. There were passengers disembarking along narrow gangplanks, and others scurrying around the dockside like tiny ants. A Rhine cruise would be out of the question during this current adventure of course. I'd be leaving Cologne the following day and heading home, so there would hardly be time for such whimsical fantasies. But having survived three weeks with her friend Joanna on board the *Oasis of the Seas,* cruising the turquoise oceans of the Caribbean, I had made the presumption that my dear wife had now managed to overcome the 'mal de mer' that for so many years had blighted her life and prevented her from accompanying me on our own little nautical adventure. So, who knows? Perhaps a romantic cruise along the Rhine might one day become a reality. I decided I would broach the subject with her the moment I arrived home.

Eight o'clock came and went and still there was no sign of Jan. I paced up and down the pedestrian square outside Cologne's central train station, checking the time on my watch every couple of minutes and cursing him under my breath. Knowing Jan's track record, I suppose I should have guessed that he'd be running late – he *was* the king of tardiness, after all. At ten-past eight I received a text from him. It said simply *'punning a kittle late, be there in ufo minutes'*. That's the annoying thing about predictive text – it will default to the most obscure word imaginable rather than suggest something obvious. Why on earth would the inventors of predictive text imagine that the word you were searching for was *'ufo'* rather than *'ten'* – especially when it precedes the word *'minutes'*? Anyway, ufo minutes later there was still no sign of Jan, so I wandered inside the station to check the arrival times of the trains from Wittlich. I stood for a while on the station concourse, staring in awe at the giant electronic display board above me. The list of destinations read like an A to Z of cities which have hosted the Eurovision Song Contest over the past thirty years – Paris, Belgrade, Lausanne, Luxembourg and Istanbul among the names on display. And as I stood there trying to spot the word 'Wittlich' among the bewildering list of destinations, I felt a tap on my shoulder.

"Sorry I'm late, matey," said Jan. "I had a row with a parking attendant after I'd parked my car in the car park at Wittlich station. The bastard made me miss my train."

"A row? What about?" I asked.

"Oh, it was nothing really. He accused me of parking my car in a space reserved for the disabled, so naturally I gave him a piece of my mind."

"And *did* you?"

"Did I what?"

"Did you park your car in a space reserved for the disabled?"

388

"Well, yes of course I did. But the only other available spaces were over the far side of the car park. The space I parked in was right next to the main entrance to the station."

"But the space was reserved for somebody disabled, Jan. The whole idea is that somebody with a disability only has to walk or manoeuvre a wheelchair a short distance to the station entrance."

"Yes, I realise that, Chris – I'm not stupid. But what this officious bastard of a parking attendant didn't appreciate was that I drive a Mercedes S-Class. You can't leave a car of that quality parked in the far corner of a car park. Someone is likely to steal it."

"And if you leave it parked in a disabled bay then the authorities are likely to have it towed away."

"I think the authorities would have more respect than that for somebody who drives a Mercedes S-Class."

I didn't pursue the conversation beyond that. When Jan has made his mind up about something there's precious little anybody can say or do to persuade him otherwise. As far as Jan was concerned, the security of his Mercedes was of far greater importance than the 'selfish' needs of disabled people – and that was that. I wasn't going to argue – it would only have set him in a bad mood for the rest of the evening. But there was a part of me that secretly hoped he'd arrive back at Wittlich station the following morning to discover his car had been impounded – that really would be a sweet irony – and as my dear old mum so often used to say: 'Parsley seed goes nine times to the devil'. [53]

The two of us headed out of the train station, across a busy main road and on to a road junction with a large department store on the corner.

---

[53] *I have no idea whether that proverb makes any sense in the context in which I've used it. I hold my mother entirely accountable for my ignorance in this matter.*

"We need to turn left here," said Jan self-assuredly. So that's what we did. We continued walking along the street for almost half a kilometre until we came to the spot where Jan expected his jazz club to be. Except it wasn't a jazz club; it was a photographic studio.

"That's strange," Jan sighed. "I could have sworn the club was somewhere along here. Maybe we should have turned *right* at the department store instead of left."

And so, the two of us retraced our steps back again, turning right instead of left once we had reached the junction with the department store on the corner. We walked for at least half a kilometre along another of Cologne's city streets – but there was no sign of a jazz club.

"I don't believe this!" said Jan, evidently frustrated by his inability to find this elusive jazz club. "Maybe it's a bit further along."

"I thought you'd been to this club before?"

"I have, many times, but I just can't remember where it is!"

"Well, you have the internet on your mobile phone, don't you? Could you not '*Google*' the name of the jazz club and find the address?"

"I don't know the name of the jazz club," Jan confessed.

Eventually, Jan decided to simply key '*jazz clubs in Cologne*' into the search engine, and sure enough he was instantly rewarded with a list of venues meeting the criteria. I waited patiently while he perused the list of jazz clubs displayed on the tiny screen.

"That's the one!" he exclaimed excitedly. "I was right all along. We should have turned left at the department store."

And so once again, Jan and I retraced our steps back to the junction where we turned left and headed back along the road we had walked along on what seemed like a thousand times already. And then suddenly, as if guided by the spirit of the great 'Bix' Beiderbecke himself, we stumbled miraculously upon the jazz club that Jan had so fervently recommended. It was two shops further along from the photographic studios.

We were greeted in the club's foyer by a tall, frail-looking man with grey skin and a gaunt face. He had a large, crooked nose and chiselled cheek bones sharp enough to open letters with. But my attention was immediately drawn to his hair. It was ginger in colour, perfectly groomed, and it looked decidedly unnatural. The fact that this man had made no attempt whatsoever to disguise the contrasting greyness of his sideburns made it blatantly obvious (to me, anyway) that he was wearing a badly-fitting toupee. Jan marched purposefully over to the man with his arm outstretched, ready to offer him a hearty handshake.

"Ruprecht!" said Jan. "It's so good to see you again, my friend." [54]

Ruprecht looked a little startled and rather bemused as he stood in the dimly-lit foyer shaking hands with Jan. And although he was clearly making an effort to feign a smile, there was an expression on his face that conveyed utter confusion – an expression that was most definitely saying: 'who the hell are *you*?' Jan too had clearly sensed that the man had no idea who he was.

"You remember me, surely?" he said. "My name is Jan – Jan Henke. We met a couple of years ago at an insurance seminar organised by our mutual accountant. If you remember rightly we had a very interesting chat during the coffee break and we exchanged business cards. I think I still have yours in my wallet."

[54] *I confess to having chuckled to myself when Jan introduced the manager of the jazz club as 'Ruprecht'. 'Ruprecht' was the name of one of Steve Martin's absurd characters in the 1988 Frank Oz comedy 'Dirty Rotten Scoundrels'. As soon as Jan mentioned the name 'Ruprecht' I had visions of Steve Martin running frantically around a room banging the base of a saucepan with a wooden spoon and shouting "Oklahoma, Oklahoma!"*

Jan fumbled around in his jacket pocket and pulled out a black leather wallet, from which he produced a rather dog-eared business card which still bore a stain from where Jan had rested his coffee cup on it during the insurance seminar he'd attended two years earlier. Poor Ruprecht the jazz club manager was slightly taken aback.

"Oh yes, I do remember you," he said, albeit somewhat unconvincingly. He was clearly lying.

"Well, since we're old acquaintances," Jan continued, "can my friend and I have free admission to the club tonight?"

I remember wondering at the time whether there was any limit to Jan's audaciousness.

"No," replied Ruprecht. "You can purchase a ticket at the cash desk like everyone else!"

Once inside the club, Jan made his way over to the bar while I searched for a couple of vacant seats. In the event, it wasn't difficult – the club was relatively quiet and there were plenty of seats to choose from. So, after some indecision on my part, I eventually settled on a table inside the *'Stube'* – a little alcove tucked away in one corner of the venue. The Stube's isolated position, I decided, was close enough to the stage to give us a good view of the band, but would allow the two of us to chat away, out of earshot of any of the other punters.

The club was everything a jazz club should be: small and intimate with dim 'mood' lighting, designed to create that perfect 'mellow' ambience. In the far corner of the room was a small stage. I use the word 'stage' reservedly because it was, in point of fact, so small that it barely qualified as being anything more than just a wooden plinth. Yet somehow, the band had managed to squeeze themselves onto it, together with keyboards, microphone stands, drum kit, and a miscellany of speakers and other assorted electrical equipment – the exact function of which will have to remain a mystery. Every square centimetre of the stage floor was occupied by something or someone – like a lifeboat crammed with passengers desperate to escape from a sinking ship. And as I sat there waiting for Jan to return from the bar, listening to the mellow sounds of the jazz band and tapping my feet to the rhythm of the music, I suddenly felt a strange sense of déjà vu. There was something about the music that seemed strangely familiar – something about the style; the arrangement; the delivery. It was less frenetic than jazz can sometimes be; a combination of guitar, keyboard, saxophone and percussion; a unique style of improvised jazz that I'd heard somewhere before. And then, through the half-light of this dimly lit jazz club, I saw a familiar face. It appeared only briefly – just as the light from a rotating glitter-ball mounted on the ceiling reflected off the burnished surface of a silver cymbal and temporarily illuminated the man's eyes, nose and cheekbones. The owner of the face was unmistakable – it was Heinrich, the 78-year-old veteran percussionist from *'Jazz zum Frühstück'* – the jazz band I had seen performing in a similarly seedy club in Bremen some four weeks earlier. And of course, as soon as I'd recognised Heinrich, it wasn't long before I managed to identify the rest of the quartet. There was *'Klavier-Klaus'* the keyboard player; Joseph (aka *'Saxophon Sepp'*) the saxophonist; and of course Volkard (or *Gittarre Volk)* – the man who made the art of playing jazz guitar seem like a casual stroll in the park on a Sunday afternoon. Yes, *Jazz zum Frühstück* were performing another of their 'one night only' events, this time at the jazz club in Cologne. And by sheer coincidence, I just happened to be there on the night in question.

Feeling a little mischievous, I concocted a devious little caper, a jolly jape; the sort that Jan would take tremendous pleasure from inflicting on others, but would be less than enamoured to find himself on the receiving end of. It wasn't long before Jan joined me at the table carrying two large glasses of ice-cold *Kölsch* – a beer which, quite frankly, has a taste not dissimilar to Zagreb tap water.

"I have a couple of bones to pick with you, Mister Henke," I said.

"Oh really? And what might they be?"

"Well firstly, you made me walk up and down the streets of Cologne looking for a jazz club that you claimed not to know the name of or the address of – and yet you had a business card in your wallet with all those details printed on it!"

Jan grinned at me inanely, looking more than a little discomfited.

"Yes, you're quite right about that, mate," he said. "I forgot I had that card in my wallet. It was only after we'd found the place that I realised it was there. Still, no harm done, eh? Walking is always good exercise and we got to explore a bit more of the city!"

"You also told me that the manager of the jazz club was a friend of yours!"

"Well, I don't think I described him as a *friend*, did I? I think the word I used was '*acquaintance*'.

"Actually, Jan, I believe you said '*I know the manager – he's a good friend of mine.*' Those, as I recall, were your exact words, old chum. A chance encounter with a stranger at an insurance seminar two years ago, who you chatted with during a coffee break and exchanged business cards with, hardly qualifies as a '*good friend*', now does it?"

Jan chuckled.

"No, mate," he said. "But you know what I'm like – I do have a tendency to exaggerate sometimes."

"Blatant fibs, Mr. Henke."

"Yes, you're right."

"The truth is, my friend – you don't actually know *anybody* in Cologne, do you? In fact, I'm prepared to bet any money you like that *I* know more people in Cologne than you do. I'm prepared to wager that there are even people in this jazz club who I'm on first-name terms with!"

Jan chuckled once again.

"Yeah, right!" he said sarcastically, "as if *you* know anybody here!"

"OK, Jan – I bet you fifty euros that I'll be able to introduce you to every member of the band during the interval."

Jan laughed again – this time rather loudly.

"Yeah, whatever!" he said – and shook my hand on the deal.

We stayed that night at the Hyatt Regency – a five-star luxury hotel situated on the west bank of the Rhine, and one of the most elegant and stylish hotels I have ever had the pleasure of staying at. It was my last night in Germany, and experiencing the sumptuous opulence of the Hyatt Regency was indeed a fitting end to my tour of this wonderful country. Unsurprisingly, Jan *didn't* manage to 'wangle a discount' – it turned out that the manager of the hotel was not a 'good friend' after all, so Jan ended up paying the full tariff. But to compensate for his disappointment, I let him off the fifty euros he owed me from our little wager. Seeing the expression on Jan's face when I introduced him to every member of *Jazz zum Frühstück* was worth far more than a mere fifty euros. It was priceless.

The two of us woke reasonably early the following morning and, after breakfast, set off towards the railway station. It was here that Jan and I parted company. Jan had to attend the farmer's mart later that morning and so was eager to get moving as early as possible. I waved him off at the platform and watched him as he boarded the crowded commuter train to Wittlich – packed solid in the morning rush hour with men and women in suits and ties and carrying cumbersome-looking briefcases. There is something terribly satisfying about watching commuters scurrying about in the morning rush hour – especially when you've nothing else to do other than wander around at your leisure. I had the best part of a day to kill, and I intended to make the most of it. It was my last day in Germany after all. So as Jan's train pulled out of the station, I set off towards the river, or more specifically, to the quayside where the pleasure cruisers were moored.

Now, I've mentioned already that I've always rather fancied a river cruise on the Rhine. Well, I'd made a decision over breakfast that morning that since this was my final day in Germany, and since Joerg Kachelmann (during his slot on 'Das Wette') had forecast 'a nice hot, sunny day' (I think those were his exact words, allowing for any minor inaccuracies in translation), I decided I would take a short boat trip as far as the neighbouring city of Bonn.

Bonn is approximately 35 kilometres south of Cologne, and there was no shortage of pleasure-boat services vying for my custom. It's not exactly a 'cruise' I'll admit, at least not in the conventional sense – but the boats operating the Cologne-Bonn service amble along the Rhine at a leisurely pace and take the best part of three hours to complete the journey. They're generally well equipped too – they have their own little bars, restaurants and games rooms, so plenty to keep me entertained along the way. And so, after paying the fare for my one-way voyage to Bonn, I clambered aboard the *Pegasus* and took my seat on the upper deck. With my sunshades at the ready and a temperate breeze gently massaging my bald patch, I waited patiently for the skipper of this splendid old veteran to fire up her engines before skilfully manoeuvring his pride and joy away from her berth at the Cologne quayside.

Bonn is another of North Rhine Westphalia's beautiful cities. It's smaller than Cologne (about a third of the size in terms of both physical area and population), and was established as long ago as 11BC when the Roman Army stationed a unit here and established a small settlement on the banks of the Rhine. The city of Bonn was the capital of the former West Germany between 1949 and 1990 and remained the official seat of government even after German reunification. It wasn't until 1999 that the German government was re-established once again at its new location in Berlin.

But the city has another claim to fame, as lovers of classical music will undoubtedly concur. Bonn is the birthplace of Ludwig van Beethoven – born here in 1770. Of course, there are other cities around the world that can claim renowned classical composers among their lists of famous or notable sons or daughters, and there's one in particular that springs immediately to mind – a city in Austria I have had the pleasure of visiting on a number of occasions.

If you didn't already know that Wolfgang Amadeus Mozart was born in Salzburg, then you'll only be five minutes into a visit there before you do. In Salzburg, Mozart is everywhere you turn. Mozart is in the street names, on billboards, on shop doorways, in museums, churches, concert halls, and in tourist souvenir shops. Simply by including the word 'Mozart' on a product's packaging, or by adding a picture of the great man, mugs, cutlery sets, boxes of chocolates, playing cards, soap bars, trinkets, penknives, children's toys, packets of biscuits, tins of sweets, dolls, and just about everything else imaginable, become mysteriously transformed into a special 'must-have' city souvenir, which somehow justifies the inflated price tag. Yes, Mozart was born in Salzburg, and for more than three hundred years the city has been milking it for all its worth. But the city of Bonn treats its association with Beethoven with far greater respect and subtlety. Whereas the ubiquitous and often tacky Mozart souvenirs seem to follow you around as you wander through Salzburg, I spent an entire afternoon wandering the streets and exploring the enchanting back alleyways of Bonn, and yet struggled to find any tourist tat relating to Ludwig van Beethoven at all – which I found somewhat surprising, given that Beethoven has arguably had a far greater influence on classical music than Mozart. [55]

Of course, it is possible to visit the house where Beethoven was born, and since I stumbled upon it during my walking tour of the city, it seemed churlish not to join the small line of visitors queuing outside the main entrance. But whereas in Salzburg, the house in which Mozart was born is painted in a hideous mustard colour and has the words '*Mozart's Geburtshaus*' emblazoned across the façade, the house in Bonn where Beethoven was born (and spent much of his childhood) is more modestly decorated. The house is a memorial site, a museum and a cultural institution and is located at number 20 *Bonngasse*. The neighbouring buildings (Bonngasse 18 and 24 to 26) accommodate the Beethoven archive research centre, a library, a publishing house and a chamber music hall.

But time was pressing on. I had a train to catch at just after six o'clock that evening and I couldn't afford to miss it. It was only a short journey – a twenty-minute hop back to Cologne, but it was just the first of many rail journeys that I'd be facing over the following eighteen hours or so, and missing this one would have had a catastrophic domino effect on my ability to make any of my later train connections.

My journey back to London was an exhausting itinerary. From Cologne, I faced a three-hour journey to Paris (Nord). From there, after waiting for more than an hour for a connecting train, I was on my way to Lille, hurtling through the French countryside under the cover of darkness. At Lille, I faced a wait of more than six hours for my onward

---

[55] *I await hate mail from Mozart aficionados with trepidation*

connection – and since the station was officially closed during the night, the stationmaster very considerately locked me in a waiting room, along with a number of other travellers facing a similar predicament. My temporary incarceration, according to the Président-Directeur Général of the SNCF, was in the interests of passenger safety – the authorities can't have us roaming around the platforms or sleeping on benches while we're waiting for our onward connections. Most of my fellow inmates were young, backpacker types – with excessive facial hair and acne that had resembled relief maps of the Himalayas carved across their cheeks and foreheads. Mercifully, I managed to fall asleep whilst seated, with my arms folded on a table in front of me and my head resting on my arms. I didn't sleep terribly well though – I woke up on a couple of occasions to the grunting sounds of an elderly Asian man who was clearly competing for the title of world snoring champion – that, and the fact that I had pins and needles in my fingertips on account of my unconventional sleeping position.

At 6.30 the following morning I boarded a train to take me on the eighty-minute hop from Lille to Calais – and from there, a P&O ferry – *'the Pride of Kent'* – which trundled its way through the choppy waters of the English Channel, arriving in Dover just before ten o'clock in the morning.

I must admit, it felt good to be back in Blighty. After thirty-two days on the road, I was back in a land of familiarity. Cars were being driven on the proper side of the road; there were zebra crossings you can step onto without running the risk of being flattened by a tram; there were people speaking to each other in a recognisable tongue; and there were signposts pointing the way to places with familiar names, their distances stated in good old-fashioned imperial miles. Yes, it was great to be back – and to celebrate my arrival I decided I'd strike up a conversation with one of my fellow countrymen by asking a passer-by for directions.

"Can you tell me where Dover railway station is please," I asked one of a group of young men standing in a queue outside the post office. He stared at me momentarily with a look of disparagement and derision before shrugging his shoulders.

"Jestem przykro ale nie rozumiem," he said.

I found my way to Dover station eventually without anybody else's help – and from there I was whisked safely and smoothly to my home in west London thanks to the combined efforts of Southeastern Trains and the London Underground. It was probably one of the least eventful of all my rail journeys – except for one exciting moment when Jan called me on my mobile phone.

"The bastards towed my car away!" he ranted. "When I got to the car-park at Wittlich station yesterday morning, my car was being loaded onto the back of a tow-truck!"

I probably shouldn't have laughed quite as loudly as I did.

As soon as I'd arrived home in the early afternoon, I stepped inside the doorway and very nearly tripped over two large suitcases which were standing in the hallway. I was surprised to find my wife and her best friend, Joanna, sitting on the sofa in the living room, both with their jackets on – as if they were just about to leave. I was delighted to see them both of course – I just hadn't expected them to be there.

"What are you two doing here?" I asked. "I thought you were going on a spa weekend to the Cotswolds – I presumed you'd be on your way by now."

"We couldn't leave before *you* came home," my wife replied.

"Well, my love, that's very sweet of you," I said. "I suppose you wanted to welcome me home and have a nice cup of tea waiting for me as soon as I stepped through the front door!"

"Well, not exactly. The reason we didn't want to head off to the Cotswolds before you came home was because I didn't want Fifi to be left home alone."

As you might well imagine, my wife's cryptic explanation confused me considerably – and I think she may have sensed my confusion.

"You'll be looking after our next-door neighbour's cat while Joanna and I are away this weekend," she explained. "Our neighbour has gone to Majorca for a few days – she's been asked to judge a knobbly knees competition in Magaluf. I told her that you would be more than happy to look after little Fifi while she's away. Didn't I mention it when we spoke a couple of days ago?"

"No, you didn't."

"Oh, I'm sorry – I thought I did," my wife replied chirpily. "Still, never mind. She won't be any bother. There's dry cat food in the kitchen cupboard and wet food pouches in the fridge. You'll find the *Jonny-Cat Clumping Litter* in a bag in the conservatory – you'll need that to top her tray up. Oh, and don't forget to keep her water bowl topped up too – especially during the night."

At that very moment, 'bloody Fifi' crept along the hallway and poked her head around the living room door. Our eyes met – and for a few seconds the two of us stared at each other. We were locked in a battle of wits; engaged in a momentary bout of psychological warfare. Which one of us would crack first? The cat squinted in a manner that was both supercilious and scornful – it was her way of letting me know that she was equally as unhappy about this little arrangement as I was.

"You don't mind looking after little Fifi do you, honey?" my wife said, in a syrupy sort of way. Without answering her question directly, I embraced my wife in a hug and gave her a kiss.

"Have a lovely time in the Cotswolds, won't you?" I said.

401

"Yes, we will," she replied.

oOo

Dear Diary,

The Beer, Cheese and Tent Report for the State of North Rhine Westphalia:

Beer: Mittenwald Brau – Kölsch:

The name Kölsch is protected by law so that only beers brewed in and around Cologne can bear the name. At first glance, it looks like any ordinary Pilsner: pale, straw-coloured and clear. But unlike many ordinary German lagers, the taste is far more delicate and refreshing – and a lot less bitter. I didn't mean what I said about it tasting like Zagreb tap water.

Cheese: Münsterkäse:

Its tang and its very flat and smooth skin are the distinctive features of this cheese. Münsterkäse cheeses are perfectly spherical and come in a variety of sizes and levels of fat content. It's a delightfully tangy cheese; ludicrously calorific and deliciously flavoursome.

Tent Stability:

I am now the proud owner of a Vaude Power-Tokee one-man ultra-light tent which I have not yet used, but fully intend to take with me on my next camping adventure. I am delighted to report that I am no longer grieving over the loss of my Windbreaker-DeLuxe.

oOo

Just Before We Say Goodbye....

A Little Note from the Author

Getting a book published in the UK is notoriously difficult, unless of course you happen to be a vacuous Z-list 'celebrity' whose recent appearance on a tawdry reality TV show is somehow enough to justify an autobiography. If that's the case, you'll have publishers tripping over each other for a slice of the action.

But for budding young authors (or even middle-aged, miserable and cantankerous ones, like me), self publishing provides something of a lifeline – a platform that allows us to reach an audience that we would otherwise have difficulty tapping into.

Now, I'm prepared to concede that the quality of work submitted by amateur authors is not always compatible with the standards set by many of the more established writers. That, I'm sure, would account for why publishers are often reluctant to take the risk. But quality aside – when you've invested such a huge amount of time in researching, writing, rewriting, editing and re-editing your own little 'magnum opus', all you really want is a little market exposure – and to find people like you, who are willing to take the time and trouble to read the damned thing.

So, I just want to say thank you. Thank you for purchasing my book, and thank you for making the effort to wade through it – it is very much appreciated. Of course, if you have enjoyed '*Tents and Tent Stability*' you may want to help me further by writing a review on the *amazon* webpage. There's no need to write a thousand-word essay – just a few lines will do very nicely. The more reviews I have, the easier it will be for other potential readers to find my book among the hundreds of thousands of tiles available.